EYEWITNESS ● HANDBOOKS

AQUARIUM
FISH

AQUARIUM FISH

DICK MILLS

Photography by
JERRY YOUNG

Editorial Consultant
DR. CHRIS ANDREWS

DORLING KINDERSLEY
London • New York • Stuttgart

DK

A DORLING KINDERSLEY BOOK

Important Notice
The publisher has made every effort to ensure that the coloration of each
fish has been reproduced precisely, but because the colour of some
species changes under the stress of photography, this may not
have been achieved in every case.

Project Editor Jane Cooke
Project Art Editor Louise Bruce
Assistant Editor Lesley Malkin
Series Editor Jonathan Metcalf
Series Art Editor Spencer Holbrook
Production Controller Adrian Gathercole

— (—

First published in Great Britain in 1993
by Dorling Kindersley Limited,
9 Henrietta Street, London WC2E 8PS

Copyright © 1993
Dorling Kindersley Limited, London
Text Copyright © 1993 Dick Mills

A CIP catalogue record for this book is available
from the British Library

ISBN 0-7513-1021-2 hardcover
ISBN 0-7513-1020-4 flexibound

— (—

Computer page make-up by Adam Moore
Text film output by The Right Type, Great Britain
Reproduced by Colourscan, Singapore
Printed and bound by Kyodo Printing Co., Singapore

CONTENTS

AUTHOR'S INTRODUCTION

There are now hundreds of strangely shaped and wonderfully coloured fish to choose for the aquarium, and caring for them makes only modest demands on time and requires little technical knowledge. Dramatic improvements in aquarium equipment and air transport have brought all fish types – freshwater and marine, tropical and coldwater – within the scope of the enthusiast.

A LL SPECIES of fish that can be kept in an aquarium fall into one of four distinct areas, listed here in order of popularity: tropical freshwater species, tropical marine species, coldwater freshwater species, and, to a far lesser extent, coldwater marine species. Fish are presented in this book within these divisions. Although many coldwater freshwater fishes, such as Koi and Goldfish, are kept in garden ponds, it is the tropical freshwater species that are the most popular, because they are relatively easy to keep.

KOI
*The result of
dedicated fish
cultivation
spanning many
centuries.*

ORIGINS OF FISHKEEPING

The art of fishkeeping has developed gradually from the basic need for food. Food fish were formerly the exclusive privilege of people living by the sea or near rivers, as the storing of live fish was impractical. Keeping live fish in captivity, therefore, became a rare luxury for inland dwellers. The first captive fishes are likely to have been members of the carp family. Over the years, fishkeepers may have learned to recognize individuals and become attached to their charges, and it is likely that an occasional genetic sport, or non-standard coloured fish, would appear and draw greater attention. Such fish would be segregated and kept for their appearance rather than their meat, and so the fishkeeping hobby was born.

THE HOBBY DEVELOPS

It is thought that the Ancient Egyptians were among the very first aquarists. Frescoes found in their tombs indicate that fish were regarded by them as sacred. The Romans kept both freshwater and marine fish species in public display aquariums, the former to sell as food and the latter as decorative status symbols.

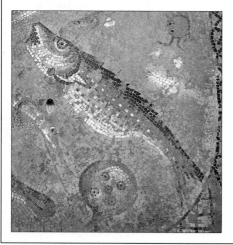

ROMAN FOUNTAIN DETAIL
*The Romans kept fish for food and for decoration;
this mosaic dates from the 4th century* AD.

PARIS EXHIBITION 1867
*Fish-fanciers gather to admire the spectacular
tropical marine aquarium.*

FISH FOLLIES
*Enthusiam for fish-
keeping led to exotic
inventions, such
as this combined
aquarium and
terrarium.*

But it was in China and Japan that
fishkeeping really developed into a
culture. In the Sung Dynasty
(AD970–1279), the keeping of red carp
was a common practice, and once regular
exports of these fish arrived in Japan in
the 1500s, their formal recognition and
appreciation was established. The
hobby reached Europe in the 17th
century, and Goldfish were introduced
to America a century later. The first
major public aquarium was erected
in the Zoological
Gardens of
London,
England,
in 1853.

NEW DISCOVERIES
*Until recent years, new
species were still
recorded with
colourful
drawings.*

MODERN FISHKEEPING

Modern fishkeepers can make a definite contribution towards improving the hobby by studying the living and breeding requirements of their fish. With better understanding, fish could be bred commercially in such quantities that natural stocks could remain untouched. Indeed, many freshwater fishes are already bred in captivity, but the breeding of marine fishes still remains experimental. However, aquarists should be aware of the reality of collecting fish in the wild. Cyanide, for example, may be used to capture reef fishes, and transportation conditions are sometimes cramped. Furthermore, there is little sense in buying a fish if it cannot adjust to aquarium living, and this is frequently true of marine fishes. Fortunately, many countries are now regulating or banning certain aquarium exports until habitats and fish stocks have recovered.

CLUB REGALIA
National fish-keeping federations work to promote the hobby.

AIMS AND LIMITATIONS

This book illustrates all of the fish commonly available to the aquarist, plus some of the more unusual species for the specialist keeper. Some juveniles (often the most popular) have been photographed for this book, and this, together with the stress of photography, means that coloration and markings may differ from those of adult specimens, or from fish in their natural environments. The mix of clear photographs and definitive text nevertheless provides everything the aquarist needs to start and stock a rewarding aquarium.

HOME SWEET HOME
Aquariums are available in many forms, including the high-tech model shown above. The hobbyist should always try to include features of the fish's natural habitat (left).

HOW THIS BOOK WORKS

THIS BOOK is arranged in four parts: tropical freshwater fishes, coldwater freshwater fishes, tropical marine fishes, and coldwater marine fishes. These are not scientific groupings, but are recognized and widely used by fishkeepers. Each section is further divided into fish families or groups, in which the species appear in alphabetical order by their scientific names. The page below explains a typical species entry.

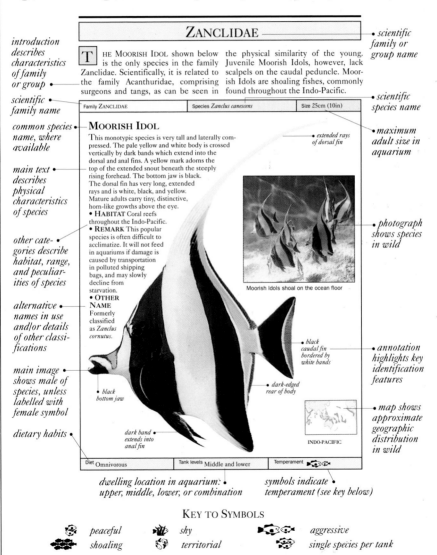

introduction describes characteristics of family or group

scientific family name

common species name, where available

main text describes physical characteristics of species

other categories describe habitat, range, and peculiarities of species

alternative names in use and/or details of other classifications

main image shows male of species, unless labelled with female symbol

dietary habits

ZANCLIDAE

THE MOORISH IDOL shown below is the only species in the family Zanclidae. Scientifically, it is related to the family Acanthuridae, comprising surgeons and tangs, as can be seen in the physical similarity of the young. Juvenile Moorish Idols, however, lack scalpels on the caudal peduncle. Moorish Idols are shoaling fishes, commonly found throughout the Indo-Pacific.

Family ZANCLIDAE	Species *Zanclus canescens*	Size 25cm (10in)

MOORISH IDOL

This monotypic species is very tall and laterally compressed. The pale yellow and white body is crossed vertically by dark bands which extend into the dorsal and anal fins. A yellow mark adorns the top of the extended snout beneath the steeply rising forehead. The bottom jaw is black. The dorsal fin has very long, extended rays and is white, black, and yellow. Mature adults carry tiny, distinctive, horn-like growths above the eye.
• **HABITAT** Coral reefs throughout the Indo-Pacific.
• **REMARK** This popular species is often difficult to acclimatize. It will not feed in aquariums if damage is caused by transportation in polluted shipping bags, and may slowly decline from starvation.
• **OTHER NAME** Formerly classified as *Zanclus cornutus*.

extended rays of dorsal fin

Moorish Idols shoal on the ocean floor

black caudal fin bordered by white bands

dark-edged rear of body

black bottom jaw

dark band extends into anal fin

INDO-PACIFIC

Diet Omnivorous	Tank levels Middle and lower	Temperament

scientific family or group name

scientific species name

maximum adult size in aquarium

photograph shows species in wild

annotation highlights key identification features

map shows approximate geographic distribution in wild

dwelling location in aquarium: upper, middle, lower, or combination

symbols indicate temperament (see key below)

KEY TO SYMBOLS

peaceful
shoaling

shy
territorial

aggressive
single species per tank

WHAT IS A FISH?

CERTAIN PARALLELS can be drawn between the structure of fish and humans: both have a skeleton supporting muscles, and a heart that supplies blood to all parts of the body. A human's five senses are also present in fish, but they are modified as required. However, the similarities end here, as fundamental changes occurred when life forms adapted to living on land. The greatest difference is in the means of motion and manoeuvrability: fish are usually propelled by movements of the tail stem (caudal peduncle), with the fins acting as stabilizers. Nostrils are normally used only for smelling and play no part in respiration, and a fish's skin is generally protected by scales, which reduce friction and protect the soft tissues from predators, parasites, and even sunburn. The position and shape of a fish's mouth help to indicate its feeding habit and dwelling level in the water.

FISH MOUTHS
Fish with upturned (superior) mouths are surface feeders; a down-turned (inferior) mouth facilitates feeding from the streambed; and a mouth situated at the tip of the snout (terminal) often indicates mid-water feeding.

dorsal fin

eye

SUPERIOR

mouth

INFERIOR

gill-cover protects gill opening

pectoral fin

pelvic, or ventral, fin

FISH COVERINGS
The majority of scale types fall into two categories: ctenoid, with small teeth on the rear edge; and cycloid, with smooth edges. Scutes are bony plates found on many catfishes.

TERMINAL

CTENOID SCALES

CYCLOID SCALES

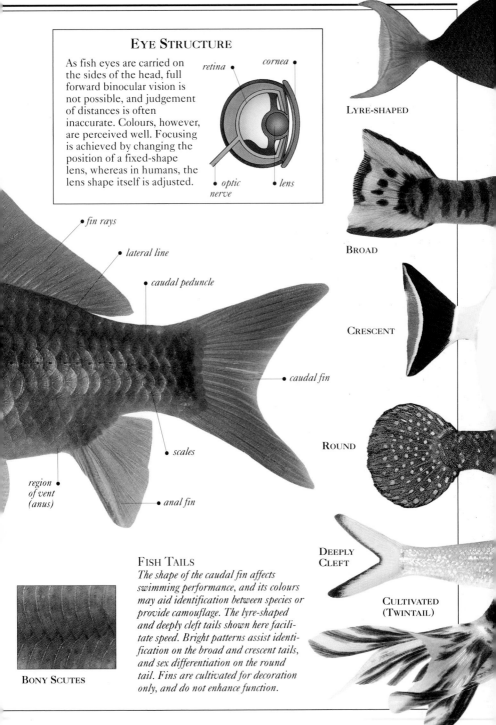

EYE STRUCTURE

As fish eyes are carried on the sides of the head, full forward binocular vision is not possible, and judgement of distances is often inaccurate. Colours, however, are perceived well. Focusing is achieved by changing the position of a fixed-shape lens, whereas in humans, the lens shape itself is adjusted.

retina •   cornea •

• optic nerve   • lens

LYRE-SHAPED

BROAD

CRESCENT

ROUND

DEEPLY CLEFT

CULTIVATED (TWINTAIL)

• fin rays

• lateral line

• caudal peduncle

• caudal fin

• scales

region of vent (anus) •

• anal fin

FISH TAILS

The shape of the caudal fin affects swimming performance, and its colours may aid identification between species or provide camouflage. The lyre-shaped and deeply cleft tails shown here facilitate speed. Bright patterns assist identification on the broad and crescent tails, and sex differentiation on the round tail. Fins are cultivated for decoration only, and do not enhance function.

BONY SCUTES

HOW FISH FUNCTION

Fish have certain specialized functions that enable them to survive in water: gills in place of lungs, swim bladders to maintain buoyancy, and the "lateral line system" to detect changes in the fish's surroundings by a form of echo location.

BREATHING

Fish "breathe" by drawing water in through the mouth and passing it over the gills. Oxygen in the water is absorbed by the gill filaments and then passed into the blood. Meanwhile, carbon dioxide and other wastes are expelled. Some species have developed extra breathing organs for collecting oxygen in stagnating waters, or in waters with decaying plants where oxygen levels are low. Members of the anabantid family, for example, have an auxiliary organ near the gills which holds atmospheric air gulped from the surface and extracts oxygen from it. This maze-like organ has prompted the popular name of "labyrinth" fishes. Some catfishes also gulp air and extract oxygen in a capillary-rich offshoot of the gut.

SWIM BLADDER

Most fish have a gas-filled bladder which acts as a buoyancy compensation device, enabling them to maintain position anywhere in the water. The bladder automatically inflates or deflates to give the fish neutral buoyancy, equalizing the fish's weight with that of the surrounding water. Some species use their swim bladder to make or to amplify sounds.

SIXTH SENSE
Fish can navigate by detecting external vibrations through tiny scale openings along the "lateral line".

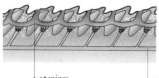

• *openings in scales*   • *nervous system*

FISH'S GILLS
Gills absorb oxygen from water as it passes into the mouth and out through the gill cavity.

water passes back out through gill slits •

• *water passes in through mouth*

oxygen is • *absorbed through gill membrane*

SIGHT AND SMELL

Sight is not as important to fish as it is to humans, as many fish can navigate and locate food in the darkest and murkiest waters by using their lateral line system (see below) to detect obstacles in their path. Fish's eyes are without eyelids because they are permanently lubricated by the surrounding water (see p.11). Fish's sense of smell is much more sensitive than humans', and extra taste buds are carried, usually on barbels and fins.

LATERAL LINE SYSTEM

A fish's nervous system is linked to the outside world through tiny perforations in a single row of scales, known as the lateral line. The row runs horizontally along the length of

lateral line scale openings shown • *on flank*

the fish. Vibrations caused by the fish's own movements are reflected back from obstacles or by other fish and are then detected by nerve endings deep inside the "portholes" in the lateral line scales.

OSMOSIS

A fish's skin acts as a semi-permeable membrane, or a one-way transfer system for water. Due to osmotic pressure, a weaker liquid will diffuse through the membrane to dilute a more concentrated one. In fresh water, the weaker liquid is the water in which the fish lives. Water constantly passes into the fish and, to avoid bursting, freshwater fishes excrete as much water as possible and drink little. Conversely, marine fishes lose water to the more concentrated sea water outside, and must drink constantly but excrete little. Few fish can pass from one type of water to the other without distress: migratory species are exceptions.

water passes through skin, diluting stronger fluid within

FRESHWATER FISH

MARINE FISH

excess water is passed out

water is drunk to replenish fluids

water passes out to dilute stronger surrounding fluid

WATER BALANCE
Freshwater fishes absorb outside water, while marine fishes lose it to the outside.

FOOD-FINDING ORGANS

A fish's ability to sense food is increased by taste buds on the ends of barbels, such as those of the catfishes, and on the hair-like cirri carried by blennies. Other fish, notably the gouramies, carry sensory cells on the tips of their pelvic fins.

distinct nostrils help locate meaty foods

LONGNOSED ELEPHANT FISH

lower jaw makes excellent digging tool

taste buds located at tips of pelvic fins

GIANT GOURAMI

PIRANHA

YARRELL'S BLENNIE

cirri may detect tastes and vibrations

barbels detect food

PORTHOLE CATFISH

ADAPTING TO THE ENVIRONMENT

THE MOST DIVERSE adaptations to the shape and appearance of fish occur in fresh waters, where fish must cope with high or low water levels, fast or still water flows, wide temperature ranges, and sparse or dense vegetation. Marine fishes adapt principally for species recognition, camouflage, and defence.

BODY SHAPE

The shape of a fish is the direct result of its environment. Fish that inhabit fast-flowing rivers, for example, are often more streamlined than the disc-shaped fish of still backwaters. Freshwater fishes may be flat-bottomed to hug the riverbed, thus avoiding being swept away by strong currents. Species with tall, thin (laterally compressed) bodies are often found living among plant stems in lakes, while fish with flat dorsal profiles swim just below the water's surface.

FUSIFORM
Basic shape for fast swimming in open waters.

TALL AND THIN
Its shape allows this fish to move easily between plants.

FLAT-BOTTOMED
Bottom-dwellers have flat ventral surfaces to hug the riverbed.

DEEP-SECTIONED
Deep, keel-like bodies house powerful muscles which enable the fish to leave the water, using their pelvic fins.

 FLAT-TOPPED
Fish of this shape swim just beneath the surface.

CYLINDRICAL
Fish with slim, sinuous bodies can hide easily among plant roots and rocks.

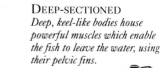

SELF-PRESERVATION

Fish have evolved defences to deal with the attentions, friendly or hostile, of other fish. Sharp, erectile fins, for example, prevent the hunted from being prised from a safe crevice or swallowed, and the flesh of some species excretes poison when danger threatens. Some fish generate electricity (which is used by other species as a navigational aid) to stun their enemies.

SURPRISE SIZE
The Porcupine-fish can inflate its body to intimidate predators.

VENOMOUS SPINES
Lionfish fin rays contain powerful poison.

SHARP SCALPELS
The retractable scalpels of surgeons and tangs can inflict severe wounds.

retractable scalpel on caudal peduncle

COLORATION

The dazzling colours of fish, so admired by aquarists, have very practical purposes: recognizing fellow species and camouflage in the face of danger are priorities, but some fish mimic the colours of other fish for predatory ends. Colours intensify at breeding times to warn off others, and patterns may also help young fish to recognize their parents.

EYE PROTECTION
Stripes hide real eyes (left), while false eyes on tails or flanks divert unwanted attention (right).

 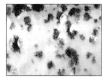

MAKING COLOUR
Colour is produced by light-reflecting crystals of guanin under the skin, or by skin pigmentation.

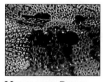

HIDE AND SEEK
Vertical stripes and blotches may conceal the outline of fish among corals and plants.

YOUNG AND OLD
The colours of juvenile marine angelfish (left) alter dramatically in adulthood (right).

 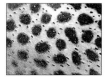

WHO'S WHO?
Colour patterns are vital for identification among the crowds of fish on coral reefs.

HOW FISH BREED

A HOST OF SUBTLE ADAPTATIONS distinguish the breeding methods of different fish families, although there are two general breeding categories. Most fishes (the "egg-layers") lay and fertilize their eggs externally; the eggs of others (the "livebearers") are fertilized and developed inside the female body. The ways in which eggs are fertilized, and young are protected and provided for, differ dramatically in the aquatic world, where predation and cannibalism are rife.

STICKLEBACK EGGS
The eggs of the Stickleback develop externally, with the eyes and backbone appearing first. The tiny fry emerge after 10–14 days.

LIVEBEARERS

The anal fin of a male livebearer is often modified to form a reproductive organ called the gonopodium. It is used to inject sperm into the female fish. Gestation takes about a month at average tropical aquarium temperatures, after which the young fry are ejected into the water ready to fend for themselves. Females of the more popular, cultivated livebearers, like guppies and swordtails, are able to store sperm internally, and can produce successive broods of fry without re-mating. These are known as ovoviviparous breeders. For species that cannot store sperm internally (viviparous breeders), mating is necessary for each brood. All developing fry receive nourishment through a type of placenta.

LIVE BIRTH
The Green Goodeid, a wild, viviparous livebearer, gives birth to multiple live young.

EGG-SCATTERING

This is the simplest form of egg-laying (or oviparous) reproduction. The eggs (ova) are ejected by the female into the water; usually after a hectic pursuit by a male, which stimulates egg release. They are fertilized by the male liquid sperm, but only the eggs that float away on currents or fall among plants or pebbles survive; the rest are soon eaten by other fish and even the parents. Many eggs are laid to increase the chances of survival.

EGG-BURYING

The water in which egg-buriers live dries up completely once a year. Species survival therefore relies on the fertilized eggs withstanding dehydration, often for months, and then hatching once re-immersed in water during the rainy season. In captivity, the eggs from these fish must be collected and stored, semi-dry, for a period before rehydration.

EGG-DEPOSITING

Egg-depositing fishes show some degree of parental protection towards their eggs after they are laid (see bottom right). They deposit them carefully on the underside of leaves, inside rocky caves, or on the leaves of overhanging plants above the water's surface. They use flat surfaces out in the open water, or sometimes a special pouch carried by the male. Egg-guarding and fry-herding are also practised by this group. Fish that exhibit parental care will often pair off naturally.

MOUTH-BROODING

Mouth-brooding females store fertilized eggs in their throats until they hatch weeks later. They may abstain from feeding until the fry are free-swimming, and, at any hint of danger, the fry seek refuge back in their mother's mouth. Mouth-brooders have no special breeding requirements apart from a separate tank. Male mouth-brooders of the Rift Valley cichlids have egg-spots on their anal fins. The female nudges these and so stimulates the release of sperm.

HIGH SECURITY
Mother's mouth is the safest place for these fry.

NEST-BUILDING

Tropical fishes build a variety of nests: some dig pits in the sand, while others build bubble-nests. Males make a nest of saliva-coated bubbles before coaxing the female beneath them (see below), where eggs are laid, fertilized, and then placed in the nest. Depending on the species, bubble-nests may be floating masses or collections of bubbles underneath plant leaves.

BREEDING IN CAPTIVITY

To produce high-quality fry, healthy parents with excellent colour, finnage, and size must be chosen for breeding. The best specimens are the result of special care, with close attention to water quality, and the feeding of live foods and sometimes vegetables. Some fish may require special water conditions to breed, and you may need to prevent parent fish from eating their own eggs or young. The sheer numbers of fry that may arise from a successful spawning should also be anticipated and provided for.

SEPARATING BREEDERS

It is advisable to establish a separate breeding aquarium where water conditions can be adjusted and where fish can mate undisturbed. The risks of egg-eating in the aquarium are increased because of the small volume of water, but furnishing the breeding tank with dense, bushy plants, or covering the floor with pebbles or marbles to hide the eggs, are ways of avoiding this behaviour. Floating plants also provide retreats for newly hatched or free-swimmimg fry. Separating the sexes (especially the egg-scatterers) before breeding improves the chances of spawning once pairs are reunited. Male egg-scatterers generally have brighter colours, longer fins, and slimmer bodies.

COURTING BEHAVIOUR
The male must coax the female beneath the bubble-nest, under the leaf, before she lays and he fertilizes the eggs.

PATERNAL CARE
This male South American cichlid guards a carpet of newly hatched eggs which have been deposited on a flat rock.

CHOOSING YOUR FISH

CHOOSING FISH for a collection involves more than simply going to the pet shop and buying the most attractive species. You should decide in advance which fish will suit your aquarium and equipment, and consider whether any species will require special care (such as being fed live foods). Tank size and water quality requirements vary from species to species. Once you are sure you have the right equipment, the criteria for purchase should be aquarium suitability, ease of care, compatibility, and physical health.

AQUARIUM SUITABILITY

Not all fish are suitable for the aquarium, despite their availability. Some grow too large too quickly, for example, while others, primarily marine fishes, never acclimatize to aquarium life. Fish are usually sold as juveniles, and it is wise to check that they will not grow too large – either for your aquarium or for smaller tank-mates that they may prey upon.

COMPATIBILITY

Fish from different parts of the world cannot necessarily be expected to live in harmony in a community tank. Those that shoal in nature, for example, should be kept in numbers in captivity, but a solitary species may pine away, even in a crowded tank. Sparring between adult males is another common aquarium problem, for example with the Siamese Fighting Fish, and marine fishes can be particularly territorial, even picking on similarly coloured fishes of other species.

GOLDFISH

PIRANHA

ANGELFISH

HUMBLE BEGINNINGS
It is important to check that your fish will not outgrow your tank. These examples show how similar-sized juveniles grow into different adult sizes.

BEWARE OF THE FISH
Smaller fish should not be kept with predators, such as the Moray Eel (above).

PERFECT HOST
A Cleaner Wrasse (right) removes parasites from other fish species.

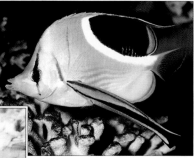

AQUARIUM SANCTUARY
A nearby bolt-hole, among rocks or in the substrate, is reassuring for many fish of a nervous disposition, such as this Yellow-headed Jawfish (left).

HEALTH CHECK POINTS

A fish may have travelled thousands of kilometres before reaching the aquarium dealer, or it may have been collected using harmful methods. Either of these factors may leave it debilitated or damaged beyond remedy. Before purchasing a fish, check that it has an effortless swimming action and that it easily maintains its position in the water. Look also for sores, pimples, wounds, and split or folded fins. Make sure, particularly with marine fishes, that they are taking food readily, and try to witness them feeding. Never buy a fish from a tank containing dead specimens.

colours should be strong, although they may vary with mood, age, and sex

eyes should be clear, not cloudy or protruding

fins of freshwater fishes should be erect

gill-covers should be closed, and not inflamed; breathing should be slow and regular

excess skin secretions may indicate infection or poor water quality

scales should be flat and intact

body should lack pimples, dents, and bumps

SIGNS OF ILL-HEALTH

A fish hiding in the corner of an aquarium may not necessarily be sick; it may simply be nocturnal and unwilling to show itself in the glare of lights. Fishes with laboured swimming actions should be avoided, but allowances can be made for extravagantly finned cultivated specimens. Folded fins on marine fishes are not always signs of ill health.

CREATIVE FISH-KEEPING

It would be wrong to stipulate exactly which species to buy, as personal tastes differ and the availability of certain species may be restricted in local areas. Stocking an aquarium is a creative process involving the purchase of fish that you admire and can adequately care for. To get maximum benefit from the space in your aquarium, buy fish that will occupy all levels and spaces in the tank. Top, middle, and bottom-dwelling species can be included for a fuller representation of the underwater world. Your aquarium may house fish from all over the world, or from one particular continent or area. Specialization often evolves over a period of years, as experience is gained and as fishkeeping tastes change.

TOP TO BOTTOM
Stock the aquarium with a range of species so that all water levels are occupied.

Giant Gourami • *Blue Gourami* •

• *Tiger Barb*   •*Red-tailed Black Shark*

STARTING AN AQUARIUM

EVERYTHING that is placed inside an aquarium alters its balance, so every action of the fishkeeper should be carefully considered. Fish need plenty of space and oxygen, as well as carefully monitored feeding and water conditions.

The modern aquarium should be geared to help meet these requirements. Only the basic aquarium system is discussed here, as specialized fish may require certain modifications, which your aquarium dealer should advise you of.

CHOOSING A DEALER

A local aquarium shop is likely to share your water supply (and any related problems), and should offer you informed advice. Try to monitor the shop's fish stocks over a period, and consider whether it has a fast turnover because of brisk trade or because the stock is dying. Ascertain whether new imports are

MODERN OUTLETS
Choose an aquarium dealer who can offer sound advice on his range of fish and fish supplies.

NEWCOMERS
Transport new fish home in bags. Equalize the water temperature by floating the bag in the tank for 10–15 minutes.

kept in quarantine before being offered for sale. Good dealers will take an interest in what you buy rather than how much you buy, and will know the requirements of every fish in their stock. They should get to know what fish you already have, and so advise you against unsuitable purchases, or let you know of new species that may be of interest. Always buy from a reputable source – cheap fish are never the bargains they appear to be.

BUYING CHECKLIST

• Do not buy fish that have recently arrived at the shop; wait until they have been quarantined and observed.

• Do not consider keeping rare, expensive, or delicate fish if you are in the early stages of fishkeeping.

• Do not be tempted to buy a sickly looking fish. It will probably not respond to any treatment offered.

• Do buy several specimens of a community species that is gregarious, or that is naturally shoaling.

• Do ascertain the dietary needs of your new fishes; if they are herbivorous, they may eat your aquarium plants.

• Do find out, before purchase, what adult size a fish will reach, and whether it requires special water conditions.

STOCKING LEVELS

A fish obviously needs enough space in which to swim freely, but the size of the aquarium and the temperature of the water also affect oxygen content, and therefore dictate the number of fish that can be accommodated. The oxygen consumption of the four main fish groups differs, partly because warmer waters carry less oxygen, and so the recommended minimum sizes of tanks differ accordingly. An aquarium measuring 60cm (24in) long and 30cm (12in) wide, with a surface area 1800cm² (288in²), is roughly adequate for tropical freshwater fishes. But an aquarium of at least 90cm (36in) by 30cm (12in) is better for coldwater freshwater and all marine fishes, which consume proportionally more oxygen.

SURFACE AREA

The depth of the tank is not relevant to the oxygen content calculations; it is the surface area of the water that is important. Tropical marine species require 300cm² (48in²) of water per 2.5cm (1in) of body length; cold-water freshwater fishes require 190cm² (30in²); and tropical freshwater fishes require 75cm² (12in²). The 60 x 30cm (24 x 12in) aquariums shown here, therefore, will hold approximately 15cm (6in) of tropical marine fishes (measured from snout to caudal peduncle), 23cm (9in) of coldwater freshwater fishes, and 60cm (24in) of tropical freshwater fishes.

TROPICAL MARINE
Water with a surface area of 1800cm² (288in²) can support one 15cm (6in) marine angelfish.

COLDWATER FRESHWATER
A surface area of 1800cm² (288in²) can support two 11.5cm (4½in) Goldfish, or one of 23cm (9in).

TROPICAL FRESHWATER
A surface area of 1800cm² (288in²) can support four 15cm (6in) catfish, or one of 60cm (24in).

UPRIGHT VERSUS HORIZONTAL
These two tanks contain the same volume of water and provide the same amount of swimming space, but because the upright tank has a smaller surface area of water compared with the horizontal tank, it will support far fewer fish.

UPRIGHT
TANK

lower oxygen levels mean fewer fish

• same volume of water as "horizontal" tank

• greater surface area than upright tank

• higher oxygen levels support many more fish

HORIZONTAL
TANK

AQUARIUM EQUIPMENT

MODERN AQUARIUM TANKS are made of glass or of one-piece moulded acrylic. They do not corrode, which is a vital advantage if you intend to keep marine fishes. Tanks come in standard sizes, described either by dimension or water capacity. They should be positioned on a firm, level surface before any water is added. The "furniture" part of decorative tanks, such as a surrounding cabinet or table top, should be resistant to condensation.

CLEAN EQUIPMENT

The aquarium must be kept clean using filters, and aerated using air pumps. Many filters work in conjunction with an air pump, which drives aquarium water through the filter. The filter rids the tank of the fish's waste products, consisting of ammonia and other toxic chemicals, and general debris. Waste is also removed by regular, partial water changes. Plants can further help to adsorb metals, nitrates, and carbon dioxide. Filtration equipment varies from simple foam filters to sophisticated "total" filter systems. Suspended matter in the water is mechanically strained out by the filter, and dissolved wastes are adsorbed within it by a special medium, such as activated carbon.

• power head drives water under gravel

covering of pea gravel •

• water is drawn through slotted plastic plates

PREPARING UNDER- GRAVEL FILTRATION

UNDER-GRAVEL FILTRATION

This system of filtration (see above) works without a filter medium. The power head drives water though the gravel, where it comes into contact with a bacterial colony living on the gravel surface. These bacteria feed on the fish's waste.

• this device pumps compressed air through the water to aerate it

AIR PUMP

DWARF SWORD- PLANT

FURNISHINGS

Freshwater aquariums look best when furnished with clusters of rocks, sunken logs, and verdant plant growth. Herbivorous fishes, however, will quickly denude a tank of plants, and some fish uproot plants and furnishings when breeding. Plastic plants can be substituted, and moulded resin replicas of logs, branches, and ornaments, which do not leach chemicals or dyes, are available. Enhance marine tanks with synthetic corals.

WATER

The majority of aquarium fishes acclimatize well to domestic water supplies, providing that precautions are taken to remove or neutralize the effect of heavy metals, chlorine, and chloramines. It is only necessary to alter the composition of water further when attempting to breed, or to keep more delicate freshwater species. Water for marine aquariums should be made up using synthetic salt mixes.

HEATING

Keep aquarium water for tropical freshwater and marine fishes constant at around 25°C (77°F). A thermostatically controlled heater will maintain this temperature level reliably. Two units can be used in large tanks to distribute heat quickly and evenly. Modern thermostats have microchip circuitry for more accurate control, and some external thermostatic controls even have memories for recording temperatures, with alarms to warn of extreme changes.

LIGHTING

Light illuminates the aquarium and provides energy for photosynthesizing aquatic plants. Tanks deeper than 38cm (15in), and those with lush plant-life, will need more lighting than is generally supplied with an aquarium. Aquariums are best lit by fluorescent tubes inside the hood; marine reef tanks require high-intensity metal halide or mercury vapour lamps. Tungsten lamps generate excessive heat but may be used to grow plants.

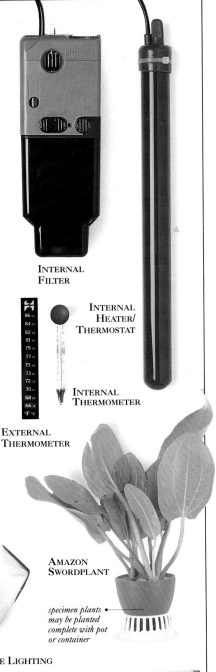

INTERNAL
FILTER

INTERNAL
HEATER/
THERMOSTAT

INTERNAL
THERMOMETER

EXTERNAL
THERMOMETER

FISH NET

AMAZON
SWORDPLANT

CABLE TIDY

• safety device for
connecting and
switching electricity

• specimen plants
may be planted
complete with pot
or container

FLUORESCENT TUBE LIGHTING

CARING FOR YOUR FISH

ONE ADVANTAGE of fishkeeping is the small amount of time required for maintenance: a few minutes each day for feeding, and perhaps an hour or so a week for cleaning. Periodic tests for water quality are advisable, especially with marine tanks, delicate fish, or when breeding, but water hardness need not unduly concern the average keeper.

Fish diseases are usually initiated by stress, often caused by a change in the aquarium environment, or by pollution from over-feeding or the decay of carcasses. Fortunately, most ailments can be diagnosed and may respond to medication or treatments.

TREATING COMMON AILMENTS

• **White Spot** (*Ichthyophthirius*) Small white spots appear on the body and fins. It can be remedied with a proprietary water treatment. The marine equivalent is *Cryptocaryon*.
• **Velvet** Similar to White Spot, but spots are smaller. All forms are caused by *Oodinium* parasites, which respond to treatment.
• **Fungus** (*Saprolegnia*) The body has "woolly" growths; remedy with a salt bath, or, for freshwater fishes, a swab with a proprietary treatment.
• **Mouth "Fungus"** This usually responds only to antibiotics, which are available from veterinary surgeons.
• **Skin and Gill Flukes** Fish scratch against objects to relieve the irritation of Skin Flukes (*Gyrodactylus*). Gill Flukes (*Dactylogyrus*) cause fish to hang, with gills inflamed, at the surface. Proprietary treatments are effective.
• **Fin-Rot** Often a secondary ailment due to poor water quality; tissue between the fin rays is gradually eroded by bacteria. Changing the water may prompt a recovery.
• **Dropsy** Scales stand out from the body and the fish becomes bloated; no cures are reliable and fish are best destroyed.

MAINTENANCE CHART

	FRESHWATER	MARINE
WATER Check temperature	daily	daily
Top up water level	weekly	weekly
Check specific gravity (using hydrometer)	not applicable	weekly
Check ammonia, nitrite, and nitrate levels (using test kit)	not applicable	before stocking tank, then periodically
Check pH (using test kit)	when breeding or specializing	weekly
Check hardness (using test kit)	when breeding or specializing	not applicable
Make partial water changes	monthly, more if required	monthly
FILTERS Clean or renew filter floss and replace carbon	as required	as required
Clean biological materials	partially every 2–3 months	partially every 2–3 months
PLANTS Trim excessive growth; remove decayed leaves	as required	not applicable
GENERAL Check health of fish	daily	daily
Scrape algae; clean light fittings; siphon out debris	as required	as required

HOSPITAL TANK

A separate tank is useful both for treating sick fishes and as quarantine quarters.

FEEDING

The types and amounts of food offered to fish are crucial, as uneaten food will rot, upsetting tank conditions. Fish should never be fed with more than they can consume within a few minutes. Any food that is not eaten will simply be left to waste, depleting the aquarium of vital oxygen. Fish will not starve if left for a week or so during vacations, providing they have been well fed beforehand. Fish foods fall into two groups: dried or prepared foods; and natural foods in the form of living creatures, seeds, or fruit. Aim to match the wild diet of a fish as closely as possible.

DRY FOODS

Multi-million-pound businesses have been established to provide modern, nutritionally balanced diets for all types of captive fish. Ants' eggs and drums of biscuit powder have become redundant, as the natural diets of fish can now be more closely matched. Whether fish are carnivorous, herbivorous, or omnivorous, adult or fry, there are convenient substitute foods available in several forms, including flakes, granules, tablets, and liquids. In addition to proteins, carbohydrates, and fats, fish require vitamins and minerals just as humans do, and many manufactured foods now have these added during the production process.

NATURAL LIVE FOODS

Freezing and freeze-drying also mean that live aquatic foods can be preserved. These are ideal, as living creatures, either water-borne or terrestrial, naturally contain all the nutrients that fish need. They also make a welcome treat, if offered only occasionally. Mosquito larvae can be collected from rain-butts, and bloodworms and water fleas are usually available from aquatic dealers.

DRY FLAKES

DRY TABLETS

DRY PELLETS

FREEZE-DRIED BRINE SHRIMP

LIVE BRINE SHRIMP

FAST FOOD
The Archerfish can leap out of the water to grab an insect with its mouth, or to project a jet of water to knock it down.

BLOOD WORMS

WATER FLEAS

MOSQUITO LARVAE

FRESHWATER HABITATS

THE PROPORTION of fresh water in the world is very small at around two per cent, but, due to its diverse location, its accessibility, and its differing qualities, the variety of freshwater fishes is very great. Freshwater fishes can cope with a wide range of water locations, qualities, and temperatures, and this adaptability and resilience has made them hardy and particularly suitable for life in the aquarium.

TYPES OF FRESH WATER

When water falls from clouds as rain, it is conditioned by the earth upon which it lands. This, in turn, affects the local fishes' tolerance of their water conditions. If water falls on granitic rock, its composition is altered very little and it remains soft. But when it permeates limestone, it absorbs calcium, which makes it alkaline and hard. Peaty soil will acidify water, as will the rotting vegetation typically found in slow-moving streams. Fishes from such streams, including the majority of aquarium fishes, such as barbs and rasboras, will, therefore, tolerate acidity in their aquarium water. Lakes with no inflow or outflow of water from rivers, as in the Rift Valley of Africa, have a high mineral content which must be emulated in

ASIAN RAINFOREST
Although they contain many aquarium fish species, waters in Southeast Asian jungles (below) usually contain much oxygen-consuming decaying vegetation. Waterfalls help boost oxygen levels.

LIFE ON THE RIVERBED
The anostomus (above) searches for food on the riverbeds of Amazonia, home to a great many tropical aquarium favourites. The stripes help it to blend in with its surroundings.

RIFT VALLEY
A vantage point by Lake Malawi in the Rift Valley of East Africa. Several of these hard-water valley lakes are home to the "Rift Valley cichlids". There are over 250 cichlid species in this lake alone.

captivity using proprietary mixes. Estuarine waters are regularly altered by tidal additions of sea water, and fish from these environments, such as the Mono and the Scat, appreciate a small addition of salt in their water. By the time rain water reaches the sea, it is of an entirely different composition. Once there, it evaporates and begins its journey back through the water cycle.

EFFECTS OF TEMPERATURE

Changes in temperature may also significantly alter the freshwater habitat: where the volume of water is small, the differences between day and night temperatures are greater. More drastic fluctuations include the melting of mountain snows, which add cool water to rivers, and the warming effect of the sun on pond water.

FRESH WATERS OF MEXICO
Lake Catemaco in Mexico has a tropical climate at an altitude of 370m (1,212ft). It contains cichlids, livebearers, and killifishes.

CHINESE SAILFIN SUCKER
This sturdy species inhabits the temperate waters of China.

FRESHWATER AQUARIUMS

THERE ARE MANY MORE options open to the freshwater fishkeeper than to the marine aquarist. The freshwater keeper can recreate the conditions of a tropical river or lake, a backwater pond, a hard-water Rift Valley lake, or a coldwater habitat. Whichever aquatic habitat you choose to create, water quality will be of great importance. Simulating the water chemistry of a location can be achieved using resins, minerals, and sometimes peat in the mechanical filter system. These will soften, harden, make alkaline, or acidify the water. Dilution by adding rainwater is one way to reduce water hardness, while soft water can be

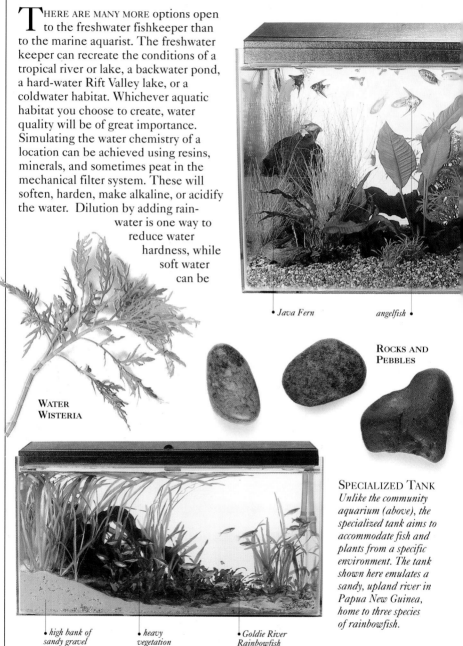

• Java Fern   angelfish •

ROCKS AND PEBBLES

WATER WISTERIA

SPECIALIZED TANK
Unlike the community aquarium (above), the specialized tank aims to accommodate fish and plants from a specific environment. The tank shown here emulates a sandy, upland river in Papua New Guinea, home to three species of rainbowfish.

• high bank of sandy gravel   • heavy vegetation   • Goldie River Rainbowfish

THE COMMUNITY COLLECTION

A range of fishes from different worldwide habitats can be mixed together in a community tank.

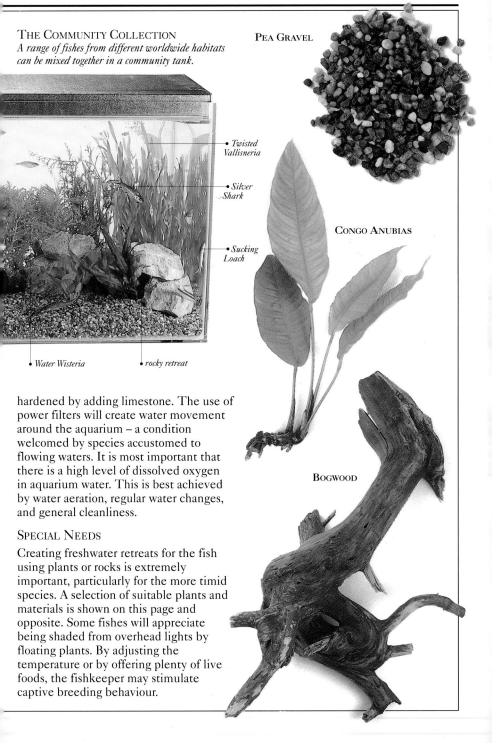

PEA GRAVEL

• *Twisted Vallisneria*

• *Silver Shark*

• *Sucking Loach*

CONGO ANUBIAS

• *Water Wisteria*   • *rocky retreat*

BOGWOOD

hardened by adding limestone. The use of power filters will create water movement around the aquarium – a condition welcomed by species accustomed to flowing waters. It is most important that there is a high level of dissolved oxygen in aquarium water. This is best achieved by water aeration, regular water changes, and general cleanliness.

SPECIAL NEEDS

Creating freshwater retreats for the fish using plants or rocks is extremely important, particularly for the more timid species. A selection of suitable plants and materials is shown on this page and opposite. Some fishes will appreciate being shaded from overhead lights by floating plants. By adjusting the temperature or by offering plenty of live foods, the fishkeeper may stimulate captive breeding behaviour.

MARINE HABITATS

COVERING approximately 77 per cent of the Earth's surface, the saltwater oceans are regarded as a highly stable environment, with only minor fluctuations in salinity. The problem that this brings to the keeper of marine fish is that these species have little tolerance to even the slightest change in water conditions, unlike their freshwater relatives. In addition, the vast ocean waters soon dilute the pollution of fish wastes and decaying organic matter. Even the largest marine aquarium cannot reproduce these self-cleansing conditions, and the water in marine tanks needs assistance if it is to support life.

SUPPLY OF SPECIES

Most marine species available for the aquarium come from shallow coastal waters near coral reefs, where fish can be captured easily. Unlike many freshwater fishes, most marine species are still caught from the wild. Despite the attraction and commercial value of

UNDERWATER TRAFFIC
Despite the apparent crowding on this Fijian reef, there is plenty of food for all.

their fantastic colours and unusual shapes, marine fishes have proved difficult to breed cost-effectively in captivity, and certainly not in the numbers required for commercial supply.

CORAL DWELLERS
Shy seahorses use corals and seaweeds to anchor themselves.

FISH PARADISE
Coral reefs, such as these off tropical islands in the South Pacific, teem with fish life.

POOLS OF LIFE

On seashores in all temperate zones, tides recede, leaving behind rock-pools, which are ecosystems in their own right. They contain easily caught fishes, colourful seaweeds and algae, and unusual invertebrates. Although rock-pool dwellers are not as brightly coloured as their tropical counterparts, their diverse sheltering and feeding techniques provide a special fascination.

SPECIALIZED FEEDING

Some marine fishes have specialized feeding habits that can cause problems for aquarists. Many species eat specific foods, such as sponges, algae, and even the coral itself. Providing these foods in captivity is difficult, and many marine fishes refuse to accept substitutes. Parrotfishes, for example, are beautiful and easy to collect, but they feed only on algae within coral rubble. Fortunately, proprietary foods are now incorporating more of these natural foods. Other fishes with specialized feeding habits, such as the sponge-eating Atlantic angelfishes and the polyp-eating butterflyfishes, can be adapted to aquarium life if captured very young. They will accept live brine shrimp and adapt to frozen food and flakes. Algae-eating pygmy angelfishes will adapt to meats, supplemented with blanched vegetables.

SAFETY IN SEAWEED

Long, tapering pipefishes hide, head-up, in grasses and slim seaweeds near the shore.

MARINE AQUARIUMS

Providing fish with the equivalent of the natural conditions found on coral reefs is the secret of successful marine fishkeeping. Controlling water-quality within very specific parameters is top of the list of priorities. The marine aquarium should be as large as possible for maximum water quality stability – a minimum of 90cm (36in) in length and 30cm (12in) in depth. At least a quarter of the water should be changed every month. The replacement water must be mixed to the correct specific gravity (tested using a hydrometer) and aerated before being added: your aquarium dealer will advise you. An efficient filtration system is also vital to control dangerous toxins. Each aquarium has an optimum fish-holding capacity, but this should be reached gradually, to allow the filtration system to cope with

• *power filter hose*   • *reef rock*

Vagabond Butterflyfish •   *Malu Anemone* •

SEASHELL

TUFA ROCK

SPECIALIZED TANK

A coldwater marine tank is an interesting, if more demanding, alternative to tropical reef aquariums. A larger tank is needed to support fishes that grow to considerable sizes. Temperature, pH, specific gravity, and salinity must all be monitored. These aquariums should be kept cool in summer.

shrimp •   • *Grey Mullet*   • *plastic seaweed*

THE COMMUNITY TANK

Choose fish for their colour, shape, or unusual behaviour, and for their utilization of swimming space. Add invertebrates, such as anemones, marine worms, and crabs for further interest.

POWER FILTER

power head

crushed coral over coral sand

HYDROMETER

• *Squirrelfish*

the increasing waste load. You can achieve additional water purification using specialized equipment, including protein skimmers, ultra-violet lamps, and ozone, an oxidizing agent.

OTHER NEEDS

Light intensity on the reef top is high, and intense lighting in the aquarium will encourage the algae required by herbivorous species. Reef aquariums should have more hideaways than fish, and the substrate should be fairly fine for certain burrowing species. Suggested materials and furnishings are illustrated on this page and opposite.

SEA SALT MIX

CRUSHED CORAL

How Fish are Grouped

ALL FISH ARE DEFINED by their scientific species name, which is recognized worldwide. Similar species are grouped into "genera", which in turn are grouped into families, as shown below. Characteristics of the groups used in this book are set out on the following pages (pp.35–45).

FISH FOSSIL
Fossils help us to trace the development of the common characteristics of a family, genus, or species.

FAMILY
A family usually contains several related genera, but sometimes only a single genus. The family name always appears in Roman type, e.g. Belontiidae.

FAMILY

GENUS/GENERA
A genus usually contains several related species, but sometimes only one. The scientific genus name always appears in italic type, e.g. *Sphaerichthys*.

Genus

SPECIES
Members of a species share similar features, and can breed together. Scientific species names consist of the genus name and species epithet, e.g. *Betta bellica*.

Species

Species

VARIETIES AND SUBSPECIES
Varieties (var.) are cultivated divisions within a species; subspecies (denoted by a second epithet on the scientific name) are usually geographically separate.

Variety (var.)

Subspecies (e.g. Trichogaster trichopterus sumatranus)

CYPRINIDS

TIGER BARB
*A diamond-shaped body
and high dorsal fin are
typical of the barbs,
the most common
tropical cyprinids.*

high dorsal fin •

• *deeply forked
caudal fin*

*well-defined •
scales*

*more colourful •
fins on males*

GROUP CHARACTERISTICS
The cyprinid family contains around
1,300 species, widely distributed on most
continents of the world. They inhabit all
types of waters, and so adapt readily to the
various water conditions that are provided
by the fishkeeper.

The body shape is conventional, with
symmetrical contours, but it may be slender
or quite deep, depending on habitat. Cyprinids have seven fins: two sets of paired fins
and three single ones. Pharyngeal teeth in
the throat grind food before it reaches the
intestine. Their arrangement provides positive identification between similar species.

Coldwater cyprinids (see pp.213–233)
include the most popular aquarium fishes of
all, the Goldfishes and Koi. Tropical cyprinids
(see pp.46–73) are divided into three main
aquarium groups: barbs, which are carp-like
fishes, inhabiting the middle and lower
water levels; danios, which are
faster swimming and prefer
the upper levels; and rasboras,
which use all levels. All
cyprinids spawn using egg-
scattering methods, and do
not usually offer parental care.

"SHARK"
*Several family members have dorsal fins
and flattened profiles similar to the true
marine sharks.*

RASBORA
*Midwater-swimming rasboras can be
either slim- or deep-bodied, brightly
coloured or
plain silver.*

DANIO
*These characins spawn easily.
They are constantly active just
below the water's surface.*

CHARACINS

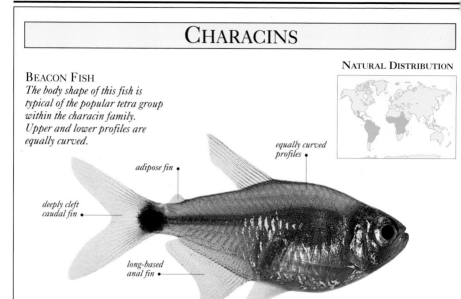

BEACON FISH
The body shape of this fish is typical of the popular tetra group within the characin family. Upper and lower profiles are equally curved.

equally curved profiles •

adipose fin •

deeply cleft caudal fin •

long-based anal fin •

DISTICHODUS
This heavily built African characin requires plenty of room.

HATCHETFISH
Deep-bodied, flat-topped characins like this are capable of leaping across the water's surface.

GROUP CHARACTERISTICS

The characin family includes around 1,300 species, distributed across Central and South America, and Africa. Most of these fishes shoal in lakes and rivers.

Body shapes and sizes vary considerably, from the 5cm- (2in-) long pencilfish to the stocky African distichodus species, which measures 40cm (16in). Piranhas and pacus are muscular and heavily built to facilitate the tearing of flesh or fruits. Other characins, in contrast, may persistently eat aquarium plants. Characins have sharp teeth in the jaws and most have an extra fin, known as the adipose fin, on the back. The family contains many popular fishes, including the tetras, of which the brilliant Neon and Cardinal Tetras are prime examples.

Most characins spawn by egg-scattering. The male may have tiny hooks on the anal fin to hold the female against him during spawning. The eggs are adhesive and, once laid, usually become lodged among plants. One notable exception is the Splashing Tetra, which deposits eggs on a firm surface out of the water, to protect them from the attentions of aquatic predators.

PENCILFISH
The coloration patterns of these spindle-shaped characins alter at night-time.

CICHLIDS

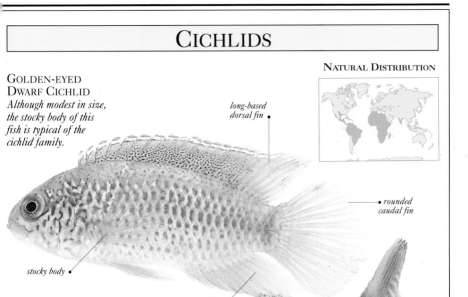

GOLDEN-EYED DWARF CICHLID
Although modest in size, the stocky body of this fish is typical of the cichlid family.

long-based dorsal fin •

NATURAL DISTRIBUTION

• *rounded caudal fin*

stocky body •

pointed anal fin on male •

GROUP CHARACTERISTICS

The 1,000 or more members of the cichlid family are native to Central and South America, Africa, Asia, and parts of the USA. Most will acclimatize well to domestic tap water, although some species, such as the Discus Fish, need carefully controlled water.

The colours, shapes, and sizes of cichlids vary enormously, although they tend to be heavily built. Some grow too large for the average community tank, while others breed readily among other fishes in any aquarium. Male cichlids from the Americas may have longer, more pointed dorsal and anal fins, while male African Rift Valley cichlids often have yellow or orange spots on the anal fin. There is plenty of opportunity for specialization within this family: Rift Valley cichlids, for example, prefer hard water and rocky furnishings. Many are herbivorous, requiring vegetable foods. Cichlids are hearty eaters, producing a lot of waste, which calls for frequent water changes. These fishes generally reproduce by egg-depositing, but they display diverse methods of breeding, all of which involve a high degree of parental care.

ANGELFISH
This aquarium favourite has a very different body shape to most cichlids.

LARGER CICHLID
Some cichlids, like this Oscar, may outgrow the average aquarium. Although large, it can become hand-tame.

DISCUS
This graceful, colourful cichlid requires soft, acidic water conditions.

ANABANTIDS

LEERI GOURAMI
An oval body and flowing fins are typical of the gracefully swimming gourami group.

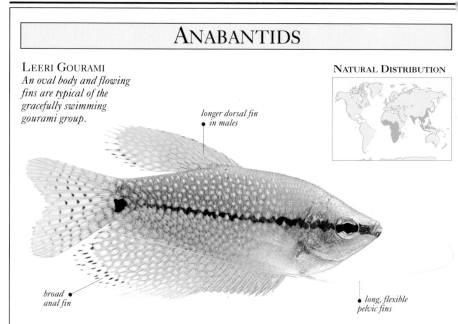

longer dorsal fin
• in males

broad •
anal fin

• long, flexible
pelvic fins

GROUP CHARACTERISTICS
Fishes within this group of families often inhabit oxygen-depleted waters of Africa and Asia. They possess an auxiliary breathing organ which enables them to use atmospheric air, gulped at the surface. This "labyrinth organ" is a folded mass of bone and capillary-rich tissue, situated internally near the gills. Its function is to store air and extract oxygen.

The Asiatic anabantids are usually peaceful and swim gracefully. Gouramies have thread-like pelvic fins with taste cells at the tips. A few other Asian species make croaking noises when they are breeding or when removed from the water. African species are larger and are stealthy predators, often with spectacular colours and patterns.

Most anabantids build floating bubble-nests in which the eggs are deposited. The male spurns the female once spawning is completed. He may even kill her as he takes on responsibility for guarding the eggs in the nest. An exception is the mouth-brooding Chocolate Gourami.

BETTA
The Siamese Fighting Fish, an aquarium-bred Betta *species, has a brighter coloration than its wild counterpart.*

CTENOPOMA
Members of the African anabantid group are usually predatory. They are, however, very colourful.

KILLIFISHES

BLUE GULARIS
This large, colourful killifish is popular for the tropical aquarium.

NATURAL DISTRIBUTION

brilliant • coloration

flat dorsal • profile indicates surface dweller

flag-like caudal fin

GROUP CHARACTERISTICS

"Killi" is a Dutch word meaning stream or brook, but the 300 killifish members of the family Cyprinodontidae in fact inhabit a great variety of waters. These include ephemeral ponds, brackish marshes, lakes, and rivers of the Americas, Africa, Asia, and warmer parts of Europe. Their small, cylindrical bodies have upturned mouths for surface-feeding. Males are usually more brilliantly coloured.

In captivity, killifishes accept most types of food. They lay eggs in plants or in the substrate. In both cases, eggs may take weeks or months to hatch, and they can survive periods of almost total dehydration. Many subspecies of various coloration have led to confusion with identification.

CATFISHES

CHOCOLATE CATFISH
This species displays the typical blotchy brown catfish coloration.

NATURAL DISTRIBUTION

barbels • surround mouth

flat ventral • surface indicates bottom dweller

bony • plates and spines on body

truncated • caudal fin

GROUP CHARACTERISTICS

The catfish family contains around 2,000 members, which comprise some of the more unique aquarium attractions: certain species swim upside-down; some can manoeuvre on land; and others can emit sound or use electricity to kill. All are from the Americas, Africa, and Asia and share the common characteristic of bottom-dwelling. Many are surprisingly gregarious and enjoy being kept in numbers, but some catfish are nocturnal, and their regular activities often go un-noticed. Catfishes are identifiable by the

barbels around their mouths which allow them to locate food in the dark. Instead of scales, the skin may be naked or covered with bony plates (or "scutes"). They often use oxygen that is gulped at the surface and extracted in the gut. Usually omnivorous, some species are herbivorous and are bought as algae controllers. Catfishes spawn in several ways, including egg-depositing and bubble-nest building.

LOACHES

COOLIE LOACH
*The elongate body of the loach
allows easy access to hiding places.*

*dark, camouflaging
stripes*

NATURAL DISTRIBUTION

*erectile
spine
beneath eye*

*pale ventral
surface*

GROUP CHARACTERISTICS

The various species of loach that are
available to the aquarist come from
India and Asia. They spend most of
their time on the bottom of river- and
stream-beds, hence their flat-
bottomed bodies. A distinctive
characteristic of this family is the
erectile spine beneath the eye. It
acts as a deterrent to predators,
but it also tends to catch in the
fishkeeper's net. The mouths of
loaches are down-turned and
carry barbels for detecting food.

Like anabantids and some catfishes,
loaches can gulp atmospheric air at the
water's surface, and extract
oxygen from it as it passes
through the gut. Many species
are nocturnal and hide among
plants and rocks by day, emerging
as darkness falls or when food
appears at close range. Their
natural diet includes worms and
insects, but most loaches will
accept prepared foods in
captivity, especially
tablets and other quick-
sinking forms.

Little is known of their
reproductive behaviour,
but loaches have been induced to
spawn in captivity by using hormone
injections. Loaches in the *Botia* genus
are long-established aquarium favourites.

CLOWN LOACH
*The flat-bottomed body
and down-turned mouth
of this loach facilitate
substrate feeding.*

ZEBRA LOACH
*Distinctive dark stripes
provide camouflage for
this loach.*

HORSEFACED LOACH
*The head of this species is longer
than those of other loaches. It may
become more active during stormy weather.*

OTHER TROPICAL EGG-LAYING SPECIES

SIAMESE TIGERFISH
A slim body enables this predatory, egg-laying species to lurk in plants.

NATURAL DISTRIBUTION

second dorsal fin contains softer rays

spiny front to dorsal fin

• powerful caudal fin

• large, predatory mouth

GROUP CHARACTERISTICS
There are many egg-laying fishes that are monotypic – occurring as a single species within their genus. Some genera contain very few representative species, and other species do not fit conveniently into the major fish groups. These miscellaneous fishes are grouped together in this book, in alphabetical order by scientific species name (see pp.180–196).

There is an extraordinary variety of fishes to choose for the aquarium within this category, from both brackish and fresh waters. They are sometimes kept by hobbyists as interim choices before graduating to more demanding marine fishkeeping.

The species in this section have been chosen to demonstrate the variety of fishes available to enliven even the smallest aquarium. Availability in local areas cannot be guaranteed, as species fluctuate in popularity.

ELEPHANT FISH
The extended lower jaw makes this unusual tropical egg-layer easily recognizable.

RAINBOWFISH
Two separate dorsal fins are a major characteristic of the rainbowfish family.

LEAF FISH
By imitating a dead leaf, this predator may drift up to its prey unnoticed.

TROPICAL LIVEBEARERS

large, flowing caudal fin

RED VEILTAIL GUPPY
Guppies, mollies, swordtails, and platys are a related group of extremely popular livebearers. The males are smaller, but more colourful than the females.

NATURAL DISTRIBUTION

rod-like anal fin on male

upturned mouth

GROUP CHARACTERISTICS
Livebearing fishes are native to the Americas, from New Jersey down to Brazil, and in east Asia. They have been introduced into other tropical areas to combat malaria, as livebearers eat the waterborne larvae of disease-carrying mosquitoes.

Females are usually longer than males, but the latter have more striking colours and patterns, and often have longer fins. Most livebearers adapt well to the aquarium, and will thrive in hard water. Feeding is uncomplicated, but these fishes appreciate the addition of vegetable matter.

A main attraction of these fishes is their propensity to breed in captivity, especially the brilliantly coloured, aquarium-developed strains of guppies, mollies, platys, and swordtails. It is advisable to move a gravid female into a separate nursery tank for birthing. This should be heavily planted to shield the young from their hungry mother.

SAILFIN MOLLY
Plenty of green matter is appreciated in the diet of this livebearer.

SWORDTAIL
The "sword-like" extension on the tail distinguishes this species.

GOODEID
Males of the family Goodeidae lack the rod-like, fertilizing anal fin of other male livebearers.

COLDWATER FRESHWATER FISHES

SARASA COMET
The Goldfish is the most popular aquarium fish of all. Red and white patches are typical of this slim-bodied cultivated strain.

long-based dorsal fin

variable colours depend on strain

large, deeply forked caudal fin

scales can be metallic, translucent, or opaque

FAMILY CHARACTERISTICS

The popularity of ornamental coldwater fishes sustained the aquarium hobby for hundreds of years until the tropical varieties were introduced in the 19th century. Coldwater aquarium species are mostly comprised of the many aquarium-cultivated varieties of the Common Goldfish (*Carassius auratus*), a member of the cyprinid family originating in Asia. A near relative in the same family, the Koi (*Cyprinus carpio*), has been developed in Japan, although it is generally kept in the outdoor pond rather than the aquarium. Goldfishes and Koi are long-lived and adapt well to aquarium and pond culture. No standard size descriptions are offered in this book as they generally grow to the limits of their environment, and no habitat is given as they are aquarium-bred.

A number of species from temperate regions of North America, Europe, and Japan are also included in this category as more recently established aquarium subjects. There may be local laws against selling some of these species or removing them from their habitat.

TWINTAIL GOLDFISH
A strain with divided anal and caudal fins.

SUNFISH
All sunfishes have a distinctive "ear-flap".

SHINER
Members of this fish group develop head tubercles when breeding.

TROPICAL MARINE FISHES

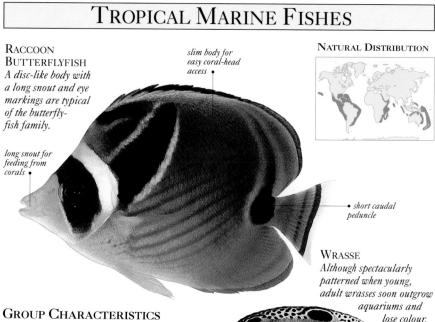

RACCOON BUTTERFLYFISH
A disc-like body with a long snout and eye markings are typical of the butterfly-fish family.

slim body for easy coral-head access

NATURAL DISTRIBUTION

long snout for feeding from corals

short caudal peduncle

WRASSE
Although spectacularly patterned when young, adult wrasses soon outgrow aquariums and lose colour.

GROUP CHARACTERISTICS

Marine fishes are perhaps the most attractive of all candidates for the aquarium, but they are also the most intolerant of changes in water quality. They form a specialized aspect of fish-keeping that should only be attempted with forethought. It is advisable to start off with the more hardy species.

Tropical marine fishes generally come from coral reefs and coastal areas throughout the tropical oceans of the world. The choice of shapes, sizes, and colours is extensive, and the question of compatibility must be considered during selection. Many marine fishes are intol-erant of other members of the same species, and they may be very territorial, so always provide hiding places. Some species form natural relationships with other fishes or invertebrates and may be kept together: anemonefishes, for example, appreciate sea anemones.

The breeding of marine fishes is frequently restricted to anemonefishes and gobies. The most popular tropical marine groups are described in this book first, followed by genera with fewer species members.

ANGELFISH
Body shape is similar to that of the butterflyfishes, but a spine is present on the gill-cover.

GOBY
Gobies are brightly coloured fishes which usually have a suction disc formed by the pelvic fins, as seen here.

COLDWATER MARINE FISHES

LONG-SPINED SEA SCORPION
The spines of this magnificent fish are poisonous to other fish and to unwary fish collectors.

bony ridges on head •

decorative dorsal • spines

flat ventral • surface

NATURAL DISTRIBUTION

GROUP CHARACTERISTICS

Fishkeepers who live within reach of the seashore are able to collect local species from rock-pools that have become isolated by receding tides. If these species outgrow the aquarium, they can easily be returned to the shore. The selection of species described in this section does not represent all temperate coastal regions, but is offered as an indication of the variety of species that can be collected directly by the fishkeeper. Generally speaking, it is likely that coldwater fishes will be rather subdued in colour compared with their tropical relatives. Mottled brown coloration is the norm.

Most coldwater marine fishes depend on rocky retreats, so you should provide these in the aquarium. A fine, deep substrate will enable burrowing fishes, like the wrasse, to feel secure. As with tropical aquariums, you can add invertebrates for interest: sea anemones, shrimps, starfish, and small crabs can all be included to enliven a coldwater marine scene. Native marine fishes can be kept fairly cheaply in a medium to large tank which must be checked for over-heating in the summer.

STICKLEBACK
These fish are easily identified by the spines and bony plates on their flanks.

LUMPSUCKER
A concealed first dorsal fin and a spiny skin characterize this unusual coldwater marine species.

CLINGFISH
Like the gobies, this fish adheres itself to surfaces using a special suction disc.

TROPICAL FRESHWATER FISHES

CYPRINIDS
BARBS, DANIOS, AND RASBORAS

T HERE ARE ABOUT 1,250 hardy, active species in the family Cyprinidae, of which barbs, danios, and rasboras are the most common. These attractive smaller cyprinids from both tropical and subtropical waters are undemanding in the aquarium and easy to feed. They breed by egg-scattering.

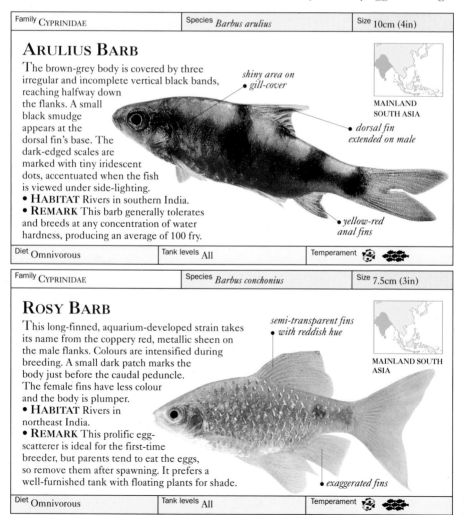

Family CYPRINIDAE	Species *Barbus arulius*	Size 10cm (4in)

ARULIUS BARB

The brown-grey body is covered by three irregular and incomplete vertical black bands, reaching halfway down the flanks. A small black smudge appears at the dorsal fin's base. The dark-edged scales are marked with tiny iridescent dots, accentuated when the fish is viewed under side-lighting.
• **HABITAT** Rivers in southern India.
• **REMARK** This barb generally tolerates and breeds at any concentration of water hardness, producing an average of 100 fry.

shiny area on gill-cover

MAINLAND SOUTH ASIA

dorsal fin extended on male

yellow-red anal fins

Diet Omnivorous	Tank levels All	Temperament

Family CYPRINIDAE	Species *Barbus conchonius*	Size 7.5cm (3in)

ROSY BARB

This long-finned, aquarium-developed strain takes its name from the coppery red, metallic sheen on the male flanks. Colours are intensified during breeding. A small dark patch marks the body just before the caudal peduncle. The female fins have less colour and the body is plumper.
• **HABITAT** Rivers in northeast India.
• **REMARK** This prolific egg-scatterer is ideal for the first-time breeder, but parents tend to eat the eggs, so remove them after spawning. It prefers a well-furnished tank with floating plants for shade.

semi-transparent fins with reddish hue

MAINLAND SOUTH ASIA

exaggerated fins

Diet Omnivorous	Tank levels All	Temperament

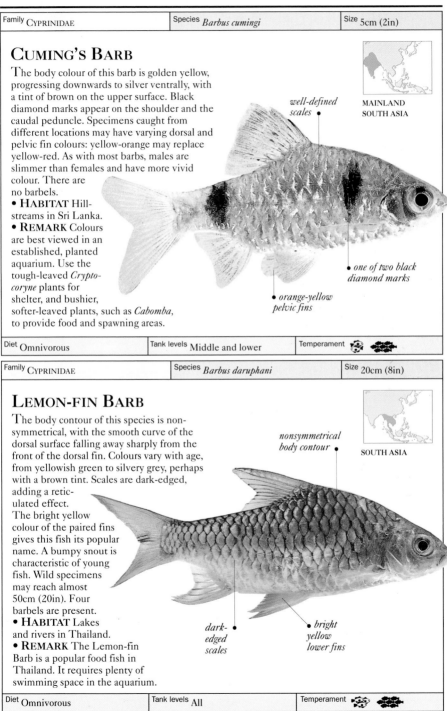

| Family CYPRINIDAE | Species *Barbus cumingi* | Size 5cm (2in) |

CUMING'S BARB

The body colour of this barb is golden yellow, progressing downwards to silver ventrally, with a tint of brown on the upper surface. Black diamond marks appear on the shoulder and the caudal peduncle. Specimens caught from different locations may have varying dorsal and pelvic fin colours: yellow-orange may replace yellow-red. As with most barbs, males are slimmer than females and have more vivid colour. There are no barbels.

• **HABITAT** Hill-streams in Sri Lanka.
• **REMARK** Colours are best viewed in an established, planted aquarium. Use the tough-leaved *Crypto-coryne* plants for shelter, and bushier, softer-leaved plants, such as *Cabomba*, to provide food and spawning areas.

well-defined scales

MAINLAND SOUTH ASIA

one of two black diamond marks

orange-yellow pelvic fins

| Diet Omnivorous | Tank levels Middle and lower | Temperament |

| Family CYPRINIDAE | Species *Barbus daruphani* | Size 20cm (8in) |

LEMON-FIN BARB

The body contour of this species is non-symmetrical, with the smooth curve of the dorsal surface falling away sharply from the front of the dorsal fin. Colours vary with age, from yellowish green to silvery grey, perhaps with a brown tint. Scales are dark-edged, adding a retic-ulated effect. The bright yellow colour of the paired fins gives this fish its popular name. A bumpy snout is characteristic of young fish. Wild specimens may reach almost 50cm (20in). Four barbels are present.

• **HABITAT** Lakes and rivers in Thailand.
• **REMARK** The Lemon-fin Barb is a popular food fish in Thailand. It requires plenty of swimming space in the aquarium.

nonsymmetrical body contour

SOUTH ASIA

dark-edged scales

bright yellow lower fins

| Diet Omnivorous | Tank levels All | Temperament |

Family CYPRINIDAE	Species *Barbus dorsalis*	Size 13cm (5in)

DORSALIS BARB

This fish's body is symmetrical and generally more elongate than most barbs. Colours vary from metallic bronze to blushing red, and the brown-green dorsal surface shades down to silver on the ventral region. The dark apex at the front of each scale is distinct.
• **HABITAT** Streams and rivers in Sri Lanka.
• **REMARK** This active species needs an efficient filtration system to keep the water clear of suspended waste matter.

erect, triangular dorsal fin is • *tinged red*

MAINLAND SOUTH ASIA

red upper part of eye •

deeply forked • *caudal fin*

extended • *snout carrying terminal mouth*

Diet Omnivorous	Tank levels All	Temperament

Family CYPRINIDAE	Species *Barbus everetti*	Size 14cm (5½in)

CLOWN BARB

The background colour of this barb is a golden brown-pink which shades to silver on the belly. Several equally spaced dark blotches appear on the flanks. Females are deeper-bodied.
• **HABITAT** Streams and rivers in Borneo, Malaysia, and Singapore.
• **REMARK** Soft water is preferable for this active fish. It is easily bred in large tanks with bushy plants.

dark patches may run • *together*

S.E. ASIA

fins are • *yellowish, tinged with red*

silver ventral • *surface*

Diet Omnivorous	Tank levels Middle and lower	Temperament

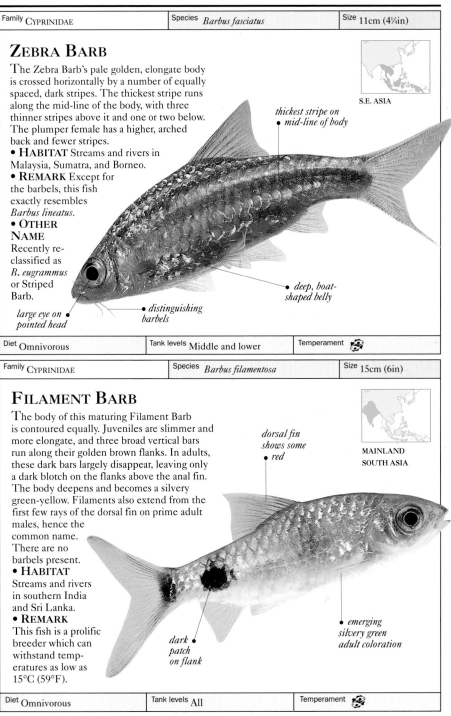

Family CYPRINIDAE	Species *Barbus fasciatus*	Size 11cm (4¼in)

ZEBRA BARB

The Zebra Barb's pale golden, elongate body is crossed horizontally by a number of equally spaced, dark stripes. The thickest stripe runs along the mid-line of the body, with three thinner stripes above it and one or two below. The plumper female has a higher, arched back and fewer stripes.
• **HABITAT** Streams and rivers in Malaysia, Sumatra, and Borneo.
• **REMARK** Except for the barbels, this fish exactly resembles *Barbus lineatus*.
• **OTHER NAME** Recently re-classified as *B. eugrammus* or Striped Barb.

S.E. ASIA

thickest stripe on mid-line of body

deep, boat-shaped belly

large eye on pointed head

distinguishing barbels

Diet Omnivorous	Tank levels Middle and lower	Temperament

Family CYPRINIDAE	Species *Barbus filamentosa*	Size 15cm (6in)

FILAMENT BARB

The body of this maturing Filament Barb is contoured equally. Juveniles are slimmer and more elongate, and three broad vertical bars run along their golden brown flanks. In adults, these dark bars largely disappear, leaving only a dark blotch on the flanks above the anal fin. The body deepens and becomes a silvery green-yellow. Filaments also extend from the first few rays of the dorsal fin on prime adult males, hence the common name. There are no barbels present.
• **HABITAT** Streams and rivers in southern India and Sri Lanka.
• **REMARK** This fish is a prolific breeder which can withstand temperatures as low as 15°C (59°F).

dorsal fin shows some red

MAINLAND SOUTH ASIA

dark patch on flank

emerging silvery green adult coloration

Diet Omnivorous	Tank levels All	Temperament

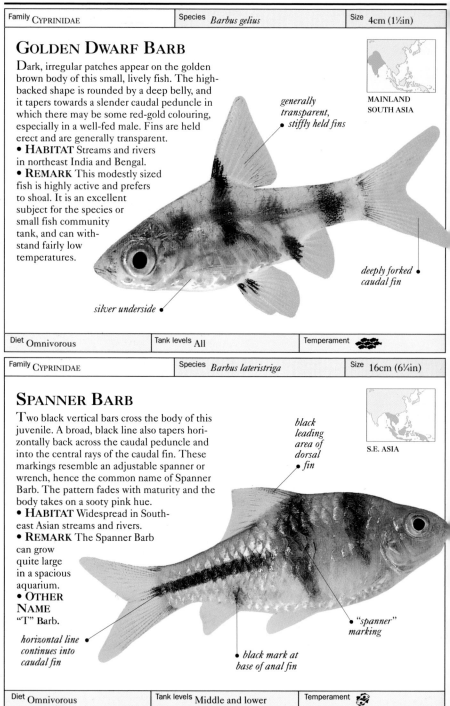

Family CYPRINIDAE	Species *Barbus gelius*	Size 4cm (1½in)

GOLDEN DWARF BARB

Dark, irregular patches appear on the golden brown body of this small, lively fish. The high-backed shape is rounded by a deep belly, and it tapers towards a slender caudal peduncle in which there may be some red-gold colouring, especially in a well-fed male. Fins are held erect and are generally transparent.
• **HABITAT** Streams and rivers in northeast India and Bengal.
• **REMARK** This modestly sized fish is highly active and prefers to shoal. It is an excellent subject for the species or small fish community tank, and can with-stand fairly low temperatures.

generally transparent, stiffly held fins

MAINLAND SOUTH ASIA

deeply forked caudal fin

silver underside

Diet Omnivorous	Tank levels All	Temperament

Family CYPRINIDAE	Species *Barbus lateristriga*	Size 16cm (6¼in)

SPANNER BARB

Two black vertical bars cross the body of this juvenile. A broad, black line also tapers hori-zontally back across the caudal peduncle and into the central rays of the caudal fin. These markings resemble an adjustable spanner or wrench, hence the common name of Spanner Barb. The pattern fades with maturity and the body takes on a sooty pink hue.
• **HABITAT** Widespread in South-east Asian streams and rivers.
• **REMARK** The Spanner Barb can grow quite large in a spacious aquarium.
• **OTHER NAME** "T" Barb.

black leading area of dorsal fin

S.E. ASIA

horizontal line continues into caudal fin

"spanner" marking

black mark at base of anal fin

Diet Omnivorous	Tank levels Middle and lower	Temperament

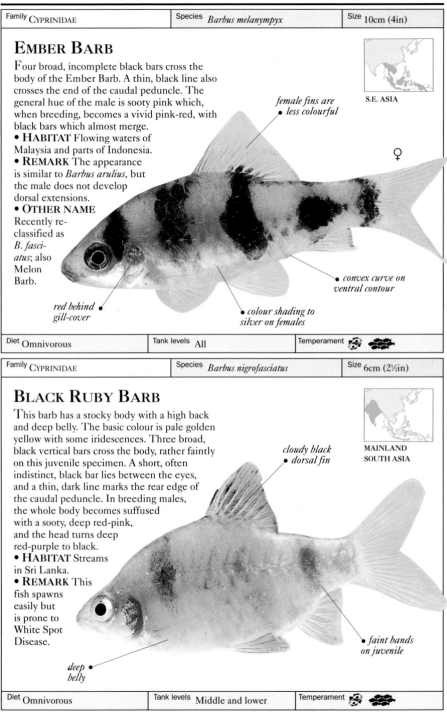

| Family CYPRINIDAE | Species *Barbus melanympyx* | Size 10cm (4in) |

EMBER BARB

Four broad, incomplete black bars cross the body of the Ember Barb. A thin, black line also crosses the end of the caudal peduncle. The general hue of the male is sooty pink which, when breeding, becomes a vivid pink-red, with black bars which almost merge.
• **HABITAT** Flowing waters of Malaysia and parts of Indonesia.
• **REMARK** The appearance is similar to *Barbus arulius*, but the male does not develop dorsal extensions.
• **OTHER NAME** Recently re-classified as *B. fasciatus*; also Melon Barb.

female fins are less colourful

S.E. ASIA

♀

convex curve on ventral contour

red behind gill-cover

colour shading to silver on females

| Diet Omnivorous | Tank levels All | Temperament |

| Family CYPRINIDAE | Species *Barbus nigrofasciatus* | Size 6cm (2½in) |

BLACK RUBY BARB

This barb has a stocky body with a high back and deep belly. The basic colour is pale golden yellow with some iridescences. Three broad, black vertical bars cross the body, rather faintly on this juvenile specimen. A short, often indistinct, black bar lies between the eyes, and a thin, dark line marks the rear edge of the caudal peduncle. In breeding males, the whole body becomes suffused with a sooty, deep red-pink, and the head turns deep red-purple to black.
• **HABITAT** Streams in Sri Lanka.
• **REMARK** This fish spawns easily but is prone to White Spot Disease.

cloudy black dorsal fin

MAINLAND SOUTH ASIA

faint bands on juvenile

deep belly

| Diet Omnivorous | Tank levels Middle and lower | Temperament |

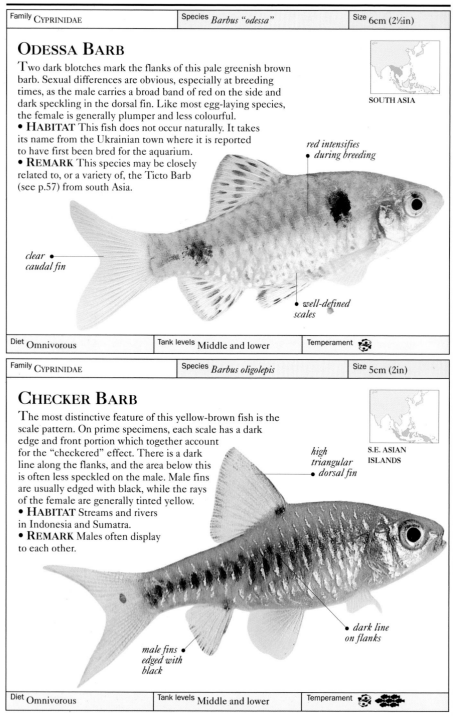

| Family CYPRINIDAE | Species Barbus "odessa" | Size 6cm (2½in) |

ODESSA BARB

Two dark blotches mark the flanks of this pale greenish brown
barb. Sexual differences are obvious, especially at breeding
times, as the male carries a broad band of red on the side and
dark speckling in the dorsal fin. Like most egg-laying species,
the female is generally plumper and less colourful.
• **HABITAT** This fish does not occur naturally. It takes
its name from the Ukrainian town where it is reported
to have first been bred for the aquarium.
• **REMARK** This species may be closely
related to, or a variety of, the Ticto Barb
(see p.57) from south Asia.

SOUTH ASIA

*red intensifies
• during breeding*

*clear •
caudal fin*

*• well-defined
scales*

| Diet Omnivorous | Tank levels Middle and lower | Temperament |

| Family CYPRINIDAE | Species Barbus oligolepis | Size 5cm (2in) |

CHECKER BARB

The most distinctive feature of this yellow-brown fish is the
scale pattern. On prime specimens, each scale has a dark
edge and front portion which together account
for the "checkered" effect. There is a dark
line along the flanks, and the area below this
is often less speckled on the male. Male fins
are usually edged with black, while the rays
of the female are generally tinted yellow.
• **HABITAT** Streams and rivers
in Indonesia and Sumatra.
• **REMARK** Males often display
to each other.

*high
triangular
• dorsal fin*

S.E. ASIAN
ISLANDS

*• dark line
on flanks*

*male fins •
edged with
black*

| Diet Omnivorous | Tank levels Middle and lower | Temperament |

| Family CYPRINIDAE | Species *Barbus pentazona johorensis* | Size 5cm (2in) |

FIVE-BANDED BARB

Five prominent dark bands vertically cross the body of this subspecies. The first passes through the eye, not quite meeting at the ventral surface. Most fins carry red shading, usually at the base; this is less evident in the caudal fin and on this juvenile. Females are plumper and less intensely coloured.
• **HABITAT** Streams in Borneo, Malaysia, and Sumatra.
• **REMARK** There are several other subspecies of *Barbus pentazona*, which can be identified by differences in the bands.

S. E. ASIA

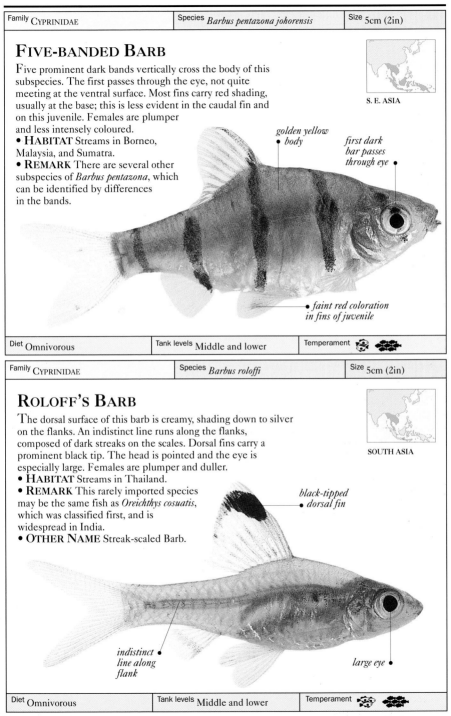

golden yellow body

first dark bar passes through eye

faint red coloration in fins of juvenile

| Diet Omnivorous | Tank levels Middle and lower | Temperament |

| Family CYPRINIDAE | Species *Barbus roloffi* | Size 5cm (2in) |

ROLOFF'S BARB

The dorsal surface of this barb is creamy, shading down to silver on the flanks. An indistinct line runs along the flanks, composed of dark streaks on the scales. Dorsal fins carry a prominent black tip. The head is pointed and the eye is especially large. Females are plumper and duller.
• **HABITAT** Streams in Thailand.
• **REMARK** This rarely imported species may be the same fish as *Oreichthys cosuatis*, which was classified first, and is widespread in India.
• **OTHER NAME** Streak-scaled Barb.

SOUTH ASIA

black-tipped dorsal fin

indistinct line along flank

large eye

| Diet Omnivorous | Tank levels Middle and lower | Temperament |

| Family CYPRINIDAE | Species *Barbus sachsi* | Size 10cm (4in) |

GOLDEN BARB

This slightly elongate fish has a narrow caudal peduncle but plump sides. The general body coloration is yellow, with silver on the ventral surface. There may be some short, dark vertical streaks or marks randomly distributed over the body, especially on juveniles (like this specimen); they usually fade with age. Female Golden Barbs are plumper.
- **HABITAT** Streams in Singapore.
- **REMARK** Differences between this species and the Schuberti Barb (below) are slight. It is thought that they might be related.

SOUTH ASIA

narrow caudal peduncle

irregular black marks

silver ventral surface

| Diet Omnivorous | Tank levels Middle and lower | Temperament |

| Family CYPRINIDAE | Species *Barbus "schuberti"* | Size 7.5cm (3in) |

SCHUBERTI BARB

A number of dark speckles appear on the dorsal surface of this species. Larger blotches run above the lateral line, and a dark blotch crosses the end of the caudal peduncle. The main colour is yellow, with metallic green along the top. On prime specimens fins are bright red and streaked with yellow, while the base of the caudal fin and the two tail lobes have bright red portions. Females are fuller.
- **HABITAT** Streams and rivers in south Asia.
- **REMARK** This fish has not been named according to strict scientific classification. Its discovery has been attributed to Mr. Thomas Schubert of the USA, but some suggest that it is a colour strain of the Golden Barb (above).

Barbs look their best in shoals

reddish eye

metallic green on flanks

SOUTH ASIA

dark blotch on caudal peduncle

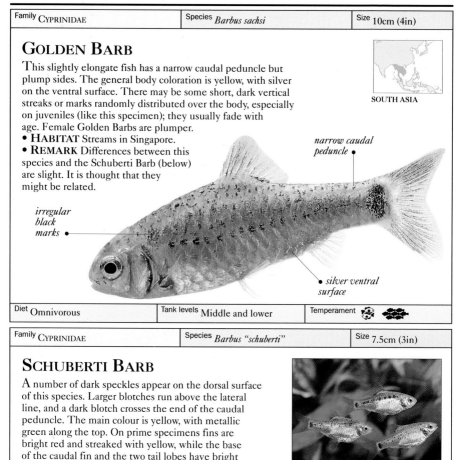

| Diet Omnivorous | Tank levels Middle and lower | Temperament |

Family CYPRINIDAE	Species *Barbus schwanenfeldi*	Size 30cm (12in)

TINFOIL BARB

The greyish brown colour on the dorsal surface of this juvenile barb shades down to shining silver flanks with well-defined scales. The triangular dorsal fin, which is black with a red base on adult fish, has a concave trailing edge. Pelvic and anal fins on mature specimens are bright red-orange, and the lesser coloured caudal fin has black top and bottom edges.
• **HABITAT** Rivers and lakes in Borneo, Sumatra, and Thailand.
• **REMARK** This active fish needs space and plenty of green matter. It is an avid consumer of duckweed.

S.E. ASIAN ISLANDS

shining silver flanks

faint black on edge of caudal fin

yellow-orange anal fin

Diet Omnivorous	Tank levels Middle and lower	Temperament

Family CYPRINIDAE	Species *Barbus semifasciolatus*	Size 7.5cm (3in)

HALF-BANDED BARB

Thin, incomplete dark lines vertically cross the olive-green body of this hardy barb. Dark speckles may generally appear on the dorsal surface. In the breeding male, all fins are red and streaked with yellow.
• **HABITAT** Streams, rivers, and paddy fields in Malaysia; also in Hong Kong and central and southern China.
• **REMARK** The Half-banded Barb is a popular aquarium fish, and is now produced in quantity by fish farms in Asia and Florida.
• **OTHER NAME** Chinese Green Barb.

SOUTH ASIA

dark vertical lines

well-defined scales

silver ventral surface

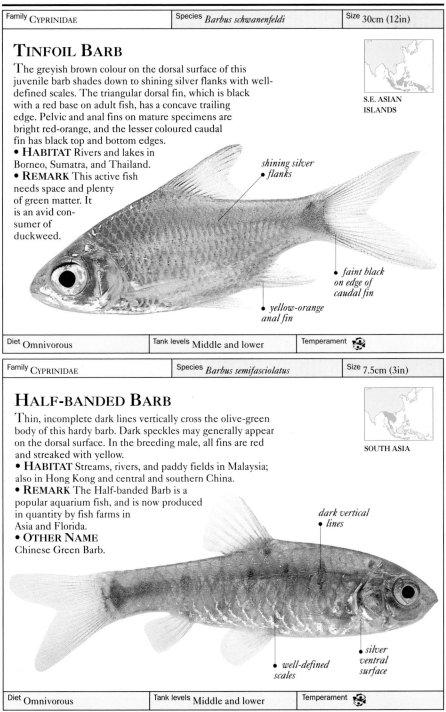

Diet Omnivorous	Tank levels Middle and lower	Temperament

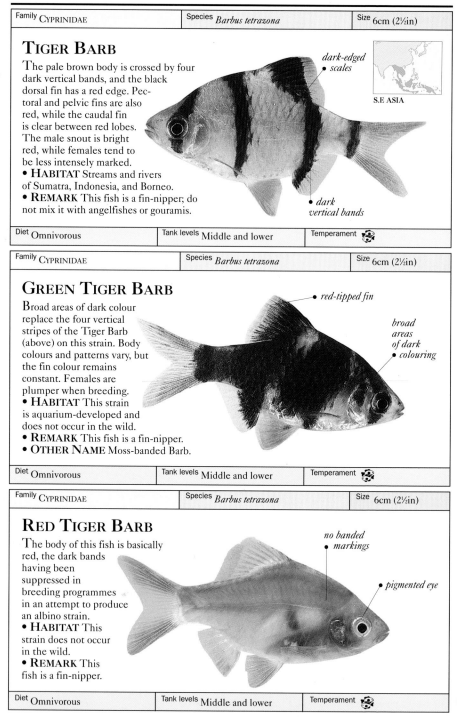

| Family CYPRINIDAE | Species *Barbus tetrazona* | Size 6cm (2½in) |

TIGER BARB

The pale brown body is crossed by four dark vertical bands, and the black dorsal fin has a red edge. Pectoral and pelvic fins are also red, while the caudal fin is clear between red lobes. The male snout is bright red, while females tend to be less intensely marked.
• **HABITAT** Streams and rivers of Sumatra, Indonesia, and Borneo.
• **REMARK** This fish is a fin-nipper; do not mix it with angelfishes or gouramis.

dark-edged scales

S.E ASIA

dark vertical bands

| Diet Omnivorous | Tank levels Middle and lower | Temperament |

| Family CYPRINIDAE | Species *Barbus tetrazona* | Size 6cm (2½in) |

GREEN TIGER BARB

Broad areas of dark colour replace the four vertical stripes of the Tiger Barb (above) on this strain. Body colours and patterns vary, but the fin colour remains constant. Females are plumper when breeding.
• **HABITAT** This strain is aquarium-developed and does not occur in the wild.
• **REMARK** This fish is a fin-nipper.
• **OTHER NAME** Moss-banded Barb.

red-tipped fin

broad areas of dark colouring

| Diet Omnivorous | Tank levels Middle and lower | Temperament |

| Family CYPRINIDAE | Species *Barbus tetrazona* | Size 6cm (2½in) |

RED TIGER BARB

The body of this fish is basically red, the dark bands having been suppressed in breeding programmes in an attempt to produce an albino strain.
• **HABITAT** This strain does not occur in the wild.
• **REMARK** This fish is a fin-nipper.

no banded markings

pigmented eye

| Diet Omnivorous | Tank levels Middle and lower | Temperament |

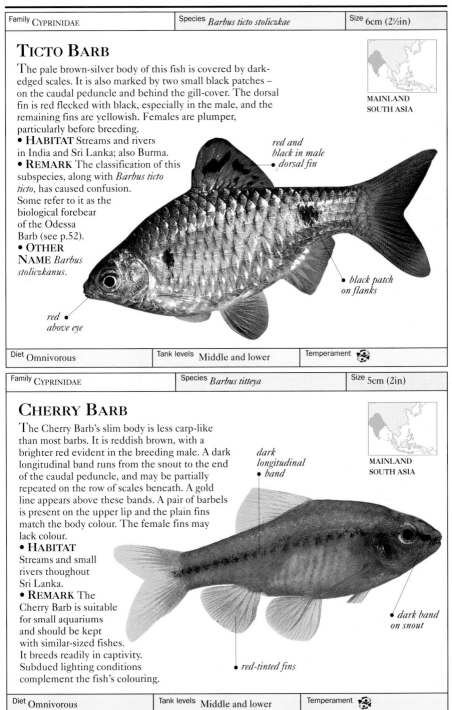

| Family CYPRINIDAE | Species *Barbus ticto stoliczkae* | Size 6cm (2½in) |

TICTO BARB

The pale brown-silver body of this fish is covered by dark-edged scales. It is also marked by two small black patches – on the caudal peduncle and behind the gill-cover. The dorsal fin is red flecked with black, especially in the male, and the remaining fins are yellowish. Females are plumper, particularly before breeding.

MAINLAND
SOUTH ASIA

• **HABITAT** Streams and rivers in India and Sri Lanka; also Burma.
• **REMARK** The classification of this subspecies, along with *Barbus ticto ticto*, has caused confusion. Some refer to it as the biological forebear of the Odessa Barb (see p.52).
• **OTHER NAME** *Barbus stoliczkanus.*

red and black in male dorsal fin

black patch on flanks

red above eye

| Diet Omnivorous | Tank levels Middle and lower | Temperament |

| Family CYPRINIDAE | Species *Barbus titteya* | Size 5cm (2in) |

CHERRY BARB

The Cherry Barb's slim body is less carp-like than most barbs. It is reddish brown, with a brighter red evident in the breeding male. A dark longitudinal band runs from the snout to the end of the caudal peduncle, and may be partially repeated on the row of scales beneath. A gold line appears above these bands. A pair of barbels is present on the upper lip and the plain fins match the body colour. The female fins may lack colour.

dark longitudinal band

MAINLAND
SOUTH ASIA

• **HABITAT** Streams and small rivers thoughout Sri Lanka.
• **REMARK** The Cherry Barb is suitable for small aquariums and should be kept with similar-sized fishes. It breeds readily in captivity. Subdued lighting conditions complement the fish's colouring.

dark band on snout

red-tinted fins

| Diet Omnivorous | Tank levels Middle and lower | Temperament |

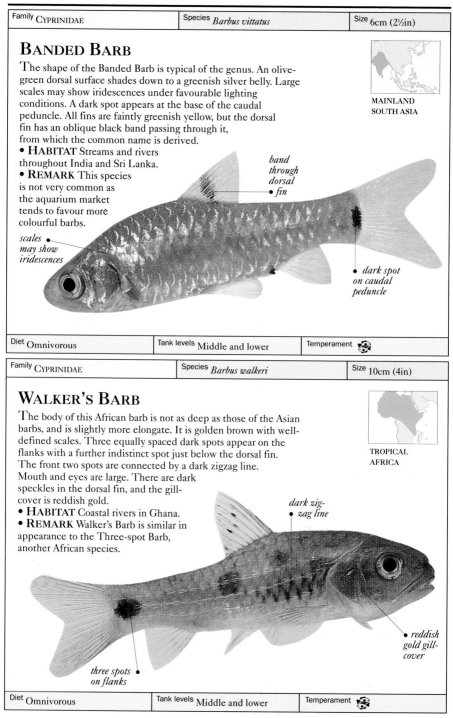

| Family CYPRINIDAE | Species *Barbus vittatus* | Size 6cm (2½in) |

BANDED BARB

The shape of the Banded Barb is typical of the genus. An olive-green dorsal surface shades down to a greenish silver belly. Large scales may show iridescences under favourable lighting conditions. A dark spot appears at the base of the caudal peduncle. All fins are faintly greenish yellow, but the dorsal fin has an oblique black band passing through it, from which the common name is derived.
• **HABITAT** Streams and rivers throughout India and Sri Lanka.
• **REMARK** This species is not very common as the aquarium market tends to favour more colourful barbs.

MAINLAND
SOUTH ASIA

band through dorsal fin

scales may show iridescences

dark spot on caudal peduncle

| Diet Omnivorous | Tank levels Middle and lower | Temperament |

| Family CYPRINIDAE | Species *Barbus walkeri* | Size 10cm (4in) |

WALKER'S BARB

The body of this African barb is not as deep as those of the Asian barbs, and is slightly more elongate. It is golden brown with well-defined scales. Three equally spaced dark spots appear on the flanks with a further indistinct spot just below the dorsal fin. The front two spots are connected by a dark zigzag line. Mouth and eyes are large. There are dark speckles in the dorsal fin, and the gill-cover is reddish gold.
• **HABITAT** Coastal rivers in Ghana.
• **REMARK** Walker's Barb is similar in appearance to the Three-spot Barb, another African species.

TROPICAL
AFRICA

dark zig-zag line

reddish gold gill-cover

three spots on flanks

| Diet Omnivorous | Tank levels Middle and lower | Temperament |

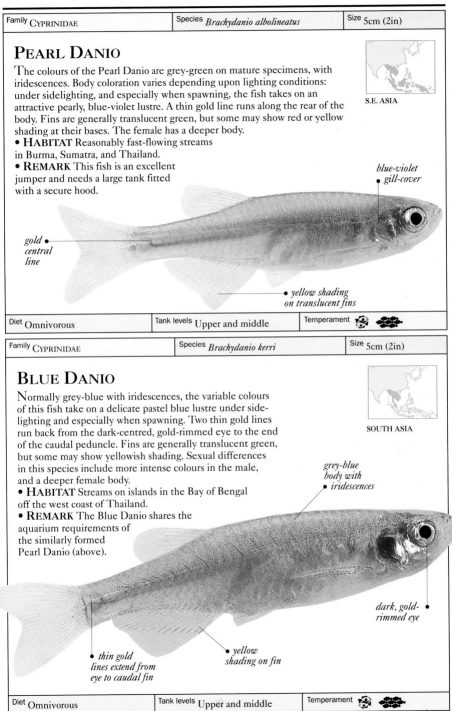

Family CYPRINIDAE	Species *Brachydanio albolineatus*	Size 5cm (2in)

PEARL DANIO

The colours of the Pearl Danio are grey-green on mature specimens, with iridescences. Body coloration varies depending upon lighting conditions: under sidelighting, and especially when spawning, the fish takes on an attractive pearly, blue-violet lustre. A thin gold line runs along the rear of the body. Fins are generally translucent green, but some may show red or yellow shading at their bases. The female has a deeper body.
• **HABITAT** Reasonably fast-flowing streams in Burma, Sumatra, and Thailand.
• **REMARK** This fish is an excellent jumper and needs a large tank fitted with a secure hood.

S.E. ASIA

blue-violet gill-cover

gold central line

yellow shading on translucent fins

Diet Omnivorous	Tank levels Upper and middle	Temperament

Family CYPRINIDAE	Species *Brachydanio kerri*	Size 5cm (2in)

BLUE DANIO

Normally grey-blue with iridescences, the variable colours of this fish take on a delicate pastel blue lustre under side-lighting and especially when spawning. Two thin gold lines run back from the dark-centred, gold-rimmed eye to the end of the caudal peduncle. Fins are generally translucent green, but some may show yellowish shading. Sexual differences in this species include more intense colours in the male, and a deeper female body.
• **HABITAT** Streams on islands in the Bay of Bengal off the west coast of Thailand.
• **REMARK** The Blue Danio shares the aquarium requirements of the similarly formed Pearl Danio (above).

SOUTH ASIA

grey-blue body with iridescences

dark, gold-rimmed eye

thin gold lines extend from eye to caudal fin

yellow shading on fin

Diet Omnivorous	Tank levels Upper and middle	Temperament

Family CYPRINIDAE	Species *Brachydanio frankei*	Size 4.5cm (1¾in)

LEOPARD DANIO

Leopard-like spots on a gold background give these fish their popular name. Of the two fish shown here, the long-finned variety has been aquarium-developed. Spots on both are smaller and closer together on the upper body, giving a darker appearance; the spots may also group together to form interrupted "lines", particularly on the caudal peduncle. Faint patterning is apparent in the yellowish anal fin and the centre of the caudal fin. The female is usually larger than the male, even outside the breeding season, with a more convex body outline.
• **HABITAT** The wild species is from southern and central India; also ranging into the Malay peninsula.
• **REMARK** The classification of this species has been argued over since its introduction to the aquarium, a process further complicated by its ready hybridization with *Brachydanio rerio* and *B. albolineatus*. Some authorities assume it to be an offspring of one of these two species.

MAINLAND SOUTH ASIA

eye set forward on small head •

yellow tint •

• cultivated trailing fins

faint • patterning on anal fin

LONG-FINNED VARIETY

upturned mouth •

WILD SPECIES

• rows of interrupted spots

♀

Diet Omnivorous	Tank level Upper	Temperament

Family CYPRINIDAE	Species *Brachydanio rerio*	Size 4.5cm (1¾in)

ZEBRA DANIO

This fish has a base colour of silver or gold, strikingly marked by
a number of bright blue or purple horizontal lines which run from
the head to the rear edge of the caudal fin. This pattern is
repeated in the anal and caudal fins; the dorsal area is yellowish
olive. The long-finned variety has been aquarium-developed.
All males are slimmer and slightly smaller than the females.
• **HABITAT** The wild species is from east India.
• **REMARK** This is a very active species, constantly on the
move in the upper levels of the water; a group is recommended. It is a prolific spawner which is good for first
breeding attempts, but precautions should be taken to
prevent egg-eating by the adults, even though the eggs
may be lodged in densely leaved plants provided for
the purpose. Selective breeding has produced
both long-finned and veil-tailed strains.

MAINLAND
SOUTH ASIA

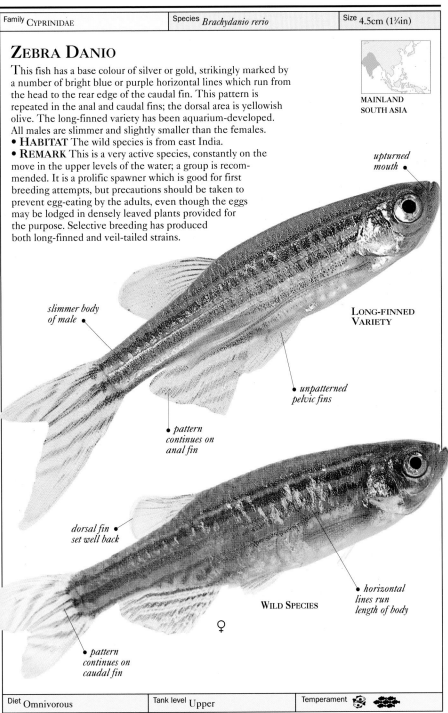

upturned mouth

slimmer body of male

LONG-FINNED
VARIETY

unpatterned pelvic fins

pattern continues on anal fin

dorsal fin set well back

horizontal lines run length of body

WILD SPECIES

♀

pattern continues on caudal fin

Diet Omnivorous	Tank level Upper	Temperament

| Family CYPRINIDAE | Species *Danio aequipinnatus* | Size 10cm (4in) |

GIANT DANIO

The Giant Danio's body is pale blue, with three or four vertical yellow lines from the gill-cover to the caudal peduncle. Females have bodies of greater depth, and their yellow lines turn up at the beginning of the caudal fin.
- **HABITAT** Hill streams of southwest India and Sri Lanka.
- **REMARK** This fish is extremely active and requires plenty of space. It looks best when kept in a shoal.
- **OTHER NAME** Formerly known as *Danio malarbaricus*.

MAINLAND
SOUTH ASIA

yellow lines begin behind gill-cover

gold-ringed eye

blue lines extend into tail

superior mouth

colourless fins

| Diet Omnivorous | Tank level Upper | Temperament |

| Family CYPRINIDAE | Species *Tanichthys albonubes* | Size 5cm (2in) |

WHITE CLOUD MOUNTAIN MINNOW

A thin gold line, overlaid by blue lines, runs from the eye to the end of the caudal peduncle, where it terminates in a dark patch surrounded by red. The dorsal, pelvic, and anal fins are edged with red, yellow, or white, and the scales are dark-edged.
- **HABITAT** Hill streams and lakes in China.
- **REMARK** A good choice for first-time breeders.

Minnows in Chinese hill stream

red and yellow in dorsal fin

gold line overlaid by blue lines

EAST ASIA

red base of caudal fin

| Diet Omnivorous | Tank level Upper | Temperament |

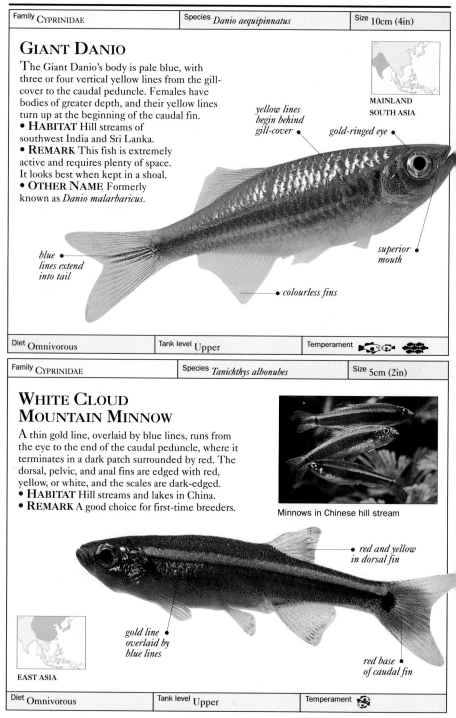

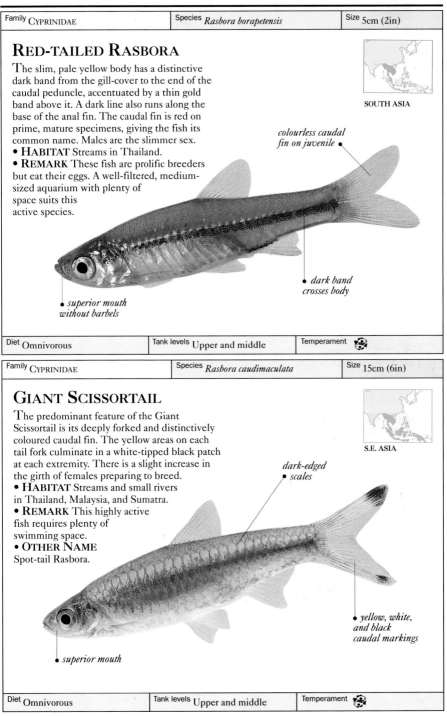

| Family CYPRINIDAE | Species *Rasbora borapetensis* | Size 5cm (2in) |

RED-TAILED RASBORA

The slim, pale yellow body has a distinctive dark band from the gill-cover to the end of the caudal peduncle, accentuated by a thin gold band above it. A dark line also runs along the base of the anal fin. The caudal fin is red on prime, mature specimens, giving the fish its common name. Males are the slimmer sex.
• **HABITAT** Streams in Thailand.
• **REMARK** These fish are prolific breeders but eat their eggs. A well-filtered, medium-sized aquarium with plenty of space suits this active species.

SOUTH ASIA

colourless caudal fin on juvenile

dark band crosses body

superior mouth without barbels

| Diet Omnivorous | Tank levels Upper and middle | Temperament |

| Family CYPRINIDAE | Species *Rasbora caudimaculata* | Size 15cm (6in) |

GIANT SCISSORTAIL

The predominant feature of the Giant Scissortail is its deeply forked and distinctively coloured caudal fin. The yellow areas on each tail fork culminate in a white-tipped black patch at each extremity. There is a slight increase in the girth of females preparing to breed.
• **HABITAT** Streams and small rivers in Thailand, Malaysia, and Sumatra.
• **REMARK** This highly active fish requires plenty of swimming space.
• **OTHER NAME** Spot-tail Rasbora.

S.E. ASIA

dark-edged scales

yellow, white, and black caudal markings

superior mouth

| Diet Omnivorous | Tank levels Upper and middle | Temperament |

Family CYPRINIDAE	Species *Rasbora daniconius*	Size 9cm (3½in)

SLENDER RASBORA

This fish has an elongate body with slight curvatures on the dorsal and ventral profiles. Its body coloration is silver with overtones of purple, green, or yellow. A blue-black line runs the length of the fish. The fins of the male have a yellowish tinge, and the female body shape is slightly deeper.
• **HABITAT** Streams and rivers of Burma, the Greater Sunda Islands, and Thailand; also Southeast India and Sri Lanka.
• **REMARK** This fish is very similar in appearance to *Rasbora einthoveni* (opposite). It will usually reach twice the given size in the wild.
• **OTHER NAME** Gold-line Rasbora.

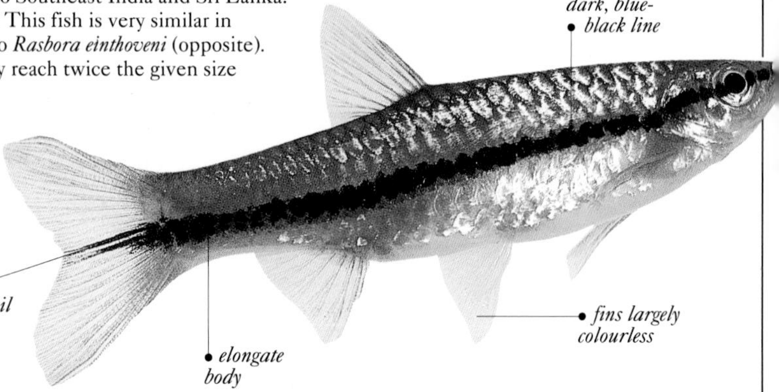

S. E. ASIA

dark, blue-black line

dark line extends into tail

fins largely colourless

elongate body

Diet Omnivorous	Tank level Middle	Temperament

Family CYPRINIDAE	Species *Rasbora dorsiocellata*	Size 6cm (2½in)

EYE-SPOT RASBORA

The coloration of this species is golden green, gradually shading down to white. The dorsal fin carries a distinctive white-edged, dark blotch; all other fins are relatively plain. The female body is deeper than the male; he may have some more definite colour in the fins.
• **HABITAT** Streams and rivers of the Malay peninsula and Sumatra.
• **REMARK** This fish is best kept in small shoals in a well-planted aquarium, where spawning may occur. A smaller subspecies, *Rasbora dorsiocellata macrophthalma*, grows to only half the size of the species shown here and has a vivid blue eye.

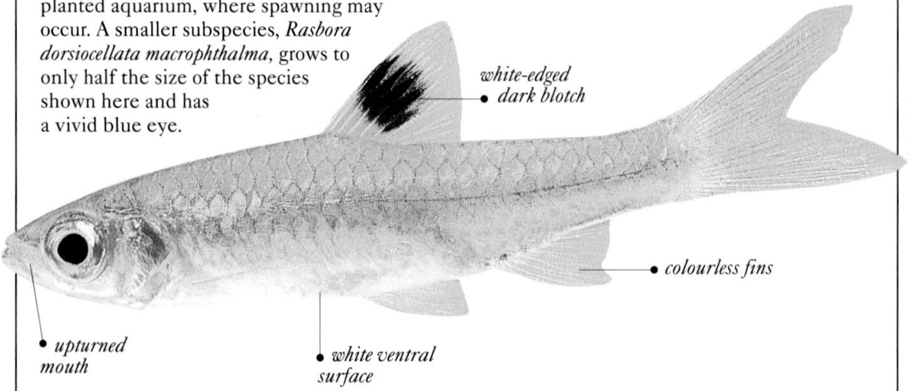

S. E. ASIA

white-edged dark blotch

colourless fins

upturned mouth

white ventral surface

Diet Omnivorous	Tank levels Upper and middle	Temperament

Family CYPRINIDAE	Species *Rasbora einthoveni*	Size 9cm (3½in)

BRILLIANT RASBORA

The body of this pinkish brown fish may carry violet overtones, depending on lighting conditions. A blue-black line runs from the tip of the snout to the rear edge of the caudal fin. Females are plumper and more deep-set than males.
• **HABITAT** Flowing and stationary waters of Borneo, Malaysia, Sumatra, and Thailand.
• **REMARK** A hardy and active shoaling species, this fish can tolerate temperatures as low as 18°C (65°F).

S. E. ASIA

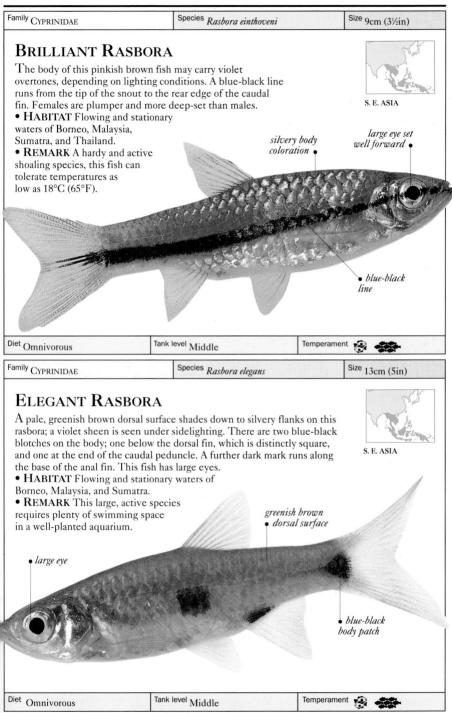

silvery body coloration

large eye set well forward

blue-black line

Diet Omnivorous	Tank level Middle	Temperament

Family CYPRINIDAE	Species *Rasbora elegans*	Size 13cm (5in)

ELEGANT RASBORA

A pale, greenish brown dorsal surface shades down to silvery flanks on this rasbora; a violet sheen is seen under sidelighting. There are two blue-black blotches on the body; one below the dorsal fin, which is distinctly square, and one at the end of the caudal peduncle. A further dark mark runs along the base of the anal fin. This fish has large eyes.
• **HABITAT** Flowing and stationary waters of Borneo, Malaysia, and Sumatra.
• **REMARK** This large, active species requires plenty of swimming space in a well-planted aquarium.

S. E. ASIA

greenish brown dorsal surface

large eye

blue-black body patch

Diet Omnivorous	Tank level Middle	Temperament

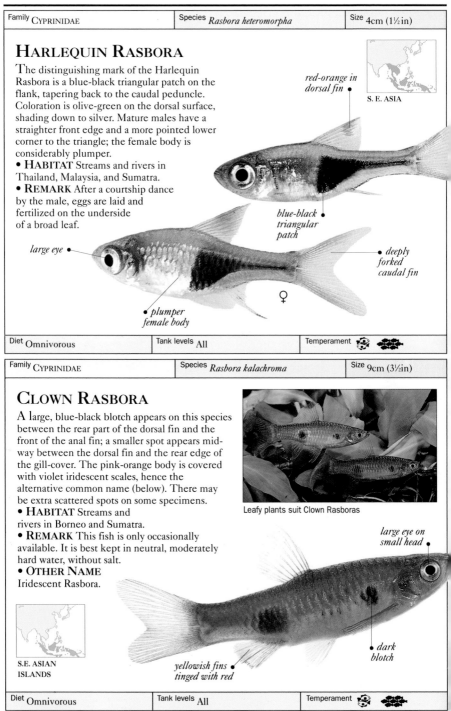

Family CYPRINIDAE	Species *Rasbora heteromorpha*	Size 4cm (1½in)

HARLEQUIN RASBORA

The distinguishing mark of the Harlequin Rasbora is a blue-black triangular patch on the flank, tapering back to the caudal peduncle. Coloration is olive-green on the dorsal surface, shading down to silver. Mature males have a straighter front edge and a more pointed lower corner to the triangle; the female body is considerably plumper.
• **HABITAT** Streams and rivers in Thailand, Malaysia, and Sumatra.
• **REMARK** After a courtship dance by the male, eggs are laid and fertilized on the underside of a broad leaf.

red-orange in dorsal fin

S. E. ASIA

blue-black triangular patch

large eye

deeply forked caudal fin

♀

plumper female body

Diet Omnivorous	Tank levels All	Temperament

Family CYPRINIDAE	Species *Rasbora kalachroma*	Size 9cm (3½in)

CLOWN RASBORA

A large, blue-black blotch appears on this species between the rear part of the dorsal fin and the front of the anal fin; a smaller spot appears midway between the rear of the dorsal fin and the rear edge of the gill-cover. The pink-orange body is covered with violet iridescent scales, hence the alternative common name (below). There may be extra scattered spots on some specimens.
• **HABITAT** Streams and rivers in Borneo and Sumatra.
• **REMARK** This fish is only occasionally available. It is best kept in neutral, moderately hard water, without salt.
• **OTHER NAME** Iridescent Rasbora.

Leafy plants suit Clown Rasboras

large eye on small head

S.E. ASIAN ISLANDS

dark blotch

yellowish fins tinged with red

Diet Omnivorous	Tank levels All	Temperament

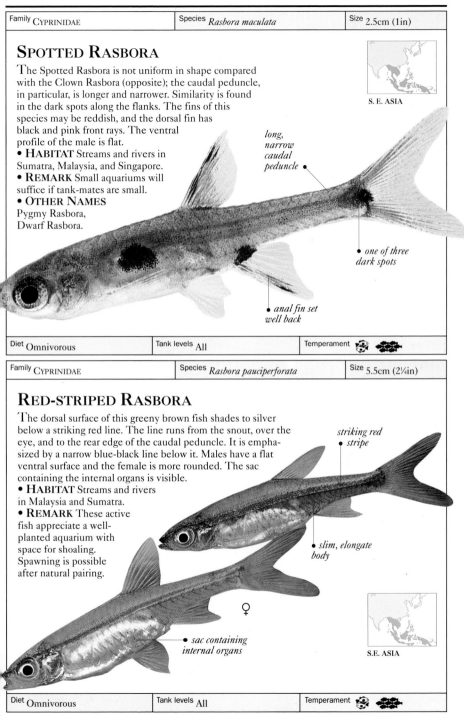

| Family CYPRINIDAE | Species *Rasbora maculata* | Size 2.5cm (1in) |

SPOTTED RASBORA

The Spotted Rasbora is not uniform in shape compared with the Clown Rasbora (opposite); the caudal peduncle, in particular, is longer and narrower. Similarity is found in the dark spots along the flanks. The fins of this species may be reddish, and the dorsal fin has black and pink front rays. The ventral profile of the male is flat.
• **HABITAT** Streams and rivers in Sumatra, Malaysia, and Singapore.
• **REMARK** Small aquariums will suffice if tank-mates are small.
• **OTHER NAMES** Pygmy Rasbora, Dwarf Rasbora.

S. E. ASIA

long, narrow caudal peduncle

one of three dark spots

anal fin set well back

| Diet Omnivorous | Tank levels All | Temperament |

| Family CYPRINIDAE | Species *Rasbora pauciperforata* | Size 5.5cm (2¼in) |

RED-STRIPED RASBORA

The dorsal surface of this greeny brown fish shades to silver below a striking red line. The line runs from the snout, over the eye, and to the rear edge of the caudal peduncle. It is emphasized by a narrow blue-black line below it. Males have a flat ventral surface and the female is more rounded. The sac containing the internal organs is visible.
• **HABITAT** Streams and rivers in Malaysia and Sumatra.
• **REMARK** These active fish appreciate a well-planted aquarium with space for shoaling. Spawning is possible after natural pairing.

striking red stripe

slim, elongate body

♀

sac containing internal organs

S.E. ASIA

| Diet Omnivorous | Tank levels All | Temperament |

Family CYPRINIDAE	Species *Rasbora trilineata*	Size 8cm (3½in)

SCISSORTAIL

The caudal fin of the Scissortail is deeply forked, and on prime specimens it is marked with bold black and white areas; other fins are colourless. Body colour is greyish green with a shiny, silvery belly. Sexual differences include the typical increase in the girth of females, and the more intense colours of breeding males.
• **HABITAT** Streams in Borneo and Sumatra; also Malaysia.
• **REMARK** This fish twitches its caudal fin in a characteristic scissor action when at rest.
• **OTHER NAME** Spot-tail Rasbora.

S.E. ASIAN ISLANDS

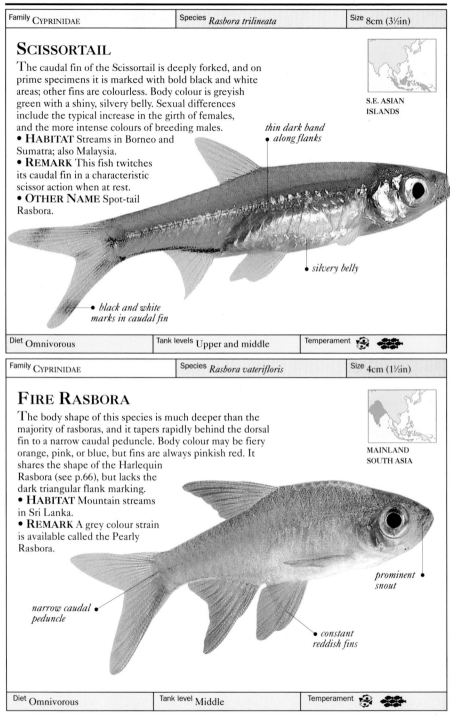

thin dark band along flanks

silvery belly

black and white marks in caudal fin

Diet Omnivorous	Tank levels Upper and middle	Temperament

Family CYPRINIDAE	Species *Rasbora vaterifloris*	Size 4cm (1½in)

FIRE RASBORA

The body shape of this species is much deeper than the majority of rasboras, and it tapers rapidly behind the dorsal fin to a narrow caudal peduncle. Body colour may be fiery orange, pink, or blue, but fins are always pinkish red. It shares the shape of the Harlequin Rasbora (see p.66), but lacks the dark triangular flank marking.
• **HABITAT** Mountain streams in Sri Lanka.
• **REMARK** A grey colour strain is available called the Pearly Rasbora.

MAINLAND SOUTH ASIA

prominent snout

narrow caudal peduncle

constant reddish fins

Diet Omnivorous	Tank level Middle	Temperament

OTHER CYPRINIDS

T HERE ARE OVER 1,500 species in the family Cyprinidae, distributed on every continent except South America and Australia. Barbs, danios, and rasboras form the largest groups of tropical cyprinids; the smaller groups, including the sharks and flying foxes, appear in this section. These fish are from a variety of climes and may require specialized water conditions.

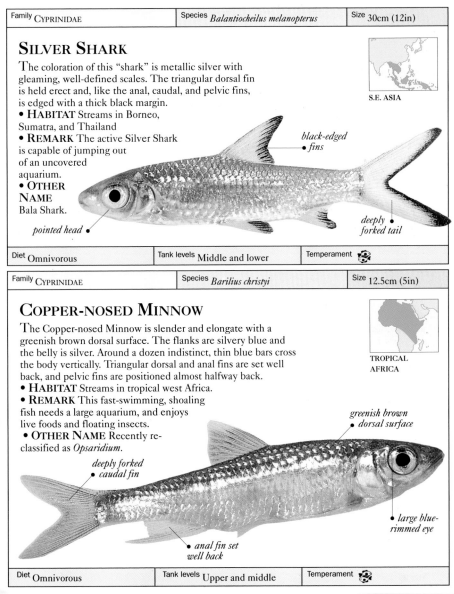

Family CYPRINIDAE	Species *Balantiocheilus melanopterus*	Size 30cm (12in)

SILVER SHARK

The coloration of this "shark" is metallic silver with gleaming, well-defined scales. The triangular dorsal fin is held erect and, like the anal, caudal, and pelvic fins, is edged with a thick black margin.
• **HABITAT** Streams in Borneo, Sumatra, and Thailand
• **REMARK** The active Silver Shark is capable of jumping out of an uncovered aquarium.
• **OTHER NAME** Bala Shark.

pointed head •

S.E. ASIA

black-edged • fins

deeply • forked tail

Diet Omnivorous	Tank levels Middle and lower	Temperament

Family CYPRINIDAE	Species *Barilius christyi*	Size 12.5cm (5in)

COPPER-NOSED MINNOW

The Copper-nosed Minnow is slender and elongate with a greenish brown dorsal surface. The flanks are silvery blue and the belly is silver. Around a dozen indistinct, thin blue bars cross the body vertically. Triangular dorsal and anal fins are set well back, and pelvic fins are positioned almost halfway back.
• **HABITAT** Streams in tropical west Africa.
• **REMARK** This fast-swimming, shoaling fish needs a large aquarium, and enjoys live foods and floating insects.
• **OTHER NAME** Recently re-classified as *Opsaridium*.

TROPICAL AFRICA

greenish brown • dorsal surface

deeply forked • caudal fin

large blue-rimmed eye •

• anal fin set well back

Diet Omnivorous	Tank levels Upper and middle	Temperament

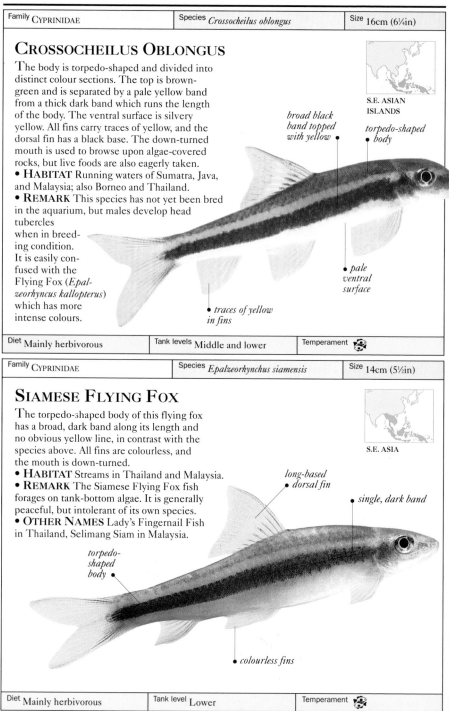

Family CYPRINIDAE	Species *Crossocheilus oblongus*	Size 16cm (6¼in)

CROSSOCHEILUS OBLONGUS

The body is torpedo-shaped and divided into distinct colour sections. The top is brown-green and is separated by a pale yellow band from a thick dark band which runs the length of the body. The ventral surface is silvery yellow. All fins carry traces of yellow, and the dorsal fin has a black base. The down-turned mouth is used to browse upon algae-covered rocks, but live foods are also eagerly taken.
• HABITAT Running waters of Sumatra, Java, and Malaysia; also Borneo and Thailand.
• REMARK This species has not yet been bred in the aquarium, but males develop head tubercles when in breed-ing condition. It is easily con-fused with the Flying Fox (*Epal-zeorhyncus kallopterus*) which has more intense colours.

S.E. ASIAN ISLANDS

broad black band topped with yellow

torpedo-shaped body

pale ventral surface

traces of yellow in fins

Diet Mainly herbivorous	Tank levels Middle and lower	Temperament

Family CYPRINIDAE	Species *Epalzeorhynchus siamensis*	Size 14cm (5½in)

SIAMESE FLYING FOX

The torpedo-shaped body of this flying fox has a broad, dark band along its length and no obvious yellow line, in contrast with the species above. All fins are colourless, and the mouth is down-turned.
• HABITAT Streams in Thailand and Malaysia.
• REMARK The Siamese Flying Fox fish forages on tank-bottom algae. It is generally peaceful, but intolerant of its own species.
• OTHER NAMES Lady's Fingernail Fish in Thailand, Selimang Siam in Malaysia.

S.E. ASIA

long-based dorsal fin

single, dark band

torpedo-shaped body

colourless fins

Diet Mainly herbivorous	Tank level Lower	Temperament

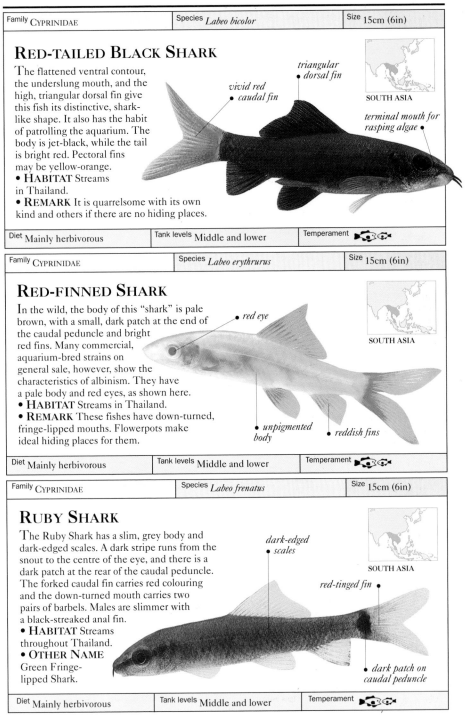

Family CYPRINIDAE	Species *Labeo bicolor*	Size 15cm (6in)

RED-TAILED BLACK SHARK

The flattened ventral contour, the underslung mouth, and the high, triangular dorsal fin give this fish its distinctive, shark-like shape. It also has the habit of patrolling the aquarium. The body is jet-black, while the tail is bright red. Pectoral fins may be yellow-orange.
• **HABITAT** Streams in Thailand.
• **REMARK** It is quarrelsome with its own kind and others if there are no hiding places.

triangular dorsal fin
vivid red caudal fin

SOUTH ASIA

terminal mouth for rasping algae

Diet Mainly herbivorous	Tank levels Middle and lower	Temperament

Family CYPRINIDAE	Species *Labeo erythrurus*	Size 15cm (6in)

RED-FINNED SHARK

In the wild, the body of this "shark" is pale brown, with a small, dark patch at the end of the caudal peduncle and bright red fins. Many commercial, aquarium-bred strains on general sale, however, show the characteristics of albinism. They have a pale body and red eyes, as shown here.
• **HABITAT** Streams in Thailand.
• **REMARK** These fishes have down-turned, fringe-lipped mouths. Flowerpots make ideal hiding places for them.

red eye

SOUTH ASIA

unpigmented body
reddish fins

Diet Mainly herbivorous	Tank levels Middle and lower	Temperament

Family CYPRINIDAE	Species *Labeo frenatus*	Size 15cm (6in)

RUBY SHARK

The Ruby Shark has a slim, grey body and dark-edged scales. A dark stripe runs from the snout to the centre of the eye, and there is a dark patch at the rear of the caudal peduncle. The forked caudal fin carries red colouring and the down-turned mouth carries two pairs of barbels. Males are slimmer with a black-streaked anal fin.
• **HABITAT** Streams throughout Thailand.
• **OTHER NAME** Green Fringe-lipped Shark.

dark-edged scales

SOUTH ASIA

red-tinged fin

dark patch on caudal peduncle

Diet Mainly herbivorous	Tank levels Middle and lower	Temperament

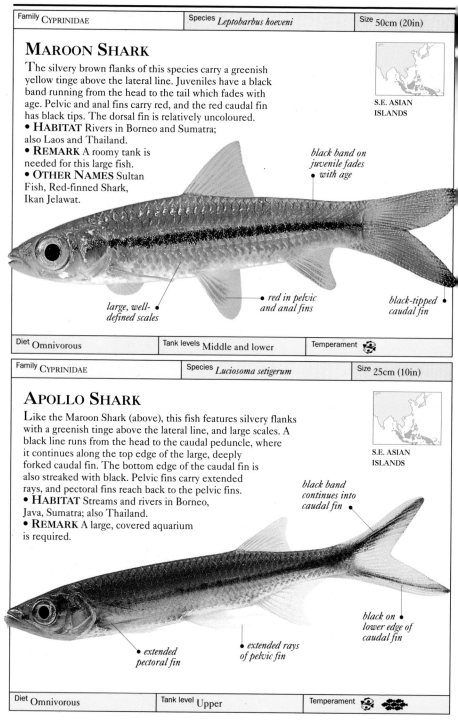

| Family CYPRINIDAE | Species *Leptobarbus hoeveni* | Size 50cm (20in) |

MAROON SHARK

The silvery brown flanks of this species carry a greenish yellow tinge above the lateral line. Juveniles have a black band running from the tail which fades with age. Pelvic and anal fins carry red, and the red caudal fin has black tips. The dorsal fin is relatively uncoloured.
- **HABITAT** Rivers in Borneo and Sumatra; also Laos and Thailand.
- **REMARK** A roomy tank is needed for this large fish.
- **OTHER NAMES** Sultan Fish, Red-finned Shark, Ikan Jelawat.

S.E. ASIAN ISLANDS

black band on juvenile fades with age

large, well-defined scales

red in pelvic and anal fins

black-tipped caudal fin

| Diet Omnivorous | Tank levels Middle and lower | Temperament |

| Family CYPRINIDAE | Species *Luciosoma setigerum* | Size 25cm (10in) |

APOLLO SHARK

Like the Maroon Shark (above), this fish features silvery flanks with a greenish tinge above the lateral line, and large scales. A black line runs from the head to the caudal peduncle, where it continues along the top edge of the large, deeply forked caudal fin. The bottom edge of the caudal fin is also streaked with black. Pelvic fins carry extended rays, and pectoral fins reach back to the pelvic fins.
- **HABITAT** Streams and rivers in Borneo, Java, Sumatra; also Thailand.
- **REMARK** A large, covered aquarium is required.

S.E. ASIAN ISLANDS

black band continues into caudal fin

black on lower edge of caudal fin

extended pectoral fin

extended rays of pelvic fin

| Diet Omnivorous | Tank level Upper | Temperament |

Family CYPRINIDAE	Species *Morulius chrysophekadion*	Size 50cm (20in)

BLACK SHARK

The colouring on this maturing Black Shark is grey-black:
on adults it is deep velvety black. The juvenile has scales
with red or gold centres, giving a speckled appearance.
The species has a large, triangular dorsal fin
resembling that of a true shark.
• **HABITAT** Various waters in Java,
Borneo, Sumatra, Thailand, Cambodia.
• **REMARK** This peaceful species
relishes algae and green foods.
• **OTHER NAME** Also classified
in the genus *Labeo*.

S. E. ASIA

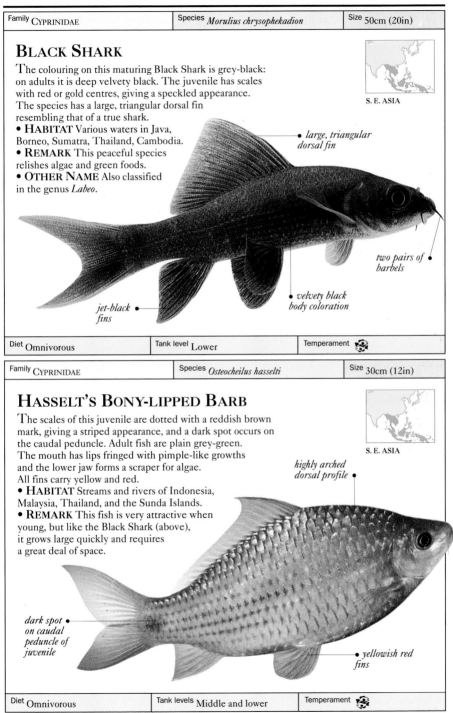

large, triangular
dorsal fin

two pairs of
barbels

velvety black
body coloration

jet-black
fins

Diet Omnivorous	Tank level Lower	Temperament

Family CYPRINIDAE	Species *Osteocheilus hasselti*	Size 30cm (12in)

HASSELT'S BONY-LIPPED BARB

The scales of this juvenile are dotted with a reddish brown
mark, giving a striped appearance, and a dark spot occurs on
the caudal peduncle. Adult fish are plain grey-green.
The mouth has lips fringed with pimple-like growths
and the lower jaw forms a scraper for algae.
All fins carry yellow and red.
• **HABITAT** Streams and rivers of Indonesia,
Malaysia, Thailand, and the Sunda Islands.
• **REMARK** This fish is very attractive when
young, but like the Black Shark (above),
it grows large quickly and requires
a great deal of space.

S. E. ASIA

highly arched
dorsal profile

dark spot
on caudal
peduncle of
juvenile

yellowish red
fins

Diet Omnivorous	Tank levels Middle and lower	Temperament

CHARACINS
SMALLER TETRAS

W HEN COMPARED TO larger characins, such as the Pacu, the diminutive size of the smaller tetras illustrates the great range within the family Characidae. Temperaments, likewise, vary in the extreme, from the tranquillity of the Neon Tetra to the ferocity of the Piranha. Native to South America and Africa, all characins make decorative additions to the aquarium – there are about 1,200 species in the wild. They have teeth in their jaws, unlike cyprinids. Many carry an additional small adipose fin behind the dorsal fin, although this is not an exclusive feature of characins (some other genera have it too, e.g. *Corydoras* catfish). Many smaller tetras are readily bred in soft waters, but very often the eggs are light-sensitive.

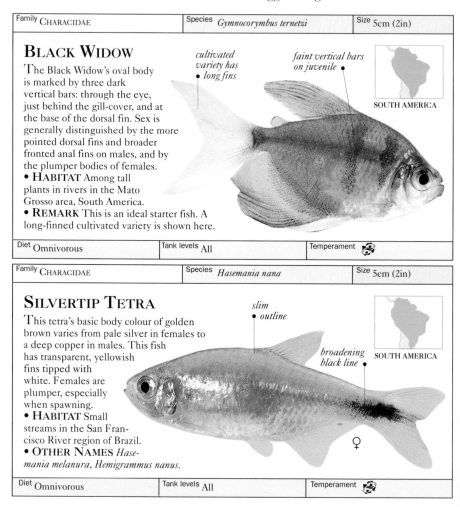

Family CHARACIDAE	Species *Gymnocorymbus ternetzi*	Size 5cm (2in)

BLACK WIDOW

The Black Widow's oval body is marked by three dark vertical bars: through the eye, just behind the gill-cover, and at the base of the dorsal fin. Sex is generally distinguished by the more pointed dorsal fins and broader fronted anal fins on males, and by the plumper bodies of females.
• HABITAT Among tall plants in rivers in the Mato Grosso area, South America.
• REMARK This is an ideal starter fish. A long-finned cultivated variety is shown here.

cultivated variety has • long fins

faint vertical bars on juvenile •

SOUTH AMERICA

Diet Omnivorous	Tank levels All	Temperament

Family CHARACIDAE	Species *Hasemania nana*	Size 5cm (2in)

SILVERTIP TETRA

This tetra's basic body colour of golden brown varies from pale silver in females to a deep copper in males. This fish has transparent, yellowish fins tipped with white. Females are plumper, especially when spawning.
• HABITAT Small streams in the San Francisco River region of Brazil.
• OTHER NAMES *Hasemania melanura, Hemigrammus nanus.*

slim • outline

broadening black line •

SOUTH AMERICA

♀

Diet Omnivorous	Tank levels All	Temperament

Family CHARACIDAE	Species *Hemigrammus caudovittatus*	Size 7.5cm (3in)

BUENOS AIRES TETRA

A thin, horizontal blue line begins behind the gill-cover of this slim fish, and tapers until obscured by a darker line, ending in the centre of the caudal fin. Male colours intensify during spawning.
• **HABITAT** Plate River basin of Argentina, Paraguay, and Brazil.
• **REMARK** It may eat soft-leaved plants.

black mark at base of caudal fin

orange-red fins

♀

SOUTH AMERICA

Diet Omnivorous	Tank levels All	Temperament

Family CHARACIDAE	Species *Hemigrammus erythrozonus*	Size 5cm (2in)

GLOWLIGHT TETRA

The upper and lower halves of the peach-coloured yet translucent Glowlight Tetra are divided by a glowing red-gold line. It starts on the snout and ends at the base of the caudal fin.
• **HABITAT** Rivers in Guyana.
• **REMARK** These small fish prefer a well-planted aquarium and soft, acid water for breeding. They will eat their eggs.

red area in dorsal fin

red-gold line

♀

SOUTH AMERICA

Diet Omnivorous	Tank levels All	Temperament

Family CHARACIDAE	Species *Hemigrammus ocellifer*	Size 5cm (2in)

BEACON FISH

The deep body outline of the Beacon Fish follows the general tetra pattern. The identifying features of this silvery grey fish are the bright red top of the eye, and the gold spot behind the adipose fin, above a dark blotch at the base of the caudal fin.
• **HABITAT** Rivers in the Amazon region and Guyana.
• **OTHER NAMES** Head and Tail-light Fish, Motorist Fish.

gold spot on caudal peduncle

red upper eye

♀

SOUTH AMERICA

Diet Omnivorous	Tank levels All	Temperament

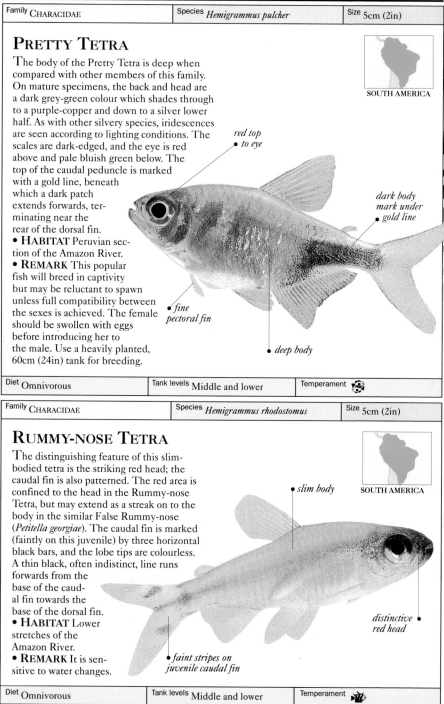

| Family CHARACIDAE | Species *Hemigrammus pulcher* | Size 5cm (2in) |

PRETTY TETRA

The body of the Pretty Tetra is deep when compared with other members of this family. On mature specimens, the back and head are a dark grey-green colour which shades through to a purple-copper and down to a silver lower half. As with other silvery species, iridescences are seen according to lighting conditions. The scales are dark-edged, and the eye is red above and pale bluish green below. The top of the caudal peduncle is marked with a gold line, beneath which a dark patch extends forwards, terminating near the rear of the dorsal fin.
• **HABITAT** Peruvian section of the Amazon River.
• **REMARK** This popular fish will breed in captivity but may be reluctant to spawn unless full compatibility between the sexes is achieved. The female should be swollen with eggs before introducing her to the male. Use a heavily planted, 60cm (24in) tank for breeding.

SOUTH AMERICA

red top to eye

dark body mark under gold line

fine pectoral fin

deep body

| Diet Omnivorous | Tank levels Middle and lower | Temperament |

| Family CHARACIDAE | Species *Hemigrammus rhodostomus* | Size 5cm (2in) |

RUMMY-NOSE TETRA

The distinguishing feature of this slim-bodied tetra is the striking red head; the caudal fin is also patterned. The red area is confined to the head in the Rummy-nose Tetra, but may extend as a streak on to the body in the similar False Rummy-nose (*Petitella georgiae*). The caudal fin is marked (faintly on this juvenile) by three horizontal black bars, and the lobe tips are colourless. A thin black, often indistinct, line runs forwards from the base of the caudal fin towards the base of the dorsal fin.
• **HABITAT** Lower stretches of the Amazon River.
• **REMARK** It is sensitive to water changes.

slim body   SOUTH AMERICA

distinctive red head

faint stripes on juvenile caudal fin

| Diet Omnivorous | Tank levels Middle and lower | Temperament |

| Family CHARACIDAE | Species *Hyphessobrycon bifasciatus* | Size 5cm (2in) |

YELLOW TETRA

The Yellow Tetra's uniformly proportioned body is typical of the genus. Adults have a lemon-gold sheen and two vertical marks just behind the gill-cover. The first mark is wedge shaped and accentuated by a golden iridescence; the other is longer, thinner, and less distinct. Occasionally, there is more gold in the dorsal area due to chemical deposits beneath the skin which reflect the light. All fins are yellowish, sometimes with a tinge of red at their bases. Males have slightly concave anal fins.
• **HABITAT** Streams, lakes, and rivers around Rio de Janeiro, Brazil.
• **REMARK** Yellow Tetras do well in a tank of small tetras and rasboras. They are fin-nippers.

lemon-gold sheen •

SOUTH AMERICA

• *faint vertical marks behind gill-cover of juvenile*

• *arrow-head patterning along lateral line*

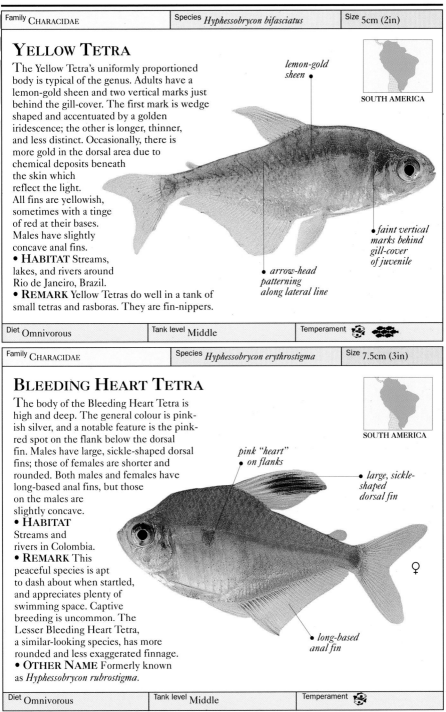

| Diet Omnivorous | Tank level Middle | Temperament |

| Family CHARACIDAE | Species *Hyphessobrycon erythrostigma* | Size 7.5cm (3in) |

BLEEDING HEART TETRA

The body of the Bleeding Heart Tetra is high and deep. The general colour is pink-ish silver, and a notable feature is the pink-red spot on the flank below the dorsal fin. Males have large, sickle-shaped dorsal fins; those of females are shorter and rounded. Both males and females have long-based anal fins, but those on the males are slightly concave.
• **HABITAT** Streams and rivers in Colombia.
• **REMARK** This peaceful species is apt to dash about when startled, and appreciates plenty of swimming space. Captive breeding is uncommon. The Lesser Bleeding Heart Tetra, a similar-looking species, has more rounded and less exaggerated finnage.
• **OTHER NAME** Formerly known as *Hyphessobrycon rubrostigma*.

SOUTH AMERICA

pink "heart" on flanks •

• *large, sickle-shaped dorsal fin*

♀

• *long-based anal fin*

| Diet Omnivorous | Tank level Middle | Temperament |

Family CHARACIDAE	Species *Hyphessobrycon flammeus*	Size 4.5cm (1¾in)

FLAME TETRA

The body shape of this fish is typical of the tetra group, with a high profile tapering evenly to the caudal peduncle. Coloration is pinkish brown with silver. On perfect specimens, two dark bars appear behind the gill-cover and extend down to the belly; the lower rear of the body carries more red. Pelvic, anal, and caudal fins are also red, edged with black, and the dorsal fin may be sooty with white streaks. A terminal mouth is situated at the tip of the snout, and an adipose fin is present. The female is less red and increases in girth when spawning.
• **HABITAT** Streams and rivers around Rio de Janeiro.
• **REMARK** *Hyphessobrycon griemi* is a similar species, but lacks the red coloration and has more white in its fins.

paler female coloration

SOUTH AMERICA

terminal mouth

red and black pelvic and anal fins

♀

increase in red towards rear

Diet Omnivorous	Tank levels All	Temperament

Family CHARACIDAE	Species *Hyphessobrycon herbertaxelrodi*	Size 4.5cm (1¾in)

BLACK NEON TETRA

This tetra is olive-green on the dorsal surface and silvery on the belly. There is an iridescent, pale green-blue line along the flanks, from the top of the eye to the caudal peduncle. Below this, a dark area gradually pales towards the lower part of the body. Fins are mostly colourless, and an adipose fin is present. Females generally have deeper bodies and increase in girth at spawning times.
• **HABITAT** Streams and rivers in the Mato Grosso region of Brazil.
• **REMARK** Soft, acid water will bring out this fish's colours.

iridescent green-blue line

SOUTH AMERICA

bright red top of eye

dark area on flanks

colourless fins

Diet Omnivorous	Tank levels All	Temperament

Family CHARACIDAE	Species *Hyphessobrycon heterorhabdus*	Size 5cm (2in)

BELGIAN FLAG TETRA

The colour of this tetra is pale greyish brown on the dorsal surface, and silver on the flanks and ventral surface. There are three lines along the body; the uppermost is red, the middle faintly gold on this specimen, and the broader bottom line is black. The gill-covers are silver. Females are much deeper in body shape.
- **HABITAT** Streams around and including the Tocantins River, lower Amazon.
- **REMARK** It resembles *Hemigrammus ulreyi*, a less commonly available species.
- **OTHER NAME** Flag Tetra.

SOUTH AMERICA

three coloured lines along the body

black spreads into caudal fin

bright red top of eye

silver ventral surface

Diet Omnivorous	Tank levels All	Temperament

Family CHARACIDAE	Species *Hyphessobrycon pulchripinnis*	Size 5cm (2in)

LEMON TETRA

The dorsal fin contains black with a yellow streak on the front edge; the adipose fin is yellow with a black edge; and the long-based anal fin has a bright yellow front and a black rear edge. General coloration is greenish yellow with a silver belly. Mature males are more intensely coloured.
- **HABITAT** Streams of the Amazon basin.
- **REMARK** This fish looks best shoaling in a well-planted tank.

SOUTH AMERICA

yellow streak in dorsal fin

front of long-based anal fin is bright yellow

visible backbone

Diet Omnivorous	Tank levels All	Temperament

Family CHARACIDAE	Species *Hyphessobrycon rosaceus*	Size 5cm (2in)

ROSY TETRA

The colouring of this species is quite similar to the Bleeding Heart Tetra (see p.77). The body of the Rosy Tetra, however, is less deep and the spot on the flank is missing. The dorsal fin is marked with red and streaked with black; that of the male is sickle shaped, well produced, and reaches back over the adipose fin in mature specimens. The pelvic and anal fins are tinged with red and tipped with white. The caudal fin has red in each lobe and a grey margin.
• **HABITAT** Guyana and lower Amazon River.
• **REMARK** Similarly coloured fishes are *Hyphessobrycon bentosi, H. erythrostigma*, and *H. ornatus*.

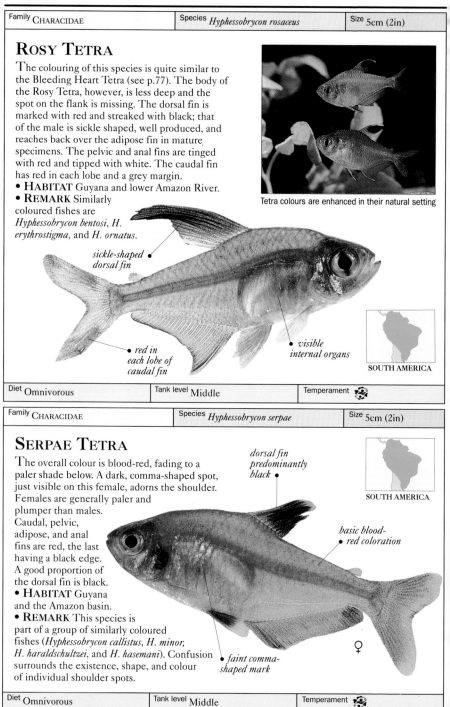

Tetra colours are enhanced in their natural setting

sickle-shaped dorsal fin

red in each lobe of caudal fin

visible internal organs

SOUTH AMERICA

Diet Omnivorous	Tank level Middle	Temperament

Family CHARACIDAE	Species *Hyphessobrycon serpae*	Size 5cm (2in)

SERPAE TETRA

The overall colour is blood-red, fading to a paler shade below. A dark, comma-shaped spot, just visible on this female, adorns the shoulder. Females are generally paler and plumper than males. Caudal, pelvic, adipose, and anal fins are red, the last having a black edge. A good proportion of the dorsal fin is black.
• **HABITAT** Guyana and the Amazon basin.
• **REMARK** This species is part of a group of similarly coloured fishes (*Hyphessobrycon callistus, H. minor, H. haraldschultzei*, and *H. hasemani*). Confusion surrounds the existence, shape, and colour of individual shoulder spots.

dorsal fin predominantly black

SOUTH AMERICA

basic blood-red coloration

faint comma-shaped mark

♀

Diet Omnivorous	Tank level Middle	Temperament

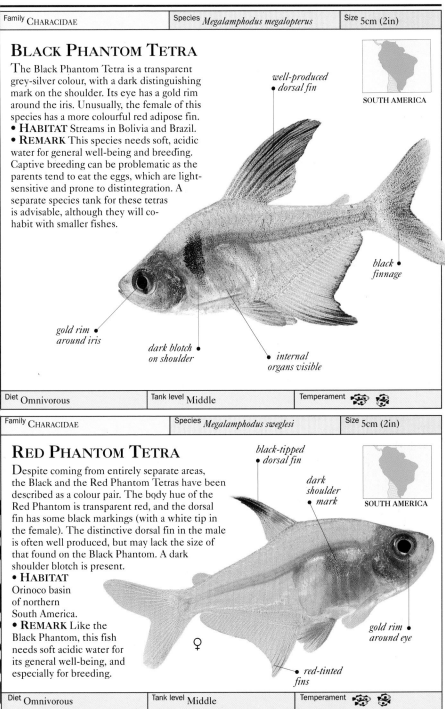

Family CHARACIDAE	Species *Megalamphodus megalopterus*	Size 5cm (2in)

BLACK PHANTOM TETRA

The Black Phantom Tetra is a transparent grey-silver colour, with a dark distinguishing mark on the shoulder. Its eye has a gold rim around the iris. Unusually, the female of this species has a more colourful red adipose fin.
• **HABITAT** Streams in Bolivia and Brazil.
• **REMARK** This species needs soft, acidic water for general well-being and breeding. Captive breeding can be problematic as the parents tend to eat the eggs, which are light-sensitive and prone to distintegration. A separate species tank for these tetras is advisable, although they will co-habit with smaller fishes.

well-produced • dorsal fin

SOUTH AMERICA

black • finnage

gold rim • around iris

dark blotch • on shoulder

internal • organs visible

Diet Omnivorous	Tank level Middle	Temperament

Family CHARACIDAE	Species *Megalamphodus sweglesi*	Size 5cm (2in)

RED PHANTOM TETRA

Despite coming from entirely separate areas, the Black and the Red Phantom Tetras have been described as a colour pair. The body hue of the Red Phantom is transparent red, and the dorsal fin has some black markings (with a white tip in the female). The distinctive dorsal fin in the male is often well produced, but may lack the size of that found on the Black Phantom. A dark shoulder blotch is present.
• **HABITAT**
Orinoco basin
of northern
South America.
• **REMARK** Like the Black Phantom, this fish needs soft acidic water for its general well-being, and especially for breeding.

black-tipped • dorsal fin

dark shoulder • mark

SOUTH AMERICA

♀

gold rim • around eye

red-tinted fins

Diet Omnivorous	Tank level Middle	Temperament

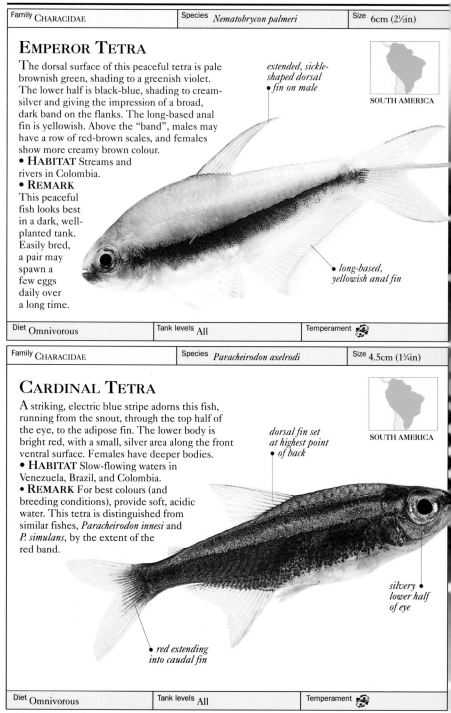

Family CHARACIDAE	Species *Nematobrycon palmeri*	Size 6cm (2½in)

EMPEROR TETRA

The dorsal surface of this peaceful tetra is pale brownish green, shading to a greenish violet. The lower half is black-blue, shading to cream-silver and giving the impression of a broad, dark band on the flanks. The long-based anal fin is yellowish. Above the "band", males may have a row of red-brown scales, and females show more creamy brown colour.
• **HABITAT** Streams and rivers in Colombia.
• **REMARK** This peaceful fish looks best in a dark, well-planted tank. Easily bred, a pair may spawn a few eggs daily over a long time.

*extended, sickle-shaped dorsal
• fin on male*

SOUTH AMERICA

• long-based, yellowish anal fin

Diet Omnivorous	Tank levels All	Temperament

Family CHARACIDAE	Species *Paracheirodon axelrodi*	Size 4.5cm (1¾in)

CARDINAL TETRA

A striking, electric blue stripe adorns this fish, running from the snout, through the top half of the eye, to the adipose fin. The lower body is bright red, with a small, silver area along the front ventral surface. Females have deeper bodies.
• **HABITAT** Slow-flowing waters in Venezuela, Brazil, and Colombia.
• **REMARK** For best colours (and breeding conditions), provide soft, acidic water. This tetra is distinguished from similar fishes, *Paracheirodon innesi* and *P. simulans*, by the extent of the red band.

*dorsal fin set at highest point
• of back*

SOUTH AMERICA

*silvery •
lower half
of eye*

*• red extending
into caudal fin*

Diet Omnivorous	Tank levels All	Temperament

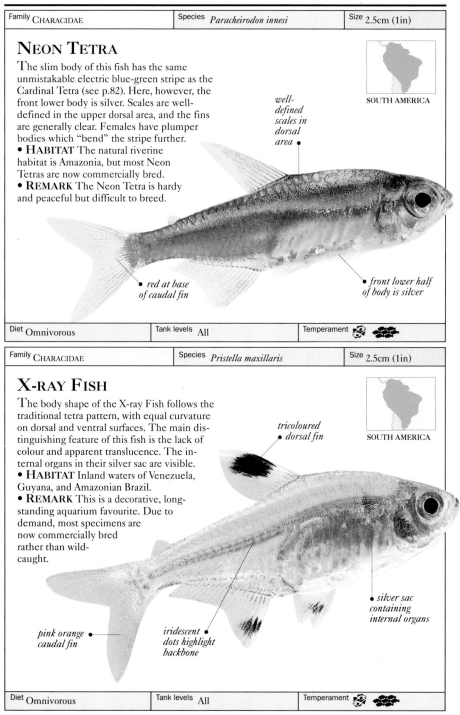

Family CHARACIDAE	Species *Paracheirodon innesi*	Size 2.5cm (1in)

NEON TETRA

The slim body of this fish has the same unmistakable electric blue-green stripe as the Cardinal Tetra (see p.82). Here, however, the front lower body is silver. Scales are well-defined in the upper dorsal area, and the fins are generally clear. Females have plumper bodies which "bend" the stripe further.
• **HABITAT** The natural riverine habitat is Amazonia, but most Neon Tetras are now commercially bred.
• **REMARK** The Neon Tetra is hardy and peaceful but difficult to breed.

well-defined scales in dorsal area

SOUTH AMERICA

red at base of caudal fin

front lower half of body is silver

Diet Omnivorous	Tank levels All	Temperament

Family CHARACIDAE	Species *Pristella maxillaris*	Size 2.5cm (1in)

X-RAY FISH

The body shape of the X-ray Fish follows the traditional tetra pattern, with equal curvature on dorsal and ventral surfaces. The main distinguishing feature of this fish is the lack of colour and apparent translucence. The internal organs in their silver sac are visible.
• **HABITAT** Inland waters of Venezuela, Guyana, and Amazonian Brazil.
• **REMARK** This is a decorative, long-standing aquarium favourite. Due to demand, most specimens are now commercially bred rather than wild-caught.

tricoloured dorsal fin

SOUTH AMERICA

silver sac containing internal organs

pink orange caudal fin

iridescent dots highlight backbone

Diet Omnivorous	Tank levels All	Temperament

OTHER CHARACINS

W HILE THE SMALLER species of the characin group (see pp.74–83) are more commonly kept in the aquarium, the species listed in this section belonging to related family groups, have equally strong claims for aquarium consideration. Hatchetfishes (Gastero-pelecidae), pencilfishes (Anostomidae), and piranhas (Serrasalmidae) are all equally interesting to keep.

Family ANOSTOMIDAE	Species *Abramites hypselonotus*	Size 13cm (5in)

MARBLED HEADSTANDER

Several broad, wavy, dark brown bands run obliquely over the pale yellowish body of this fish. A dark horizontal line runs from the tip of the snout back through the eye. Dorsal, pelvic, and adipose fins carry brown markings, and the base of the caudal peduncle has a dark edge.
• **HABITAT** Streams and rivers of the Orinoco and Amazon river systems.
• **REMARK** This species swims and rests head-down in the typical manner of the Anostomidae family. A diet with a high vegetable content is recommended: it will devour aquarium plants. It may also be slightly intolerant of its own kind.
• **OTHER NAMES** High-backed Headstander, Striped Headstander. Formerly classified as *Abramites microcephalus.*

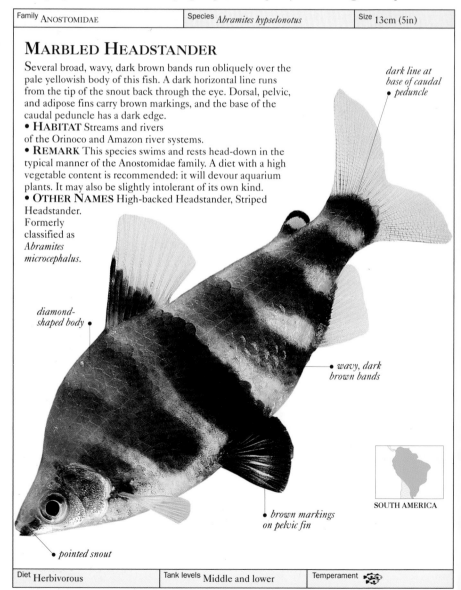

dark line at base of caudal peduncle

diamond-shaped body

wavy, dark brown bands

pointed snout

brown markings on pelvic fin

SOUTH AMERICA

Diet Herbivorous	Tank levels Middle and lower	Temperament

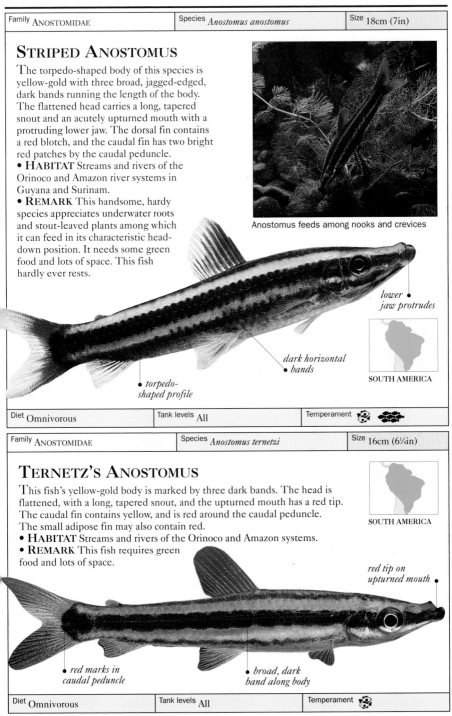

Family ANOSTOMIDAE	Species *Anostomus anostomus*	Size 18cm (7in)

STRIPED ANOSTOMUS

The torpedo-shaped body of this species is
yellow-gold with three broad, jagged-edged,
dark bands running the length of the body.
The flattened head carries a long, tapered
snout and an acutely upturned mouth with a
protruding lower jaw. The dorsal fin contains
a red blotch, and the caudal fin has two bright
red patches by the caudal peduncle.
• HABITAT Streams and rivers of the
Orinoco and Amazon river systems in
Guyana and Surinam.
• REMARK This handsome, hardy
species appreciates underwater roots
and stout-leaved plants among which
it can feed in its characteristic head-
down position. It needs some green
food and lots of space. This fish
hardly ever rests.

Anostomus feeds among nooks and crevices

lower jaw protrudes

dark horizontal bands

SOUTH AMERICA

torpedo-shaped profile

Diet Omnivorous	Tank levels All	Temperament

Family ANOSTOMIDAE	Species *Anostomus ternetzi*	Size 16cm (6¼in)

TERNETZ'S ANOSTOMUS

This fish's yellow-gold body is marked by three dark bands. The head is
flattened, with a long, tapered snout, and the upturned mouth has a red tip.
The caudal fin contains yellow, and is red around the caudal peduncle.
The small adipose fin may also contain red.
• HABITAT Streams and rivers of the Orinoco and Amazon systems.
• REMARK This fish requires green
food and lots of space.

SOUTH AMERICA

red tip on upturned mouth

red marks in caudal peduncle

broad, dark band along body

Diet Omnivorous	Tank levels All	Temperament

Family CHARACIDAE	Species *Aphyocharax anisitsi*	Size 5.5cm (2¼in)

BLOODFIN

As the name suggests, red is normally present in the fins of this silvery flanked species. The colour is not, however, very apparent on this juvenile. The male anal fin carries tiny hooks to assist in spawning, which may become entangled in an aquarium net.
• **HABITAT** Streams and rivers of Argentina and Paraguay.
• **REMARK** Bloodfins should be kept in shoals. They breed freely but may eat their own eggs.
• **OTHER NAMES** Argentine Bloodfin, Red-finned Characin, Red-finned Tetra. Formerly classified as *Aphyocharax rubripinnis*.

SOUTH AMERICA

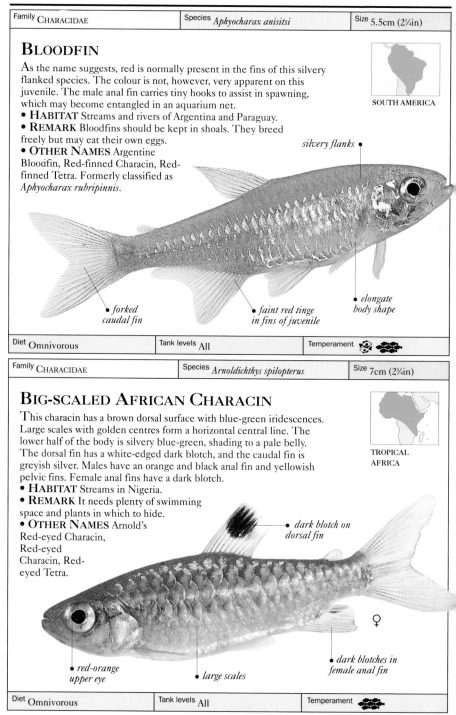

silvery flanks

forked caudal fin

faint red tinge in fins of juvenile

elongate body shape

Diet Omnivorous	Tank levels All	Temperament

Family CHARACIDAE	Species *Arnoldichthys spilopterus*	Size 7cm (2¾in)

BIG-SCALED AFRICAN CHARACIN

This characin has a brown dorsal surface with blue-green iridescences. Large scales with golden centres form a horizontal central line. The lower half of the body is silvery blue-green, shading to a pale belly. The dorsal fin has a white-edged dark blotch, and the caudal fin is greyish silver. Males have an orange and black anal fin and yellowish pelvic fins. Female anal fins have a dark blotch.
• **HABITAT** Streams in Nigeria.
• **REMARK** It needs plenty of swimming space and plants in which to hide.
• **OTHER NAMES** Arnold's Red-eyed Characin, Red-eyed Characin, Red-eyed Tetra.

TROPICAL AFRICA

dark blotch on dorsal fin

♀

red-orange upper eye

large scales

dark blotches in female anal fin

Diet Omnivorous	Tank levels All	Temperament

Family CHARACIDAE	Species *Astyanax fasciatus mexicanus*	Size 9cm (3½in)

BLIND CAVE FISH

The head of this unusual fish is notable for the absence of eyes. The body has a highly arched dorsal profile and is almost featureless, being plain pink with a silvery sheen. Fins contain some colouring.
• **HABITAT** Underground cave waters in Mexico.
• **REMARK** The eyes of this species have become superfluous as it navigates in totally dark underground waters using its lateral line system. It is content in a community tank, and rocky caves make appropriate additions.
• **OTHER NAME** Formerly classified as *Anoptichthys jordani*.

CENTRAL AMERICA

pink body has silvery sheen

head without eyes

fins almost colourless

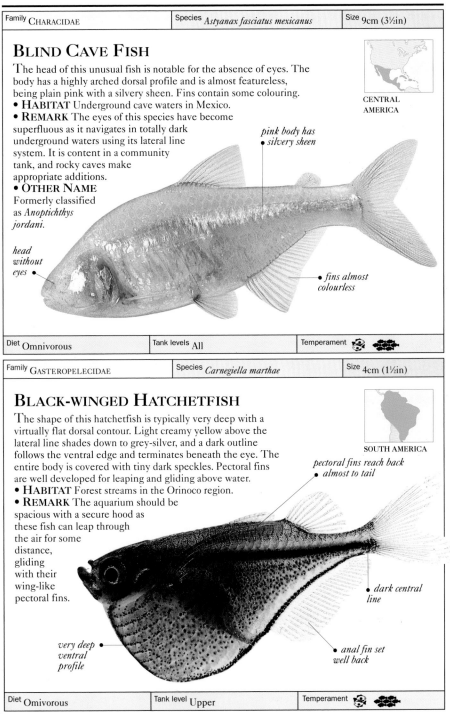

Diet Omnivorous	Tank levels All	Temperament

Family GASTEROPELECIDAE	Species *Carnegiella marthae*	Size 4cm (1½in)

BLACK-WINGED HATCHETFISH

The shape of this hatchetfish is typically very deep with a virtually flat dorsal contour. Light creamy yellow above the lateral line shades down to grey-silver, and a dark outline follows the ventral edge and terminates beneath the eye. The entire body is covered with tiny dark speckles. Pectoral fins are well developed for leaping and gliding above water.
• **HABITAT** Forest streams in the Orinoco region.
• **REMARK** The aquarium should be spacious with a secure hood as these fish can leap through the air for some distance, gliding with their wing-like pectoral fins.

SOUTH AMERICA

pectoral fins reach back almost to tail

dark central line

very deep ventral profile

anal fin set well back

Diet Omivorous	Tank level Upper	Temperament

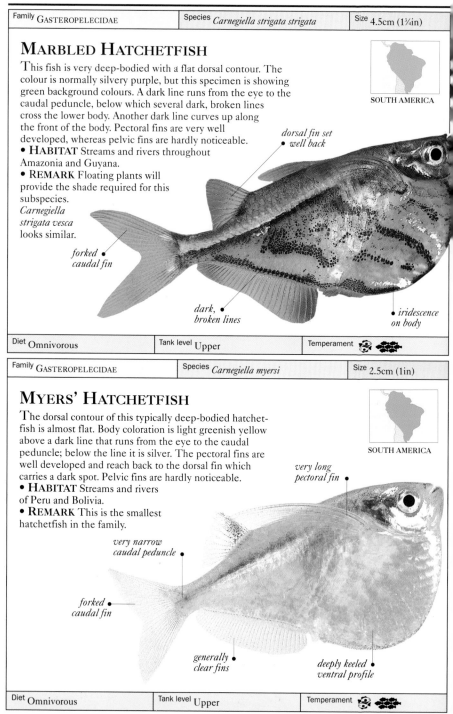

| Family GASTEROPELECIDAE | Species *Carnegiella strigata strigata* | Size 4.5cm (1¾in) |

MARBLED HATCHETFISH

This fish is very deep-bodied with a flat dorsal contour. The colour is normally silvery purple, but this specimen is showing green background colours. A dark line runs from the eye to the caudal peduncle, below which several dark, broken lines cross the lower body. Another dark line curves up along the front of the body. Pectoral fins are very well developed, whereas pelvic fins are hardly noticeable.
• **HABITAT** Streams and rivers throughout Amazonia and Guyana.
• **REMARK** Floating plants will provide the shade required for this subspecies. *Carnegiella strigata vesca* looks similar.

SOUTH AMERICA

dorsal fin set well back

forked caudal fin

dark, broken lines

iridescence on body

| Diet Omnivorous | Tank level Upper | Temperament |

| Family GASTEROPELECIDAE | Species *Carnegiella myersi* | Size 2.5cm (1in) |

MYERS' HATCHETFISH

The dorsal contour of this typically deep-bodied hatchet-fish is almost flat. Body coloration is light greenish yellow above a dark line that runs from the eye to the caudal peduncle; below the line it is silver. The pectoral fins are well developed and reach back to the dorsal fin which carries a dark spot. Pelvic fins are hardly noticeable.
• **HABITAT** Streams and rivers of Peru and Bolivia.
• **REMARK** This is the smallest hatchetfish in the family.

SOUTH AMERICA

very long pectoral fin

very narrow caudal peduncle

forked caudal fin

generally clear fins

deeply keeled ventral profile

| Diet Omnivorous | Tank level Upper | Temperament |

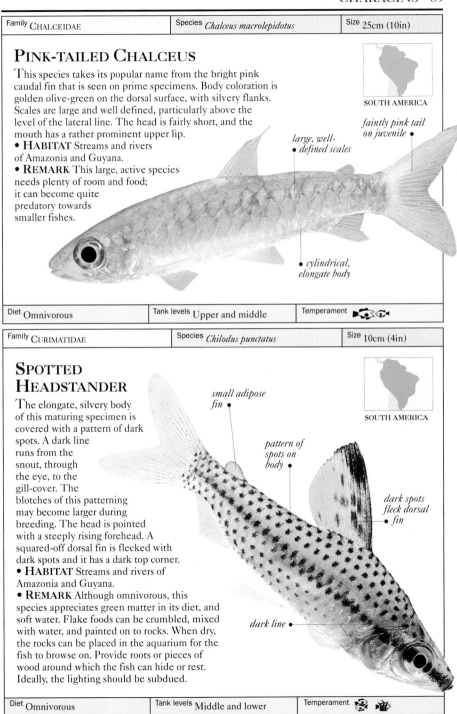

| Family CHALCEIDAE | Species *Chalceus macrolepidotus* | Size 25cm (10in) |

PINK-TAILED CHALCEUS

This species takes its popular name from the bright pink
caudal fin that is seen on prime specimens. Body coloration is
golden olive-green on the dorsal surface, with silvery flanks.
Scales are large and well defined, particularly above the
level of the lateral line. The head is fairly short, and the
mouth has a rather prominent upper lip.
• **HABITAT** Streams and rivers
of Amazonia and Guyana.
• **REMARK** This large, active species
needs plenty of room and food;
it can become quite
predatory towards
smaller fishes.

SOUTH AMERICA

*faintly pink tail
on juvenile*

*large, well-
defined scales*

*cylindrical,
elongate body*

| Diet Omnivorous | Tank levels Upper and middle | Temperament |

| Family CURIMATIDAE | Species *Chilodus punctatus* | Size 10cm (4in) |

SPOTTED HEADSTANDER

The elongate, silvery body
of this maturing specimen is
covered with a pattern of dark
spots. A dark line
runs from the
snout, through
the eye, to the
gill-cover. The
blotches of this patterning
may become larger during
breeding. The head is pointed
with a steeply rising forehead. A
squared-off dorsal fin is flecked with
dark spots and it has a dark top corner.
• **HABITAT** Streams and rivers of
Amazonia and Guyana.
• **REMARK** Although omnivorous, this
species appreciates green matter in its diet, and
soft water. Flake foods can be crumbled, mixed
with water, and painted on to rocks. When dry,
the rocks can be placed in the aquarium for the
fish to browse on. Provide roots or pieces of
wood around which the fish can hide or rest.
Ideally, the lighting should be subdued.

*small adipose
fin*

SOUTH AMERICA

*pattern of
spots on
body*

*dark spots
fleck dorsal
fin*

dark line

| Diet Omnivorous | Tank levels Middle and lower | Temperament |

Family SERRASALMIDAE	Species *Colossoma bidens*	Size 40cm (16in)

PACU

The shape of this fish resembles that of the Piranha (see p.105). The chest area, the lower edge of the gill-cover, and the pectoral, pelvic, and anal fins are red. The rest of the body is silver with faint dark spots above the lateral line. There are teeth in the mouth, but the head is not as large as those of its carnivorous relatives. Anal and caudal fins have black edges.
• **HABITAT** Guapore River, on the borders of Bolivia and Brazil.
• **REMARK** The Pacu's diet consists of fruit and vegetable matter. This species can be confused with *Colossoma brachipomum*.

SOUTH AMERICA

dark blotch on caudal • peduncle

large eye • set well forward

Diet Herbivorous	Tank levels Upper and middle	Temperament

Family LEBIASINIDAE	Species *Copeina guttata*	Size 15cm (6in)

RED-SPOTTED COPEINA

The body of this species features a green-brown dorsal surface with darker flanks, and a light yellowish ventral surface. Each large scale has a red marking at its forward apex, giving the fish the spotted appearance which is reflected in its common name.
• **HABITAT** Streams and rivers of central Amazonia.
• **REMARK** This species is relatively easy to keep and breeds readily. Eggs are laid in a hollow and guarded by the male.

SOUTH AMERICA

upturned mouth on small head •

• red-orange edges on pelvic and anal fins

Diet Omnivorous	Tank levels Upper and middle	Temperament

| Family LEBIASINIDAE | Species *Copella arnoldi* | Size 8cm (3¼in) |

SPLASHING TETRA

This creamy yellow young female carries large, iridescent scales.
A dark line runs from the snout, through the eye, to the gill-cover.
The caudal fin is distinctly forked. Fins of mature males are more
extravagantly produced and are yellowish with red marks.

• **HABITAT** Rivers and streams in Guyana and around
the mouth of the Amazon River.

• **REMARK** This fish lays its
eggs on the underside of
overhanging plants and
the male splashes them
to keep them moist.

SOUTH AMERICA

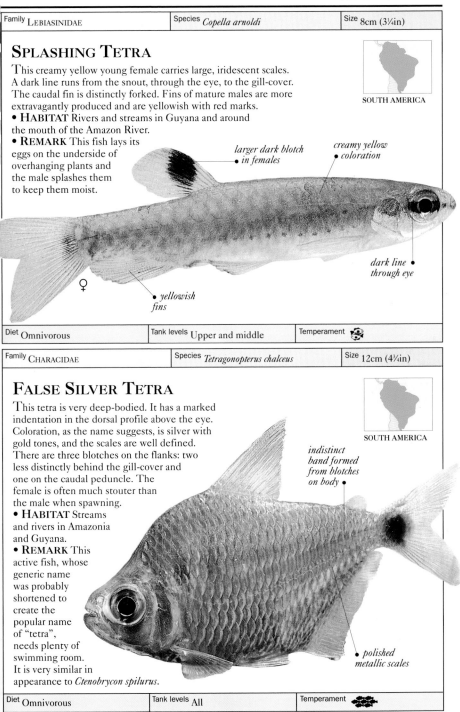

larger dark blotch in females

creamy yellow coloration

dark line through eye

♀

yellowish fins

| Diet Omnivorous | Tank levels Upper and middle | Temperament |

| Family CHARACIDAE | Species *Tetragonopterus chalceus* | Size 12cm (4¾in) |

FALSE SILVER TETRA

This tetra is very deep-bodied. It has a marked
indentation in the dorsal profile above the eye.
Coloration, as the name suggests, is silver with
gold tones, and the scales are well defined.
There are three blotches on the flanks: two
less distinctly behind the gill-cover and
one on the caudal peduncle. The
female is often much stouter than
the male when spawning.

• **HABITAT** Streams
and rivers in Amazonia
and Guyana.

• **REMARK** This
active fish, whose
generic name
was probably
shortened to
create the
popular name
of "tetra",
needs plenty of
swimming room.
It is very similar in
appearance to *Ctenobrycon spilurus*.

SOUTH AMERICA

indistinct band formed from blotches on body

polished metallic scales

| Diet Omnivorous | Tank levels All | Temperament |

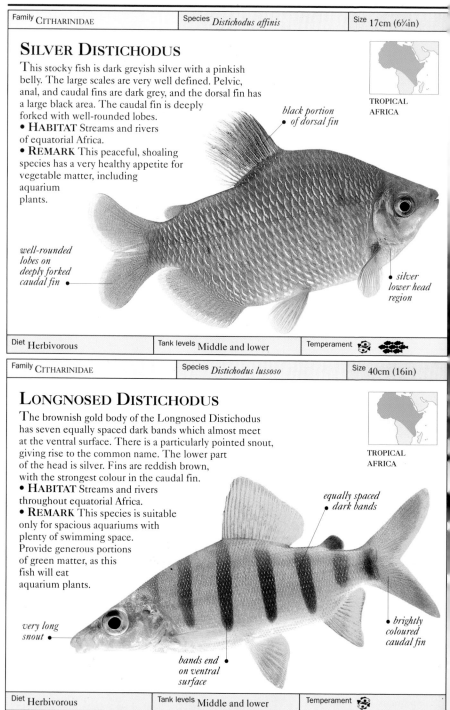

| Family CITHARINIDAE | Species *Distichodus affinis* | Size 17cm (6¾in) |

SILVER DISTICHODUS

This stocky fish is dark greyish silver with a pinkish belly. The large scales are very well defined. Pelvic, anal, and caudal fins are dark grey, and the dorsal fin has a large black area. The caudal fin is deeply forked with well-rounded lobes.
• **HABITAT** Streams and rivers of equatorial Africa.
• **REMARK** This peaceful, shoaling species has a very healthy appetite for vegetable matter, including aquarium plants.

TROPICAL AFRICA

black portion of dorsal fin

well-rounded lobes on deeply forked caudal fin

silver lower head region

| Diet Herbivorous | Tank levels Middle and lower | Temperament |

| Family CITHARINIDAE | Species *Distichodus lussoso* | Size 40cm (16in) |

LONGNOSED DISTICHODUS

The brownish gold body of the Longnosed Distichodus has seven equally spaced dark bands which almost meet at the ventral surface. There is a particularly pointed snout, giving rise to the common name. The lower part of the head is silver. Fins are reddish brown, with the strongest colour in the caudal fin.
• **HABITAT** Streams and rivers throughout equatorial Africa.
• **REMARK** This species is suitable only for spacious aquariums with plenty of swimming space. Provide generous portions of green matter, as this fish will eat aquarium plants.

TROPICAL AFRICA

equally spaced dark bands

very long snout

brightly coloured caudal fin

bands end on ventral surface

| Diet Herbivorous | Tank levels Middle and lower | Temperament |

| Family CITHARINIDAE | Species *Distichodus noboli* | Size 17cm (6¾in) |

NOBOL'S DISTICHODUS

This greyish silver fish is decorated with large, well-defined, bright silver scales and randomly sprinkled silver iridescences. The lower part of the relatively small head is silver. Dorsal, anal, and caudal fins are grey, and the dorsal fin has a black and red front portion. A small adipose fin is present.
• **HABITAT** Streams and rivers of equatorial Africa.
• **REMARK** This species is one of the smallest in the *Distichodus* genus, which contains around 30 species. It is similar to *Distichodus notospilus*.

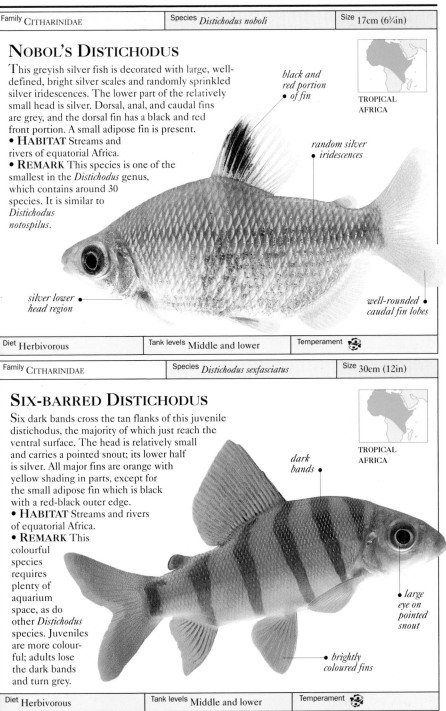

black and red portion of fin

TROPICAL AFRICA

random silver iridescences

silver lower head region

well-rounded caudal fin lobes

| Diet Herbivorous | Tank levels Middle and lower | Temperament |

| Family CITHARINIDAE | Species *Distichodus sexfasciatus* | Size 30cm (12in) |

SIX-BARRED DISTICHODUS

Six dark bands cross the tan flanks of this juvenile distichodus, the majority of which just reach the ventral surface. The head is relatively small and carries a pointed snout; its lower half is silver. All major fins are orange with yellow shading in parts, except for the small adipose fin which is black with a red-black outer edge.
• **HABITAT** Streams and rivers of equatorial Africa.
• **REMARK** This colourful species requires plenty of aquarium space, as do other *Distichodus* species. Juveniles are more colourful; adults lose the dark bands and turn grey.

dark bands

TROPICAL AFRICA

large eye on pointed snout

brightly coloured fins

| Diet Herbivorous | Tank levels Middle and lower | Temperament |

Family GASTEROPELECIDAE	Species *Gasteropelecus sternicla*	Size 6cm (2½in)

SILVER HATCHETFISH

The hatchetfish's contour is very deep and keel-like. The silver body is marked by a thin dark line on the rear two-thirds of the flanks. Pectoral fins are large and wing-like, contrasting with the rudimentary pelvic fins. The large eyes are set well forward on a small head, and the mouth is upturned.
• **HABITAT** Surface of water, usually among plants, in the Amazon basin and north to Guyana.
• **REMARK** The deep body houses powerful muscles which enable the pectoral fins to be carried stiffly and act as wings. The fish arches its body to achieve speed and sometimes to leave the water.

wing-like pectoral fin

SOUTH AMERICA

deeply forked caudal fin

long-based anal fin

keel-like body contour

Diet Insectivorous	Tank level Upper	Temperament

Family ALESTIDAE	Species *Lepidarchus adonis*	Size 3cm (1¼in)

ADONIS

As this silvery yellow fish is translucent it may pick up background colours. The male has dark blotching to the rear of the dorsal and anal fins. The anal, dorsal, and caudal fins of both sexes are finely marked with dark horizontal stripes.
• **HABITAT** Streams in Ghana and Liberia.
• **REMARK** An excellent aquarium subject, the Adonis is quite easy to breed in soft water in a well-planted tank. It produces a small number of light-sensitive eggs. First foods should be small, newly hatched brine shrimp. Keep these fish alone, or with other undemanding species, such as pencilfishes.

TROPICAL AFRICA

elongate body

large eye

sac containing internal organs

dark stripe on anal fin

Diet Omnivorous	Tank levels All	Temperament

Family ANOSTOMIDAE	Species *Leporinus desmotes*	Size 22cm (8¾in)

BLACK AND YELLOW LEPORINUS

Several sooty black bands encircle the body at intervals, beginning at the tip of the snout and ending at the caudal peduncle. The background colour is yellowish white. There is a faint amount of ground colour on the centre of the middle three bands. The terminal mouth resembles that of a hare, hence the name *Leporinus* (Latin for young hare).
• **HABITAT** Slow streams in the Amazon basin, from Guyana to the Plate River.
• **REMARK** The genus, although omnivorous, still requires plenty of vegetable matter. Plants are therefore at risk.

SOUTH AMERICA

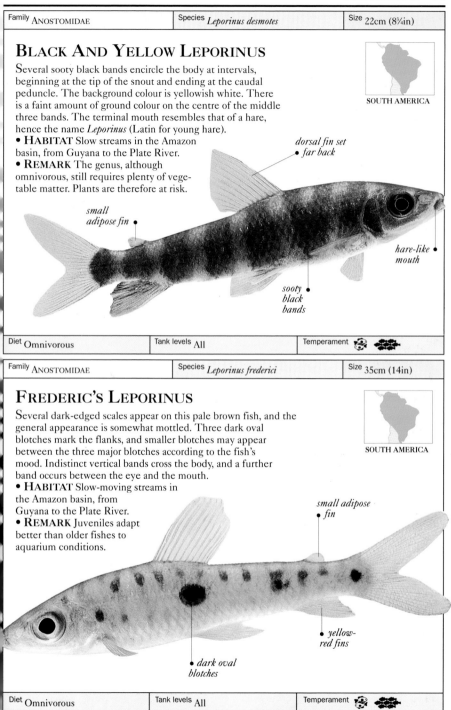

dorsal fin set • far back

small adipose fin •

hare-like • mouth

sooty black bands

Diet Omnivorous	Tank levels All	Temperament

Family ANOSTOMIDAE	Species *Leporinus frederici*	Size 35cm (14in)

FREDERIC'S LEPORINUS

Several dark-edged scales appear on this pale brown fish, and the general appearance is somewhat mottled. Three dark oval blotches mark the flanks, and smaller blotches may appear between the three major blotches according to the fish's mood. Indistinct vertical bands cross the body, and a further band occurs between the eye and the mouth.
• **HABITAT** Slow-moving streams in the Amazon basin, from Guyana to the Plate River.
• **REMARK** Juveniles adapt better than older fishes to aquarium conditions.

SOUTH AMERICA

small adipose • fin

yellow-red fins

• dark oval blotches

Diet Omnivorous	Tank levels All	Temperament

Family ANOSTOMIDAE	Species *Leporinus octofasciatum*	Size 15cm (6in)

EIGHT-BANDED LEPORINUS

The number of vertical bands on this characin appears
to vary, with some ground colour in the dark bands as in
the Black and Yellow Leporinus (see p.95). Fins are
mainly colourless, but the anal, pelvic, and dorsal
fins carry some black, and the adipose fin
has a black margin. Like many genus
members, patterns may fade with age.
• **HABITAT** Slow-moving
Amazonian streams, from
Guyana to the Plate River.

SOUTH AMERICA

vertical bands •

large, dark-rimmed eye •

black margin in adipose fin •

terminal mouth on small head •

• *black tint in anal fins*

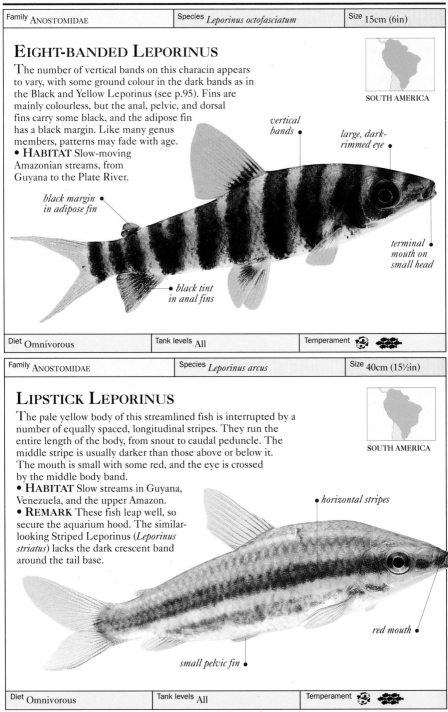

Diet Omnivorous	Tank levels All	Temperament

Family ANOSTOMIDAE	Species *Leporinus arcus*	Size 40cm (15½in)

LIPSTICK LEPORINUS

The pale yellow body of this streamlined fish is interrupted by a
number of equally spaced, longitudinal stripes. They run the
entire length of the body, from snout to caudal peduncle. The
middle stripe is usually darker than those above or below it.
The mouth is small with some red, and the eye is crossed
by the middle body band.
• **HABITAT** Slow streams in Guyana,
Venezuela, and the upper Amazon.
• **REMARK** These fish leap well, so
secure the aquarium hood. The similar-
looking Striped Leporinus (*Leporinus
striatus*) lacks the dark crescent band
around the tail base.

SOUTH AMERICA

• *horizontal stripes*

red mouth •

small pelvic fin •

Diet Omnivorous	Tank levels All	Temperament

| Family SERRASALMIDAE | Species *Metynnis hypsauchen* | Size 14cm (5½in) |

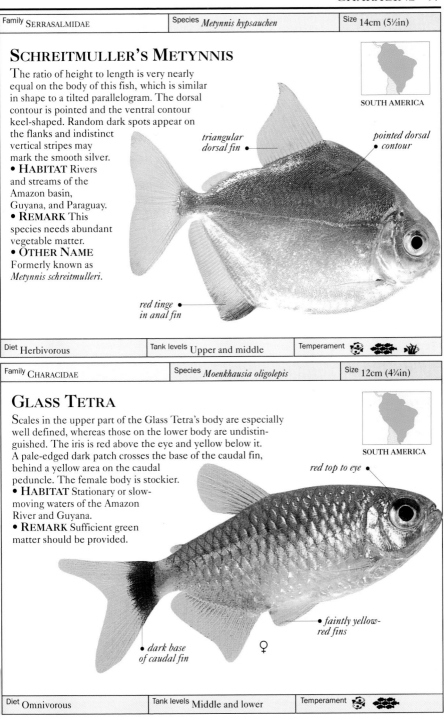

SCHREITMULLER'S METYNNIS

The ratio of height to length is very nearly
equal on the body of this fish, which is similar
in shape to a tilted parallelogram. The dorsal
contour is pointed and the ventral contour
keel-shaped. Random dark spots appear on
the flanks and indistinct
vertical stripes may
mark the smooth silver.
• HABITAT Rivers
and streams of the
Amazon basin,
Guyana, and Paraguay.
• REMARK This
species needs abundant
vegetable matter.
• OTHER NAME
Formerly known as
Metynnis schreitmulleri.

SOUTH AMERICA

*triangular
dorsal fin* •

*pointed dorsal
• contour*

*red tinge •
in anal fin*

| Diet Herbivorous | Tank levels Upper and middle | Temperament |

| Family CHARACIDAE | Species *Moenkhausia oligolepis* | Size 12cm (4¾in) |

GLASS TETRA

Scales in the upper part of the Glass Tetra's body are especially
well defined, whereas those on the lower body are undistin-
guished. The iris is red above the eye and yellow below it.
A pale-edged dark patch crosses the base of the caudal fin,
behind a yellow area on the caudal
peduncle. The female body is stockier.
• HABITAT Stationary or slow-
moving waters of the Amazon
River and Guyana.
• REMARK Sufficient green
matter should be provided.

SOUTH AMERICA

red top to eye •

*• faintly yellow-
red fins*

*• dark base
of caudal fin*

♀

| Diet Omnivorous | Tank levels Middle and lower | Temperament |

Family CHARACIDAE	Species *Moenkhausia pittieri*	Size 6cm (2½in)

DIAMOND TETRA

The coloration of the Diamond Tetra is greenish blue-grey
on the dorsal surface, and silver and white below. The
iridescences are the fish's prime attraction; they are best
appreciated under side-lighting. This juvenile has
a dark line which runs along the flanks and
terminates at the caudal peduncle. Adult
fins are bluish and edged with white; the
dorsal fin of mature males is markedly
sickle-shaped. Pelvic fins are long,
and the caudal fin is deeply forked.
The top of the eye is red.

SOUTH AMERICA

*sickle-shaped
• dorsal fin*

- **HABITAT** Lake Valencia,
Venezuela.
- **REMARK**
This species
looks its best
shoaling in a well-
planted tank. An
active swimmer,
it needs plenty
of space. It may
be slow to mature.

*bright
red top
of eye*

*dark line •
on juvenile*

*• iridescences
on flanks*

Diet Omnivorous	Tank level Middle	Temperament

Family SERRASALMIDAE	Species *Mylossoma pluriventre*	Size 20cm (8in)

SILVER DOLLAR

*small black-tipped
• dorsal fin*

The shape of this tetra is deep and the
ventral region is especially keel-like. Coloration is silvery with small scales adding a polished effect. On the rear of the gill-cover there is a
small black blotch, and, in juveniles, there may
be dark vertical bands
and a second dark
blotch midway along
the flanks. The broad
anal fin and paddle-
shaped caudal fin have
red-orange edges.

SOUTH AMERICA

- **HABITAT** Open
waters in the southern
Amazon, Paraguay, and
the River Plate.
- **REMARK** The
vegetarian habits of this
fish mean that aquarium
plants, especially softer-
leaved species, are at risk.
- **OTHER NAME** Formerly
known as *Mylossoma argenteum*.

*• straight edge
of caudal fin*

*• small,
smooth scales*

Diet Herbivorous	Tank level Middle	Temperament

Family CITHARINIDAE	Species *Nannaethiops unitaeniatus*	Size 6cm (2½in)

ONE-LINED AFRICAN TETRA

A dark line, topped by a metallic gold streak, runs from the snout to the end of the caudal fin of this elongate fish. The dorsal surface is greenish yellow-brown, and the ventral region is silvery gold. At spawning times the male develops red coloration in the square dorsal fin and in upper areas of the caudal fin.
• **HABITAT** Streams and rivers of equatorial Africa.
• **REMARK** This peaceful, rather shy species does best in a fairly spacious tank with small fishes and bushy plants.

TROPICAL
AFRICA

square
dorsal
• *fin*

well-
defined
• *scales*

gold rim
around
eye •

• *dark line
extends into
caudal fin*

• *silvery gold
flanks*

Diet Omnivorous	Tank levels Middle and lower	Temperament

Family LEBIASINIDAE	Species *Nannostomus beckfordi aripirangensis*	Size 6cm (2½in)

GOLDEN PENCILFISH

As the name suggests, this fish is pencil-shaped. The dorsal surface is golden brown, which is intensified on mature specimens. The underside is silver below a wide, dark band running from the snout to the caudal fin and ending between two red patches. A gold band runs immediately above the black band. All fins, except the pectorals, have some some red colour.
• **HABITAT** The island of Aripiranga in the lower Amazon region.
• **REMARK** The coloration of pencilfishes changes into blotchy patterns at night.
• **OTHER NAMES** Formerly classified in the *Nannobrycon* and *Poecilobrycon* genera.

SOUTH AMERICA

red coloration
• *in fins*

• *red patches
at base of
caudal fin*

dark band •

Diet Omnivorous	Tank level Middle	Temperament

Family LEBIASINIDAE	Species *Nannostomus beckfordi*	Size 6cm (2½in)

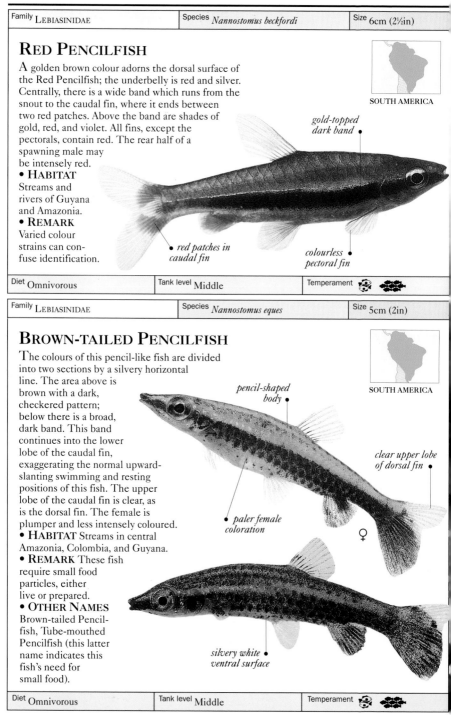

RED PENCILFISH

A golden brown colour adorns the dorsal surface of the Red Pencilfish; the underbelly is red and silver. Centrally, there is a wide band which runs from the snout to the caudal fin, where it ends between two red patches. Above the band are shades of gold, red, and violet. All fins, except the pectorals, contain red. The rear half of a spawning male may be intensely red.
• **HABITAT** Streams and rivers of Guyana and Amazonia.
• **REMARK** Varied colour strains can confuse identification.

SOUTH AMERICA

gold-topped dark band •

• *red patches in caudal fin*

colourless • *pectoral fin*

Diet Omnivorous	Tank level Middle	Temperament

Family LEBIASINIDAE	Species *Nannostomus eques*	Size 5cm (2in)

BROWN-TAILED PENCILFISH

The colours of this pencil-like fish are divided into two sections by a silvery horizontal line. The area above is brown with a dark, checkered pattern; below there is a broad, dark band. This band continues into the lower lobe of the caudal fin, exaggerating the normal upward-slanting swimming and resting positions of this fish. The upper lobe of the caudal fin is clear, as is the dorsal fin. The female is plumper and less intensely coloured.
• **HABITAT** Streams in central Amazonia, Colombia, and Guyana.
• **REMARK** These fish require small food particles, either live or prepared.
• **OTHER NAMES** Brown-tailed Pencilfish, Tube-mouthed Pencilfish (this latter name indicates this fish's need for small food).

SOUTH AMERICA

pencil-shaped body •

clear upper lobe of dorsal fin •

• *paler female coloration*

♀

silvery white • *ventral surface*

Diet Omnivorous	Tank level Middle	Temperament

| Family LEBIASINIDAE | Species *Nannostomus trifasciatus* | Size 5cm (2in) |

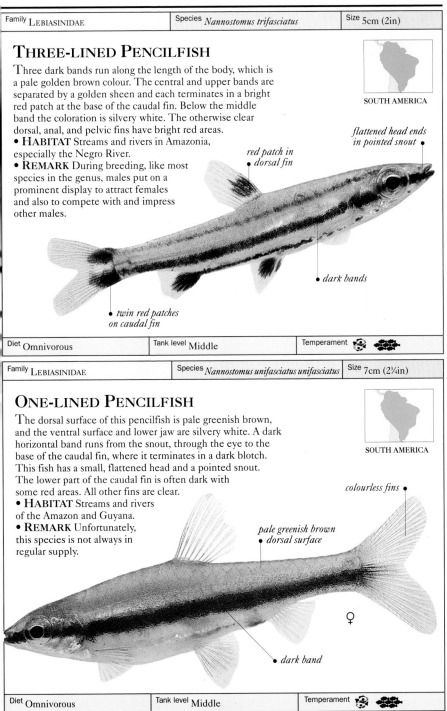

SOUTH AMERICA

THREE-LINED PENCILFISH

Three dark bands run along the length of the body, which is a pale golden brown colour. The central and upper bands are separated by a golden sheen and each terminates in a bright red patch at the base of the caudal fin. Below the middle band the coloration is silvery white. The otherwise clear dorsal, anal, and pelvic fins have bright red areas.
• **HABITAT** Streams and rivers in Amazonia, especially the Negro River.
• **REMARK** During breeding, like most species in the genus, males put on a prominent display to attract females and also to compete with and impress other males.

flattened head ends in pointed snout •

red patch in • dorsal fin

• dark bands

• twin red patches on caudal fin

| Diet Omnivorous | Tank level Middle | Temperament |

| Family LEBIASINIDAE | Species *Nannostomus unifasciatus unifasciatus* | Size 7cm (2¾in) |

SOUTH AMERICA

ONE-LINED PENCILFISH

The dorsal surface of this pencilfish is pale greenish brown, and the ventral surface and lower jaw are silvery white. A dark horizontal band runs from the snout, through the eye to the base of the caudal fin, where it terminates in a dark blotch. This fish has a small, flattened head and a pointed snout. The lower part of the caudal fin is often dark with some red areas. All other fins are clear.
• **HABITAT** Streams and rivers of the Amazon and Guyana.
• **REMARK** Unfortunately, this species is not always in regular supply.

colourless fins •

pale greenish brown • dorsal surface

♀

• dark band

| Diet Omnivorous | Tank level Middle | Temperament |

Family CHARACIDAE	Species *Poptella orbicularis*	Size 12cm (4¾in)

SALMON DISCUS

The main colour of this disc-shaped fish is silver, but various reflected colours, including green, may be evident, depending on lighting conditions. Pinks and violet hues are common, hence the popular name. The scales are large, and two indistinct, dark vertical stripes are situated by the shoulder. A dark horizontal line runs from the rearmost stripe back to the caudal peduncle. All fins are colourless.

• **HABITAT** Widespread in rivers and streams from Guyana down to the Paraguay River in Paraguay.

• **REMARKS** This active species lives happily in a shoal, especially in a spacious aquarium. The Salmon Discus tends to eat soft-leaved plants, so vegetable matter should be included in this fish's diet.

• **OTHER NAMES** Disc Tetra; formerly classified as *Ephippicharax*.

SOUTH AMERICA

violet and green hues

colourless fins

heavily built body

Diet Omnivorous	Tank level Middle	Temperament

Family CHARACIDAE	Species *Prionobrama filigera*	Size 6cm (2½in)

GLASS BLOODFIN

The streamlined shape of this fish is very similar to the true Bloodfin (see p.86). Coloration is translucent blue-grey. The male's pelvic and long-based anal fins have long, white front rays, and his anal fin may show a dark line behind the white. Male caudal fins are deep red, whereas females have a reddish area at the base of the caudal fin.

• **HABITAT** Madeira River region of Brazil in the Amazon basin.

• **REMARK** This active fish likes to shoal beneath floating plants or in currents from the filter's output. It will breed easily if soft water is provided.

• **OTHER NAME** Translucent Bloodfin.

SOUTH AMERICA

streamlined shape

semi-transparent body

♀ *reddish female caudal fin*

long first ray of anal fin

Diet Omnivorous	Tank levels Upper and middle	Temperament

Family CHARACIDAE	Species *Pseudocorynopoma doriae*	Size 8cm (3¼in)

DRAGON-FINNED CHARACIN

The dorsal and anal fins of this characin are wide, and are produced into black-tinted filamentous rays, particularly in the male. Coloration is silver, with a darker line running from midway along the body back to the base of the caudal fin. The caudal fin is deeply forked and tipped with black.
• **HABITAT** Streams and rivers of Argentina, Paraguay, Uruguay, and southern Brazil.
• **REMARK** This fish requires space and plants. Prior to spawning, the male dances, head-down, around the female.

black tinted rays of dorsal • fin

SOUTH AMERICA

♀

caudal • fin tipped with black

deep ventral profile

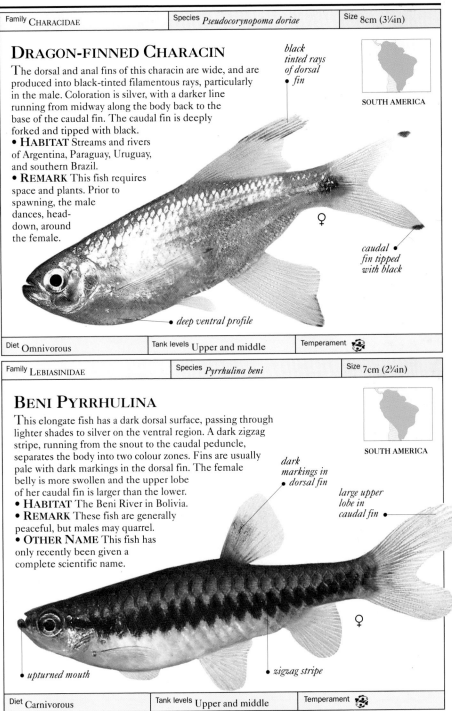

Diet Omnivorous	Tank levels Upper and middle	Temperament

Family LEBIASINIDAE	Species *Pyrrhulina beni*	Size 7cm (2¾in)

BENI PYRRHULINA

This elongate fish has a dark dorsal surface, passing through lighter shades to silver on the ventral region. A dark zigzag stripe, running from the snout to the caudal peduncle, separates the body into two colour zones. Fins are usually pale with dark markings in the dorsal fin. The female belly is more swollen and the upper lobe of her caudal fin is larger than the lower.
• **HABITAT** The Beni River in Bolivia.
• **REMARK** These fish are generally peaceful, but males may quarrel.
• **OTHER NAME** This fish has only recently been given a complete scientific name.

dark markings in • dorsal fin

SOUTH AMERICA

large upper lobe in caudal fin •

♀

• upturned mouth

• zigzag stripe

Diet Carnivorous	Tank levels Upper and middle	Temperament

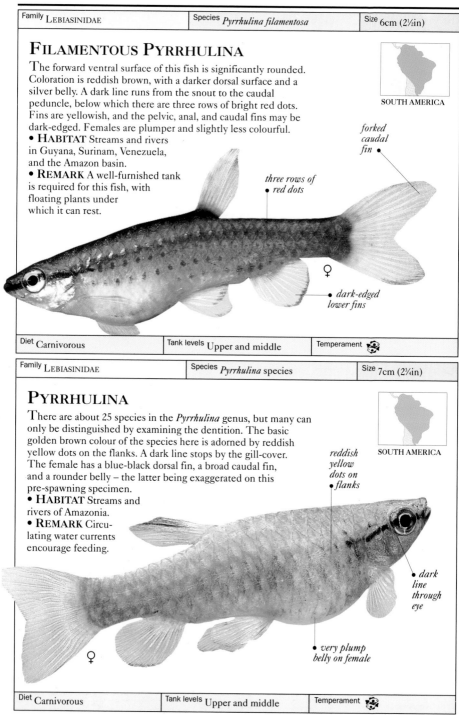

Family LEBIASINIDAE	Species *Pyrrhulina filamentosa*	Size 6cm (2½in)

FILAMENTOUS PYRRHULINA

The forward ventral surface of this fish is significantly rounded. Coloration is reddish brown, with a darker dorsal surface and a silver belly. A dark line runs from the snout to the caudal peduncle, below which there are three rows of bright red dots. Fins are yellowish, and the pelvic, anal, and caudal fins may be dark-edged. Females are plumper and slightly less colourful.
• **HABITAT** Streams and rivers in Guyana, Surinam, Venezuela, and the Amazon basin.
• **REMARK** A well-furnished tank is required for this fish, with floating plants under which it can rest.

SOUTH AMERICA

forked caudal fin •

three rows of • red dots

♀

• dark-edged lower fins

Diet Carnivorous	Tank levels Upper and middle	Temperament

Family LEBIASINIDAE	Species *Pyrrhulina* species	Size 7cm (2¾in)

PYRRHULINA

There are about 25 species in the *Pyrrhulina* genus, but many can only be distinguished by examining the dentition. The basic golden brown colour of the species here is adorned by reddish yellow dots on the flanks. A dark line stops by the gill-cover. The female has a blue-black dorsal fin, a broad caudal fin, and a rounder belly – the latter being exaggerated on this pre-spawning specimen.
• **HABITAT** Streams and rivers of Amazonia.
• **REMARK** Circulating water currents encourage feeding.

reddish yellow dots on • flanks

SOUTH AMERICA

• dark line through eye

♀

• very plump belly on female

Diet Carnivorous	Tank levels Upper and middle	Temperament

Family SERRASALMIDAE	Species *Serrasalmus nattereri*	Size 30cm (12in)

RED-BELLIED PIRANHA

The body of this Piranha is deeply oval and heavily built. Coloration is mainly steely grey, shading down through silvery grey flanks to a bright, orange-red chest and underbelly. Iridescences cover the flanks. Juveniles carry faint dark spots on the flanks which fade with age, and they lack the red and steely grey colourings. The adult is snub-nosed and the lower jaw projects further than the top jaw. Both jaws contain very sharp teeth.

SOUTH AMERICA

• **HABITAT** Rivers from Guyana to the River Plate.
• **REMARK** Due to their growth potential, Piranhas need plenty of space and food. These notoriously predatory fishes should be handled with extreme caution. A shoal of adults looks good in a well-filtered and well-aerated species aquarium; they may spawn if well fed.
• **OTHER NAME** Also-classified as *Taddyella*.

faint spots fade with age

JUVENILE

silver sheen

heavily built body

iridescences on flanks

ADULT

projecting lower jaw filled with sharp teeth

orange-red underside

long-based, concave anal fin

Diet Carnivorous	Tank levels Middle and lower	Temperament

Family CHARACIDAE	Species *Thayeria boehlkei*	Size 7.5cm (3in)

PENGUIN FISH

The common name of this fish is due to its predominantly black and white colouring. Faint olive-green on the dorsal surface shades down to silver on the belly. A dark, blurred band runs from the rear of the gill-cover, across the body, and down into the lower lobe of the caudal fin, where it is bordered by white. Females share the markings but are plumper at spawning time.
• **HABITAT** Streams in Brazil.
• **REMARK** This fish swims pointing head-upwards.

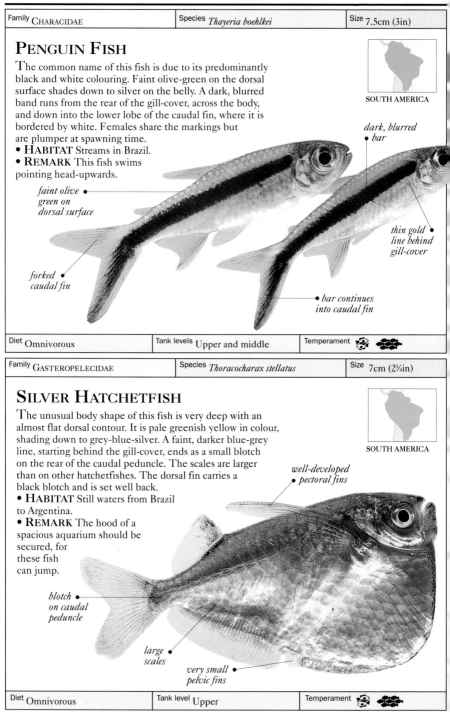

dark, blurred bar

faint olive green on dorsal surface

thin gold line behind gill-cover

forked caudal fin

bar continues into caudal fin

Diet Omnivorous	Tank levels Upper and middle	Temperament

Family GASTEROPELECIDAE	Species *Thoracocharax stellatus*	Size 7cm (2¾in)

SILVER HATCHETFISH

The unusual body shape of this fish is very deep with an almost flat dorsal contour. It is pale greenish yellow in colour, shading down to grey-blue-silver. A faint, darker blue-grey line, starting behind the gill-cover, ends as a small blotch on the rear of the caudal peduncle. The scales are larger than on other hatchetfishes. The dorsal fin carries a black blotch and is set well back.
• **HABITAT** Still waters from Brazil to Argentina.
• **REMARK** The hood of a spacious aquarium should be secured, for these fish can jump.

well-developed pectoral fins

blotch on caudal peduncle

large scales

very small pelvic fins

Diet Omnivorous	Tank level Upper	Temperament

CICHLIDS
SMALLER CICHLIDS

T HE FAMILY CICHLIDAE contains a large number of mostly heavy bodied fishes which are widely distributed throughout Central and South America, tropical Africa and, to a lesser extent, southern Asia. They generally live in still or slow-moving waters, sheltering among rocks and vegetation. As males vigorously defend their territory in the wild, a single pair is usually suitable for the average aquarium. Some cichlids dig to lay their eggs in the substrate, so rooted plants in the tank will be prone to damage. The smaller cichlids, or dwarf cichlids, include *Apistogramma* and *Pelvicachromis* species. They tend to be secretive spawners, often laying their eggs inside caves or, in the aquarium equivalent, in an overturned flowerpot.

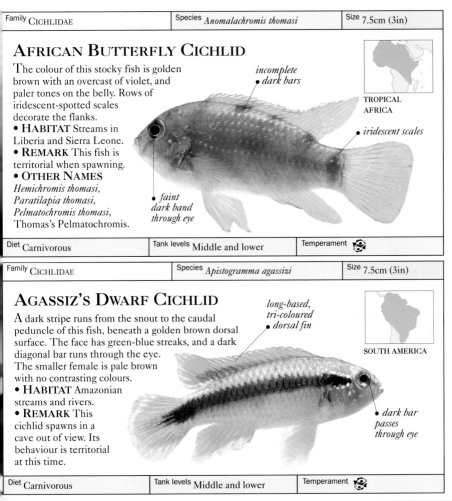

Family CICHLIDAE	Species *Anomalachromis thomasi*	Size 7.5cm (3in)

AFRICAN BUTTERFLY CICHLID

The colour of this stocky fish is golden brown with an overcast of violet, and paler tones on the belly. Rows of iridescent-spotted scales decorate the flanks.
• **HABITAT** Streams in Liberia and Sierra Leone.
• **REMARK** This fish is territorial when spawning.
• **OTHER NAMES** *Hemichromis thomasi, Paratilapia thomasi, Pelmatochromis thomasi,* Thomas's Pelmatochromis.

incomplete dark bars

TROPICAL AFRICA

iridescent scales

faint dark band through eye

Diet Carnivorous	Tank levels Middle and lower	Temperament

Family CICHLIDAE	Species *Apistogramma agassizi*	Size 7.5cm (3in)

AGASSIZ'S DWARF CICHLID

A dark stripe runs from the snout to the caudal peduncle of this fish, beneath a golden brown dorsal surface. The face has green-blue streaks, and a dark diagonal bar runs through the eye. The smaller female is pale brown with no contrasting colours.
• **HABITAT** Amazonian streams and rivers.
• **REMARK** This cichlid spawns in a cave out of view. Its behaviour is territorial at this time.

long-based, tri-coloured dorsal fin

SOUTH AMERICA

dark bar passes through eye

Diet Carnivorous	Tank levels Middle and lower	Temperament

Family CICHLIDAE	Species *Apistogramma cacatuoides*	Size 7.5cm (3in)

COCKATOO DWARF CICHLID

The most distinctive characteristics of this species are the fins. The dorsal fin has extended rays like the crest of a cockatoo, and the caudal fin has red and black markings. Body coloration is greyish green. A wide, dark band runs horizontally along the flanks, and repeated, broken lines run beneath this. Females have dark bars through the eyes and lesser finnage.
• **HABITAT** Streams and rivers of Peruvian Amazonia.
• **REMARK** One male of this species is best kept with several females in a modestly sized aquarium.
• **OTHER NAME** Crested Dwarf Cichlid.

SOUTH AMERICA

dorsal fin carries extended rays

greyish green body coloration

red and black marks on caudal fin

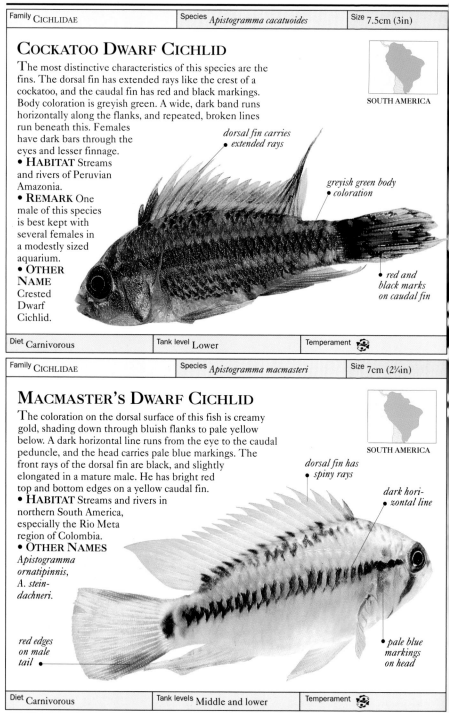

Diet Carnivorous	Tank level Lower	Temperament

Family CICHLIDAE	Species *Apistogramma macmasteri*	Size 7cm (2¾in)

MACMASTER'S DWARF CICHLID

The coloration on the dorsal surface of this fish is creamy gold, shading down through bluish flanks to pale yellow below. A dark horizontal line runs from the eye to the caudal peduncle, and the head carries pale blue markings. The front rays of the dorsal fin are black, and slightly elongated in a mature male. He has bright red top and bottom edges on a yellow caudal fin.
• **HABITAT** Streams and rivers in northern South America, especially the Rio Meta region of Colombia.
• **OTHER NAMES** *Apistogramma ornatipinnis, A. stein-dachneri.*

SOUTH AMERICA

dorsal fin has spiny rays

dark hori-zontal line

red edges on male tail

pale blue markings on head

Diet Carnivorous	Tank levels Middle and lower	Temperament

| Family CICHLIDAE | Species *Apistogramma nijsseni* | Size 5cm (2in) |

NIJSSEN'S DWARF CICHLID

The coloration of this cichlid is greenish yellow with bluish flanks. Depending on the mood and condition of the fish, a number of dark bands cross the body vertically, and a dark diagonal band reaches from the eye across the gill-cover. On the best specimens, the dorsal fin is blue with a red and yellow edge, and the rounded edge of the tail is bright red. Females are less intensely coloured.
• **HABITAT** Streams and rivers of central and northern South America.
• **REMARK** Like all species in the genus, this fish becomes very territorial when breeding.

SOUTH AMERICA

long-based • dorsal fin

• rounded caudal fin

• bluish flanks

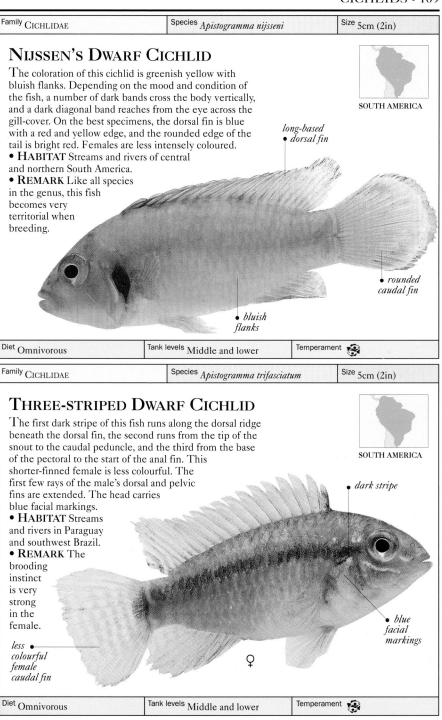

| Diet Omnivorous | Tank levels Middle and lower | Temperament |

| Family CICHLIDAE | Species *Apistogramma trifasciatum* | Size 5cm (2in) |

THREE-STRIPED DWARF CICHLID

The first dark stripe of this fish runs along the dorsal ridge beneath the dorsal fin, the second runs from the tip of the snout to the caudal peduncle, and the third from the base of the pectoral to the start of the anal fin. This shorter-finned female is less colourful. The first few rays of the male's dorsal and pelvic fins are extended. The head carries blue facial markings.
• **HABITAT** Streams and rivers in Paraguay and southwest Brazil.
• **REMARK** The brooding instinct is very strong in the female.

SOUTH AMERICA

• dark stripe

• blue facial markings

less • colourful female caudal fin

♀

| Diet Omnivorous | Tank levels Middle and lower | Temperament |

Family CICHLIDAE	Species *Crenicara filamentosa*	Size 7.5cm (3in)

CHECKERBOARD CICHLID

This fish gets its name from the horizontal pattern of dark blotches checkering its flanks. Greenish blue lines, more apparent under sidelighting, run either side of the blotches. The fins are speckled in red, edged in light blue, and terminate in extended filaments. Under the eye there is a red line and a dark band extending from the snout to the end of the gill-cover.
• **HABITAT** Rivers in the Orinoco region.
• **REMARK** This shy species does best in soft, acid water, around rocks and at the bases of plants. It prefers live foods.

SOUTH AMERICA

extended filaments

red line under eye

equally spaced blotches

lyre-shaped caudal fin

Diet Carnivorous	Tank level Lower	Temperament

Family CICHLIDAE	Species *Nannacara anomala*	Size 7.5cm (3in)

GOLDEN-EYED DWARF CICHLID

The colour of this stocky fish is usually golden brown with greenish blue iridescent scales on the flanks. Darker markings may appear, depending on its mood. The head is rounded with a large golden eye and greenish blue facial markings. The female has a plainer yellow coloration.
• **HABITAT** Streams and rivers in Guyana, South America.
• **REMARK** The female often takes on a pattern of blotches when spawning.

SOUTH AMERICA

rayed dorsal fin

arched dorsal surface

green-blue iridescent scales

plain yellow colouring in female

♀

Diet Carnivorous	Tank level Lower	Temperament

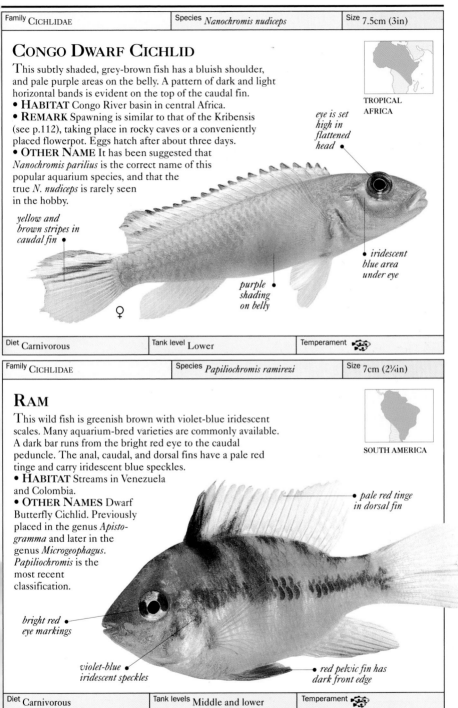

Family CICHLIDAE	Species *Nanochromis nudiceps*	Size 7.5cm (3in)

CONGO DWARF CICHLID

This subtly shaded, grey-brown fish has a bluish shoulder, and pale purple areas on the belly. A pattern of dark and light horizontal bands is evident on the top of the caudal fin.
• **HABITAT** Congo River basin in central Africa.
• **REMARK** Spawning is similar to that of the Kribensis (see p.112), taking place in rocky caves or a conveniently placed flowerpot. Eggs hatch after about three days.
• **OTHER NAME** It has been suggested that *Nanochromis parilius* is the correct name of this popular aquarium species, and that the true *N. nudiceps* is rarely seen in the hobby.

TROPICAL AFRICA

eye is set high in flattened head

yellow and brown stripes in caudal fin

iridescent blue area under eye

♀

purple shading on belly

Diet Carnivorous	Tank level Lower	Temperament

Family CICHLIDAE	Species *Papiliochromis ramirezi*	Size 7cm (2¾in)

RAM

This wild fish is greenish brown with violet-blue iridescent scales. Many aquarium-bred varieties are commonly available. A dark bar runs from the bright red eye to the caudal peduncle. The anal, caudal, and dorsal fins have a pale red tinge and carry iridescent blue speckles.
• **HABITAT** Streams in Venezuela and Colombia.
• **OTHER NAMES** Dwarf Butterfly Cichlid. Previously placed in the genus *Apistogramma* and later in the genus *Microgeophagus*. *Papiliochromis* is the most recent classification.

SOUTH AMERICA

pale red tinge in dorsal fin

bright red eye markings

violet-blue iridescent speckles

red pelvic fin has dark front edge

Diet Carnivorous	Tank levels Middle and lower	Temperament

Family CICHLIDAE	Species *Pelvicachromis pulcher*	Size 10cm (4in)

KRIBENSIS

The dorsal and ventral body contours of this fish are equal in the male, but slightly heavier around the ventral region in the female. Colours are divided into two distinct halves by a dark band which runs from the snout, along the length of the body, and into the central rays of the caudal fin. The lower half of the body is silvery pink-violet in the male, whereas the belly of the female takes on a rich purple-plum colour. The female has gold areas both above and below the eye, and both sexes have light bars across the forehead. The male dorsal fin is pointed, with some dark shading and a red-gold outer edging. The female dorsal fin is rounded and carries dark spots in the rear. Pelvic fins of the Kribensis are bluish red, except on a spawning female, whose fins are sooty black.
• **HABITAT** Niger River delta in west Africa.
• **REMARK** The Kribensis is a secretive, yet prolific, spawner. Water pH may have a bearing on proportion of sexes within a brood.

TROPICAL
AFRICA

*dark band
runs from
snout to*
• *caudal fin*

♀

*olive-green upper
dorsal surface*
• *on male*

dark spots •
*in upper lobe
of female fin*

pointed •
*dorsal fin
of male*

• *bluish red
pelvic fins*

• *caudal fins have
dark central rays*

Diet Omnivorous	Tank levels Middle and lower	Temperament

CICHLIDS
LARGER CICHLIDS

THE LARGER, STOCKY members of the family Cichlidae are chosen both for their interesting breeding habits and for their majestic, sturdy appearance. Many species, such as the angelfishes and discus fishes from South America, have attractive patterns and make excellent display specimens for large aquariums. A high level of parental care is involved in the breeding of all well-established cichlids, and they are often territorial at this time as a result. Spawning sites are carefully chosen, cleaned, and guarded. As with many other large species, these fish have hearty appetites, so an efficient filtration system and frequent partial water changes are important. Water quality is not critical for most of these species, excluding the discus fish.

Family CICHLIDAE	Species *Aequidens maronii*	Size 10cm (4in)

KEYHOLE CICHLID

A dark, curving bar passes through the eye of this stockily built fish, connecting the front of the dorsal fin with the lower edge of the gill-cover. Background coloration is generally a creamy pale brown, but it may change to a mottled brown when the fish is disturbed. The dark blotch which gives the fish its common name appears on the flanks beneath the dorsal fin. It resembles the shape of a keyhole more closely on juvenile specimens.
• **HABITAT** Streams and rivers in Guyana.
• **REMARK** Unlike most cichlids, this fish is extremely peaceful, even shy. After spawning, which takes place on a flat rock in open water, the young may stay with the parents for several months.

Male adults have pointed dorsal and anal fins

dark bar passes through • eye

• *clear caudal fin*

"keyhole" • marking

SOUTH AMERICA

Diet Omnivorous	Tank level Lower	Temperament

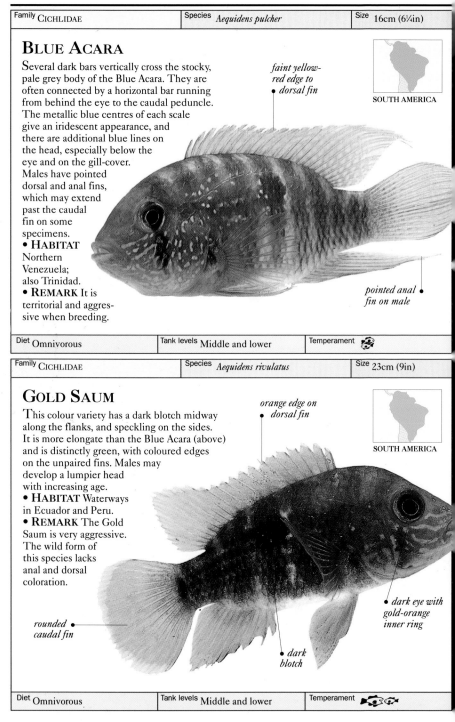

Family CICHLIDAE	Species *Aequidens pulcher*	Size 16cm (6¼in)

BLUE ACARA

Several dark bars vertically cross the stocky, pale grey body of the Blue Acara. They are often connected by a horizontal bar running from behind the eye to the caudal peduncle. The metallic blue centres of each scale give an iridescent appearance, and there are additional blue lines on the head, especially below the eye and on the gill-cover. Males have pointed dorsal and anal fins, which may extend past the caudal fin on some specimens.
• **HABITAT** Northern Venezuela; also Trinidad.
• **REMARK** It is territorial and aggressive when breeding.

faint yellow-red edge to dorsal fin

SOUTH AMERICA

pointed anal fin on male

Diet Omnivorous	Tank levels Middle and lower	Temperament

Family CICHLIDAE	Species *Aequidens rivulatus*	Size 23cm (9in)

GOLD SAUM

This colour variety has a dark blotch midway along the flanks, and speckling on the sides. It is more elongate than the Blue Acara (above) and is distinctly green, with coloured edges on the unpaired fins. Males may develop a lumpier head with increasing age.
• **HABITAT** Waterways in Ecuador and Peru.
• **REMARK** The Gold Saum is very aggressive. The wild form of this species lacks anal and dorsal coloration.

orange edge on dorsal fin

SOUTH AMERICA

rounded caudal fin

dark eye with gold-orange inner ring

dark blotch

Diet Omnivorous	Tank levels Middle and lower	Temperament

Family CICHLIDAE	Species *Astronotus ocellatus*	Size 28cm (11¼in)

RED OSCAR

This Red or Tiger Oscar is a domestic variety bred to increase the distribution of red pigment. The wild variety has irregular dark blotches and rust-coloured markings. The head of this specimen is grey with less red coloration and a large, fleshy lipped mouth. The fins are functional rather than decorative; dorsal and anal fins are wider at the rear and the caudal fin is rounded and paddle-shaped.
• **HABITAT** Rivers in Amazonia and Guyana.
• **REMARK** A favourite pet despite its rapid rate of growth and large appetite, the Oscar needs regular, thorough water changes. It spawns prolifically and is likely to produce around 3,000 fry. If fed from the hand, it will readily become tame.
• **OTHER NAME** Velvet Cichlid.

Marble-patterned juvenile Oscars

white edging on dorsal fin

narrow front of dorsal fin

fleshy lipped mouth

dark margin on anal fin

dark pelvic fins

eye has dark centre and red rim

SOUTH AMERICA

Diet Carnivorous	Tank levels Middle and lower	Temperament

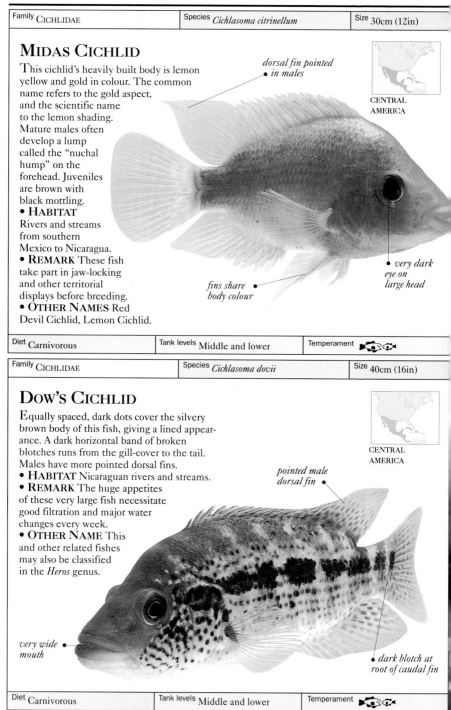

| Family CICHLIDAE | Species *Cichlasoma citrinellum* | Size 30cm (12in) |

MIDAS CICHLID

This cichlid's heavily built body is lemon yellow and gold in colour. The common name refers to the gold aspect, and the scientific name to the lemon shading. Mature males often develop a lump called the "nuchal hump" on the forehead. Juveniles are brown with black mottling.
• **HABITAT** Rivers and streams from southern Mexico to Nicaragua.
• **REMARK** These fish take part in jaw-locking and other territorial displays before breeding.
• **OTHER NAMES** Red Devil Cichlid, Lemon Cichlid.

dorsal fin pointed in males

CENTRAL AMERICA

very dark eye on large head

fins share body colour

| Diet Carnivorous | Tank levels Middle and lower | Temperament |

| Family CICHLIDAE | Species *Cichlasoma dovii* | Size 40cm (16in) |

DOW'S CICHLID

Equally spaced, dark dots cover the silvery brown body of this fish, giving a lined appearance. A dark horizontal band of broken blotches runs from the gill-cover to the tail. Males have more pointed dorsal fins.
• **HABITAT** Nicaraguan rivers and streams.
• **REMARK** The huge appetites of these very large fish necessitate good filtration and major water changes every week.
• **OTHER NAME** This and other related fishes may also be classified in the *Heros* genus.

CENTRAL AMERICA

pointed male dorsal fin

very wide mouth

dark blotch at root of caudal fin

| Diet Carnivorous | Tank levels Middle and lower | Temperament |

Family CICHLIDAE	Species *Cichlasoma maculicauda*	Size 30cm (12in)

BLACK-BELT CICHLID

Dark speckles cluster sporadically on the silver-blue body of this cichlid, particularly on the mid-section and on the caudal peduncle. The front part of the head and the base of the pectoral fin are marked with carmine-red, and speckles of this colour appear above the gill-cover. Dorsal and anal fins of the male are pointed.
• **HABITAT** Rivers and streams from southern Mexico to Panama.

dark vertical bar • created by dots

CENTRAL AMERICA

red in • caudal fin

• carmine-red colouring

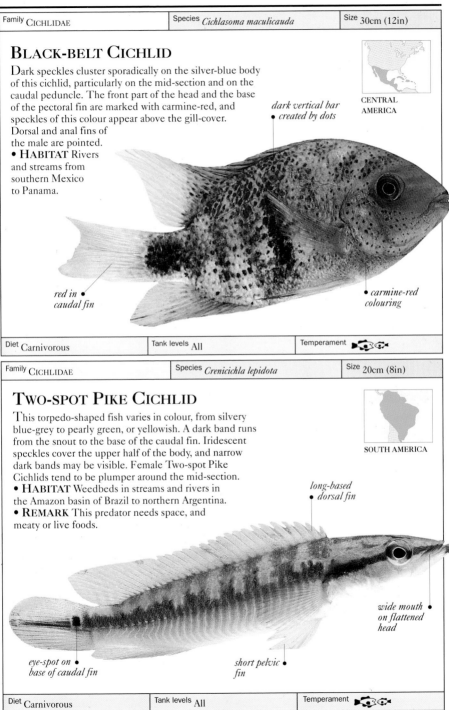

Diet Carnivorous	Tank levels All	Temperament

Family CICHLIDAE	Species *Crenicichla lepidota*	Size 20cm (8in)

TWO-SPOT PIKE CICHLID

This torpedo-shaped fish varies in colour, from silvery blue-grey to pearly green, or yellowish. A dark band runs from the snout to the base of the caudal fin. Iridescent speckles cover the upper half of the body, and narrow dark bands may be visible. Female Two-spot Pike Cichlids tend to be plumper around the mid-section.
• **HABITAT** Weedbeds in streams and rivers in the Amazon basin of Brazil to northern Argentina.
• **REMARK** This predator needs space, and meaty or live foods.

SOUTH AMERICA

long-based • dorsal fin

wide mouth • on flattened head

eye-spot on • base of caudal fin

short pelvic • fin

Diet Carnivorous	Tank levels All	Temperament

Family CICHLIDAE	Species *Etroplus maculatus*	Size 8cm (3¼in)

ORANGE CHROMIDE

This golden yellow fish is covered with tiny red dots
which may spread into the fins. A central black blotch
appears on the flanks. Anal and pelvic fins may be darker
than shown. Males and females are alike.

• **HABITAT** Coastal brackish rivers
of southern India and Sri Lanka.

• **REMARK** Eggs are laid
on hard surfaces –
flowerpots are ideal.
Keep in a species
tank or with
similarly-
sized fish.

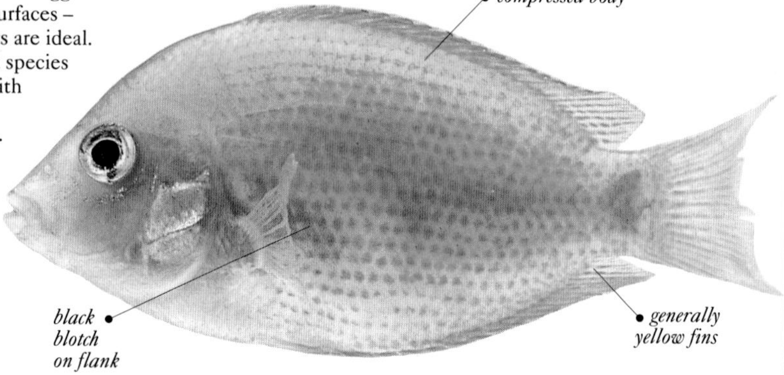

MAINLAND
SOUTH ASIA

*oval, laterally
compressed body*

*black
blotch
on flank*

*generally
yellow fins*

Diet Carnivorous	Tank levels Middle and lower	Temperament

Family CICHLIDAE	Species *Geophagus daemon*	Size 15cm (6in)

SLENDER GEOPHAGUS

This fish is slimmer than other members of the genus. The
body is blue-grey, and the upper flanks are tinged with yellow
and clearly marked with dark, diamond-shaped blotches.

• **HABITAT** Rivers and streams of the lower
Amazon region, and the Negro River.

• **REMARK** *Geophagus* means earth-
eater, and refers to
the fish's habit of
sifting sand and
gravel for
worms or
insect
larvae.

SOUTH
AMERICA

*two red sections
on eye*

*pointed
anal fin
on male*

*long rays in
pelvic fins*

Diet Omnivorous	Tank level Lower	Temperament

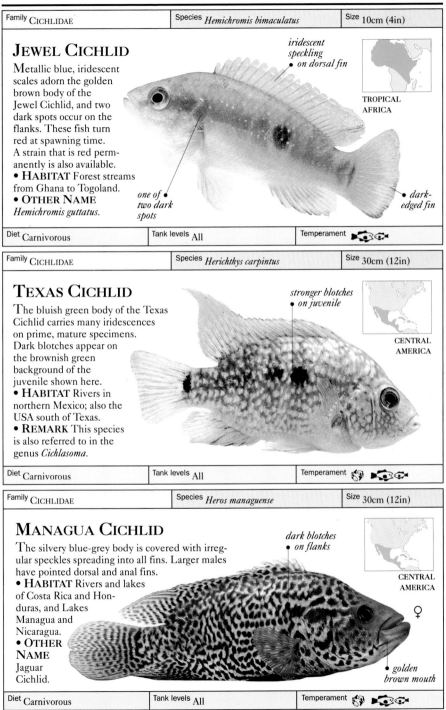

| Family CICHLIDAE | Species *Hemichromis bimaculatus* | Size 10cm (4in) |

JEWEL CICHLID

Metallic blue, iridescent
scales adorn the golden
brown body of the
Jewel Cichlid, and two
dark spots occur on the
flanks. These fish turn
red at spawning time.
A strain that is red permanently is also available.
• **HABITAT** Forest streams
from Ghana to Togoland.
• **OTHER NAME**
Hemichromis guttatus.

iridescent speckling on dorsal fin

TROPICAL AFRICA

one of two dark spots

dark-edged fin

| Diet Carnivorous | Tank levels All | Temperament |

| Family CICHLIDAE | Species *Herichthys carpintus* | Size 30cm (12in) |

TEXAS CICHLID

The bluish green body of the Texas
Cichlid carries many iridescences
on prime, mature specimens.
Dark blotches appear on
the brownish green
background of the
juvenile shown here.
• **HABITAT** Rivers in
northern Mexico; also the
USA south of Texas.
• **REMARK** This species
is also referred to in the
genus *Cichlasoma.*

stronger blotches on juvenile

CENTRAL AMERICA

| Diet Carnivorous | Tank levels All | Temperament |

| Family CICHLIDAE | Species *Heros managuense* | Size 30cm (12in) |

MANAGUA CICHLID

The silvery blue-grey body is covered with irreg-
ular speckles spreading into all fins. Larger males
have pointed dorsal and anal fins.
• **HABITAT** Rivers and lakes
of Costa Rica and Hon-
duras, and Lakes
Managua and
Nicaragua.
• **OTHER
NAME**
Jaguar
Cichlid.

dark blotches on flanks

CENTRAL AMERICA

♀

golden brown mouth

| Diet Carnivorous | Tank levels All | Temperament |

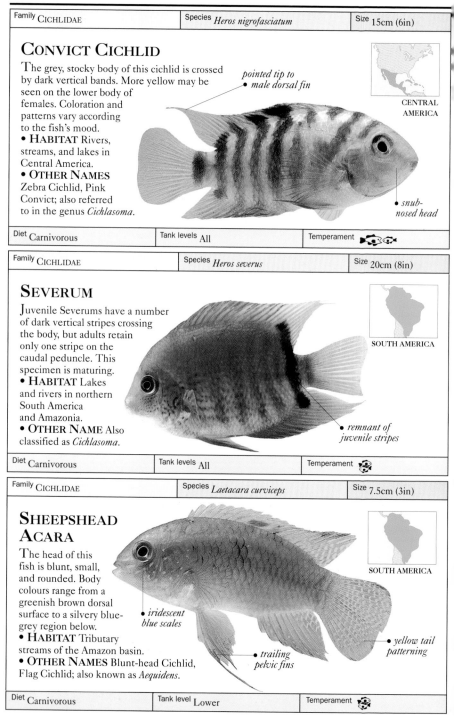

Family CICHLIDAE	Species *Heros nigrofasciatum*	Size 15cm (6in)

CONVICT CICHLID

The grey, stocky body of this cichlid is crossed by dark vertical bands. More yellow may be seen on the lower body of females. Coloration and patterns vary according to the fish's mood.
• **HABITAT** Rivers, streams, and lakes in Central America.
• **OTHER NAMES** Zebra Cichlid, Pink Convict; also referred to in the genus *Cichlasoma*.

pointed tip to male dorsal fin

CENTRAL AMERICA

snub-nosed head

Diet Carnivorous	Tank levels All	Temperament

Family CICHLIDAE	Species *Heros severus*	Size 20cm (8in)

SEVERUM

Juvenile Severums have a number of dark vertical stripes crossing the body, but adults retain only one stripe on the caudal peduncle. This specimen is maturing.
• **HABITAT** Lakes and rivers in northern South America and Amazonia.
• **OTHER NAME** Also classified as *Cichlasoma*.

SOUTH AMERICA

remnant of juvenile stripes

Diet Carnivorous	Tank levels All	Temperament

Family CICHLIDAE	Species *Laetacara curviceps*	Size 7.5cm (3in)

SHEEPSHEAD ACARA

The head of this fish is blunt, small, and rounded. Body colours range from a greenish brown dorsal surface to a silvery blue-grey region below.
• **HABITAT** Tributary streams of the Amazon basin.
• **OTHER NAMES** Blunt-head Cichlid, Flag Cichlid; also known as *Aequidens*.

SOUTH AMERICA

iridescent blue scales

trailing pelvic fins

yellow tail patterning

Diet Carnivorous	Tank level Lower	Temperament

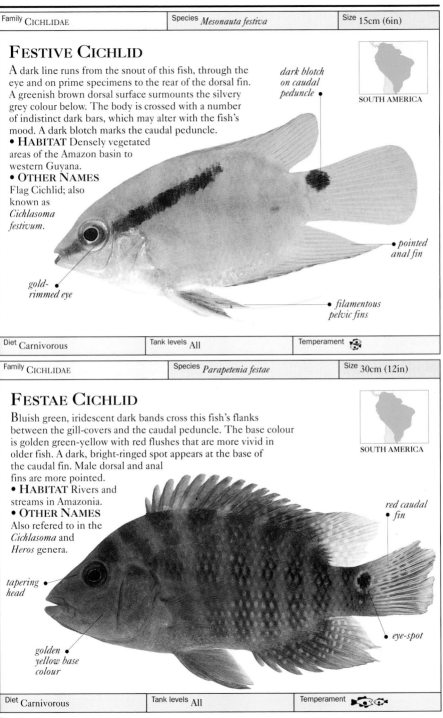

| Family CICHLIDAE | Species *Mesonauta festiva* | Size 15cm (6in) |

FESTIVE CICHLID

A dark line runs from the snout of this fish, through the eye and on prime specimens to the rear of the dorsal fin. A greenish brown dorsal surface surmounts the silvery grey colour below. The body is crossed with a number of indistinct dark bars, which may alter with the fish's mood. A dark blotch marks the caudal peduncle.
• **HABITAT** Densely vegetated areas of the Amazon basin to western Guyana.
• **OTHER NAMES** Flag Cichlid; also known as *Cichlasoma festivum*.

dark blotch on caudal peduncle

SOUTH AMERICA

• pointed anal fin

gold-rimmed eye

• filamentous pelvic fins

| Diet Carnivorous | Tank levels All | Temperament |

| Family CICHLIDAE | Species *Parapetenia festae* | Size 30cm (12in) |

FESTAE CICHLID

Bluish green, iridescent dark bands cross this fish's flanks between the gill-covers and the caudal peduncle. The base colour is golden green-yellow with red flushes that are more vivid in older fish. A dark, bright-ringed spot appears at the base of the caudal fin. Male dorsal and anal fins are more pointed.
• **HABITAT** Rivers and streams in Amazonia.
• **OTHER NAMES** Also refered to in the *Cichlasoma* and *Heros* genera.

SOUTH AMERICA

red caudal • fin

tapering • head

• eye-spot

golden • yellow base colour

| Diet Carnivorous | Tank levels All | Temperament |

FRESHWATER ANGELFISHES

T HE BODY SHAPE of the freshwater angelfish is unlike that of other members of the cichlid family: it is disc-like and laterally compressed, with long trailing fins which add considerably to its height. There are two species of wild angelfishes: *Pterophyllum altum* (below), and *P. scalare* (opposite), from which colour varieties have been developed (see pp.124–125). Angelfishes are popular because of their elegant outlines and graceful swimming action, and also for their intense parental care during breeding. Both parents guard and fan water over the eggs, which are laid on leaves and stems.

Family CICHLIDAE	Species *Pterophyllum altum*	Size 12.5cm (5in)

DEEP ANGELFISH

The natural coloration of this wild angelfish is brownish silver with several dark vertical bands which cross the body and enter the dorsal and anal fins. There may be some dark speckling between these bands. The distinguishing feature of this species is the distinct notch in the forehead outline above the snout. Dorsal and anal fins are long and carry extended filaments on adults. Pelvic fin rays extend well below the anal fin. Rays also extend from the top and bottom of the caudal fin.
• **HABITAT** Reedbeds of the Orinoco River system.
• **REMARK** The shape of this species enables it to move adeptly in and out of reed-stems, while its coloration camouflages it perfectly when at rest among the plants. A deep tank is needed to contain this fish comfortably. It is imported less frequently than *Pterophyllum scalare* (opposite), which is bred commercially in large numbers.

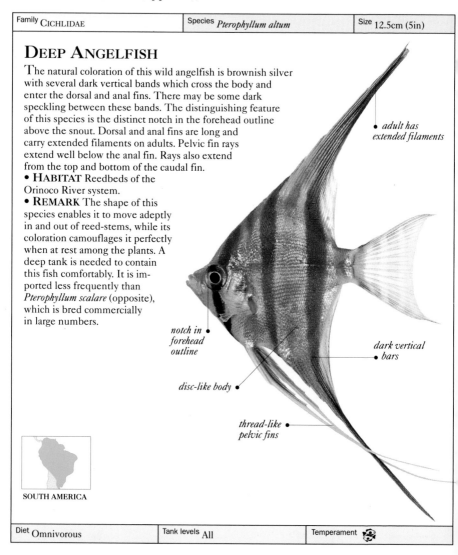

• *adult has extended filaments*

notch in forehead outline

dark vertical bars

disc-like body

thread-like pelvic fins

SOUTH AMERICA

Diet Omnivorous	Tank levels All	Temperament

Family CICHLIDAE	Species *Pterophyllum scalare*	Size 12.5cm (5in)

ANGELFISH

The colour of the wild form of this angelfish is silver with several dark vertical bands that enter the dorsal and anal fins. As with the Deep Angelfish (opposite), occasional dark speckling occurs between these bands. The fin structure is also similar: dorsal and anal fins are long with filaments extending from the tips in mature adults. The juvenile wild fish is shown here. Selective breeding programmes have resulted in many different colour strains of this species, some of which are shown below and overleaf. Sexual differences are not obvious.

• **HABITAT** Reedbeds of the Amazon and Negro Rivers.

• **REMARK** This species spawns readily and shows excellent parental care. A deep tank is required for these angelfish to develop fully.

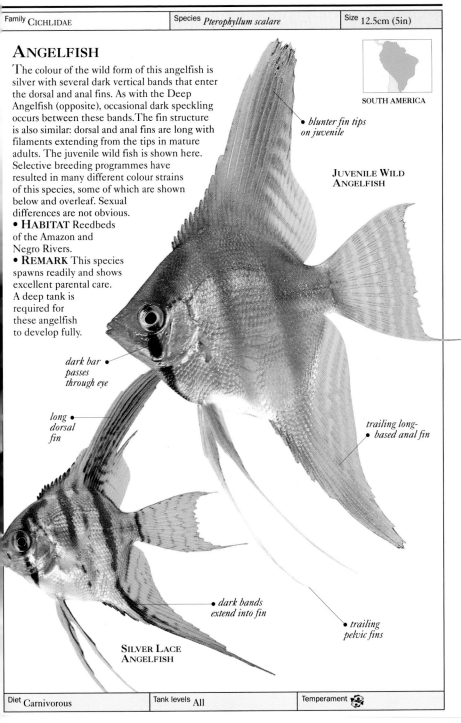

SOUTH AMERICA

• *blunter fin tips on juvenile*

JUVENILE WILD ANGELFISH

dark bar passes through eye •

long • dorsal fin

• *trailing long-based anal fin*

• *dark bands extend into fin*

• *trailing pelvic fins*

SILVER LACE ANGELFISH

Diet Carnivorous	Tank levels All	Temperament

Family CICHLIDAE	Species *Pterophyllum scalare*	Size 11cm (4¼in)

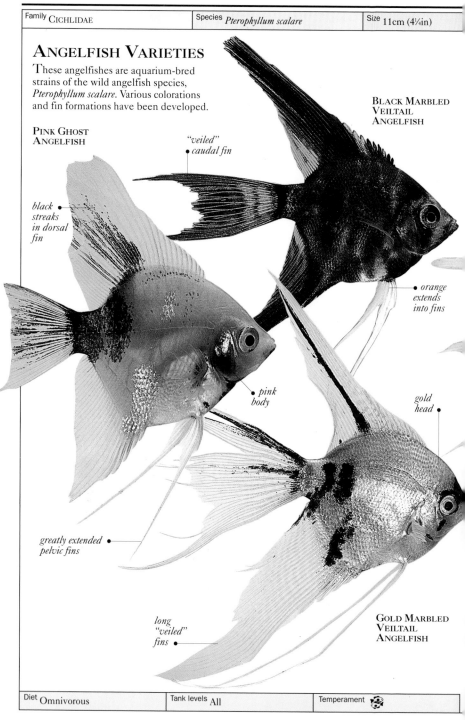

ANGELFISH VARIETIES

These angelfishes are aquarium-bred strains of the wild angelfish species, *Pterophyllum scalare*. Various colorations and fin formations have been developed.

BLACK MARBLED VEILTAIL ANGELFISH

PINK GHOST ANGELFISH

"veiled" caudal fin

black streaks in dorsal fin

orange extends into fins

pink body

gold head

greatly extended pelvic fins

long "veiled" fins

GOLD MARBLED VEILTAIL ANGELFISH

Diet Omnivorous	Tank levels All	Temperament

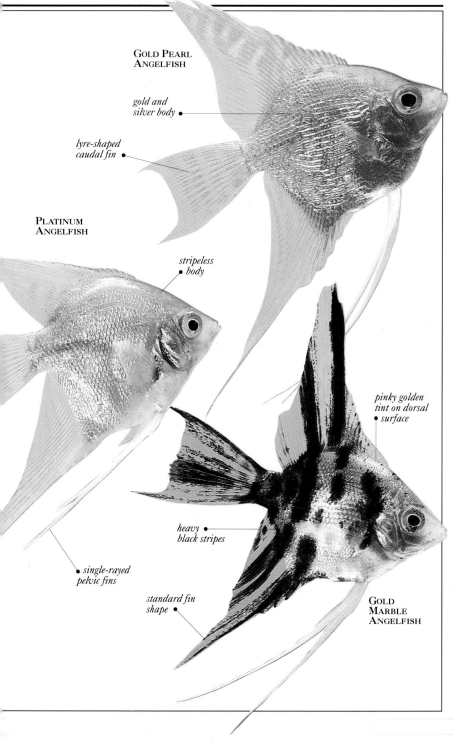

GOLD PEARL
ANGELFISH

gold and
silver body

lyre-shaped
caudal fin

PLATINUM
ANGELFISH

stripeless
body

pinky golden
tint on dorsal
surface

heavy
black stripes

single-rayed
pelvic fins

standard fin
shape

GOLD
MARBLE
ANGELFISH

DISCUS FISHES

L IKE THE FRESHWATER angelfishes (see p.122), the shape of discus fishes is uncharacteristic of the family Cichlidae to which they belong. Discus fishes are for the specialist fishkeeper, as they require highly specific water conditions: water must be soft, slightly acidic, and filtered through peat Several aquarium-bred subspecies of varying colours are available.

Family CICHLIDAE	Species *Symphysodon aequifasciata*	Size 20cm (8in)

BLUE DISCUS

The body of the discus fish is round, laterally compressed and, as the name suggests, disc-like. Dorsal and anal fins are very long-based, almost reaching back to the caudal fin, and it may be noted that the ovipositor of the female is rounded. Many aquarium-developed strains have been bred from the wild *Symphysodon* genus and their coloration varies, as can be seen here, opposite, and on p.128. On the Blue Discus, the variety shown here, dark vertical bars (seen more clearly on the adult) are overlaid with a pattern of blue wavy lines that extend into the dorsal and anal fins.

• **HABITAT** Rivers and lakes of Amazonia.

• **REMARK** This splendid fish requires high quality water and a separate and secluded aquarium. Fry are best left with the parents for the first weeks as they feed from the parents' skin secretions.

Discus fry feeding on skin secretions

• *wavy blue lines extend into dorsal fin*

steeply • rising forehead

SOUTH AMERICA

• *dark inner margin in anal fin*

Diet Carnivorous	Tank levels Middle and lower	Temperament 🐟 🐟

Family CICHLIDAE	Species *Symphysodon* var.	Size 20cm (8in)

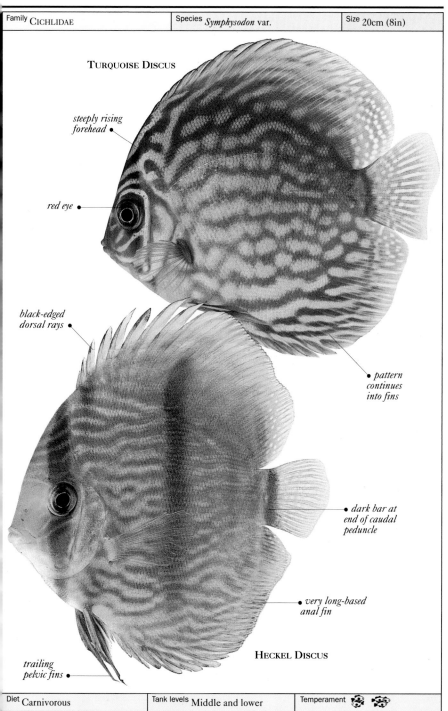

TURQUOISE DISCUS

steeply rising
forehead •

red eye •

black-edged
dorsal rays •

• pattern
continues
into fins

• dark bar at
end of caudal
peduncle

• very long-based
anal fin

HECKEL DISCUS

trailing
pelvic fins •

Diet Carnivorous	Tank levels Middle and lower	Temperament

Family CICHLIDAE	Species *Symphysodon aequifasciata*	Size 20cm (8in)

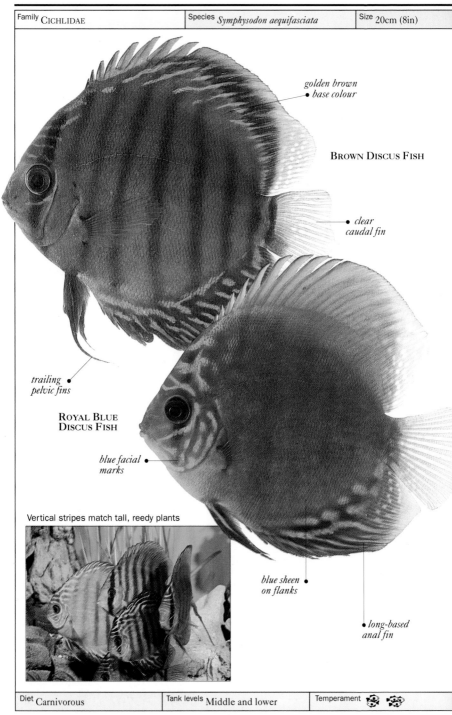

golden brown
• base colour

BROWN DISCUS FISH

• clear
caudal fin

trailing •
pelvic fins

ROYAL BLUE
DISCUS FISH

blue facial •
marks

Vertical stripes match tall, reedy plants

blue sheen •
on flanks

• long-based
anal fin

Diet Carnivorous	Tank levels Middle and lower	Temperament

Family CICHLIDAE	Species *Thorichthys meeki*	Size 15cm (6in)

FIREMOUTH

The distinguishing feature of the species is the fiery
red colour of the lower mouth and chest region, which is
especially vivid in this male. The general coloration is
brown-grey with clearly defined scales. There is a dark
spot on the gill-cover and more spots along the flanks.
These spots may extend into dark vertical stripes if the
fish is stressed. Dorsal and anal fins are long-based
and very pointed on the male.
• **HABITAT** Streams and
rivers in Guatemala, and
Yucatan in Mexico.
• **REMARK** The
Firemouth can be
aggressive, and is
best kept in a
well-planted
tank with other
large fishes.
• **OTHER
NAME** Formerly
classified as
Cichlasoma meeki.

CENTRAL
AMERICA

*dark blotches
• along flanks*

*steeply rising
forehead •*

*• fiery red
chest region*

dark fin streaks

Diet Carnivorous	Tank levels Middle and lower	Temperament

Family CICHLIDAE	Species *Tilapia mariae*	Size 30cm (12in)

TIGER TILAPIA

Juveniles of this species are greenish silver, marked by several
vertical dark stripes. Some strains have a blotch in the dorsal
fin. This male adult is dark greenish yellow, with blotches
replacing the bars. All fins have some dark speckling. Male
dorsal and anal fins are longer.
• **HABITAT** Inland waters
from Niger to Cameroon.
• **REMARK** This fish
forages in the sub-
strate and eats
plants: install
a "gravel-
tidy" if a
biological
filter sys-
tem is
used. The
character-
istic hollow
belly is not
a sign
of poor
health.

*red edge to
• dorsal fin*

TROPICAL
AFRICA

*horizontal row •
of dark blotches*

*• clear
pectoral fins*

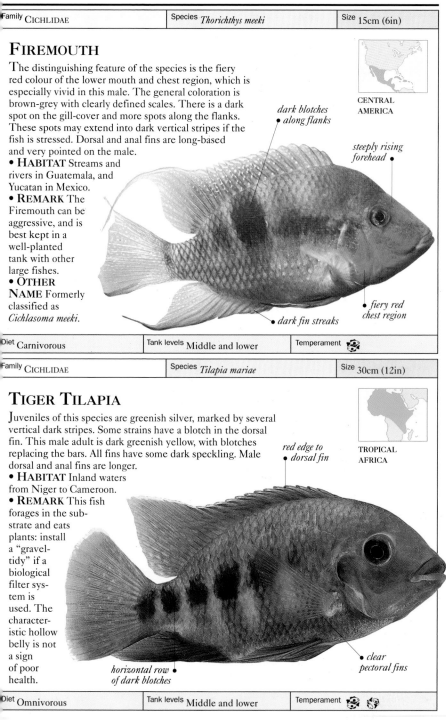

Diet Omnivorous	Tank levels Middle and lower	Temperament

CICHLIDS
RIFT VALLEY CICHLIDS

F ISHES FROM the Rift Valley lakes in Africa are popular for two reasons: they are brightly coloured and, being members of the cichlid family, they show interesting breeding characteristics. While most are specific to their lake, different colour specimens are found at different locations.

Family CICHLIDAE	Species *Aulonacara nyassae*	Size 15cm (6in)

PEACOCK CICHLID

This fish has many colour variations which are categorized with various, as yet unvalidated, scientific names. The basic colour of *Aulonacara nyassae* is electric blue, covered with a pattern of dark vertical stripes. Females and young males are more subdued in colour.
• **HABITAT** Endemic to rocky areas of Lake Malawi (formerly Lake Nyassa).
• **REMARK** These fish exist peacefully in a large aquarium. Their water should be alkaline; special "Malawi Salt Mixes" are commercially available.

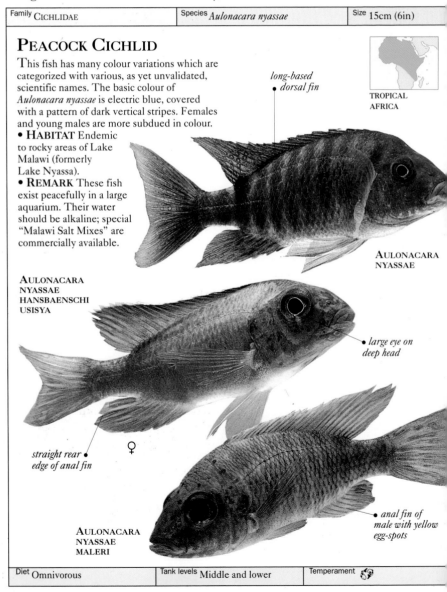

TROPICAL AFRICA

long-based dorsal fin

AULONACARA NYASSAE

AULONACARA NYASSAE HANSBAENSCHI USISYA

large eye on deep head

straight rear edge of anal fin

♀

AULONACARA NYASSAE MALERI

anal fin of male with yellow egg-spots

Diet Omnivorous	Tank levels Middle and lower	Temperament

Family CICHLIDAE	Species *Cyprichromis leptosoma*	Size 13cm (5in)

SLENDER CICHLID

The body is elongate, as the popular name suggests. The lower part of the head is pale yellow, and a small, yellow saddle occurs on the upper part of the caudal peduncle. Dorsal and anal fins are blue-black with a pale inner edge.
• HABITAT Endemic to Lake Tanganyika, where it lives in shoals high up in the water column.
• REMARK Males are intolerant of each other but a large aquarium will support a number of specimens.

well-defined scales

TROPICAL AFRICA

pointed head carrying large eye and terminal mouth

lemon-yellow caudal fin with pale blue edges

blue-black anal fin

Diet Plankton	Tank level Middle	Temperament

Family CICHLIDAE	Species *Cyrtocara ahli*	Size 17cm (6¾in)

AHL'S HAPLOCHROMIS

The metallic blue body of this cichlid is crossed by eight to ten indistinct dark vertical bars. The dorsal fin is very long-based with a white margin; the anal fin has yellow-gold shading, and the first rays of the pelvic fins are often kept white and white.
• HABITAT Open waters of Lake Malawi.
• REMARK This species will devour other fishes, so it should be fed well and kept with equally sized fishes in a rocky environment.
• OTHER NAMES Also referred to in the *Haplochromis* genus, some consider this species synonymous with *Cyrtocara jacksoni*.

laterally compressed body

TROPICAL AFRICA

metallic blue coloration

slightly elongated snout

Diet Piscivorous	Tank levels Middle and lower	Temperament

Family CICHLIDAE	Species *Cyrtocara polystigma*	Size 25cm (10in)

POLYSTIGMA

A long-standing Rift Valley favourite, and reportedly the first of these lake fishes to be bred in captivity, the Polystigma has a pale coloration, overlaid with large brown blotches and a sprinkling of reddish brown dots. Prime males are usually more intensely coloured.
• **HABITAT** Rocky shores of Lake Malawi.
• **REMARK** Spawning follows the typical mouth-brooding pattern, with the female incubating the eggs in her throat. This fish requires a large, rock-furnished aquarium.
• **OTHER NAMES** Leopard Cichlid; also referred to in the *Haplochromis* genus.

TROPICAL AFRICA

large brown • blotching

long, sloping • forehead above gold-rimmed eye

• speckling continues into all fins

Diet Omnivorous	Tank levels Middle and lower	Temperament

Family CICHLIDAE	Species *Julidochromis dickfeldi*	Size 10cm (4in)

DICKFELD'S JULIE

The cylindrical, pale white-brown body of this julie displays three distinctive, equally spaced dark bands – the lowest occupying the mid-line of the fish. A few dark lines also cross the forehead. Females may be larger.
• **HABITAT** Rocky shores of Lake Tanganyika.
• **REMARK** Smaller tanks with rocky retreats will suffice for this fish.
• **OTHER NAME** Brown Julie.

TROPICAL AFRICA

dark fins with pale blue connecting • tissue

• white-brown body

• long-based anal fin

Diet Omnivorous	Tank level Lower	Temperament

Family CICHLIDAE	Species *Julidochromis marlieri*	Size 13cm (5in)

MARLIER'S JULIE

The cylindrical body of this fish is golden brown with three dark bands running along its length. The bands are crossed vertically at regular intervals by indistinct dark bars reaching almost to the ventral surface. Another dark bar runs from the corner of the mouth to the base of the pectoral fin.
• **HABITAT** Rocky shores of Lake Tanganyika.
• **REMARK** This species, together with *Julidochromis ornatus*, is the most colourful of the genus.

gold stripe runs through centre of dorsal fin •

TROPICAL AFRICA

golden inner ring of eye •

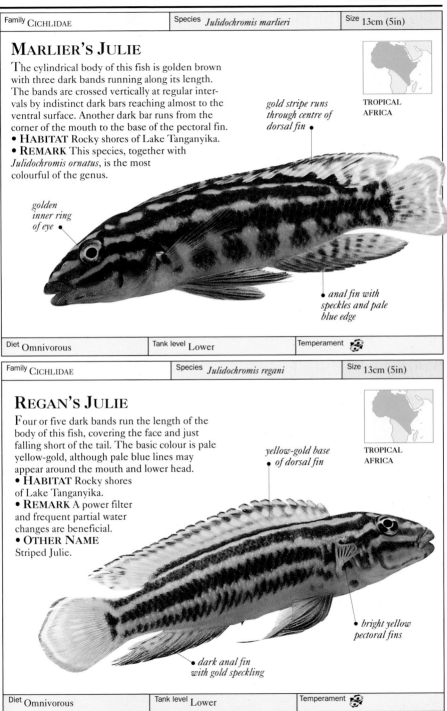

• anal fin with speckles and pale blue edge

Diet Omnivorous	Tank level Lower	Temperament

Family CICHLIDAE	Species *Julidochromis regani*	Size 13cm (5in)

REGAN'S JULIE

Four or five dark bands run the length of the body of this fish, covering the face and just falling short of the tail. The basic colour is pale yellow-gold, although pale blue lines may appear around the mouth and lower head.
• **HABITAT** Rocky shores of Lake Tanganyika.
• **REMARK** A power filter and frequent partial water changes are beneficial.
• **OTHER NAME** Striped Julie.

yellow-gold base • of dorsal fin

TROPICAL AFRICA

bright yellow pectoral fins

• dark anal fin with gold speckling

Diet Omnivorous	Tank level Lower	Temperament

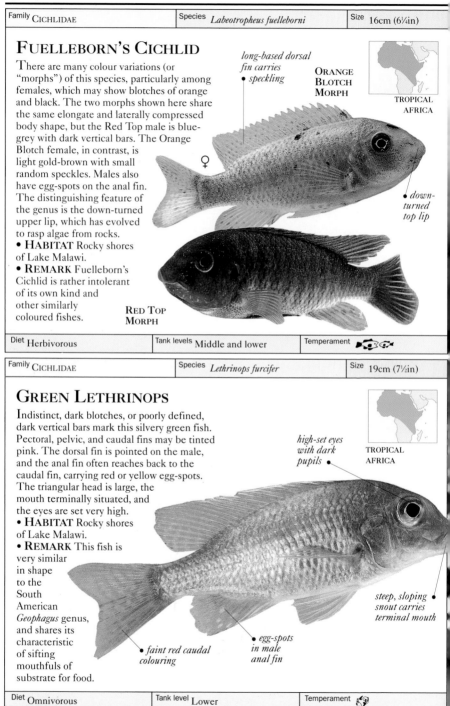

Family CICHLIDAE	Species *Labeotropheus fuelleborni*	Size 16cm (6¼in)

FUELLEBORN'S CICHLID

There are many colour variations (or "morphs") of this species, particularly among females, which may show blotches of orange and black. The two morphs shown here share the same elongate and laterally compressed body shape, but the Red Top male is blue-grey with dark vertical bars. The Orange Blotch female, in contrast, is light gold-brown with small random speckles. Males also have egg-spots on the anal fin. The distinguishing feature of the genus is the down-turned upper lip, which has evolved to rasp algae from rocks.
• **HABITAT** Rocky shores of Lake Malawi.
• **REMARK** Fuelleborn's Cichlid is rather intolerant of its own kind and other similarly coloured fishes.

long-based dorsal fin carries
• speckling

ORANGE BLOTCH MORPH

TROPICAL AFRICA

♀

• down-turned top lip

RED TOP MORPH

Diet Herbivorous	Tank levels Middle and lower	Temperament

Family CICHLIDAE	Species *Lethrinops furcifer*	Size 19cm (7½in)

GREEN LETHRINOPS

Indistinct, dark blotches, or poorly defined, dark vertical bars mark this silvery green fish. Pectoral, pelvic, and caudal fins may be tinted pink. The dorsal fin is pointed on the male, and the anal fin often reaches back to the caudal fin, carrying red or yellow egg-spots. The triangular head is large, the mouth terminally situated, and the eyes are set very high.
• **HABITAT** Rocky shores of Lake Malawi.
• **REMARK** This fish is very similar in shape to the South American *Geophagus* genus, and shares its characteristic of sifting mouthfuls of substrate for food.

high-set eyes with dark pupils •

TROPICAL AFRICA

steep, sloping snout carries terminal mouth •

• faint red caudal colouring

• egg-spots in male anal fin

Diet Omnivorous	Tank level Lower	Temperament

Family CICHLIDAE	Species *Melanochromis auratus*	Size 13cm (5in)

AURATUS

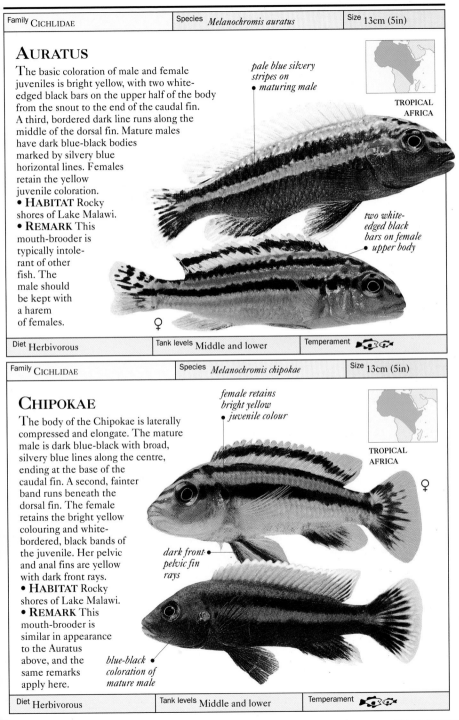

The basic coloration of male and female juveniles is bright yellow, with two white-edged black bars on the upper half of the body from the snout to the end of the caudal fin. A third, bordered dark line runs along the middle of the dorsal fin. Mature males have dark blue-black bodies marked by silvery blue horizontal lines. Females retain the yellow juvenile coloration.
• **HABITAT** Rocky shores of Lake Malawi.
• **REMARK** This mouth-brooder is typically intolerant of other fish. The male should be kept with a harem of females.

pale blue silvery stripes on • maturing male

TROPICAL AFRICA

two white-edged black bars on female • upper body

Diet Herbivorous	Tank levels Middle and lower	Temperament

Family CICHLIDAE	Species *Melanochromis chipokae*	Size 13cm (5in)

CHIPOKAE

The body of the Chipokae is laterally compressed and elongate. The mature male is dark blue-black with broad, silvery blue lines along the centre, ending at the base of the caudal fin. A second, fainter band runs beneath the dorsal fin. The female retains the bright yellow colouring and white-bordered, black bands of the juvenile. Her pelvic and anal fins are yellow with dark front rays.
• **HABITAT** Rocky shores of Lake Malawi.
• **REMARK** This mouth-brooder is similar in appearance to the Auratus above, and the same remarks apply here.

female retains bright yellow • juvenile colour

TROPICAL AFRICA

dark front • pelvic fin rays

blue-black • coloration of mature male

Diet Herbivorous	Tank levels Middle and lower	Temperament

Family CICHLIDAE	Species *Melanochromis johanni*	Size 13cm (5in)

JOHANNI

The coloration of mature males is a combination of blue, black, and brown with one silvery, pale blue line running across the forehead, over the top of the eye, and along the body above the mid-line. A second line appears below the mid-line. The long-based dorsal fin is dark blue with a pale shade at the base. Females, like the specimen here, have a brownish yellow coloration and faint, dark brown bands on the body.

• **HABITAT** Rocky shores of Lake Malawi.

• **REMARK** Colours of the genus vary from species to species, and from fish to fish within the species.

• **OTHER NAME** *Pseudotropheus daviesi*.

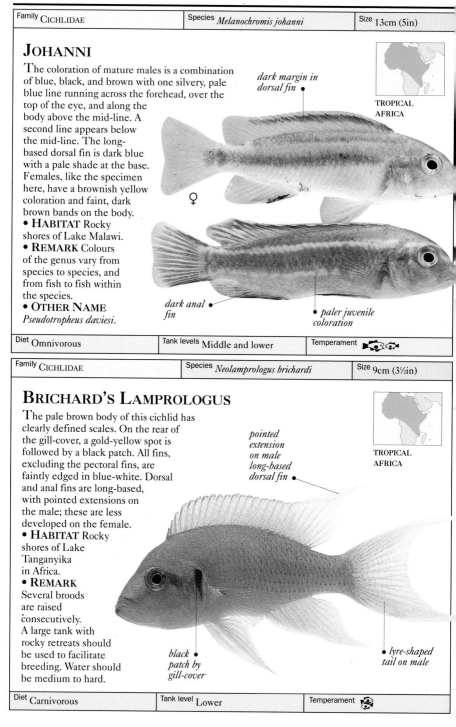

dark margin in dorsal fin

TROPICAL AFRICA

♀

dark anal fin

paler juvenile coloration

Diet Omnivorous	Tank levels Middle and lower	Temperament

Family CICHLIDAE	Species *Neolamprologus brichardi*	Size 9cm (3½in)

BRICHARD'S LAMPROLOGUS

The pale brown body of this cichlid has clearly defined scales. On the rear of the gill-cover, a gold-yellow spot is followed by a black patch. All fins, excluding the pectoral fins, are faintly edged in blue-white. Dorsal and anal fins are long-based, with pointed extensions on the male; these are less developed on the female.

• **HABITAT** Rocky shores of Lake Tanganyika in Africa.

• **REMARK** Several broods are raised consecutively. A large tank with rocky retreats should be used to facilitate breeding. Water should be medium to hard.

pointed extension on male long-based dorsal fin

TROPICAL AFRICA

black patch by gill-cover

lyre-shaped tail on male

Diet Carnivorous	Tank level Lower	Temperament

Family CICHLIDAE	Species *Neolamprologus leleupi*	Size 9cm (3½in)

LEMON CICHLID

The shape of the Lemon Cichlid is similar to that of fishes
from the lake-sharing genus *Julidochromis*. The fins share the
bright yellow body colour, with a hint of dark shading along
the rear edges. The dorsal fin is long-based, and pelvic and
anal fins are slightly trailing. The caudal fin is broad.
• **HABITAT** Rocky shallows of Lake Tanganyika.
• **REMARK** There are several colour strains, often in
shades nearer to orange than the popular name
suggests: for example, *Neolamprologus
leleupi leleupi* and *N. leleupi
longior*. Sexing is
difficult.

TROPICAL
AFRICA

broad caudal fin •

*trailing
pelvic fins*

Diet Carnivorous	Tank level Lower	Temperament

Family CICHLIDAE	Species *Pseudotropheus elongatus*	Size 10cm (4in)

SLENDER MBUNA

This species shows varying colours according to its mood. The
body is elongate and generally sooty blue-black. From behind
the gill-covers a number of incomplete, pale blue vertical bands
cross the body. The long-based dorsal fin is dark-edged.
• **HABITAT** Rocky shores of Lake Malawi.
• **REMARK** Hard water and rocky furnishings with algae
are required. Males and females part company after
mating, the female incubating the eggs in her throat.

TROPICAL
AFRICA

*dark eye with inner
gold ring* •

*long-based
dorsal fin* •

*pale
blue band*

*dark-edged
fins*

Diet Omnivorous	Tank levels Middle and lower	Temperament

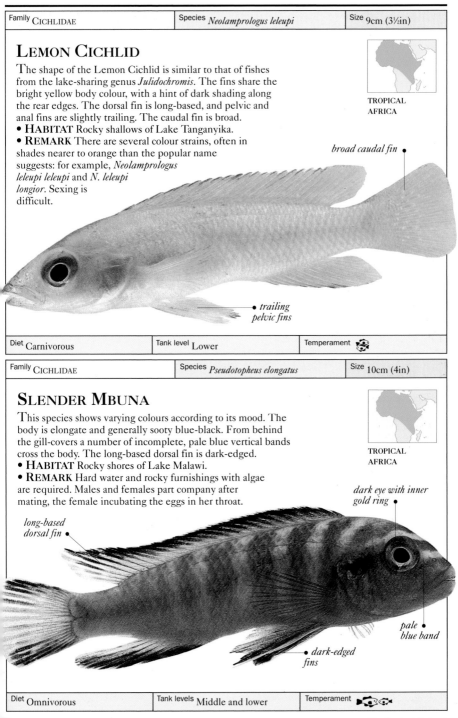

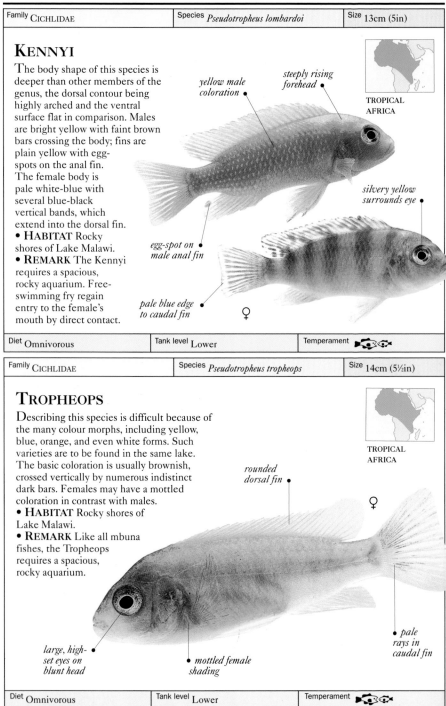

Family CICHLIDAE	Species *Pseudotropheus lombardoi*	Size 13cm (5in)

KENNYI

The body shape of this species is deeper than other members of the genus, the dorsal contour being highly arched and the ventral surface flat in comparison. Males are bright yellow with faint brown bars crossing the body; fins are plain yellow with egg-spots on the anal fin. The female body is pale white-blue with several blue-black vertical bands, which extend into the dorsal fin.
• **HABITAT** Rocky shores of Lake Malawi.
• **REMARK** The Kennyi requires a spacious, rocky aquarium. Free-swimming fry regain entry to the female's mouth by direct contact.

yellow male coloration •

steeply rising forehead •

TROPICAL AFRICA

silvery yellow surrounds eye •

egg-spot on • male anal fin

pale blue edge to caudal fin •

♀

Diet Omnivorous	Tank level Lower	Temperament

Family CICHLIDAE	Species *Pseudotropheus tropheops*	Size 14cm (5½in)

TROPHEOPS

Describing this species is difficult because of the many colour morphs, including yellow, blue, orange, and even white forms. Such varieties are to be found in the same lake. The basic coloration is usually brownish, crossed vertically by numerous indistinct dark bars. Females may have a mottled coloration in contrast with males.
• **HABITAT** Rocky shores of Lake Malawi.
• **REMARK** Like all mbuna fishes, the Tropheops requires a spacious, rocky aquarium.

rounded dorsal fin •

♀

TROPICAL AFRICA

pale rays in caudal fin

large, high-set eyes on blunt head •

• mottled female shading

Diet Omnivorous	Tank level Lower	Temperament

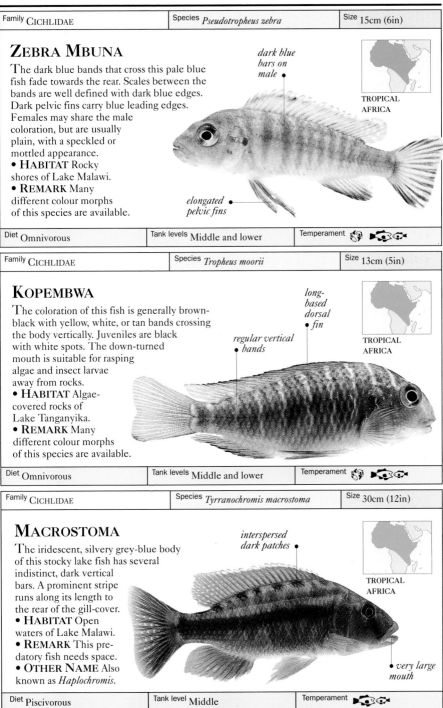

| Family CICHLIDAE | Species *Pseudotropheus zebra* | Size 15cm (6in) |

ZEBRA MBUNA

The dark blue bands that cross this pale blue fish fade towards the rear. Scales between the bands are well defined with dark blue edges. Dark pelvic fins carry blue leading edges. Females may share the male coloration, but are usually plain, with a speckled or mottled appearance.
• **HABITAT** Rocky shores of Lake Malawi.
• **REMARK** Many different colour morphs of this species are available.

dark blue bars on male

TROPICAL AFRICA

elongated pelvic fins

| Diet Omnivorous | Tank levels Middle and lower | Temperament |

| Family CICHLIDAE | Species *Tropheus moorii* | Size 13cm (5in) |

KOPEMBWA

The coloration of this fish is generally brown-black with yellow, white, or tan bands crossing the body vertically. Juveniles are black with white spots. The down-turned mouth is suitable for rasping algae and insect larvae away from rocks.
• **HABITAT** Algae-covered rocks of Lake Tanganyika.
• **REMARK** Many different colour morphs of this species are available.

long-based dorsal fin

regular vertical bands

TROPICAL AFRICA

| Diet Omnivorous | Tank levels Middle and lower | Temperament |

| Family CICHLIDAE | Species *Tyrranochromis macrostoma* | Size 30cm (12in) |

MACROSTOMA

The iridescent, silvery grey-blue body of this stocky lake fish has several indistinct, dark vertical bars. A prominent stripe runs along its length to the rear of the gill-cover.
• **HABITAT** Open waters of Lake Malawi.
• **REMARK** This predatory fish needs space.
• **OTHER NAME** Also known as *Haplochromis*.

interspersed dark patches

TROPICAL AFRICA

very large mouth

| Diet Piscivorous | Tank level Middle | Temperament |

ANABANTIDS

A NABANTIDS often inhabit oxygen-depleted waters of Africa and Southeast Asia. To survive, they have developed an auxiliary breathing organ (the labyrinth organ) which is a folded mass of respiratory tissue situated near the gills. Air is gulped at the surface and stored in this organ, which then extracts the oxygen. This enables certain anabantids to travel overland to nearby waters. The males of one well-known anabantid, the Siamese Fighting Fish, are put together to fight as a sport in their native Thailand.

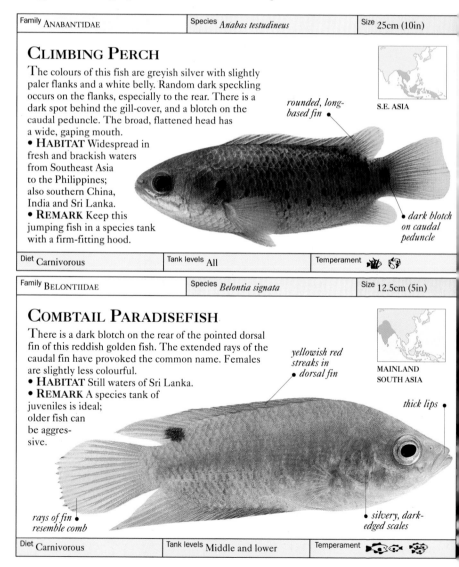

Family ANABANTIDAE	Species *Anabas testudineus*	Size 25cm (10in)

CLIMBING PERCH

The colours of this fish are greyish silver with slightly paler flanks and a white belly. Random dark speckling occurs on the flanks, especially to the rear. There is a dark spot behind the gill-cover, and a blotch on the caudal peduncle. The broad, flattened head has a wide, gaping mouth.
• **HABITAT** Widespread in fresh and brackish waters from Southeast Asia to the Philippines; also southern China, India and Sri Lanka.
• **REMARK** Keep this jumping fish in a species tank with a firm-fitting hood.

rounded, long-based fin

S.E. ASIA

dark blotch on caudal peduncle

Diet Carnivorous	Tank levels All	Temperament

Family BELONTIIDAE	Species *Belontia signata*	Size 12.5cm (5in)

COMBTAIL PARADISEFISH

There is a dark blotch on the rear of the pointed dorsal fin of this reddish golden fish. The extended rays of the caudal fin have provoked the common name. Females are slightly less colourful.
• **HABITAT** Still waters of Sri Lanka.
• **REMARK** A species tank of juveniles is ideal; older fish can be aggressive.

yellowish red streaks in dorsal fin

MAINLAND SOUTH ASIA

thick lips

rays of fin resemble comb

silvery, dark-edged scales

Diet Carnivorous	Tank levels Middle and lower	Temperament

Family BELONTIIDAE	Species *Betta bellica*	Size 11cm (4½in)

SLENDER BETTA

The colour of this fish is reddish brown with green or purple iridescent scales. The scales create a metallic sheen, especially under sidelighting. The head is pale with a marbled patterning, and the eye is set forward.
• **HABITAT** Streams and still waters in Southeast Asia.
• **REMARK** Males are likely to quarrel with each other.
• **OTHER NAME** Slim Fighting Fish.

dorsal fin set well back

S.E. ASIAN ISLANDS

slight point on rounded caudal fin

pale head with marbled pattern

iridescent scales

very long-based anal fin

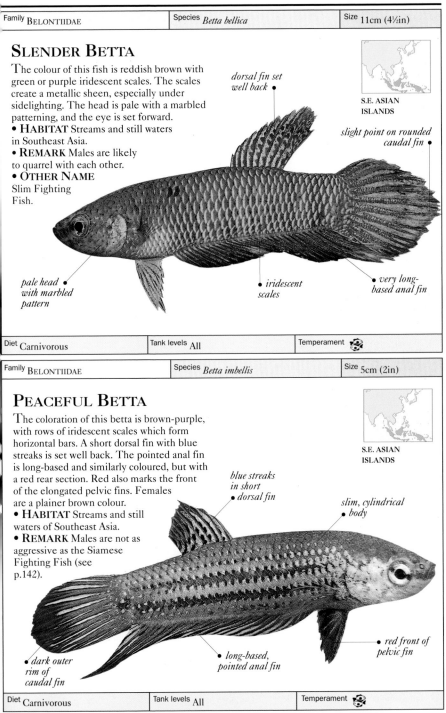

Diet Carnivorous	Tank levels All	Temperament

Family BELONTIIDAE	Species *Betta imbellis*	Size 5cm (2in)

PEACEFUL BETTA

The coloration of this betta is brown-purple, with rows of iridescent scales which form horizontal bars. A short dorsal fin with blue streaks is set well back. The pointed anal fin is long-based and similarly coloured, but with a red rear section. Red also marks the front of the elongated pelvic fins. Females are a plainer brown colour.
• **HABITAT** Streams and still waters of Southeast Asia.
• **REMARK** Males are not as aggressive as the Siamese Fighting Fish (see p.142).

S.E. ASIAN ISLANDS

blue streaks in short dorsal fin

slim, cylindrical body

dark outer rim of caudal fin

long-based, pointed anal fin

red front of pelvic fin

Diet Carnivorous	Tank levels All	Temperament

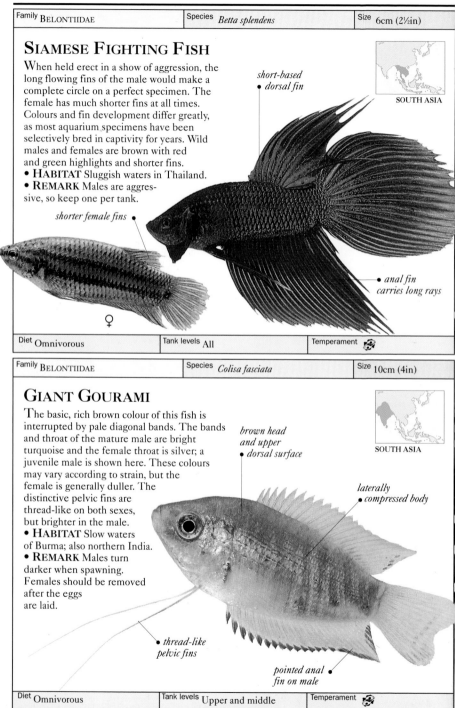

Family BELONTIIDAE	Species *Betta splendens*	Size 6cm (2½in)

SIAMESE FIGHTING FISH

When held erect in a show of aggression, the long flowing fins of the male would make a complete circle on a perfect specimen. The female has much shorter fins at all times. Colours and fin development differ greatly, as most aquarium specimens have been selectively bred in captivity for years. Wild males and females are brown with red and green highlights and shorter fins.
• **HABITAT** Sluggish waters in Thailand.
• **REMARK** Males are aggressive, so keep one per tank.

*short-based
• dorsal fin*

SOUTH ASIA

shorter female fins •

♀

*• anal fin
carries long rays*

Diet Omnivorous	Tank levels All	Temperament

Family BELONTIIDAE	Species *Colisa fasciata*	Size 10cm (4in)

GIANT GOURAMI

The basic, rich brown colour of this fish is interrupted by pale diagonal bands. The bands and throat of the mature male are bright turquoise and the female throat is silver; a juvenile male is shown here. These colours may vary according to strain, but the female is generally duller. The distinctive pelvic fins are thread-like on both sexes, but brighter in the male.
• **HABITAT** Slow waters of Burma; also northern India.
• **REMARK** Males turn darker when spawning. Females should be removed after the eggs are laid.

*brown head
and upper
• dorsal surface*

SOUTH ASIA

*laterally
• compressed body*

*• thread-like
pelvic fins*

*pointed anal •
fin on male*

Diet Omnivorous	Tank levels Upper and middle	Temperament

Family BELONTIIDAE	Species *Colisa labiosa*	Size 8cm (3¼in)

THICKLIPPED GOURAMI

Although similar to the Giant Gourami (see p.142), the bands on the body of this species are narrower and more numerous. There is a dark mark at the centre of each band on adult specimens, creating the impression of a dark line along the flanks. The upturned mouth has well-formed lips, as the popular name suggests.

• **HABITAT** Sluggish backwaters of Burma; also found in northern India.

• **REMARK** During spawning, the male turns dark chocolate-brown. This fish is good for the community aquarium and a very prolific breeder; around 600 eggs are laid in a floating bubble-nest.

pointed dorsal fin on male, with orange-red edging

SOUTH ASIA

pale turquoise throat on juvenile male

narrow bands on flanks

Diet Omnivorous	Tank levels All	Temperament

Family BELONTIIDAE	Species *Colisa lalia*	Size 5cm (2in)

DWARF GOURAMI

The silvery grey of this oval gourami is marked with numerous red and blue vertical stripes. The lower head and throat region are a uniform turquoise. Orange, thread-like pelvic fins carry sensory cells at their tips and are used to help locate food. During spawning, the brilliant colour of the male becomes even more intense. Females are less colourful and plumper.

• **HABITAT** Sluggish backwaters of northern India.

• **REMARK** These popular aquarium fish breed in bubble-nests. They are peaceful in the community tank, but the male can become pugnacious towards the female after spawning, and towards other fishes which venture too near to the nest.

long-based fin contains red and blue speckling

MAINLAND SOUTH ASIA

superior mouth

thread-like pelvic fin carries taste cells

red-edged fin

Diet Omnivorous	Tank levels All	Temperament

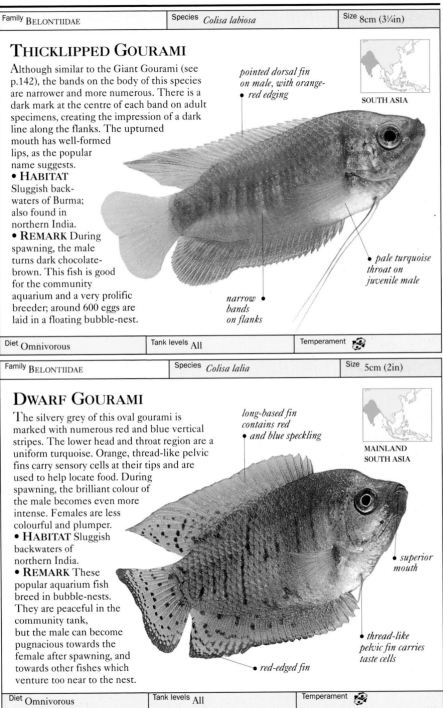

Family ANABANTIDAE	Species *Ctenopoma acutirostre*	Size 15cm (6in)

SPOTTED CLIMBING PERCH

The greenish brown oval body of the Spotted Climbing Perch is covered with leopard-like spots, and a single dark spot marks the base of the caudal fin. The mouth can be exended to form a tube with which the fish engulfs prey. The head is sharply pointed, with a con- cave upper surface and a convex lower surface. Dorsal and anal fins are spiny and reach back almost to the caudal fin. The caudal peduncle is virtually absent.
• **HABITAT** Sluggish streams in Zaire, central Africa.
• **REMARK** This fish should not be kept with smaller species. It requires a large, well-planted tank and live foods.
• **OTHER NAME** Leopard Bushfish.

TROPICAL AFRICA

single dark spot

concave upper surface

dark speckling on pelvic fins

Diet Carnivorous	Tank levels Middle and lower	Temperament

Family ANABANTIDAE	Species *Ctenopoma ansorgei*	Size 7.5cm (3in)

ORNATE CTENOPOMA

This fish is dark brown above the mid-line, changing to dull orange below. Many vertical blue-black, often discreet, bands cross the body. Faint dark markings occur around the eye and on the gill-cover. The "ornate" anal and dorsal fins are long-based and may be more pointed in the male. Male colours intensify during breeding.
• **HABITAT** Sluggish waters of Zaire.
• **REMARK** Live foods and a heavily planted aquarium may encourage breeding in a bubble-nest.
• **OTHER NAME** Orange Bushfish.

TROPICAL AFRICA

discreet dark bands

anal fin more pointed in male

mouth slightly upturned

orange and black in pelvic fins

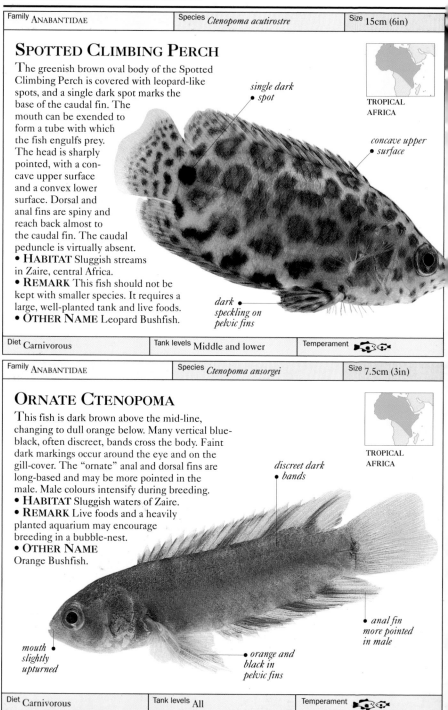

Diet Carnivorous	Tank levels All	Temperament

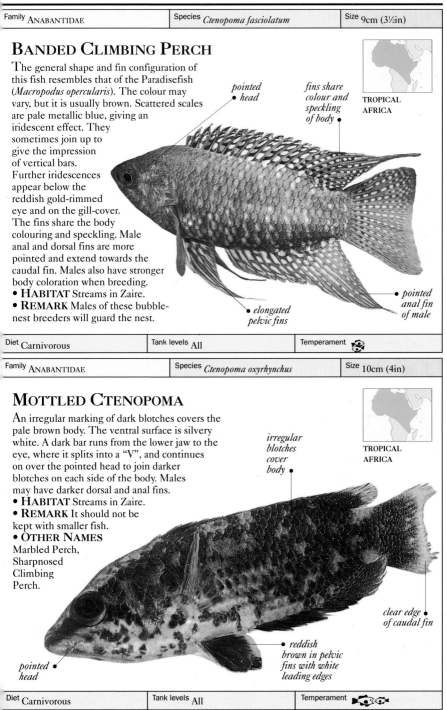

Family ANABANTIDAE	Species *Ctenopoma fasciolatum*	Size 9cm (3½in)

BANDED CLIMBING PERCH

The general shape and fin configuration of this fish resembles that of the Paradisefish (*Macropodus opercularis*). The colour may vary, but it is usually brown. Scattered scales are pale metallic blue, giving an iridescent effect. They sometimes join up to give the impression of vertical bars. Further iridescences appear below the reddish gold-rimmed eye and on the gill-cover. The fins share the body colouring and speckling. Male anal and dorsal fins are more pointed and extend towards the caudal fin. Males also have stronger body coloration when breeding.
• **HABITAT** Streams in Zaire.
• **REMARK** Males of these bubble-nest breeders will guard the nest.

pointed
head

fins share
colour and
speckling
of body

TROPICAL
AFRICA

elongated
pelvic fins

pointed
anal fin
of male

Diet Carnivorous	Tank levels All	Temperament

Family ANABANTIDAE	Species *Ctenopoma oxyrhynchus*	Size 10cm (4in)

MOTTLED CTENOPOMA

An irregular marking of dark blotches covers the pale brown body. The ventral surface is silvery white. A dark bar runs from the lower jaw to the eye, where it splits into a "V", and continues on over the pointed head to join darker blotches on each side of the body. Males may have darker dorsal and anal fins.
• **HABITAT** Streams in Zaire.
• **REMARK** It should not be kept with smaller fish.
• **OTHER NAMES** Marbled Perch, Sharpnosed Climbing Perch.

irregular
blotches
cover
body

TROPICAL
AFRICA

clear edge
of caudal fin

pointed
head

reddish
brown in pelvic
fins with white
leading edges

Diet Carnivorous	Tank levels All	Temperament

Family HELOSTOMATIDAE	Species *Helostoma temmincki*	Size 20cm (8in)

KISSING GOURAMI

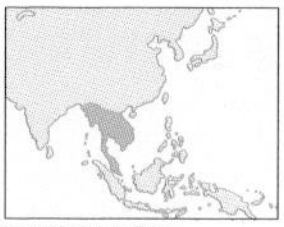

The natural coloration of this oval species is silver-green with rows of tiny dark dots. More commonly available aquarium-bred varieties, as shown here, are a pale rose-pink. The pointed head carries a thick-lipped mouth which is puckered to resemble a "kissing" posture. Dorsal and anal fins are long-based, equal in length, and have spines running two-thirds their length.
• HABITAT Streams and rivers in Thailand; also Borneo, Java, and Sumatra.
• REMARK The "kissing" behaviour of adults occurs when the fish are grazing algae, or when two fish are contesting a territory.

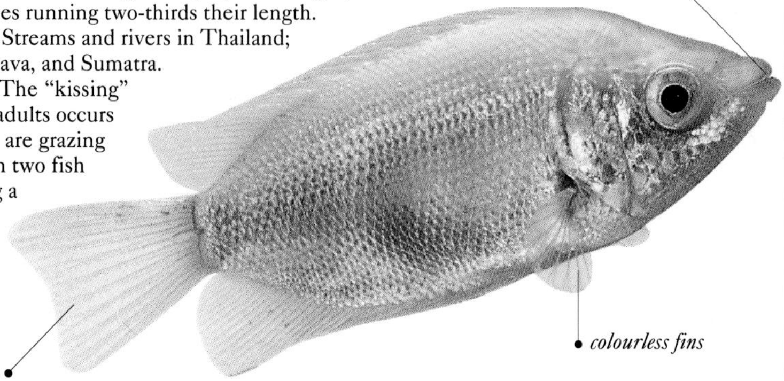

SOUTH ASIA

terminal, thick-lipped mouth •

• colourless fins

straight rear • edge of caudal fin

Diet Omnivorous	Tank levels All	Temperament

Family BELONTIIDAE	Species *Macropodus cupanus*	Size 7.5cm (3in)

SPIKETAILED PARADISEFISH

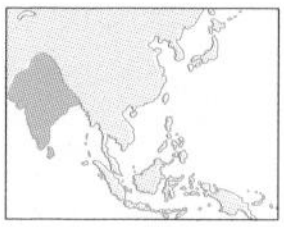

As the common name suggests, the caudal fin of this fish tapers to a central spike. Coloration on prime, contented specimens is golden-brown, emphasized by well-defined scales; long-based dorsal and anal fins are edged in blue and red respectively. There may be a dark blotch or vertical band on the caudal peduncle. Females turn brown-black when spawning.
• HABITAT Streams and ditches in India and Sri Lanka.
• REMARK It spawns beneath a bubble-nest, submerged in a cave or beneath a leaf.
• OTHER NAME Recently re-classified as *Pseudosphronemus*.

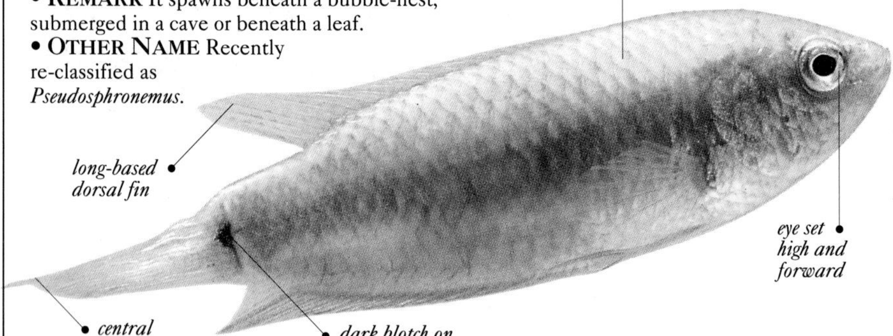

MAINLAND SOUTH ASIA

well-defined • scales

long-based • dorsal fin

eye set • high and forward

• central tail spike

• dark blotch on caudal peduncle

Diet Carnivorous	Tank levels All	Temperament

Family OSPHRONEMIDAE	Species *Osphronemus goramy*	Size 60cm (24in)

GOURAMI

The wild juvenile shown here has a silvery bronze-grey body crossed by dark vertical bars. The golden colour variety beneath is also young. The heads of both are pointed and the eyes set well forward. The adult is grey with well-defined scales and has a pale grey area on the head above a relatively small eye. Its large, upturned mouth carries fleshy lips. The pelvic fins are filamentous.

• **HABITAT** Rivers and lakes of the Greater Sunda Islands.

• **REMARK** Like the Oscar (see p.115), this species is more attractive when young, and soon outgrows the average aquarium. It is best kept with large fishes and provided with plenty of green food.

An adult Gourami will outgrow the average tank

large, upturned mouth

WILD JUVENILE

dark vertical bars

golden body of cultivated fish

bronze-tinted fins

GOLDEN JUVENILE

trailing filaments on pelvic fin

S.E. ASIA

Diet Herbivorous	Tank levels All	Temperament

Family BELONTIIDAE	Species *Sphaerichthys osphromenoides*	Size 8cm (3¼in)

CHOCOLATE GOURAMI

The oval body of the Chocolate Gourami is pointed, curving to a long snout and a short, tapering caudal peduncle. Pale-edged scales feature against a dark, chocolate-brown body. Dorsal and anal fins run about half the length of the body. The head is marked with two distinct cream lines, one from the mouth to the bottom of the eye and the other above the eye and across the head. More cream vertical bands cross the body further back.
• **HABITAT** Slow-moving waters in Borneo, Malaysia, and Sumatra.
• **REMARK** This shy fish is a mouth-brooder. Live foods are required.

cream line
above eye

S.E. ASIA

• *pelvic fin has filamentous extension*

• *clear caudal fin*

• *vertical cream lines cross body*

Diet Omnivorous	Tank levels Middle and lower	Temperament

Family BELONTIIDAE	Species *Trichogaster leeri*	Size 11cm (4¼in)

LACE GOURAMI

The elongate oval body is somewhat obscured by the broad anal fin. A mosaic of spots covers the silvery orange body and fins, and an uneven dark line joins the snout to the caudal peduncle. Males have longer dorsal fins, and bright orange on the throat, chest, pelvic fins, and front of the anal fin.
• **HABITAT** Slow-moving waters in Borneo, Malaysia, and Sumatra.
• **OTHER NAMES** Pearl, Mosaic, and Leeri Gourami.

lace-like
• *patterning*

S.E. ASIA

• *thread-like pelvic fin*

trailing filaments
• *on male anal fin*

Diet Omnivorous	Tank levels Upper and middle	Temperament

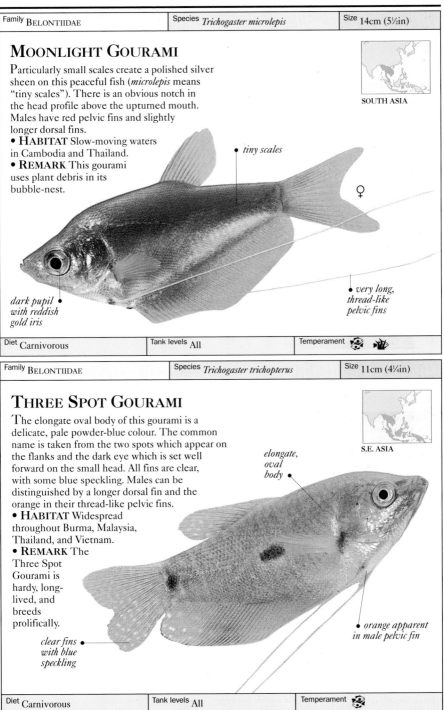

Family BELONTIIDAE	Species *Trichogaster microlepis*	Size 14cm (5½in)

MOONLIGHT GOURAMI

Particularly small scales create a polished silver sheen on this peaceful fish (*microlepis* means "tiny scales"). There is an obvious notch in the head profile above the upturned mouth. Males have red pelvic fins and slightly longer dorsal fins.
• **HABITAT** Slow-moving waters in Cambodia and Thailand.
• **REMARK** This gourami uses plant debris in its bubble-nest.

SOUTH ASIA

tiny scales

♀

very long, thread-like pelvic fins

dark pupil with reddish gold iris

Diet Carnivorous	Tank levels All	Temperament

Family BELONTIIDAE	Species *Trichogaster trichopterus*	Size 11cm (4¼in)

THREE SPOT GOURAMI

The elongate oval body of this gourami is a delicate, pale powder-blue colour. The common name is taken from the two spots which appear on the flanks and the dark eye which is set well forward on the small head. All fins are clear, with some blue speckling. Males can be distinguished by a longer dorsal fin and the orange in their thread-like pelvic fins.
• **HABITAT** Widespread throughout Burma, Malaysia, Thailand, and Vietnam.
• **REMARK** The Three Spot Gourami is hardy, long-lived, and breeds prolifically.

S.E. ASIA

elongate, oval body

orange apparent in male pelvic fin

clear fins with blue speckling

Diet Carnivorous	Tank levels All	Temperament

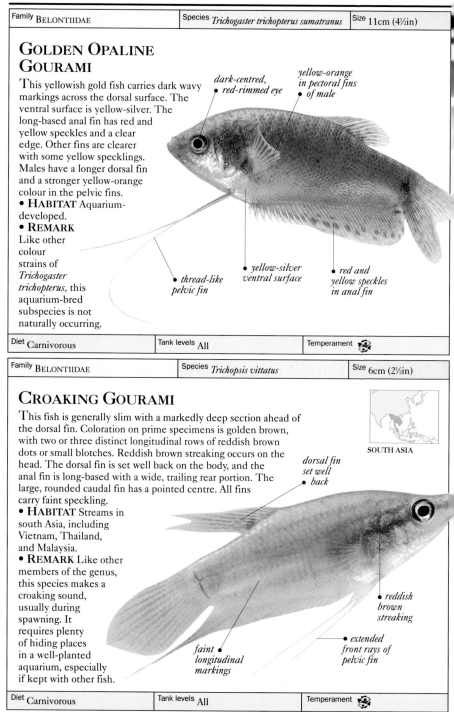

Family BELONTIIDAE	Species *Trichogaster trichopterus sumatranus*	Size 11cm (4½in)

GOLDEN OPALINE GOURAMI

This yellowish gold fish carries dark wavy markings across the dorsal surface. The ventral surface is yellow-silver. The long-based anal fin has red and yellow speckles and a clear edge. Other fins are clearer with some yellow specklings. Males have a longer dorsal fin and a stronger yellow-orange colour in the pelvic fins.
• **HABITAT** Aquarium-developed.
• **REMARK** Like other colour strains of *Trichogaster trichopterus*, this aquarium-bred subspecies is not naturally occurring.

dark-centred, red-rimmed eye

yellow-orange in pectoral fins of male

thread-like pelvic fin

yellow-silver ventral surface

red and yellow speckles in anal fin

Diet Carnivorous	Tank levels All	Temperament

Family BELONTIIDAE	Species *Trichopsis vittatus*	Size 6cm (2¼in)

CROAKING GOURAMI

This fish is generally slim with a markedly deep section ahead of the dorsal fin. Coloration on prime specimens is golden brown, with two or three distinct longitudinal rows of reddish brown dots or small blotches. Reddish brown streaking occurs on the head. The dorsal fin is set well back on the body, and the anal fin is long-based with a wide, trailing rear portion. The large, rounded caudal fin has a pointed centre. All fins carry faint speckling.
• **HABITAT** Streams in south Asia, including Vietnam, Thailand, and Malaysia.
• **REMARK** Like other members of the genus, this species makes a croaking sound, usually during spawning. It requires plenty of hiding places in a well-planted aquarium, especially if kept with other fish.

SOUTH ASIA

dorsal fin set well back

reddish brown streaking

extended front rays of pelvic fin

faint longitudinal markings

Diet Carnivorous	Tank levels All	Temperament

KILLIFISHES

KILLIFISHES BELONG TO the family Cyprinodontidae, and are also known by the alternative common name of egg-laying tooth carps. They inhabit fresh waters of the tropical Americas, Africa, Asia, and southwestern Europe. Some killifish species inhabit small bodies of water which dry up at certain times of the year; they lay eggs that can survive almost total dehydration. Adult males are usually larger, with longer fins, and are more brilliantly coloured. All these fish will accept almost any food in captivity.

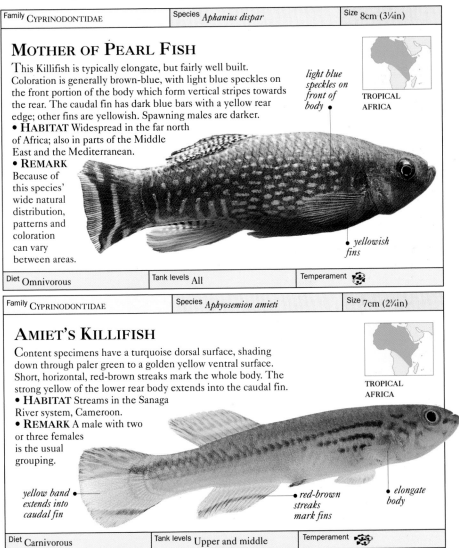

Family CYPRINODONTIDAE	Species *Aphanius dispar*	Size 8cm (3¼in)

MOTHER OF PEARL FISH

This Killifish is typically elongate, but fairly well built. Coloration is generally brown-blue, with light blue speckles on the front portion of the body which form vertical stripes towards the rear. The caudal fin has dark blue bars with a yellow rear edge; other fins are yellowish. Spawning males are darker.
• **HABITAT** Widespread in the far north of Africa; also in parts of the Middle East and the Mediterranean.
• **REMARK** Because of this species' wide natural distribution, patterns and coloration can vary between areas.

light blue speckles on front of body •

TROPICAL AFRICA

• *yellowish fins*

Diet Omnivorous	Tank levels All	Temperament

Family CYPRINODONTIDAE	Species *Aphyosemion amieti*	Size 7cm (2¾in)

AMIET'S KILLIFISH

Content specimens have a turquoise dorsal surface, shading down through paler green to a golden yellow ventral surface. Short, horizontal, red-brown streaks mark the whole body. The strong yellow of the lower rear body extends into the caudal fin.
• **HABITAT** Streams in the Sanaga River system, Cameroon.
• **REMARK** A male with two or three females is the usual grouping.

TROPICAL AFRICA

yellow band extends into caudal fin •

• *red-brown streaks mark fins*

• *elongate body*

Diet Carnivorous	Tank levels Upper and middle	Temperament

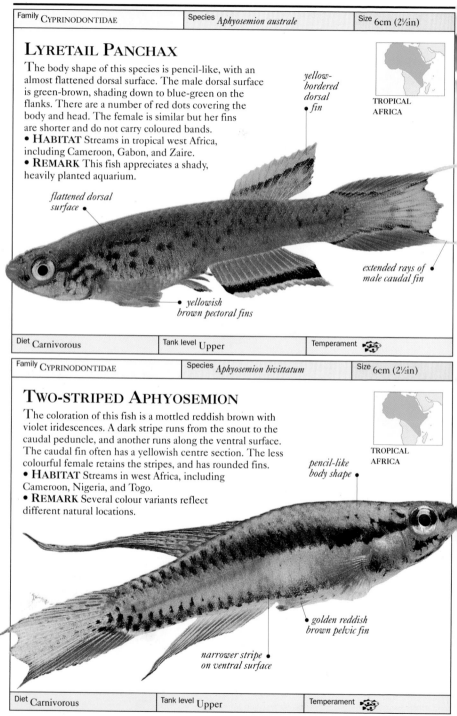

Family CYPRINODONTIDAE	Species *Aphyosemion australe*	Size 6cm (2½in)

LYRETAIL PANCHAX

The body shape of this species is pencil-like, with an almost flattened dorsal surface. The male dorsal surface is green-brown, shading down to blue-green on the flanks. There are a number of red dots covering the body and head. The female is similar but her fins are shorter and do not carry coloured bands.
• **HABITAT** Streams in tropical west Africa, including Cameroon, Gabon, and Zaire.
• **REMARK** This fish appreciates a shady, heavily planted aquarium.

yellow-bordered dorsal fin

TROPICAL AFRICA

flattened dorsal surface

extended rays of male caudal fin

yellowish brown pectoral fins

Diet Carnivorous	Tank level Upper	Temperament

Family CYPRINODONTIDAE	Species *Aphyosemion bivittatum*	Size 6cm (2½in)

TWO-STRIPED APHYOSEMION

The coloration of this fish is a mottled reddish brown with violet iridescences. A dark stripe runs from the snout to the caudal peduncle, and another runs along the ventral surface. The caudal fin often has a yellowish centre section. The less colourful female retains the stripes, and has rounded fins.
• **HABITAT** Streams in west Africa, including Cameroon, Nigeria, and Togo.
• **REMARK** Several colour variants reflect different natural locations.

pencil-like body shape

TROPICAL AFRICA

golden reddish brown pelvic fin

narrower stripe on ventral surface

Diet Carnivorous	Tank level Upper	Temperament

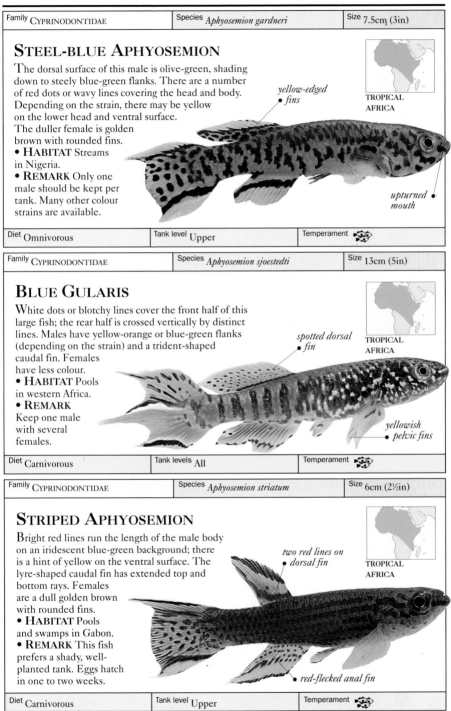

| Family CYPRINODONTIDAE | Species *Aphyosemion gardneri* | Size 7.5cm (3in) |

STEEL-BLUE APHYOSEMION

The dorsal surface of this male is olive-green, shading down to steely blue-green flanks. There are a number of red dots or wavy lines covering the head and body. Depending on the strain, there may be yellow on the lower head and ventral surface. The duller female is golden brown with rounded fins.
• **HABITAT** Streams in Nigeria.
• **REMARK** Only one male should be kept per tank. Many other colour strains are available.

yellow-edged fins

TROPICAL AFRICA

upturned mouth

| Diet Omnivorous | Tank level Upper | Temperament |

| Family CYPRINODONTIDAE | Species *Aphyosemion sjoestedti* | Size 13cm (5in) |

BLUE GULARIS

White dots or blotchy lines cover the front half of this large fish; the rear half is crossed vertically by distinct lines. Males have yellow-orange or blue-green flanks (depending on the strain) and a trident-shaped caudal fin. Females have less colour.
• **HABITAT** Pools in western Africa.
• **REMARK** Keep one male with several females.

spotted dorsal fin

TROPICAL AFRICA

yellowish pelvic fins

| Diet Carnivorous | Tank levels All | Temperament |

| Family CYPRINODONTIDAE | Species *Aphyosemion striatum* | Size 6cm (2½in) |

STRIPED APHYOSEMION

Bright red lines run the length of the male body on an iridescent blue-green background; there is a hint of yellow on the ventral surface. The lyre-shaped caudal fin has extended top and bottom rays. Females are a dull golden brown with rounded fins.
• **HABITAT** Pools and swamps in Gabon.
• **REMARK** This fish prefers a shady, well-planted tank. Eggs hatch in one to two weeks.

two red lines on dorsal fin

TROPICAL AFRICA

red-flecked anal fin

| Diet Carnivorous | Tank level Upper | Temperament |

Family CYPRINODONTIDAE	Species *Aphyosemion walkeri*	Size 6.5cm (2½in)

WALKER'S APHYOSEMION

This fish is yellowish green with blue tones. A number of vertical red-brown streaks cover the body, and longitudinal streaking occurs behind the gill-cover and on the head. Dorsal and anal fins oppose each other and contain yellow or orange mid-sections and red-brown edges.
• **HABITAT** Forest streams of Ghana and the Ivory Coast.
• **REMARK** The eggs require around two months in damp peat moss before re-immersion activates hatching.

red-brown margins in dorsal fin

TROPICAL AFRICA

red-brown spots in caudal fin

upturned mouth

very small pelvic fin

Diet Carnivorous	Tank levels All	Temperament

Family CYPRINODONTIDAE	Species *Aplocheilus dayi*	Size 7cm (2¾in)

CEYLON KILLIFISH

The Ceylon Killifish is golden yellow and is decorated with blue-green iridescences along the flanks, which may form the occasional vertical streak. The head is flattened and the red-lipped mouth is wide. A small dorsal fin is set well back, and that of the female has a dark blotch at the base. The caudal fin is yellow with red markings. Males have more pointed dorsal and anal fins.
• **HABITAT** Streams and ditches in southern India and Sri Lanka.
• **REMARK** This surface-dweller likes floating plants in which to rest. The eggs, laid over a period of days, hatch after around two weeks.

Surface-dwelling killifish rest in plants

red-lipped mouth

blue-green iridescent spots

MAINLAND SOUTH ASIA

rounded caudal fin with distinctive markings

Diet Carnivorous	Tank level Upper	Temperament

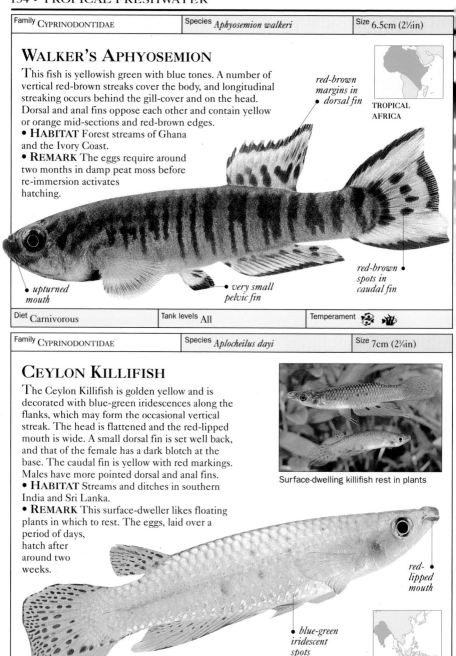

Family CYPRINODONTIDAE	Species *Cynolebias bokermani*	Size 5cm (2in)

BOKERMAN'S CYNOLEBIAS

The deepest part of this fish lies in front of the dorsal and
anal fins. A greenish golden brown colouring contrasts with
a pale yellowish ventral surface. Several pale blue-green
lines run vertically behind the metallic blue gill-cover.
There are a number of pale speckles along the top of
the body which continue into the dorsal and caudal fins.
• **HABITAT** Isolated pools near the Brazilian coast.
• **REMARK** Eggs require
around two months of
storage in damp peat
moss before re-
immersion to
hatch.

SOUTH AMERICA

*greenish
golden brown
dorsal
surface*

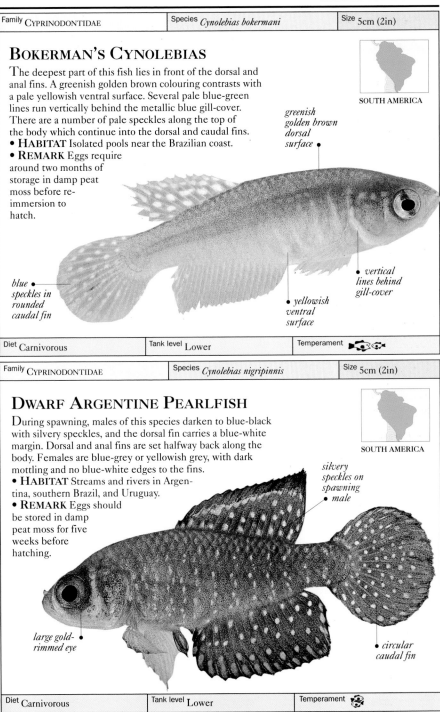

*blue
speckles in
rounded
caudal fin*

*yellowish
ventral
surface*

*vertical
lines behind
gill-cover*

Diet Carnivorous	Tank level Lower	Temperament

Family CYPRINODONTIDAE	Species *Cynolebias nigripinnis*	Size 5cm (2in)

DWARF ARGENTINE PEARLFISH

During spawning, males of this species darken to blue-black
with silvery speckles, and the dorsal fin carries a blue-white
margin. Dorsal and anal fins are set halfway back along the
body. Females are blue-grey or yellowish grey, with dark
mottling and no blue-white edges to the fins.
• **HABITAT** Streams and rivers in Argentina, southern Brazil, and Uruguay.
• **REMARK** Eggs should
be stored in damp
peat moss for five
weeks before
hatching.

SOUTH AMERICA

*silvery
speckles on
spawning
male*

*large gold-
rimmed eye*

*circular
caudal fin*

Diet Carnivorous	Tank level Lower	Temperament

Family CYPRINODONTIDAE	Species *Epiplatys fasciolatus*	Size 8cm (3¼in)

BANDED EPIPLATYS

The male of this species is yellowish brown, shading to a pale ventral surface. The flanks may take on a bluish sheen in reflected light. A number of greenish golden dots cover the body, forming an oblique pattern, and the flanks may show red dots. In mature fish, fins are generally greenish yellow with red dots. The dorsal and anal fins are set well back and the dorsal surface has a bluish tint. The female coloration is much more drab.

TROPICAL AFRICA

• **HABITAT** Streams in Liberia, Nigeria, and Sierra Leone.
• **REMARK** The Banded Epiplatys appreciates a shady, heavily planted aquarium. Although all killi-fish prefer live foods, they will accept flake foods. Eggs are laid in plants.

dark-lipped mouth

well-defined scales

lighter ventral surface

♀

rounded caudal fin

dorsal and anal fins set well back

bluish sheen on male flanks

Diet Carnivorous	Tank level Upper	Temperament

Family CYPRINODONTIDAE	Species *Jordanella floridae*	Size 7.5cm (3in)

AMERICAN FLAGFISH

The greenish blue body of this fish is covered with alternating rows of blue-green and red dots in a horizontal pattern reminiscent of the stripes in the flag of the USA. A dark blotch often appears on the flanks below the dorsal fin, but is more noticeable in the duller female. The female dorsal fin has a dark blotch at the rear.

red in dorsal fin

UNITED STATES

• **HABITAT** Heavily vegetated ponds and lakes in Florida; also Mexico.
• **REMARK** It appreciates vegetable matter and its preferred water temperature is around 20°C (68°F). The body shape does not conform to the family group standard.

clear pectoral fin

Diet Omnivorous	Tank levels All	Temperament

Family CYPRINODONTIDAE	Species *Pachypanchax playfairii*	Size 7.5cm (3in)

PLAYFAIR'S PANCHAX

The male is yellowish brown, shading to a paler belly. A number of equally spaced red dots cover the body and may be interspersed with iridescences. Fins are greenish yellow with red dots, but the pectoral and pelvic fins contain yellow tints. The female is less brightly coloured, and has a dark area at the base of the dorsal fin.
• **HABITAT** Streams in East Africa; also Madagascar, Zanzibar, and the Seychelles.
• **REMARK** It appreciates a shady, planted aquarium. Scales are raised, resembling the fish disease "dropsy", but this is normal for the species.

TROPICAL AFRICA

slightly raised scales

round caudal fin

yellowish pelvic fins

reddish edge on anal fin

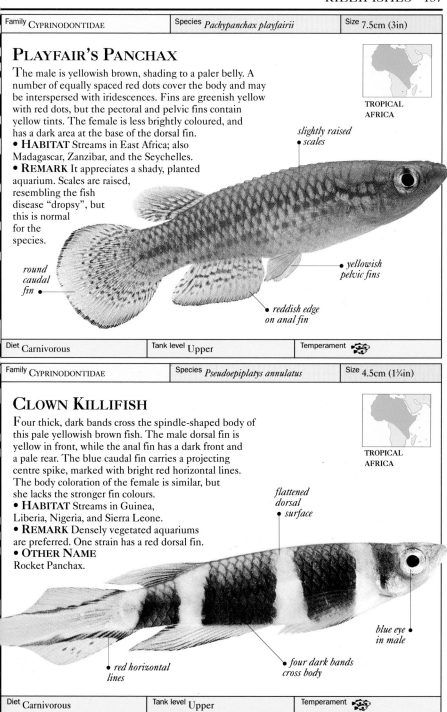

Diet Carnivorous	Tank level Upper	Temperament

Family CYPRINODONTIDAE	Species *Pseudoepiplatys annulatus*	Size 4.5cm (1¾in)

CLOWN KILLIFISH

Four thick, dark bands cross the spindle-shaped body of this pale yellowish brown fish. The male dorsal fin is yellow in front, while the anal fin has a dark front and a pale rear. The blue caudal fin carries a projecting centre spike, marked with bright red horizontal lines. The body coloration of the female is similar, but she lacks the stronger fin colours.
• **HABITAT** Streams in Guinea, Liberia, Nigeria, and Sierra Leone.
• **REMARK** Densely vegetated aquariums are preferred. One strain has a red dorsal fin.
• **OTHER NAME** Rocket Panchax.

TROPICAL AFRICA

flattened dorsal surface

blue eye in male

red horizontal lines

four dark bands cross body

Diet Carnivorous	Tank level Upper	Temperament

CATFISHES

T HERE ARE AROUND 30 catfish families containing some 2,000 species. They are widely distributed, primarily in Africa, South America, and Southeast Asia. These bottom-dwellers are often nocturnal and have barbels on their down-turned mouths, which assist in detecting food. Many catfish are covered by bony plates, or scutes, and some utilize atmospheric air.

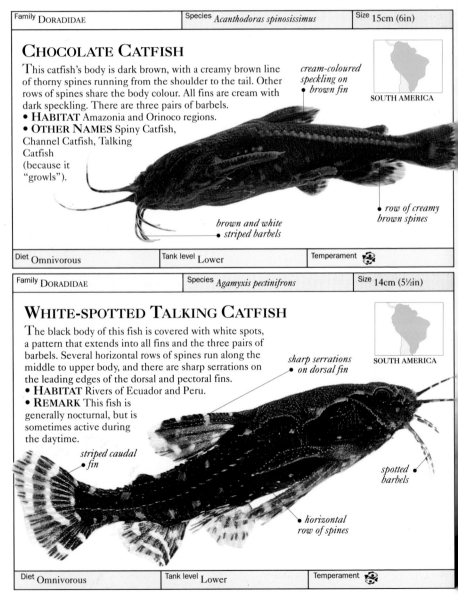

Family DORADIDAE	Species *Acanthodoras spinosissimus*	Size 15cm (6in)

CHOCOLATE CATFISH

This catfish's body is dark brown, with a creamy brown line of thorny spines running from the shoulder to the tail. Other rows of spines share the body colour. All fins are cream with dark speckling. There are three pairs of barbels.
• **HABITAT** Amazonia and Orinoco regions.
• **OTHER NAMES** Spiny Catfish, Channel Catfish, Talking Catfish (because it "growls").

cream-coloured speckling on • brown fin

SOUTH AMERICA

• row of creamy brown spines

brown and white • striped barbels

Diet Omnivorous	Tank level Lower	Temperament

Family DORADIDAE	Species *Agamyxis pectinifrons*	Size 14cm (5½in)

WHITE-SPOTTED TALKING CATFISH

The black body of this fish is covered with white spots, a pattern that extends into all fins and the three pairs of barbels. Several horizontal rows of spines run along the middle to upper body, and there are sharp serrations on the leading edges of the dorsal and pectoral fins.
• **HABITAT** Rivers of Ecuador and Peru.
• **REMARK** This fish is generally nocturnal, but is sometimes active during the daytime.

sharp serrations • on dorsal fin

SOUTH AMERICA

striped caudal • fin

spotted • barbels

• horizontal row of spines

Diet Omnivorous	Tank level Lower	Temperament

Family DORADIDAE	Species *Amblydoras hancocki*	Size 13cm (5in)

HANCOCK'S AMBLYDORAS

The colour of this fish can vary, but it is usually dark brown with darker, irregular blotches. A line of whitish spines runs along the lateral line, accentuated by a dark border beneath. The first one or two rays of the erect dorsal fin are dark. The whole body is covered with bony plates, and the head appears wrinkled. There are three pairs of long white and brown barbels.
• **HABITAT** Rivers of Brazil, Peru, and Guyana.
• **REMARK** A well-planted aquarium with retreats formed from roots or rocks will suit this species.

SOUTH AMERICA

• *dark rays in erect dorsal fin*

speckled body
• *coloration*

• *row of whitish spines*

• *three pairs of barbels*

Diet Omnivorous	Tank level Lower	Temperament

Family LORICARIIDAE	Species *Ancistrus temmincki*	Size 14cm (5½in)

TEMMINCK'S BRISTLENOSE

Small, pale spots cover the body of this fish and extend into the fins. The eyes are set well back on the large head, which, as the name suggests, carries distinctive growths of tentacles on the upper surface of the snout. Females have a single row of "bristles" between the eyes, and males have a double row which may form a "Y" shape. Tentacles are always prominent at spawning time. The mouth forms a sucker-like disc.
• **HABITAT** Fast-flowing waters in Guyana.
• **REMARK** Usually kept to remove algae, this fish needs a well-oxygenated, well-planted aquarium and blanched green vegetables.

SOUTH AMERICA

bristles on upper snout •

underslung •
mouth

♀

• *pectoral fin extends past pelvic fin*

Diet Herbivorous	Tank level Lower	Temperament

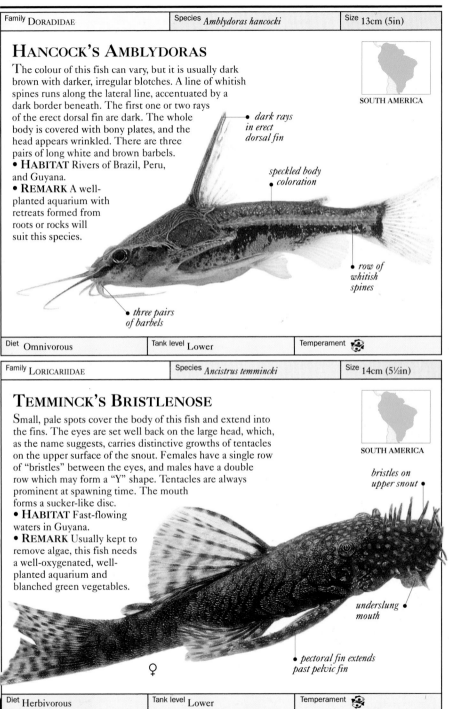

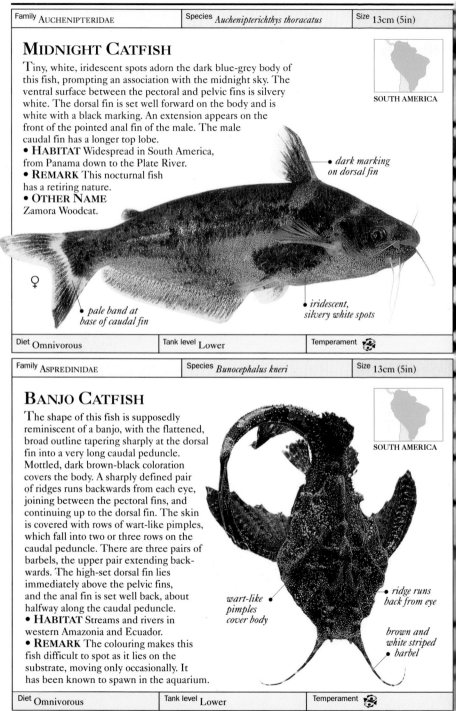

| Family AUCHENIPTERIDAE | Species *Auchenipterichthys thoracatus* | Size 13cm (5in) |

MIDNIGHT CATFISH

Tiny, white, iridescent spots adorn the dark blue-grey body of this fish, prompting an association with the midnight sky. The ventral surface between the pectoral and pelvic fins is silvery white. The dorsal fin is set well forward on the body and is white with a black marking. An extension appears on the front of the pointed anal fin of the male. The male caudal fin has a longer top lobe.
• **HABITAT** Widespread in South America, from Panama down to the Plate River.
• **REMARK** This nocturnal fish has a retiring nature.
• **OTHER NAME** Zamora Woodcat.

SOUTH AMERICA

dark marking on dorsal fin

♀

pale band at base of caudal fin

iridescent, silvery white spots

| Diet Omnivorous | Tank level Lower | Temperament |

| Family ASPREDINIDAE | Species *Bunocephalus kneri* | Size 13cm (5in) |

BANJO CATFISH

The shape of this fish is supposedly reminiscent of a banjo, with the flattened, broad outline tapering sharply at the dorsal fin into a very long caudal peduncle. Mottled, dark brown-black coloration covers the body. A sharply defined pair of ridges runs backwards from each eye, joining between the pectoral fins, and continuing up to the dorsal fin. The skin is covered with rows of wart-like pimples, which fall into two or three rows on the caudal peduncle. There are three pairs of barbels, the upper pair extending backwards. The high-set dorsal fin lies immediately above the pelvic fins, and the anal fin is set well back, about halfway along the caudal peduncle.
• **HABITAT** Streams and rivers in western Amazonia and Ecuador.
• **REMARK** The colouring makes this fish difficult to spot as it lies on the substrate, moving only occasionally. It has been known to spawn in the aquarium.

SOUTH AMERICA

ridge runs back from eye

wart-like pimples cover body

brown and white striped barbel

| Diet Omnivorous | Tank level Lower | Temperament |

| Family CALLICHTHYIDAE | Species *Callichthys callichthys* | Size 18cm (7in) |

HASSAR

The overlapping bony scutes of this catfish species are particularly prominent. They form two rows behind the gill-cover, making a herringbone pattern. General body colour is dull brown-grey. The head is broad and shallow, and the highly mobile eyes often move independently of each other.
• **HABITAT** Rivers in Brazil.
• **REMARK** It spawns differently from other catfishes: a bubble-nest is built underneath vegetation, to which the eggs are attached until hatching occurs. Males guard the nest.
• **OTHER NAME** Slender Armoured Catfish.

SOUTH AMERICA

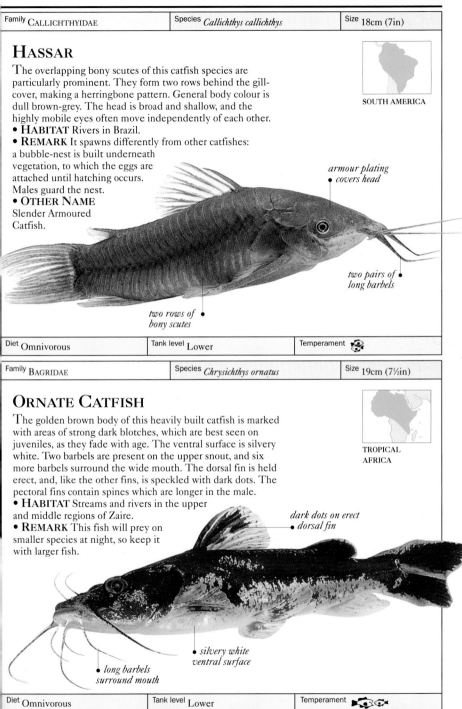

armour plating covers head

two pairs of long barbels

two rows of bony scutes

| Diet Omnivorous | Tank level Lower | Temperament |

| Family BAGRIDAE | Species *Chrysichthys ornatus* | Size 19cm (7½in) |

ORNATE CATFISH

The golden brown body of this heavily built catfish is marked with areas of strong dark blotches, which are best seen on juveniles, as they fade with age. The ventral surface is silvery white. Two barbels are present on the upper snout, and six more barbels surround the wide mouth. The dorsal fin is held erect, and, like the other fins, is speckled with dark dots. The pectoral fins contain spines which are longer in the male.
• **HABITAT** Streams and rivers in the upper and middle regions of Zaire.
• **REMARK** This fish will prey on smaller species at night, so keep it with larger fish.

TROPICAL AFRICA

dark dots on erect dorsal fin

silvery white ventral surface

long barbels surround mouth

| Diet Omnivorous | Tank level Lower | Temperament |

Family CLARIIDAE	Species *Clarias batrachus*	Size 55cm (22in)

WALKING CATFISH

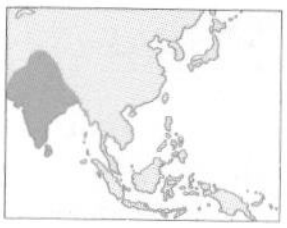

The wild form of this eel-shaped catfish is greenish brown
with speckling. The piebald strain shown here, and a gold
strain, have become increasingly popular with aquarists. The
pectoral fins contain poisonous spines which are especially
stout on the male. Pelvic fins remain small.
• **HABITAT** India and Sri Lanka; also Malaysia.
• **REMARK** This fish can exit the water and
migrate by storing air in a special respiratory
organ. Banned in several American states
as a threat to native fishes, it requires
spacious quarters and a heavy
hood. It grows very large.

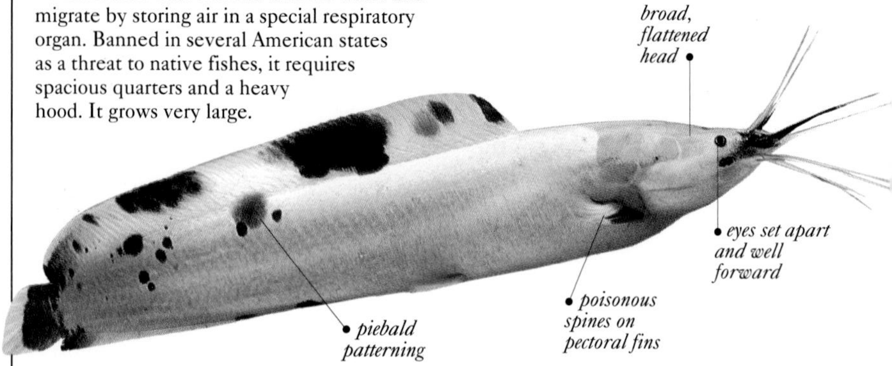

**MAINLAND
SOUTH ASIA**

*broad,
flattened
head*

*eyes set apart
and well
forward*

*poisonous
spines on
pectoral fins*

*piebald
patterning*

Diet Omnivorous	Tank level Lower	Temperament

Family CALLICHTHYIDAE	Species *Dianema longibarbis*	Size 10cm (4in)

PORTHOLE CATFISH

The cylindrical body is covered by two rows of bony
scutes behind the gill-cover. They are not as prominent
as on those of other family members. The pinky grey
colour gives way to a lighter ventral surface; dark
speckling is concentrated above the mid-line. A
terminal mouth carries two pairs of barbels which
are held out in front of the fish as it swims.
• **HABITAT** Amazon basin.
• **REMARK** This shoaling fish is usually
long-lived in the aquarium. It uses a
bubble-nest when breeding, but
rarely spawns in captivity.

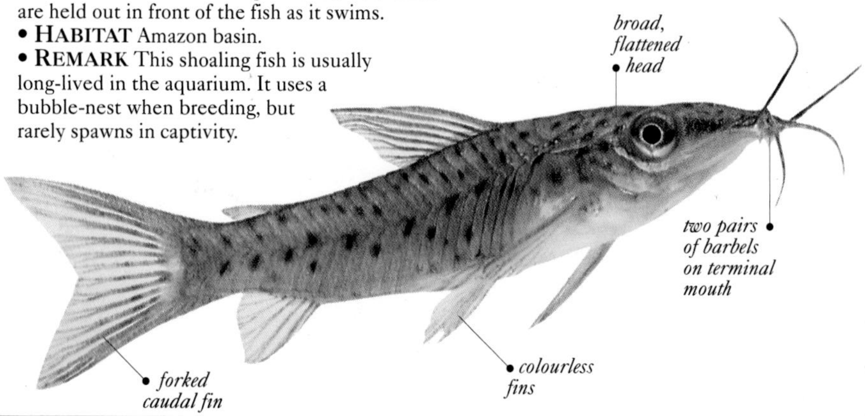

SOUTH AMERICA

*broad,
flattened
head*

*two pairs
of barbels
on terminal
mouth*

*forked
caudal fin*

*colourless
fins*

Diet Omnivorous	Tank level Middle	Temperament

| Family CALLICHTHYIDAE | Species *Dianema urostriata* | Size 13cm (5in) |

STRIPE-TAILED CATFISH

The fins of this fish are colourless, except for the caudal fin which carries black and white stripes, hence the common name. Two rows of bony scutes cover the body. A creamy grey-brown shades to a lighter colour on the belly and below the head. Speckling may be difficult to determine on the deep body tone.
• **HABITAT** Widespread in the Amazon basin.
• **REMARK** This is an active shoaling fish, especially after dark. It may not be readily available.
• **OTHER NAME** Flagtail Porthole Catfish.

SOUTH AMERICA

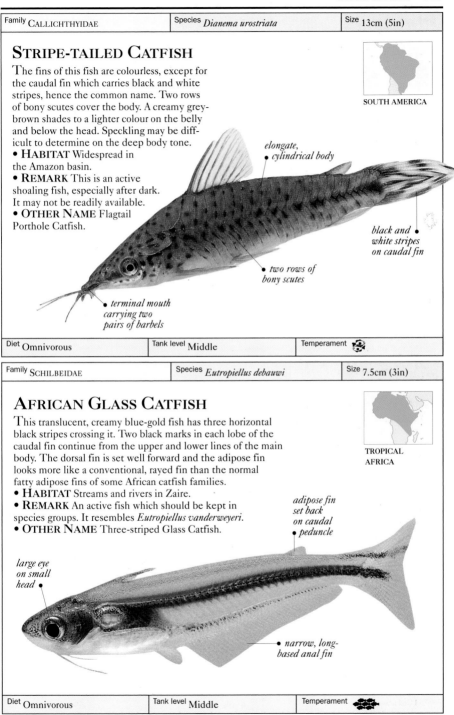

elongate, cylindrical body

black and white stripes on caudal fin

two rows of bony scutes

terminal mouth carrying two pairs of barbels

| Diet Omnivorous | Tank level Middle | Temperament |

| Family SCHILBEIDAE | Species *Eutropiellus debauwi* | Size 7.5cm (3in) |

AFRICAN GLASS CATFISH

This translucent, creamy blue-gold fish has three horizontal black stripes crossing it. Two black marks in each lobe of the caudal fin continue from the upper and lower lines of the main body. The dorsal fin is set well forward and the adipose fin looks more like a conventional, rayed fin than the normal fatty adipose fins of some African catfish families.
• **HABITAT** Streams and rivers in Zaire.
• **REMARK** An active fish which should be kept in species groups. It resembles *Eutropiellus vanderweyeri*.
• **OTHER NAME** Three-striped Glass Catfish.

TROPICAL AFRICA

adipose fin set back on caudal peduncle

large eye on small head

narrow, long-based anal fin

| Diet Omnivorous | Tank level Middle | Temperament |

| Family LORICARIIDAE | Species *Farlowella acus* | Size 20cm (8in) |

TWIG CATFISH

This elongate catfish is brown with a dark line along the flanks, from the tip of the snout to the the caudal fin. Its underside is pale and its fin rays are speckled. Bony scutes cover the body. The snout develops bristles in the mature male.
• **HABITAT** Rivers in central and south Brazil.
• **REMARK** This catfish can be bred in the aquarium; eggs are laid on a firm, clean surface and are guarded by the male. It requires extra green foods, as there is rarely sufficient algae in the aquarium.

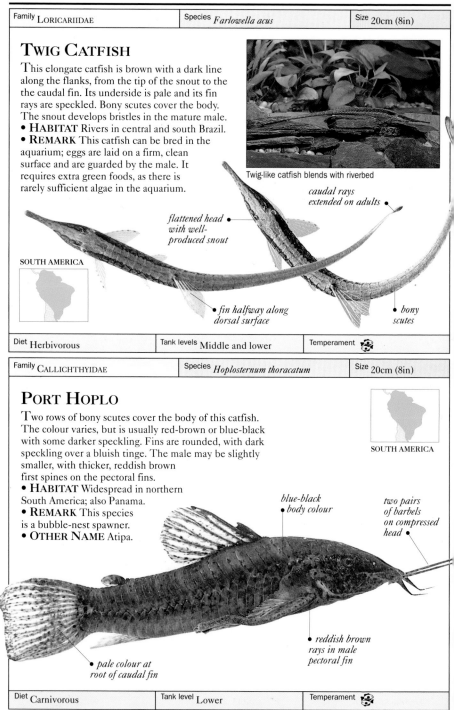

Twig-like catfish blends with riverbed

caudal rays extended on adults

flattened head with well-produced snout

SOUTH AMERICA

fin halfway along dorsal surface

bony scutes

| Diet Herbivorous | Tank levels Middle and lower | Temperament |

| Family CALLICHTHYIDAE | Species *Hoplosternum thoracatum* | Size 20cm (8in) |

PORT HOPLO

Two rows of bony scutes cover the body of this catfish. The colour varies, but is usually red-brown or blue-black with some darker speckling. Fins are rounded, with dark speckling over a bluish tinge. The male may be slightly smaller, with thicker, reddish brown first spines on the pectoral fins.
• **HABITAT** Widespread in northern South America; also Panama.
• **REMARK** This species is a bubble-nest spawner.
• **OTHER NAME** Atipa.

SOUTH AMERICA

blue-black body colour

two pairs of barbels on compressed head

pale colour at root of caudal fin

reddish brown rays in male pectoral fin

| Diet Carnivorous | Tank level Lower | Temperament |

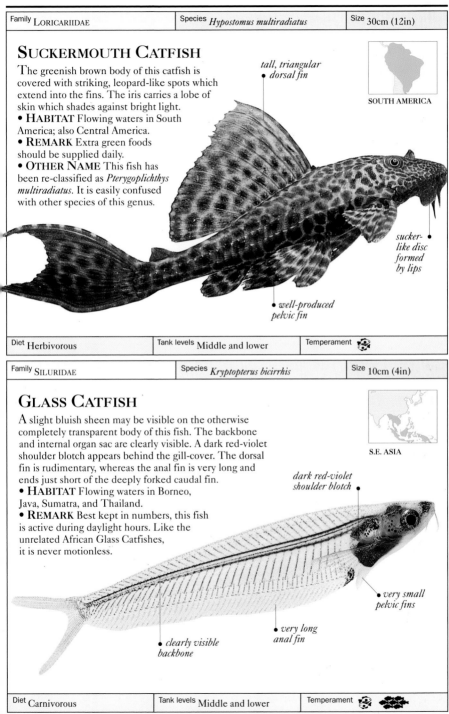

Family LORICARIIDAE	Species *Hypostomus multiradiatus*	Size 30cm (12in)

SUCKERMOUTH CATFISH

The greenish brown body of this catfish is covered with striking, leopard-like spots which extend into the fins. The iris carries a lobe of skin which shades against bright light.
• **HABITAT** Flowing waters in South America; also Central America.
• **REMARK** Extra green foods should be supplied daily.
• **OTHER NAME** This fish has been re-classified as *Pterygoplichthys multiradiatus*. It is easily confused with other species of this genus.

tall, triangular dorsal fin

SOUTH AMERICA

sucker-like disc formed by lips

well-produced pelvic fin

Diet Herbivorous	Tank levels Middle and lower	Temperament

Family SILURIDAE	Species *Kryptopterus bicirrhis*	Size 10cm (4in)

GLASS CATFISH

A slight bluish sheen may be visible on the otherwise completely transparent body of this fish. The backbone and internal organ sac are clearly visible. A dark red-violet shoulder blotch appears behind the gill-cover. The dorsal fin is rudimentary, whereas the anal fin is very long and ends just short of the deeply forked caudal fin.
• **HABITAT** Flowing waters in Borneo, Java, Sumatra, and Thailand.
• **REMARK** Best kept in numbers, this fish is active during daylight hours. Like the unrelated African Glass Catfishes, it is never motionless.

S.E. ASIA

dark red-violet shoulder blotch

very small pelvic fins

clearly visible backbone

very long anal fin

Diet Carnivorous	Tank levels Middle and lower	Temperament

| Family BAGRIDAE | Species *Leiocassis siamensis* | Size 14cm (5½in) |

BUMBLEBEE CATFISH

This catfish's stocky body is dark brown with pale, irregular
bars and patching. The pattern continues into the fins. An
adipose fin is present which is more long-based and fleshy
than the dorsal fin. The dorsal fin carries a pale crescent
shape in the centre. There are four pairs of barbels.
• **HABITAT** Rivers and streams throughout Thailand.
• **REMARK** Nocturnal and normally peaceful,
it may devour smaller fishes.
• **OTHER NAME** Barred
Siamese Catfish.

SOUTH ASIA

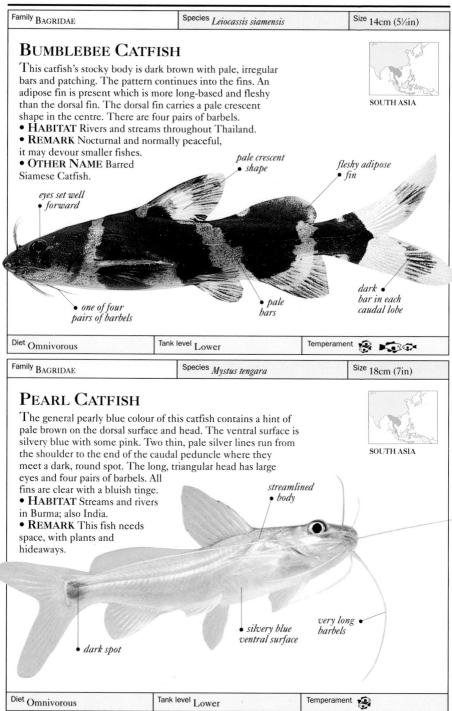

pale crescent
• shape

fleshy adipose
• fin

eyes set well
• forward

one of four
pairs of barbels

pale
bars

dark
bar in each
caudal lobe

| Diet Omnivorous | Tank level Lower | Temperament |

| Family BAGRIDAE | Species *Mystus tengara* | Size 18cm (7in) |

PEARL CATFISH

The general pearly blue colour of this catfish contains a hint of
pale brown on the dorsal surface and head. The ventral surface is
silvery blue with some pink. Two thin, pale silver lines run from
the shoulder to the end of the caudal peduncle where they
meet a dark, round spot. The long, triangular head has large
eyes and four pairs of barbels. All
fins are clear with a bluish tinge.
• **HABITAT** Streams and rivers
in Burma; also India.
• **REMARK** This fish needs
space, with plants and
hideaways.

SOUTH ASIA

streamlined
• body

dark spot

silvery blue
ventral surface

very long
barbels

| Diet Omnivorous | Tank level Lower | Temperament |

Family LORICARIIDAE	Species *Otocinclus affinis*	Size 5cm (2in)

DWARF SUCKER CATFISH

This species has an elongate, almost tadpole-like, shape. Its markings consist of dark mottled shades on the dorsal surface, and a dark band which runs from the snout, through the eye, to the end of the caudal peduncle, where it terminates in a distinctive blotch. The lower half of the body is pale. The disc-shaped sucker, which gives this fish its common name, is carried underneath the long snout. Speckling appears in the dorsal, anal, and caudal fins.
• **HABITAT** Running waters in Brazil.
• **REMARK** The Dwarf Sucker Catfish spends much time rasping algae off all surfaces, including the tank sides where it is often seen clinging to the glass. The sucker mouth also acts as an anchor in fast-flowing waters.

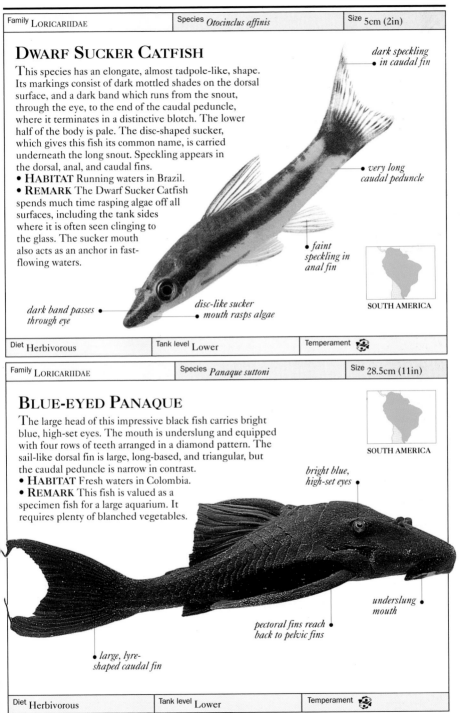

dark speckling in caudal fin

very long caudal peduncle

faint speckling in anal fin

SOUTH AMERICA

dark band passes through eye

disc-like sucker mouth rasps algae

Diet Herbivorous	Tank level Lower	Temperament

Family LORICARIIDAE	Species *Panaque suttoni*	Size 28.5cm (11in)

BLUE-EYED PANAQUE

The large head of this impressive black fish carries bright blue, high-set eyes. The mouth is underslung and equipped with four rows of teeth arranged in a diamond pattern. The sail-like dorsal fin is large, long-based, and triangular, but the caudal peduncle is narrow in contrast.
• **HABITAT** Fresh waters in Colombia.
• **REMARK** This fish is valued as a specimen fish for a large aquarium. It requires plenty of blanched vegetables.

SOUTH AMERICA

bright blue, high-set eyes

underslung mouth

pectoral fins reach back to pelvic fins

large, lyre-shaped caudal fin

Diet Herbivorous	Tank level Lower	Temperament

Family LORICARIIDAE	Species *Peckoltia pulcher*	Size 10cm (4in)

PRETTY PECKOLTIA

Narrow pale grey bands vertically cross the blue-black body of this species. The mottled coloration continues into all fins. The bony scutes, which replace long scales, often carry bristles. When held erect, the dorsal fin is flag-like. Pectoral and pelvic fins are wing-like, and the caudal fin is forked and terminates in sharp tips which make it almost lyre-shaped. The underslung mouth forms a sucker-disc.
• **HABITAT** Negro River, Amazonia.
• **REMARK** This attractive species is a useful algae-eater and a good community fish, although it does require space.

SOUTH AMERICA

mottled skin coloration •

dark vertical stripes •

• *wing-like pectoral fin*

Diet Herbivorous	Tank level Lower	Temperament

Family PIMELODIDAE	Species *Phractocephalus hemiliopterus*	Size 120cm (47in)

RED-TAILED CATFISH

The upper part of this bulky fish, including the top lip, is grey-black with small, darker specklings. The lower body, including the lower lip and three pairs of long barbels, is white. The distinguishing orange-red caudal fin is spade-like and rounded. Juveniles, as seen here, may be more intensely coloured.
• **HABITAT** Widespread throughout the Amazonian areas of Peru, Guyana, and Brazil.
• **REMARK** The adult form is more suitable for the public aquarium. It feeds heavily on live and dead fishes and other meat, and eventually outgrows even the largest home aquarium. Although it preys on smaller fish, it has a peaceful disposition.

SOUTH AMERICA

long barbels •

grey-black upper body •

• *white lower body*

• *orange-red caudal fin*

Diet Omnivorous	Tank levels Middle and lower	Temperament

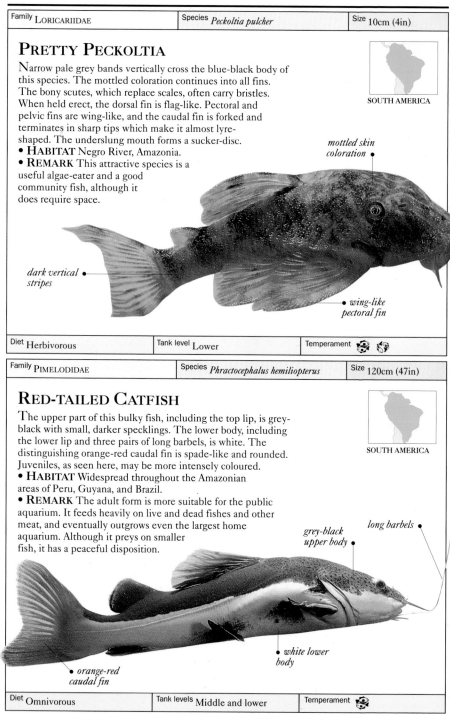

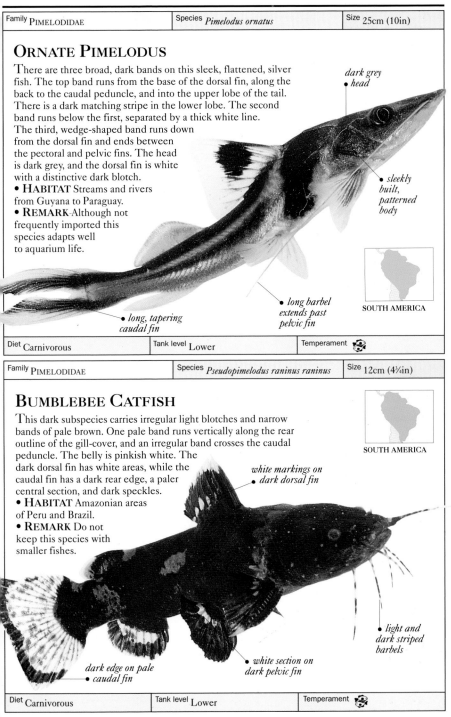

| Family PIMELODIDAE | Species *Pimelodus ornatus* | Size 25cm (10in) |

ORNATE PIMELODUS

There are three broad, dark bands on this sleek, flattened, silver fish. The top band runs from the base of the dorsal fin, along the back to the caudal peduncle, and into the upper lobe of the tail. There is a dark matching stripe in the lower lobe. The second band runs below the first, separated by a thick white line. The third, wedge-shaped band runs down from the dorsal fin and ends between the pectoral and pelvic fins. The head is dark grey, and the dorsal fin is white with a distinctive dark blotch.
• HABITAT Streams and rivers from Guyana to Paraguay.
• REMARK Although not frequently imported this species adapts well to aquarium life.

dark grey
• head

• sleekly built, patterned body

SOUTH AMERICA

• long barbel extends past pelvic fin

• long, tapering caudal fin

| Diet Carnivorous | Tank level Lower | Temperament |

| Family PIMELODIDAE | Species *Pseudopimelodus raninus raninus* | Size 12cm (4¾in) |

BUMBLEBEE CATFISH

This dark subspecies carries irregular light blotches and narrow bands of pale brown. One pale band runs vertically along the rear outline of the gill-cover, and an irregular band crosses the caudal peduncle. The belly is pinkish white. The dark dorsal fin has white areas, while the caudal fin has a dark rear edge, a paler central section, and dark speckles.
• HABITAT Amazonian areas of Peru and Brazil.
• REMARK Do not keep this species with smaller fishes.

SOUTH AMERICA

white markings on
• dark dorsal fin

• light and dark striped barbels

dark edge on pale
• caudal fin

• white section on dark pelvic fin

| Diet Carnivorous | Tank level Lower | Temperament |

Family PIMELODIDAE	Species *Pseudoplatystoma fasciata*	Size 90cm (35in)

TIGER SHOVELNOSE CATFISH

Dark grey on the dorsal surface of this catfish leads down to silvery white on the belly. Equally spaced dark bands encircle the body vertically, stopping at the ventral surface. The large head is broad and flattened, with a shallow sloping forehead. Speckled fins are surprisingly small. The deeply forked caudal fin is not used in locomotion; instead the body undulates to drive the fish forward at high speed. There are three pairs of highly extended barbels present.

• **HABITAT** Rivers of Venezuela and Peru.
• **REMARK** This nocturnal, predatory fish is suitable only for large display aquariums.

SOUTH AMERICA

equally spaced • dark stripes

high-set • eyes

anal fin set far back

extended • barbels

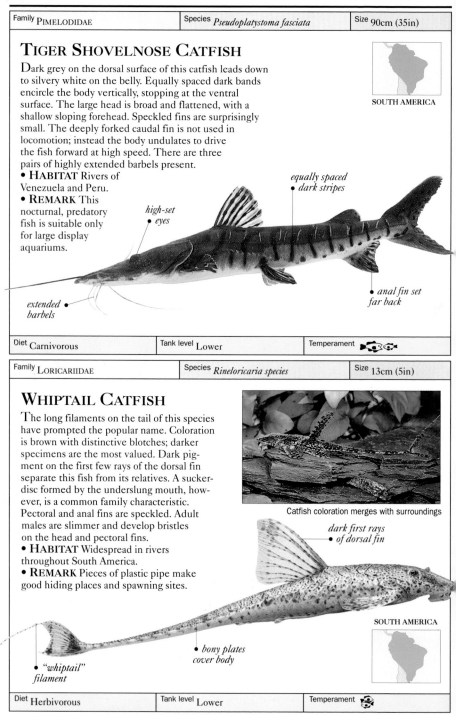

Diet Carnivorous	Tank level Lower	Temperament

Family LORICARIIDAE	Species *Rineloricaria species*	Size 13cm (5in)

WHIPTAIL CATFISH

The long filaments on the tail of this species have prompted the popular name. Coloration is brown with distinctive blotches; darker specimens are the most valued. Dark pigment on the first few rays of the dorsal fin separate this fish from its relatives. A suckerdisc formed by the underslung mouth, however, is a common family characteristic. Pectoral and anal fins are speckled. Adult males are slimmer and develop bristles on the head and pectoral fins.

• **HABITAT** Widespread in rivers throughout South America.
• **REMARK** Pieces of plastic pipe make good hiding places and spawning sites.

Catfish coloration merges with surroundings

dark first rays • of dorsal fin

SOUTH AMERICA

bony plates cover body

"whiptail" filament

Diet Herbivorous	Tank level Lower	Temperament

| Family MOCHOKIDAE | Species *Synodontis angelicus* | Size 20cm (8in) |

ANGEL CATFISH

Juveniles of this species are black and covered with white spots. In adulthood the body turns dull grey with fewer spots. The long-based adipose fin is typical of the family and carries spots only in the juvenile, as shown here. Sexual differences are apparent solely on the adult: the female has a more rounded body, and the male colour may be intensified. A down-turned mouth carries three pairs of barbels.
• **HABITAT** Slow moving waters in Zaire.
• **REMARK** It cannot now be exported from Zaire and has become highly priced.
• **OTHER NAME** Polka-dot Synodontis.

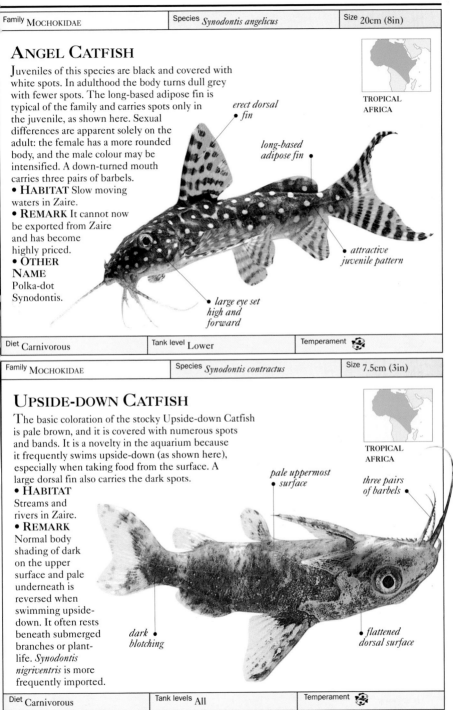

TROPICAL AFRICA

erect dorsal fin

long-based adipose fin

attractive juvenile pattern

large eye set high and forward

| Diet Carnivorous | Tank level Lower | Temperament |

| Family MOCHOKIDAE | Species *Synodontis contractus* | Size 7.5cm (3in) |

UPSIDE-DOWN CATFISH

The basic coloration of the stocky Upside-down Catfish is pale brown, and it is covered with numerous spots and bands. It is a novelty in the aquarium because it frequently swims upside-down (as shown here), especially when taking food from the surface. A large dorsal fin also carries the dark spots.
• **HABITAT** Streams and rivers in Zaire.
• **REMARK** Normal body shading of dark on the upper surface and pale underneath is reversed when swimming upside-down. It often rests beneath submerged branches or plant-life. *Synodontis nigriventris* is more frequently imported.

TROPICAL AFRICA

pale uppermost surface

three pairs of barbels

dark blotching

flattened dorsal surface

| Diet Carnivorous | Tank levels All | Temperament |

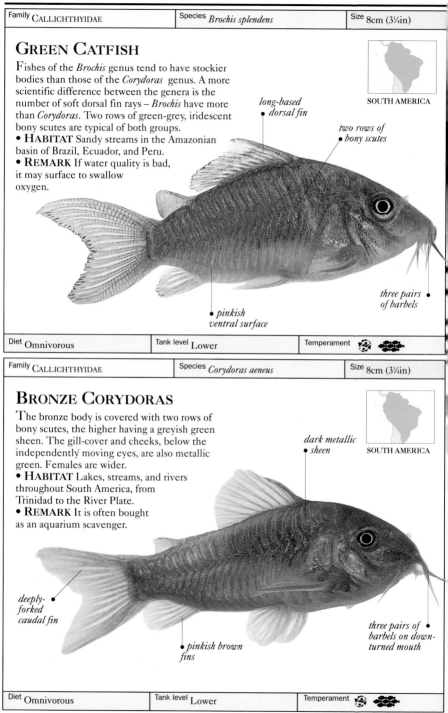

Family CALLICHTHYIDAE	Species *Brochis splendens*	Size 8cm (3¼in)

GREEN CATFISH

Fishes of the *Brochis* genus tend to have stockier bodies than those of the *Corydoras* genus. A more scientific difference between the genera is the number of soft dorsal fin rays – *Brochis* have more than *Corydoras*. Two rows of green-grey, iridescent bony scutes are typical of both groups.
• HABITAT Sandy streams in the Amazonian basin of Brazil, Ecuador, and Peru.
• REMARK If water quality is bad, it may surface to swallow oxygen.

SOUTH AMERICA

long-based
• dorsal fin

two rows of
• bony scutes

three pairs •
of barbels

• pinkish
ventral surface

Diet Omnivorous	Tank level Lower	Temperament

Family CALLICHTHYIDAE	Species *Corydoras aeneus*	Size 8cm (3¼in)

BRONZE CORYDORAS

The bronze body is covered with two rows of bony scutes, the higher having a greyish green sheen. The gill-cover and cheeks, below the independently moving eyes, are also metallic green. Females are wider.
• HABITAT Lakes, streams, and rivers throughout South America, from Trinidad to the River Plate.
• REMARK It is often bought as an aquarium scavenger.

dark metallic
• sheen

SOUTH AMERICA

deeply-
forked
caudal fin

three pairs of •
barbels on down-
turned mouth

• pinkish brown
fins

Diet Omnivorous	Tank level Lower	Temperament

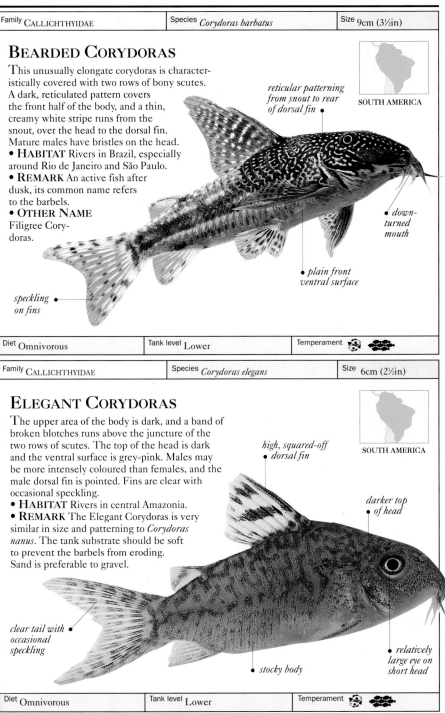

Family CALLICHTHYIDAE	Species *Corydoras barbatus*	Size 9cm (3½in)

BEARDED CORYDORAS

This unusually elongate corydoras is characteristically covered with two rows of bony scutes. A dark, reticulated pattern covers the front half of the body, and a thin, creamy white stripe runs from the snout, over the head to the dorsal fin. Mature males have bristles on the head.
• **HABITAT** Rivers in Brazil, especially around Rio de Janeiro and São Paulo.
• **REMARK** An active fish after dusk, its common name refers to the barbels.
• **OTHER NAME** Filigree Corydoras.

SOUTH AMERICA

reticular patterning from snout to rear of dorsal fin

down-turned mouth

plain front ventral surface

speckling on fins

Diet Omnivorous	Tank level Lower	Temperament

Family CALLICHTHYIDAE	Species *Corydoras elegans*	Size 6cm (2¼in)

ELEGANT CORYDORAS

The upper area of the body is dark, and a band of broken blotches runs above the juncture of the two rows of scutes. The top of the head is dark and the ventral surface is grey-pink. Males may be more intensely coloured than females, and the male dorsal fin is pointed. Fins are clear with occasional speckling.
• **HABITAT** Rivers in central Amazonia.
• **REMARK** The Elegant Corydoras is very similar in size and patterning to *Corydoras nanus*. The tank substrate should be soft to prevent the barbels from eroding. Sand is preferable to gravel.

SOUTH AMERICA

high, squared-off dorsal fin

darker top of head

clear tail with occasional speckling

stocky body

relatively large eye on short head

Diet Omnivorous	Tank level Lower	Temperament

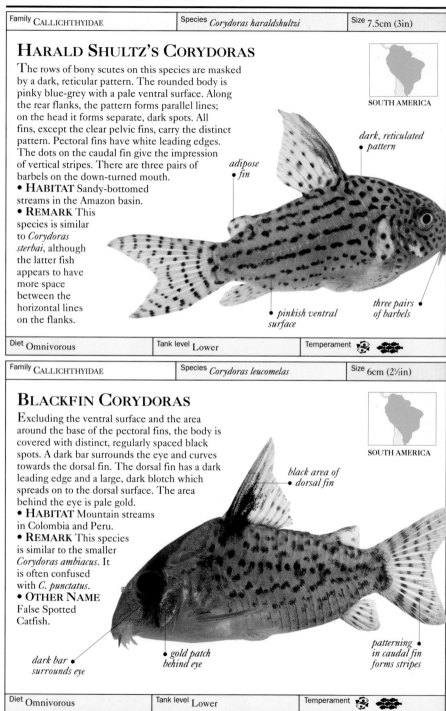

| Family CALLICHTHYIDAE | Species *Corydoras haraldshultzi* | Size 7.5cm (3in) |

HARALD SHULTZ'S CORYDORAS

The rows of bony scutes on this species are masked by a dark, reticular pattern. The rounded body is pinky blue-grey with a pale ventral surface. Along the rear flanks, the pattern forms parallel lines; on the head it forms separate, dark spots. All fins, except the clear pelvic fins, carry the distinct pattern. Pectoral fins have white leading edges. The dots on the caudal fin give the impression of vertical stripes. There are three pairs of barbels on the down-turned mouth.
• **HABITAT** Sandy-bottomed streams in the Amazon basin.
• **REMARK** This species is similar to *Corydoras sterbai*, although the latter fish appears to have more space between the horizontal lines on the flanks.

SOUTH AMERICA

dark, reticulated pattern

adipose fin

three pairs of barbels

pinkish ventral surface

| Diet Omnivorous | Tank level Lower | Temperament |

| Family CALLICHTHYIDAE | Species *Corydoras leucomelas* | Size 6cm (2½in) |

BLACKFIN CORYDORAS

Excluding the ventral surface and the area around the base of the pectoral fins, the body is covered with distinct, regularly spaced black spots. A dark bar surrounds the eye and curves towards the dorsal fin. The dorsal fin has a dark leading edge and a large, dark blotch which spreads on to the dorsal surface. The area behind the eye is pale gold.
• **HABITAT** Mountain streams in Colombia and Peru.
• **REMARK** This species is similar to the smaller *Corydoras ambiacus*. It is often confused with *C. punctatus*.
• **OTHER NAME** False Spotted Catfish.

SOUTH AMERICA

black area of dorsal fin

dark bar surrounds eye

gold patch behind eye

patterning in caudal fin forms stripes

| Diet Omnivorous | Tank level Lower | Temperament |

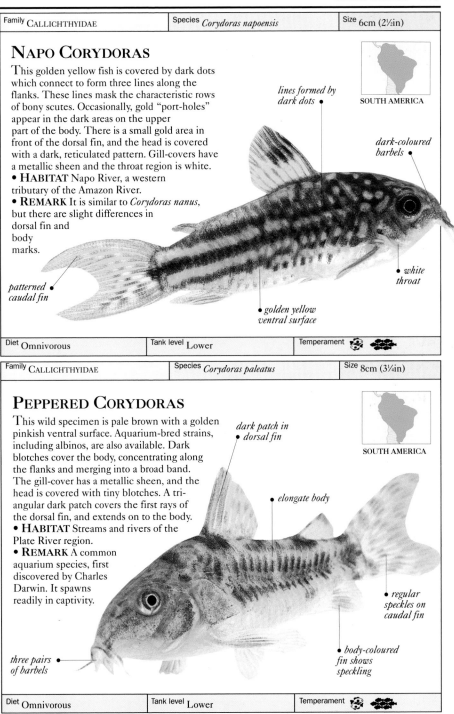

| Family CALLICHTHYIDAE | Species *Corydoras napoensis* | Size 6cm (2½in) |

NAPO CORYDORAS

This golden yellow fish is covered by dark dots which connect to form three lines along the flanks. These lines mask the characteristic rows of bony scutes. Occasionally, gold "port-holes" appear in the dark areas on the upper part of the body. There is a small gold area in front of the dorsal fin, and the head is covered with a dark, reticulated pattern. Gill-covers have a metallic sheen and the throat region is white.
• **HABITAT** Napo River, a western tributary of the Amazon River.
• **REMARK** It is similar to *Corydoras nanus*, but there are slight differences in dorsal fin and body marks.

lines formed by dark dots

SOUTH AMERICA

dark-coloured barbels

white throat

patterned caudal fin

golden yellow ventral surface

| Diet Omnivorous | Tank level Lower | Temperament |

| Family CALLICHTHYIDAE | Species *Corydoras paleatus* | Size 8cm (3¼in) |

PEPPERED CORYDORAS

This wild specimen is pale brown with a golden pinkish ventral surface. Aquarium-bred strains, including albinos, are also available. Dark blotches cover the body, concentrating along the flanks and merging into a broad band. The gill-cover has a metallic sheen, and the head is covered with tiny blotches. A triangular dark patch covers the first rays of the dorsal fin, and extends on to the body.
• **HABITAT** Streams and rivers of the Plate River region.
• **REMARK** A common aquarium species, first discovered by Charles Darwin. It spawns readily in captivity.

dark patch in dorsal fin

SOUTH AMERICA

elongate body

regular speckles on caudal fin

three pairs of barbels

body-coloured fin shows speckling

| Diet Omnivorous | Tank level Lower | Temperament |

LOACHES

MEMBERS OF THE family Cobitidae are distributed from North Africa to Eurasia and the Pacific Rim. Their mouths carry barbels, and some species have an erectile spine beneath each eye. The ventral surface is flattened as they are bottom-dwellers. As loaches are shy, nocturnal creatures, they may need coaxing into view with favourite worm-type live foods.

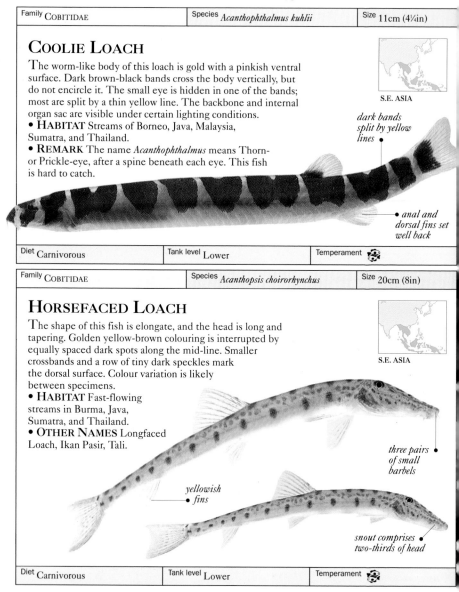

Family COBITIDAE	Species *Acanthophthalmus kuhlii*	Size 11cm (4¼in)

COOLIE LOACH

The worm-like body of this loach is gold with a pinkish ventral surface. Dark brown-black bands cross the body vertically, but do not encircle it. The small eye is hidden in one of the bands; most are split by a thin yellow line. The backbone and internal organ sac are visible under certain lighting conditions.
• **HABITAT** Streams of Borneo, Java, Malaysia, Sumatra, and Thailand.
• **REMARK** The name *Acanthophthalmus* means Thorn- or Prickle-eye, after a spine beneath each eye. This fish is hard to catch.

S.E. ASIA

dark bands split by yellow lines •

• *anal and dorsal fins set well back*

Diet Carnivorous	Tank level Lower	Temperament

Family COBITIDAE	Species *Acanthopsis choirorhynchus*	Size 20cm (8in)

HORSEFACED LOACH

The shape of this fish is elongate, and the head is long and tapering. Golden yellow-brown colouring is interrupted by equally spaced dark spots along the mid-line. Smaller crossbands and a row of tiny dark speckles mark the dorsal surface. Colour variation is likely between specimens.
• **HABITAT** Fast-flowing streams in Burma, Java, Sumatra, and Thailand.
• **OTHER NAMES** Longfaced Loach, Ikan Pasir, Tali.

S.E. ASIA

three pairs of small barbels

yellowish • fins

snout comprises two-thirds of head

Diet Carnivorous	Tank level Lower	Temperament

Family COBITIDAE	Species *Botia horae*	Size 10cm (4in)

SKUNK LOACH

The perfectly streamlined body of this loach is creamy grey, with a paler silvery colour on the lower flanks and ventral surface. A dark stripe runs the length of the body along the dorsal surface, and a band encircles the caudal peduncle. Scales are very small and the skin has a matt finish.
• **HABITAT** Streams and rivers in Thailand; also northern India.
• **REMARK** The Skunk Loach normally rests during the day among plants or retreats.
• **OTHER NAME** Hora's Loach; recently re-classified as *Botia morleti*.

SOUTH ASIA

dark line along dorsal ridge

faintly coloured fins

small, dark centre of eye

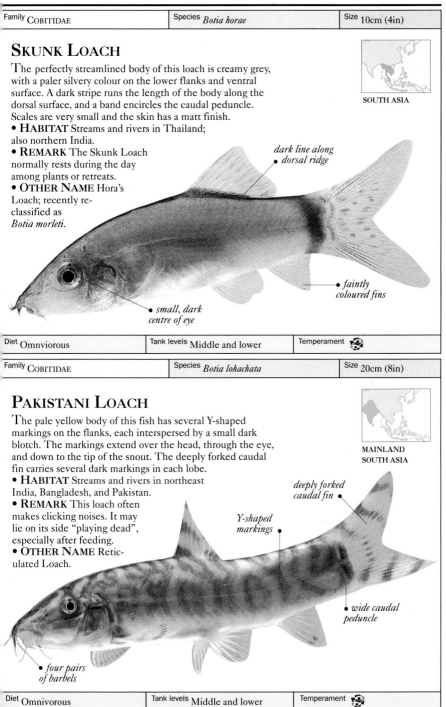

Diet Omnviorous	Tank levels Middle and lower	Temperament

Family COBITIDAE	Species *Botia lohachata*	Size 20cm (8in)

PAKISTANI LOACH

The pale yellow body of this fish has several Y-shaped markings on the flanks, each interspersed by a small dark blotch. The markings extend over the head, through the eye, and down to the tip of the snout. The deeply forked caudal fin carries several dark markings in each lobe.
• **HABITAT** Streams and rivers in northeast India, Bangladesh, and Pakistan.
• **REMARK** This loach often makes clicking noises. It may lie on its side "playing dead", especially after feeding.
• **OTHER NAME** Reticulated Loach.

MAINLAND SOUTH ASIA

deeply forked caudal fin

Y-shaped markings

wide caudal peduncle

four pairs of barbels

Diet Omnivorous	Tank levels Middle and lower	Temperament

Family COBITIDAE	Species *Botia macracantha*	Size 30cm (12in)

CLOWN LOACH

Three black bands cross the orange, arched
body of this fish. Pectoral, pelvic, and caudal
fins are red-orange; the dorsal and anal fins
are black with paler edges. Small scales
give the fish a very smooth, matt finish.
There is an erectile spine in front of
the eye, which may snag in an
aquarium net.
• **HABITAT** Streams
in Indonesia and
Sumatra; also
Borneo.
• **REMARK**
This fish
should be
kept in
numbers.

pale edge to dorsal fin

S.E. ASIAN ISLANDS

forked red caudal fin

erectile spine

four pairs of barbels

third stripe extends on to anal fin

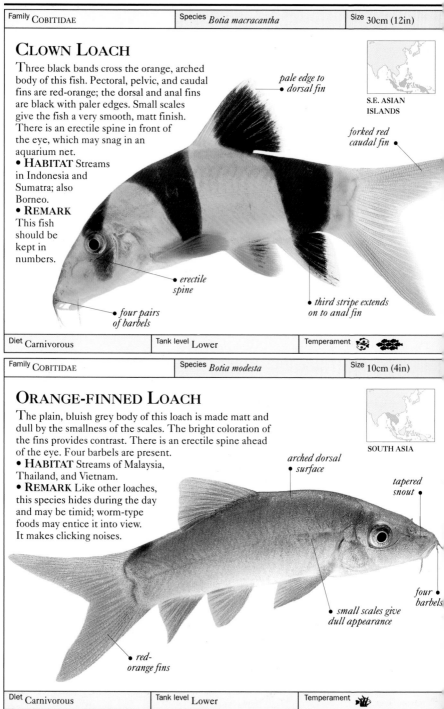

Diet Carnivorous	Tank level Lower	Temperament

Family COBITIDAE	Species *Botia modesta*	Size 10cm (4in)

ORANGE-FINNED LOACH

The plain, bluish grey body of this loach is made matt and
dull by the smallness of the scales. The bright coloration of
the fins provides contrast. There is an erectile spine ahead
of the eye. Four barbels are present.
• **HABITAT** Streams of Malaysia,
Thailand, and Vietnam.
• **REMARK** Like other loaches,
this species hides during the day
and may be timid; worm-type
foods may entice it into view.
It makes clicking noises.

SOUTH ASIA

arched dorsal surface

tapered snout

four barbels

small scales give dull appearance

red-orange fins

Diet Carnivorous	Tank level Lower	Temperament

Family COBITIDAE	Species *Botia sidthimunki*	Size 7.5cm (3in)

DWARF CHAINED LOACH

A dark chain-link pattern overlays the top half of this pale, metallic gold fish; in mature specimens the pattern might reach further down the flanks. The bottom of the chain forms a dark line from snout to caudal fin. The ventral surface is white-gold. All fins, excluding the caudal, are clear.
• **HABITAT** Streams in Thailand.
• **REMARK** This fish often "rests" by perching upon its pelvic fins.

dark chain-link pattern

SOUTH ASIA

four pairs of barbels

Diet Omnivorous	Tank level Lower	Temperament

Family COBITIDAE	Species *Botia striata*	Size 7.5cm (3in)

ZEBRA LOACH

Equally spaced, oblique dark bands run over the entire body of this fish; forwards over the head region and backwards along the flanks. The ventral surface is yellow-gold. The blunt head carries three pairs of barbels. All fins are marked with indistinct dark stripes, the most obvious on the large caudal fin.
• **HABITAT** Streams in southern India.
• **REMARK** It is more active after dark.

black bands divided by gold lines

MAINLAND SOUTH ASIA

Diet Omnivorous	Tank level Lower	Temperament

Family COBITIDAE	Species *Misgurnus anguillicaudatus*	Size 10cm (4in)

JAPANESE WEATHERFISH

The highly elongate body of this species is coloured golden brown with dark speckles. Dorsal and pelvic fins are set back on the body.
• **HABITAT** Streams in northeast Asia, including central China.
• **REMARK** It becomes active when barometric pressure is low.

small, rounded fins

EAST ASIA

cylindrical body

Diet Omnivorous	Tank level Lower	Temperament

OTHER TROPICAL EGG-LAYING FISHES

T HERE ARE MANY tropical egg-laying fishes that are monotypic (meaning they are the sole species in a genus), and several genera that contain very few species. These smaller, diverse groups, which often contain more unusual fishes, including spiny eels, glassfish, and the rainbowfish with two dorsal fins, have been grouped together in the following section.

Family BADIDAE	Species *Badis badis*	Size 6.5cm (2½in)

BADIS

The coloration of this fish is highly variable as it changes to suit its environment (an alternative popular name is the Dwarf Chameleon Fish). The basic colour is brown, which changes to a red and blue speckled pattern on a contented specimen. Females are less brightly coloured, especially at breeding times when male colours intensify dramatically.
• **HABITAT** Still waters in India.
• **REMARK** These secretive spawners stick eggs to cave ceilings after male displays of strength. They prefer live food.
• **OTHER NAME** Formerly classified in the family Nandidae.

MAINLAND
SOUTH ASIA

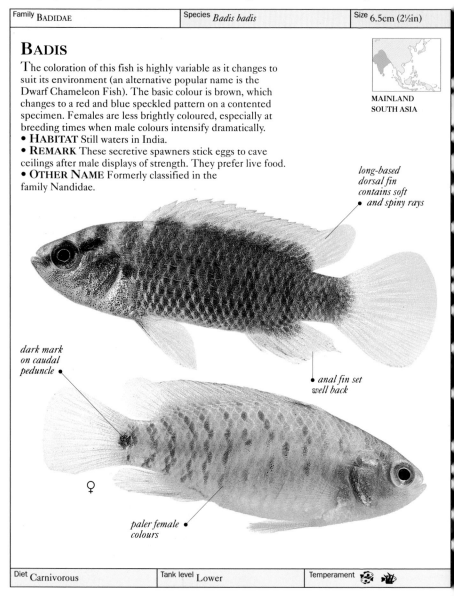

long-based
dorsal fin
contains soft
and spiny rays

dark mark
on caudal
peduncle

anal fin set
well back

♀

paler female
colours

Diet Carnivorous	Tank level Lower	Temperament

Family ATHERINIDAE	Species *Bedotia geayi*	Size 10cm (4in)

MADAGASCAR RAINBOWFISH

The colour of this slim fish is pale greenish yellow with a
bluish violet sheen apparent under sidelighting. A dark line
runs from the snout to the caudal fin. The first of two dorsal
fins is usually folded down. The second dorsal fin and the
anal fin are set well back: those of the male are dark with
orangey yellow streaks and a dark margin; the female's
only carry the dark edge.
• **HABITAT** Streams in Madagascar.
• **REMARK** This active shoaling
species needs plenty of
space. It will tolerate
hard water.

TROPICAL
AFRICA

*first dorsal fin
• folded down*

*superior •
mouth on
small head*

*• dark line runs
length of body*

*yellowish orange •
streaks in male
anal fin*

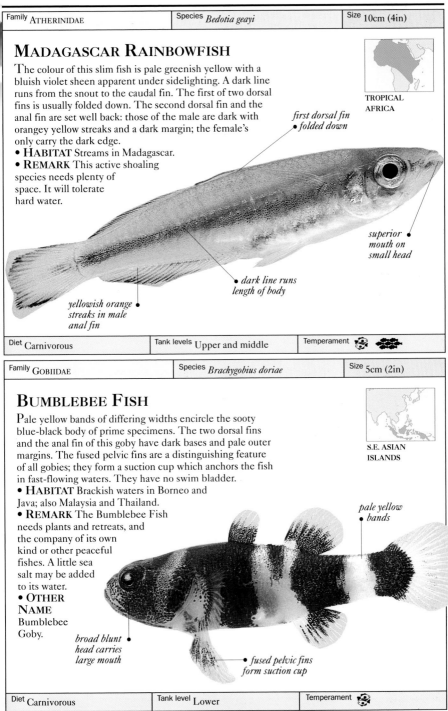

Diet Carnivorous	Tank levels Upper and middle	Temperament

Family GOBIIDAE	Species *Brachygobius doriae*	Size 5cm (2in)

BUMBLEBEE FISH

Pale yellow bands of differing widths encircle the sooty
blue-black body of prime specimens. The two dorsal fins
and the anal fin of this goby have dark bases and pale outer
margins. The fused pelvic fins are a distinguishing feature
of all gobies; they form a suction cup which anchors the fish
in fast-flowing waters. They have no swim bladder.
• **HABITAT** Brackish waters in Borneo and
Java; also Malaysia and Thailand.
• **REMARK** The Bumblebee Fish
needs plants and retreats, and
the company of its own
kind or other peaceful
fishes. A little sea
salt may be added
to its water.
• **OTHER
NAME**
Bumblebee
Goby.

S.E. ASIAN
ISLANDS

*pale yellow
• bands*

*broad blunt •
head carries
large mouth*

*• fused pelvic fins
form suction cup*

Diet Carnivorous	Tank level Lower	Temperament

Family CENTROPOMIDAE	Species *Chanda ranga*	Size 7cm (2¾in)

INDIAN GLASSFISH

Coloration is virtually non-existent on this fish, except for a
yellowish tinge, enhanced with iridescent blue under sidelighting. Background colours tend to be reflected. The gill-
cover and the lateral line are highlighted in silver, and a
silvery sac covers the internal organs. The front of the
dorsal fin is spiny. Sexual differences are subtle.
• **HABITAT** Primarily estuarine waters
of Burma and Thailand, despite
the name; also India.
• **REMARK** A separate species
tank would suit this fish well.

SOUTH ASIA

spiny front
part of dorsal
• fin

caudal •
fin deeply
forked

silver •
lateral line

upturned •
mouth

Diet Carnivorous	Tank level Middle	Temperament

Family CHANNIDAE	Species *Channa asiatica*	Size 30cm (12in)

SNAKEHEAD

This young Snakehead is a pinkish golden colour with
numerous faint, equally spaced dark bars. The adult
is brown-grey with iridescent spots. The head on all
specimens is long, blunt, and rounded. The dorsal fin
is extremely long-based, with the similar anal fin about
two-thirds its length. All fins are greyish in colour.
• **HABITAT** Rivers and lakes in southern China.
• **REMARK** This predatory species has an auxiliary
breathing organ (similar to that of the Anabantidae,
a family in which it was once classified)
which enables it to
breathe atmospheric
air. It requires
meaty foods.

EAST ASIA

equally spaced
dark bars on
• juvenile

large eye on •
narrow head

• heavy
cylindrical
body

greyish fins •

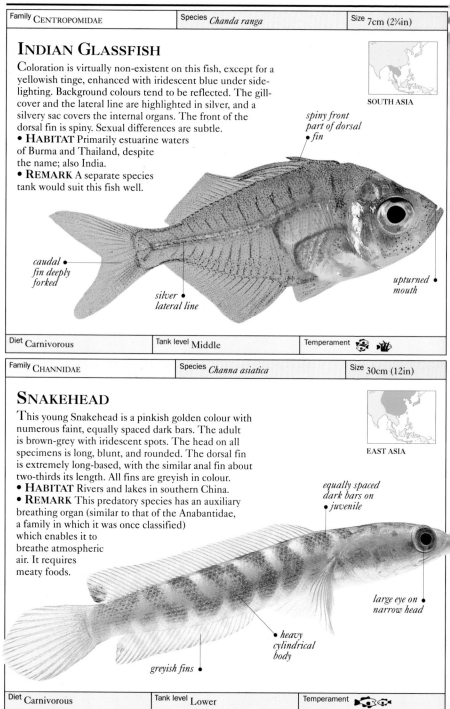

Diet Carnivorous	Tank level Lower	Temperament

Family LOBOTIDAE	Species *Datnioides microlepis*	Size 40cm (16in)

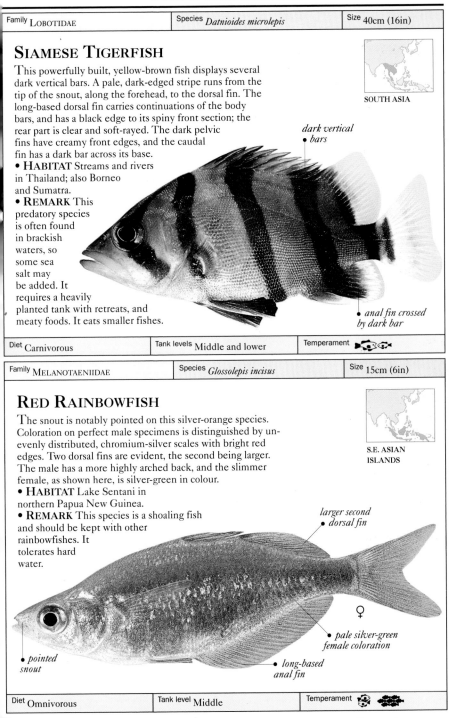

SOUTH ASIA

SIAMESE TIGERFISH

This powerfully built, yellow-brown fish displays several
dark vertical bars. A pale, dark-edged stripe runs from the
tip of the snout, along the forehead, to the dorsal fin. The
long-based dorsal fin carries continuations of the body
bars, and has a black edge to its spiny front section; the
rear part is clear and soft-rayed. The dark pelvic
fins have creamy front edges, and the caudal
fin has a dark bar across its base.
• **HABITAT** Streams and rivers
in Thailand; also Borneo
and Sumatra.
• **REMARK** This
predatory species
is often found
in brackish
waters, so
some sea
salt may
be added. It
requires a heavily
planted tank with retreats, and
meaty foods. It eats smaller fishes.

dark vertical bars

anal fin crossed by dark bar

Diet Carnivorous	Tank levels Middle and lower	Temperament

Family MELANOTAENIIDAE	Species *Glossolepis incisus*	Size 15cm (6in)

S.E. ASIAN
ISLANDS

RED RAINBOWFISH

The snout is notably pointed on this silver-orange species.
Coloration on perfect male specimens is distinguished by un-
evenly distributed, chromium-silver scales with bright red
edges. Two dorsal fins are evident, the second being larger.
The male has a more highly arched back, and the slimmer
female, as shown here, is silver-green in colour.
• **HABITAT** Lake Sentani in
northern Papua New Guinea.
• **REMARK** This species is a shoaling fish
and should be kept with other
rainbowfishes. It
tolerates hard
water.

larger second dorsal fin

♀

pale silver-green female coloration

pointed snout

long-based anal fin

Diet Omnivorous	Tank level Middle	Temperament

Family MORMYRIDAE	Species *Gnathonemus petersi*	Size 23cm (9in)

LONGNOSED ELEPHANT FISH

The head of this species forms approximately a quarter of the body length. The finger-like lower jaw is unusually extended, giving rise to the common name. The long head is balanced by a long, narrow caudal peduncle. Coloration is very dark grey, with two whitish, bracket-shaped marks on the flanks between the dorsal and anal fins, which are set very far back on the body. The narrow caudal fin is deeply forked. Pectoral fins are flipper-like, and the pelvic fins are small.

• **HABITAT** Rivers in Nigeria, Cameroon, and Zaire.

• **REMARK** This nocturnal species emits electrical impulses which enable it to navigate in the dark or in muddy waters. It is highly sensitive to water quality changes, and has been used to monitor water quality in industrial contexts.

• **OTHER NAMES** Peter's Elephant-nose, Ubangi Mormyrid.

deeply forked caudal fin

long, narrow caudal peduncle

long-based anal fin is set well back

bracket-shaped whitish mark on flank

long, finger-like lower jaw

The jaw extension is used to plough for food in the substrate

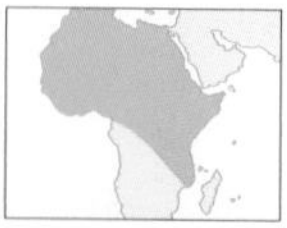

TROPICAL
AFRICA

Diet Carnivorous	Tank level Lower	Temperament

Family GYRINOCHEILIDAE	Species *Gyrinocheilus aymonieri*	Size 25cm (10in)

CHINESE SUCKING LOACH

The colour of this elongate fish is brown with dark-edged scales.
A dark band runs from the snout to the caudal peduncle. The
underslung mouth forms a sucking disc with which the fish rasps
algae. It breathes through special slits in the head while remaining
fixed on to surfaces such as the tank glass.

SOUTH ASIA

• **HABITAT** Streams and rivers in Thailand and Laos.
• **REMARK** This is one of the best algae-consuming, tank-
cleaning fishes. As well as algae,
it feeds on withered lettuce
leaves and will take dried
food. The common name is
misleading, as the fish is
not a loach, nor does it
come from China. It may
become aggressive
with age.

broad dark
• band

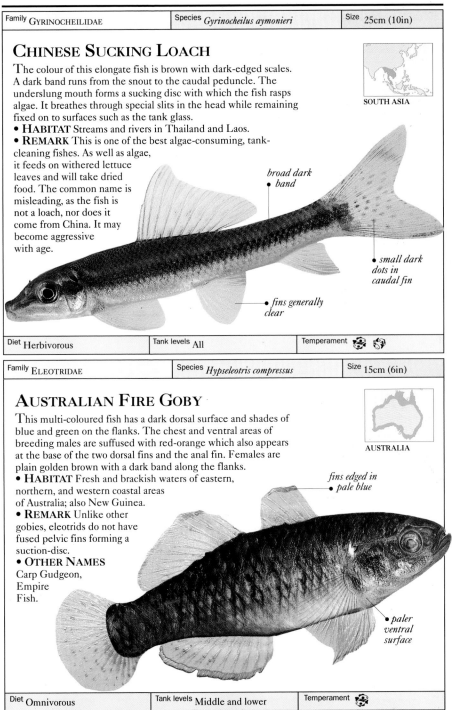

• small dark
dots in
caudal fin

• *fins generally
clear*

Diet Herbivorous	Tank levels All	Temperament

Family ELEOTRIDAE	Species *Hypseleotris compressus*	Size 15cm (6in)

AUSTRALIAN FIRE GOBY

This multi-coloured fish has a dark dorsal surface and shades of
blue and green on the flanks. The chest and ventral areas of
breeding males are suffused with red-orange which also appears
at the base of the two dorsal fins and the anal fin. Females are
plain golden brown with a dark band along the flanks.

AUSTRALIA

• **HABITAT** Fresh and brackish waters of eastern,
northern, and western coastal areas
of Australia; also New Guinea.

*fins edged in
• pale blue*

• **REMARK** Unlike other
gobies, eleotrids do not have
fused pelvic fins forming a
suction-disc.
• **OTHER NAMES**
Carp Gudgeon,
Empire
Fish.

*• paler
ventral
surface*

Diet Omnivorous	Tank levels Middle and lower	Temperament

Family MELANOTAENIIDAE	Species *Iriatherina werneri*	Size 4cm (1¾in)

THREADFIN RAINBOWFISH

The highly elongated fins are the most attractive features of the Threadfin Rainbowfish. The first, round-tipped dorsal fin is held high, and the second contains sooty black, thread-like rays. Pelvic fins are also black and thread-like, and the anal fin carries black extensions. The lyre-shaped caudal fin has rays trailing from the tips. The basic body coloration of mature specimens is golden brown-silver, with a bluish shine on the dorsal ridge. They also carry fine, reddish brown vertical lines.
• **HABITAT** Still waters in swamps and rivers in Papua New Guinea; also northern Australia.
• **REMARK** It should be kept in small groups in slightly soft, acid water, especially when breeding. Eggs can be laid in bushy plants or artificial nylon mops, and should be hatched separately.

S.E. ASIAN ISLANDS

long, thread-like fin rays

lyre-shaped caudal fin

dark-centred golden eye

black extensions on anal fin

Diet Carnivorous	Tank levels Upper and middle	Temperament

Family LEPISOSTEIDAE	Species *Lepisosteus osseus*	Size 150cm (60in)

GARPIKE

The colour of this elongate fish is green-brown on the dorsal surface, shading down through paler tones to yellow below. A broad dark band of blotches runs from the snout to the caudal peduncle. There may be dark patterning on the unpaired fins. Tooth-filled jaws occupy over half the length of the flattened head. Dorsal and anal fins are set very far back on the body.
• **HABITAT** Lakes of North America, from the Great Lakes southwards to Mexico.
• **REMARK** Only young specimens can be kept in the aquarium, either alone or with carefully selected tank-mates.

UNITED STATES

long, tooth-filled jaws

yellow ventral surface

pelvic fin halfway along body

dark band of blotches

Diet Carnivorous	Tank level Upper	Temperament

Family MASTACEMBELIDAE	Species *Mastacembelus armatus*	Size 75cm (30in)

SPINY EEL

The upper parts of this elongate species are golden brown, and the lower parts are dark brown. Two rows of oval blotches appear on the ventral surface. Dorsal, anal, and caudal fins form one complete unit, encircling the rear.
• HABITAT Weedy streambeds in India; also Thailand and Sumatra.
• REMARK Usually nocturnal, this eel will burrow in the substrate. Offer it worms.

dark brown band

MAINLAND SOUTH ASIA

stripe hides small eye

oval blotches on ventral surface

Diet Carnivorous	Tank level Lower	Temperament

Family MASTACEMBELIDAE	Species *Mastacembelus circumcinctus*	Size 20cm (8in)

LARGE SPINY EEL

The bottom two-thirds of this golden brown fish are crossed vertically by dark bars which, at their widest point, form an interrupted line along the flanks. The dorsal fin is preceded by a row of tiny spines or finlets.
• HABITAT Streambeds in Thailand.
• REMARK It should only be kept with larger fishes or with its own kind.

SOUTH ASIA

dark, interrupted line

fins encircle rear half of body

Diet Carnivorous	Tank level Lower	Temperament

Family MASTACEMBELIDAE	Species *Mastacembelus erythrotaenia*	Size 20cm (8in)

FIRE EEL

A number of discontinuous, fiery red lines run horizontally along this deep brown-black eel. The edge of the caudal fin is also red, and red facial markings may contain some yellow.
• HABITAT Streambeds throughout Southeast Asia.
• REMARK This attractive species is often kept as a prize specimen in its own aquarium: it should never be kept with smaller fishes.

brown-black coloration

S.E. ASIA

discontinuous red lines

red-yellow facial markings

Diet Carnivorous	Tank level Lower	Temperament

Family MELANOTAENIIDAE	Species *Melanotaenia boesmani*	Size 10cm (4in)

BOESMAN'S RAINBOWFISH

The front part of the two-toned body is greyish blue, the rear plain yellow. Like most rainbowfishes, there are two separate dorsal fins. The rear dorsal fin and the anal fin are pale-edged and long-based, sharing the yellow coloration of the caudal fin. Males are generally more colourful.
• **HABITAT** Streams and lakes in Papua New Guinea.
• **REMARK** This fish prefers hard, fairly alkaline water.
• **OTHER NAME** Formerly classified in the family Atherinidae.

S.E. ASIAN ISLANDS

acutely pointed snout

yellow in caudal fin

pale-edged anal fin

greyish pelvic fin

Diet Omnivorous	Tank level Middle	Temperament

Family MELANOTAENIIDAE	Species *Melanotaenia herbertaxelrodi*	Size 9cm (3½in)

HERBERT AXELROD'S RAINBOWFISH

This pale grey-blue juvenile male carries yellowish tints towards the dorsal and ventral surfaces. Darker blue bands run from the eye to the caudal peduncle. The second dorsal and anal fins have yellow at their bases; the remaining fins are relatively colourless. Mature specimens, especially males, are a more intense yellow colour.
• **HABITAT** Streams and lakes in Papua New Guinea.
• **REMARK** This increasingly popular species is named after the American fish-collector and publisher, Dr. Herbert Axelrod.

S.E. ASIAN ISLANDS

darkish blue band

yellowish tint on juvenile

rounded caudal fin

large eye on small head

yellow base of anal fin

Diet Omnivorous	Tank level Middle	Temperament

| Family MELANOTAENIIDAE | Species *Melanotaenia lacustris* | Size 10cm (4in) |

LAKE KATUBU RAINBOWFISH

A darkish blue band runs from the mid-point along the flanks of this juvenile fish to the end of the caudal peduncle; the basic body colour is pale grey-blue. In mature specimens, the upper half of the body is a deep greenish blue and the lower half is paler. Males are generally more intensely coloured.
• **HABITAT** Lake Katubu, southern Papua New Guinea.
• **REMARK** The specific name of this species, *lacustris*, indicates a lake habitat, rather than a stream or river. It is very similar in shape to the Australian rainbowfishes.

S.E. ASIAN ISLANDS

clearly defined scales

large eye set well forward

forked caudal fin

paler juvenile colour

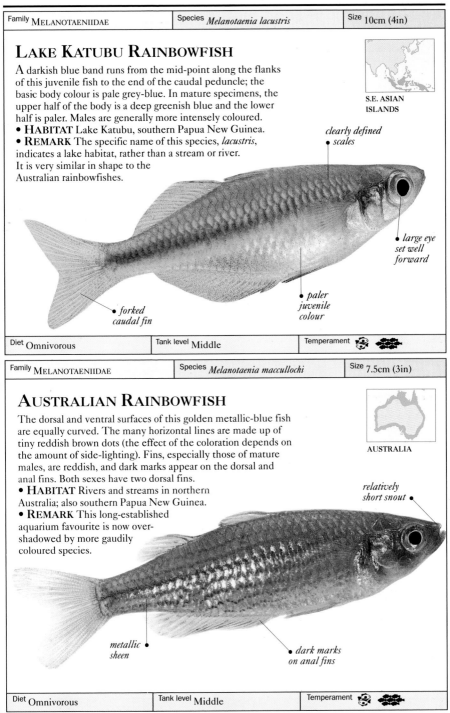

| Diet Omnivorous | Tank level Middle | Temperament |

| Family MELANOTAENIIDAE | Species *Melanotaenia maccullochi* | Size 7.5cm (3in) |

AUSTRALIAN RAINBOWFISH

The dorsal and ventral surfaces of this golden metallic-blue fish are equally curved. The many horizontal lines are made up of tiny reddish brown dots (the effect of the coloration depends on the amount of side-lighting). Fins, especially those of mature males, are reddish, and dark marks appear on the dorsal and anal fins. Both sexes have two dorsal fins.
• **HABITAT** Rivers and streams in northern Australia; also southern Papua New Guinea.
• **REMARK** This long-established aquarium favourite is now over-shadowed by more gaudily coloured species.

AUSTRALIA

relatively short snout

metallic sheen

dark marks on anal fins

| Diet Omnivorous | Tank level Middle | Temperament |

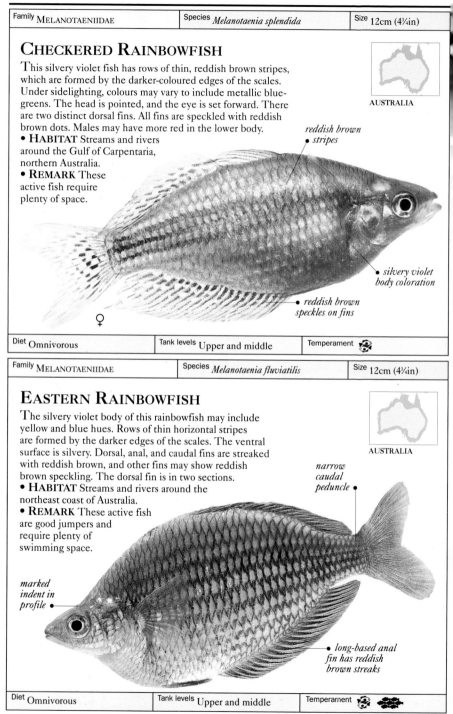

| Family MELANOTAENIIDAE | Species *Melanotaenia splendida* | Size 12cm (4¾in) |

CHECKERED RAINBOWFISH

This silvery violet fish has rows of thin, reddish brown stripes, which are formed by the darker-coloured edges of the scales. Under sidelighting, colours may vary to include metallic blue-greens. The head is pointed, and the eye is set forward. There are two distinct dorsal fins. All fins are speckled with reddish brown dots. Males may have more red in the lower body.
• **HABITAT** Streams and rivers around the Gulf of Carpentaria, northern Australia.
• **REMARK** These active fish require plenty of space.

AUSTRALIA

reddish brown stripes

silvery violet body coloration

reddish brown speckles on fins

♀

| Diet Omnivorous | Tank levels Upper and middle | Temperament |

| Family MELANOTAENIIDAE | Species *Melanotaenia fluviatilis* | Size 12cm (4¾in) |

EASTERN RAINBOWFISH

The silvery violet body of this rainbowfish may include yellow and blue hues. Rows of thin horizontal stripes are formed by the darker edges of the scales. The ventral surface is silvery. Dorsal, anal, and caudal fins are streaked with reddish brown, and other fins may show reddish brown speckling. The dorsal fin is in two sections.
• **HABITAT** Streams and rivers around the northeast coast of Australia.
• **REMARK** These active fish are good jumpers and require plenty of swimming space.

AUSTRALIA

narrow caudal peduncle

marked indent in profile

long-based anal fin has reddish brown streaks

| Diet Omnivorous | Tank levels Upper and middle | Temperament |

Family NANDIDAE	Species *Monocirrhus polyacanthus*	Size 10cm (4in)

SOUTH AMERICAN LEAF FISH

The colour of this fish varies according to its need for camouflage. It is generally golden brown, with darker brown irregular blotches, which give the appearance of a decaying leaf. The mouth is very large and can be opened out to form a "funnel" for consuming food. A thin, dark horizontal line crosses the flanks, and there are two similar dark lines on the head which make a "V" shape, with the eye at their forward meeting point. The long-based dorsal fin is spiny, and the caudal fin is often held closed when swimming in the characteristic head-down position.

• **HABITAT** Streams and rivers of Amazonia and Guyana.

• **REMARK** This species drifts up to unsuspecting prey disguised as a dead leaf, and then engulfs its victim using its protruding mouth. It requires many plants in which to lurk, and plenty of fishes on which it can prey. Eggs are laid on flat surfaces and the fry must be well fed on live foods.

Long chin growth resembles a leaf stem

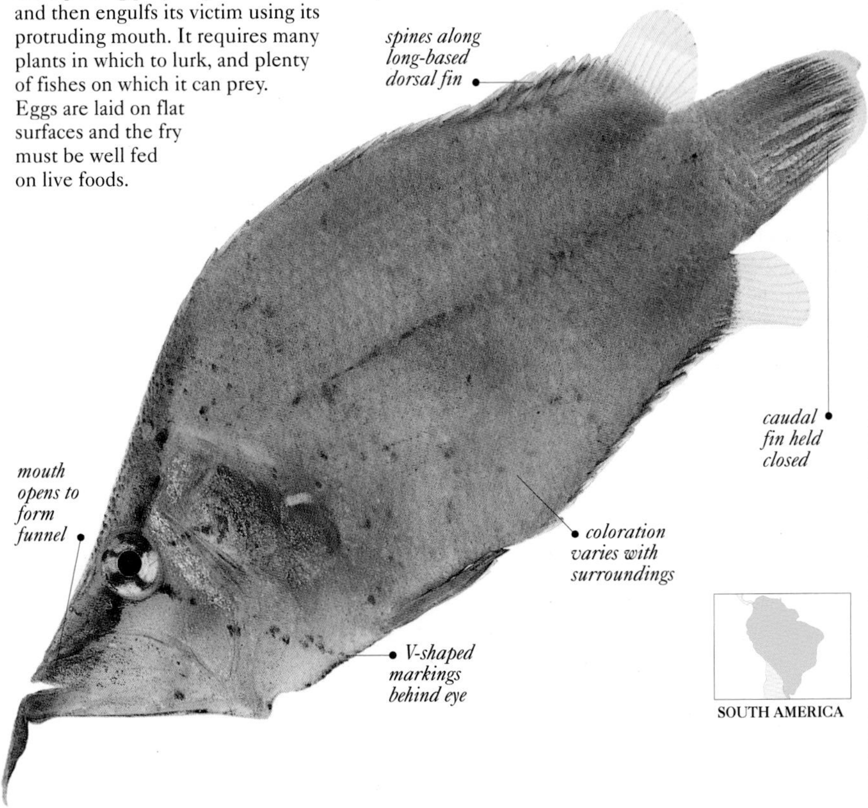

spines along long-based dorsal fin

caudal fin held closed

mouth opens to form funnel

coloration varies with surroundings

V-shaped markings behind eye

SOUTH AMERICA

Diet Carnivorous	Tank levels All	Temperament

| Family MONODACTYLIDAE | Species *Monodactylus argenteus* | Size 23cm (9in) |

MONO

The body of this disc-shaped fish is laterally compressed, like the freshwater angelfishes (see p.122). Very small scales cover a silver body. A dark bar passes through the large eye. Another slightly thinner bar runs down from the front of the dorsal fin. The highly arched lateral line is visible. Unpaired fins are yellowish orange, the dorsal and anal fins having black front edges.
• **HABITAT** Coastal waters, including harbours, from India to Tahiti, the Philippines and Australia.
• **REMARK** Best kept in shoals in a large, brackish water tank. It will eat tank plants.
• **OTHER NAMES** Fingerfish, Malayan Angelfish.

visible lateral line

INDO-PACIFIC

dark bar through eye

yellowish orange caudal fin

black-edged anal fin

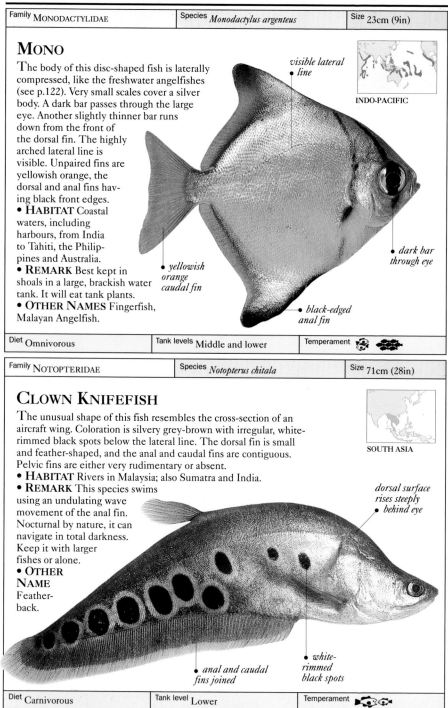

| Diet Omnivorous | Tank levels Middle and lower | Temperament |

| Family NOTOPTERIDAE | Species *Notopterus chitala* | Size 71cm (28in) |

CLOWN KNIFEFISH

The unusual shape of this fish resembles the cross-section of an aircraft wing. Coloration is silvery grey-brown with irregular, white-rimmed black spots below the lateral line. The dorsal fin is small and feather-shaped, and the anal and caudal fins are contiguous. Pelvic fins are either very rudimentary or absent.
• **HABITAT** Rivers in Malaysia; also Sumatra and India.
• **REMARK** This species swims using an undulating wave movement of the anal fin. Nocturnal by nature, it can navigate in total darkness. Keep it with larger fishes or alone.
• **OTHER NAME** Featherback.

SOUTH ASIA

dorsal surface rises steeply behind eye

anal and caudal fins joined

white-rimmed black spots

| Diet Carnivorous | Tank level Lower | Temperament |

Family ORYZIATIDAE	Species *Oryzias melastigma*	Size 4cm (1¼in)

BLACK-SPOTTED MEDAKA

This fish is pale silver with a bluish iridescence that is enhanced under sidelighting. The backbone is visible, and the small dorsal fin is set very far back on the body.
• **HABITAT** Fresh and brackish waters of eastern India and Sri Lanka; also Burma, Indonesia, and Malaysia.
• **REMARK** Following spawning, fertilized eggs hang from the female's vent in a grape-like bunch, and brush off on to plants. Keep with non-aggressive fishes, or in a species tank.
• **OTHER NAME** Formerly classifed in the family Cyprinodontidae. Also known as Rice-fish.

small dorsal fin set well • back

MAINLAND
SOUTH ASIA

• backbone visible beneath skin

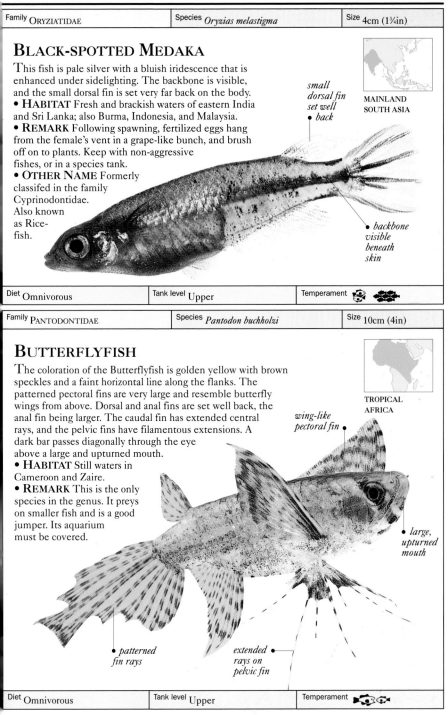

Diet Omnivorous	Tank level Upper	Temperament

Family PANTODONTIDAE	Species *Pantodon buchholzi*	Size 10cm (4in)

BUTTERFLYFISH

The coloration of the Butterflyfish is golden yellow with brown speckles and a faint horizontal line along the flanks. The patterned pectoral fins are very large and resemble butterfly wings from above. Dorsal and anal fins are set well back, the anal fin being larger. The caudal fin has extended central rays, and the pelvic fins have filamentous extensions. A dark bar passes diagonally through the eye above a large and upturned mouth.
• **HABITAT** Still waters in Cameroon and Zaire.
• **REMARK** This is the only species in the genus. It preys on smaller fish and is a good jumper. Its aquarium must be covered.

TROPICAL
AFRICA

wing-like pectoral fin •

• large, upturned mouth

• patterned fin rays

extended • rays on pelvic fin

Diet Omnivorous	Tank level Upper	Temperament

Family SCATOPHAGIDAE	Species *Scatophagus argus*	Size 30cm (12in)

SCAT

The oblong shape of the Scat is emphasized by the position of the fins. Coloration is a mix of streaky brown and gold, with numerous dark, round spots. On adults (see inset), two dark vertical lines mark the forehead, and a golden streak runs behind the gill-cover. Red markings appear on the dorsal surface. The long-based brown and gold dorsal fin has a spiny front section and a soft rear.

• **HABITAT** Coastal and estuarine waters from India to Tahiti, and the Philippines.

• **REMARK** The Scat is a true scavenger, readily eating aquarium plants. Vegetables and space are essential, and sea salt should be added to the water.

Adult Scat feeding on plant life

semi-clear caudal fin

INDO-PACIFIC

spiny front of anal fin

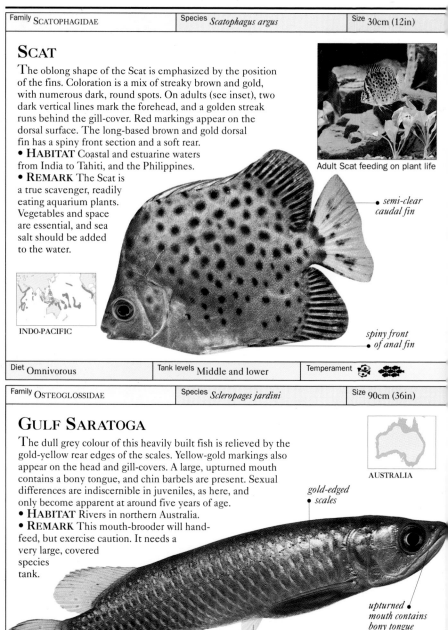

Diet Omnivorous	Tank levels Middle and lower	Temperament

Family OSTEOGLOSSIDAE	Species *Scleropages jardini*	Size 90cm (36in)

GULF SARATOGA

The dull grey colour of this heavily built fish is relieved by the gold-yellow rear edges of the scales. Yellow-gold markings also appear on the head and gill-covers. A large, upturned mouth contains a bony tongue, and chin barbels are present. Sexual differences are indiscernible in juveniles, as here, and only become apparent at around five years of age.

• **HABITAT** Rivers in northern Australia.

• **REMARK** This mouth-brooder will hand-feed, but exercise caution. It needs a very large, covered species tank.

AUSTRALIA

gold-edged scales

upturned mouth contains bony tongue

very small pelvic fin

Diet Carnivorous	Tank levels All	Temperament

Family GOBIIDAE	Species *Stigmatogobius sadanundio*	Size 8.5cm (3¼in)

SPOTTED GOBY

There are two dorsal fins on this grey-blue fish: the first consists of about six stiffly held rays (often with a black blotch); the second is equal in length to the long-based anal fin. Both carry dark spots. Females lack the longer fins and are yellowish in colour.

S.E. ASIAN ISLANDS

• **HABITAT** Fresh and brackish waters in Borneo, Java, and Sumatra; also the Philippines.
• **REMARK** This fish may benefit from a teaspoonful of sea salt per five litres (one gallon) of tank water. Breeding is by secretive egg-depositing, often on the ceilings of caves – and plenty of retreats are required. It is peaceful, but territorial.
• **OTHER NAME** Knight Goby.

erect front dorsal rays

silver underside

rounded caudal fin

fins larger on male

Diet Carnivorous	Tank level Lower	Temperament

Family ATHERINIDAE	Species *Telmatherina ladigesi*	Size 7cm (2¾in)

CELEBES RAINBOWFISH

The colour of this species varies according to lighting conditions, but is essentially pale yellow-gold, shading down to a silver belly. An iridescent, pale blue-green line runs along the flanks to the caudal peduncle. The first of two dorsal fins is small, but the second has long black and yellow filaments which are longer in the male. Males also have filamentous extensions to the anal fin. Females are less colourful.

S.E. ASIAN ISLANDS

well-developed filaments on second dorsal fin

• **HABITAT** Streams and estuarine waters in Indonesia.
• **REMARK** Unlike many Asian fishes, this species adapts to hard water very well. Additions of sea salt may be beneficial.

blue rim on large, dark-centred eye

pale blue-green line

Diet Omnivorous	Tank levels Upper and middle	Temperament

| Family TOXOTIDAE | Species *Toxotes jaculator* | Size 25cm (10in) |

ARCHERFISH

The head of this fish is long and tapered, and the lower lip protrudes. The body appears shortened due to the set-back dorsal and anal fins. Coloration is silver with dark blotches on the flanks and in the dorsal and anal fins.
• **HABITAT** Coastal regions and estuarine rivers, from East Africa to Australia.
• **REMARK** The fascination of this species is its ability to shoot down perching insects with well-aimed spit. It is able to judge the exact location of the victim despite refraction at the water's surface, and can leap at prey resting up to 30cm (12in) out of the water.

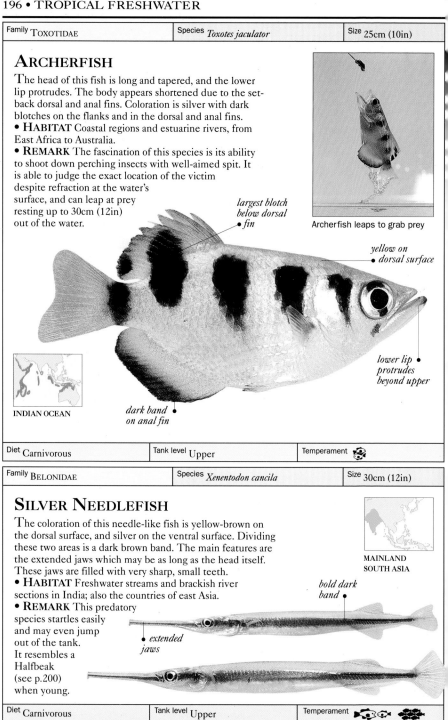

Archerfish leaps to grab prey

largest blotch below dorsal fin

yellow on dorsal surface

lower lip protrudes beyond upper

INDIAN OCEAN

dark band on anal fin

| Diet Carnivorous | Tank level Upper | Temperament |

| Family BELONIDAE | Species *Xenentodon cancila* | Size 30cm (12in) |

SILVER NEEDLEFISH

The coloration of this needle-like fish is yellow-brown on the dorsal surface, and silver on the ventral surface. Dividing these two areas is a dark brown band. The main features are the extended jaws which may be as long as the head itself. These jaws are filled with very sharp, small teeth.
• **HABITAT** Freshwater streams and brackish river sections in India; also the countries of east Asia.
• **REMARK** This predatory species startles easily and may even jump out of the tank. It resembles a Halfbeak (see p.200) when young.

MAINLAND SOUTH ASIA

bold dark band

extended jaws

| Diet Carnivorous | Tank level Upper | Temperament |

LIVEBEARERS

L IVEBEARERS ARE distinguished by their method of reproduction, in which eggs are fertilized and developed inside the female body. In the family Goodeidae, the developing young receive direct nourishment from the female. Most livebearers come from Central America and a few are from east Asia. They are hardy fish which adapt readily to water changes.

Family POECILIIDAE	Species *Alfaro cultratus*	Size 9cm (3½in)

KNIFE LIVEBEARER

The coloration of the Knife Livebearer is silvery yellow-brown with a metallic blue sheen under sidelighting. The dorsal surface is darker. A rounded dorsal fin is set halfway along the body and, as with other members of the family, anal fins differ between sexes. The anal fin of the slightly smaller male is modified to form a gonopodium, while the female anal fin is fan-shaped. All fins are yellowish, and the caudal fin may have a dark edge.
• **HABITAT** Streams in Costa Rica, Guatemala, Panama, and Nicaragua.
• **REMARK** This is a rather aggressive fish which appreciates a well-planted aquarium. Plants also provide refuge for the fry from their hungry parents.

CENTRAL
AMERICA

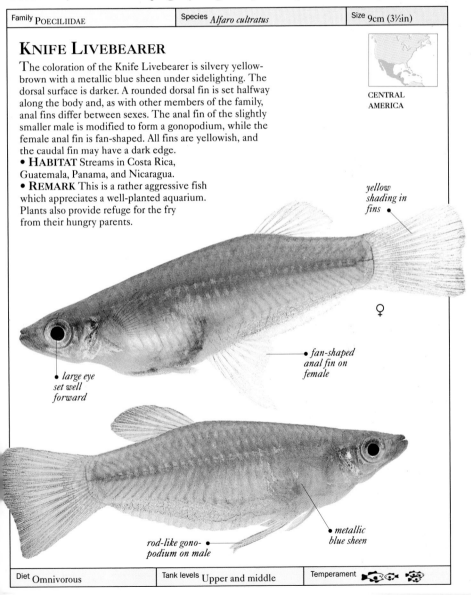

yellow shading in fins

♀

fan-shaped anal fin on female

• *large eye set well forward*

rod-like gono-podium on male

metallic blue sheen

Diet Omnivorous	Tank levels Upper and middle	Temperament

Family GOODEIDAE	Species *Allotoca dugesi*	Size 6cm (2¼in)

GOLDEN BUMBLEBEE GOODEID

This fish has a stocky, elongate body with a narrow caudal
peduncle. The coloration on the lower flanks is golden yellow
on the male, and bluish, sometimes with dark bars, on the
female. The male anal fin is not rod-like as with most other
livebearers, but the female's is typically fan-shaped. A bluish
band runs horizontally on both sexes, from behind the gill-
cover to the caudal peduncle.
• **HABITAT** Streams and rivers in the central
highlands of Mexico.
• **REMARK** Females of
the family Goodeidae
cannot store sperm like
Poeciliidae species, so
mating is required
for each
brood.

CENTRAL
AMERICA

*dorsal fin set
• well back*

*blue horizontal
band •*

*• golden
coloration on
lower flank*

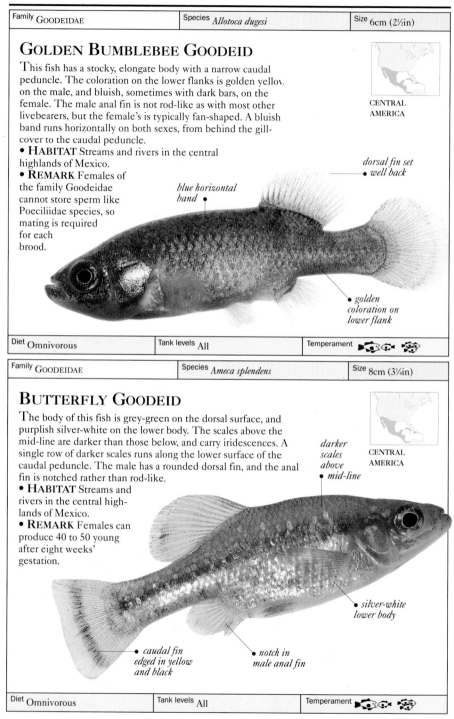

Diet Omnivorous	Tank levels All	Temperament

Family GOODEIDAE	Species *Ameca splendens*	Size 8cm (3¼in)

BUTTERFLY GOODEID

The body of this fish is grey-green on the dorsal surface, and
purplish silver-white on the lower body. The scales above the
mid-line are darker than those below, and carry iridescences. A
single row of darker scales runs along the lower surface of the
caudal peduncle. The male has a rounded dorsal fin, and the anal
fin is notched rather than rod-like.
• **HABITAT** Streams and
rivers in the central highlands of Mexico.
• **REMARK** Females can
produce 40 to 50 young
after eight weeks'
gestation.

*darker
scales
above
• mid-line*

CENTRAL
AMERICA

*• silver-white
lower body*

*• caudal fin
edged in yellow
and black*

*• notch in
male anal fin*

Diet Omnivorous	Tank levels All	Temperament

| Family POECILIIDAE | Species *Brachyrhaphis roseni* | Size 5cm (2in) |

CARDINAL BRACHY

On the best specimens, body coloration is greenish brown on the dorsal surface, with greenish yellow-gold flanks, and a silver belly. Flanks are crossed vertically by thin, equally spaced dark bars that run the full depth of the body in front of the dorsal fin. The male dorsal fin is yellow and red with a dark outer edge, and his gonopodium is long and yellow. The female has a fan-shaped anal fin.
• **HABITAT** Streams in Costa Rica and Panama.
• **REMARK** This species was introduced to the hobby in 1988. A well-planted aquarium is necessary to protect the fry from their cannibalistic parents.

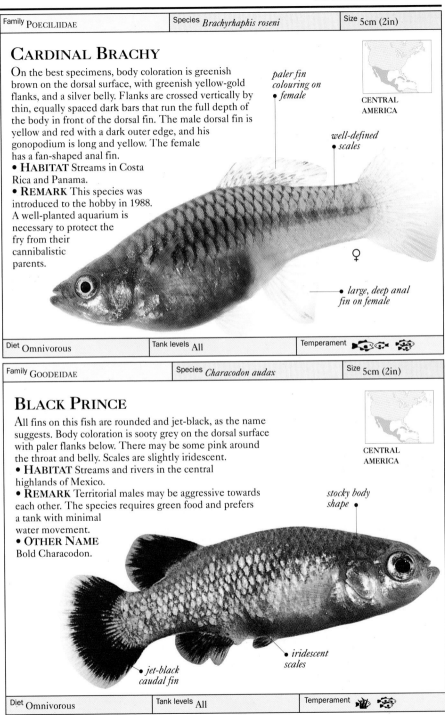

paler fin colouring on • *female*

CENTRAL AMERICA

well-defined • *scales*

♀

• *large, deep anal fin on female*

| Diet Omnivorous | Tank levels All | Temperament |

| Family GOODEIDAE | Species *Characodon audax* | Size 5cm (2in) |

BLACK PRINCE

All fins on this fish are rounded and jet-black, as the name suggests. Body coloration is sooty grey on the dorsal surface with paler flanks below. There may be some pink around the throat and belly. Scales are slightly iridescent.
• **HABITAT** Streams and rivers in the central highlands of Mexico.
• **REMARK** Territorial males may be aggressive towards each other. The species requires green food and prefers a tank with minimal water movement.
• **OTHER NAME** Bold Characodon.

CENTRAL AMERICA

stocky body shape •

• *jet-black caudal fin*

• *iridescent scales*

| Diet Omnivorous | Tank levels All | Temperament |

Family HEMIRHAMPHIDAE	Species *Dermogenys pusillus*	Size 6cm (2½in)

WRESTLING HALFBEAK

The lower jaws of these two slender male fish are extended to approximately twice the length of the upper jaw for surface feeding. Coloration is greenish yellow-gold, with patches of blue. The male anal fin appears to be folded, and that of the female is fan-shaped.
• **HABITAT** Streams and rivers in Indonesia, Java, Malaysia, Sumatra, and Thailand.
• **REMARK** Keep a male and two or three females in a group; males tend to fight by locking jaws with each other.

S. E. ASIA

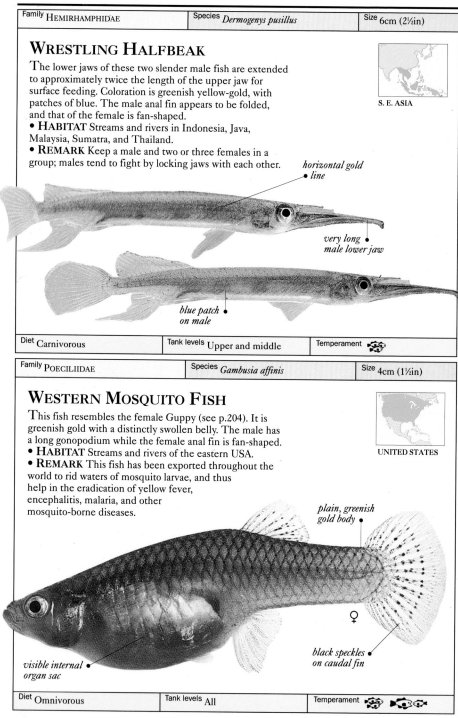

horizontal gold line

very long male lower jaw

blue patch on male

Diet Carnivorous	Tank levels Upper and middle	Temperament

Family POECILIIDAE	Species *Gambusia affinis*	Size 4cm (1½in)

WESTERN MOSQUITO FISH

This fish resembles the female Guppy (see p.204). It is greenish gold with a distinctly swollen belly. The male has a long gonopodium while the female anal fin is fan-shaped.
• **HABITAT** Streams and rivers of the eastern USA.
• **REMARK** This fish has been exported throughout the world to rid waters of mosquito larvae, and thus help in the eradication of yellow fever, encephalitis, malaria, and other mosquito-borne diseases.

UNITED STATES

plain, greenish gold body

♀

visible internal organ sac

black speckles on caudal fin

Diet Omnivorous	Tank levels All	Temperament

Family POECILIIDAE	Species *Heterandria bimaculata*	Size 7cm (2¾in)

TWO-SPOT LIVEBEARER

The coloration of this species varies: these specimens are found in mountain streams and are greenish golden brown with a bluish sheen; those from standing waters on plains carry more speckling. All scales are dark-edged. Two dark blotches are normally present, one on either side of the caudal peduncle. The dorsal fin bears a speckled pattern.
- **HABITAT** Streams, rivers, and lakes in Mexico and neighbouring Central American countries.
- **REMARK** This aggressive species is a prolific breeder.
- **OTHER NAMES** Bimac, Pseudo Helleri, *Pseudoxiphophorus*.

CENTRAL AMERICA

long-based dorsal fin

long male gonopodium

dark-edged scales

♀

dark blotch on caudal peduncle

Diet Omnivorous	Tank levels All	Temperament

Family POECILIIDAE	Species *Heterandria formosa*	Size 2cm (¾in)

MOSQUITO FISH

This fish has a dark horizontal band and speckles on the dorsal surface. The belly and ventral surface are silvery white. The male has a long gonopodium.
- **HABITAT** Still waters in South Carolina, Florida, Georgia, and Louisiana in the USA.
- **REMARK** Keep this fish in a species tank and offer a varied diet.
- **OTHER NAMES** Dwarf Livebearer, Dwarf Top Minnow.

UNITED STATES

dark blotch on dorsal fin

dark horizontal band

♀

silvery white ventral surface

Diet Omnivorous	Tank levels All	Temperament

Family POECILIIDAE	Species *Poecilia nigrofasciata*	Size 6cm (2⅓in)

HUMPBACKED LIMIA

The humped back of this species is accentuated by the decorative dorsal fin. This fish has silvery blue flanks, which are crossed vertically by dark bands. The "hump" is pronounced only on mature males, and the lower rear section of his body is keel-shaped. Females have deeper bellies and their vertical bars are shorter and broader.
• **HABITAT** Streams and rivers on Haiti in the Caribbean Sea.
• **OTHER NAME** This fish was previously classified in the *Limia* genus.

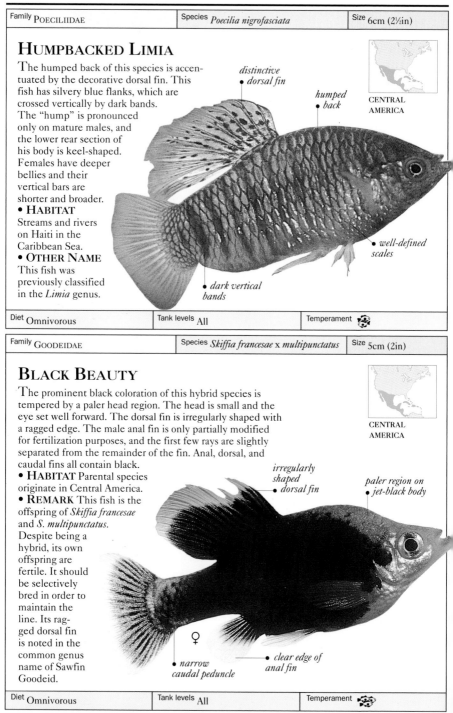

distinctive dorsal fin

humped back

CENTRAL AMERICA

well-defined scales

dark vertical bands

Diet Omnivorous	Tank levels All	Temperament

Family GOODEIDAE	Species *Skiffia francesae* x *multipunctatus*	Size 5cm (2in)

BLACK BEAUTY

The prominent black coloration of this hybrid species is tempered by a paler head region. The head is small and the eye set well forward. The dorsal fin is irregularly shaped with a ragged edge. The male anal fin is only partially modified for fertilization purposes, and the first few rays are slightly separated from the remainder of the fin. Anal, dorsal, and caudal fins all contain black.
• **HABITAT** Parental species originate in Central America.
• **REMARK** This fish is the offspring of *Skiffia francesae* and *S. multipunctatus*. Despite being a hybrid, its own offspring are fertile. It should be selectively bred in order to maintain the line. Its ragged dorsal fin is noted in the common genus name of Sawfin Goodeid.

irregularly shaped dorsal fin

paler region on jet-black body

CENTRAL AMERICA

♀

narrow caudal peduncle

clear edge of anal fin

Diet Omnivorous	Tank levels All	Temperament

Family GOODEIDAE	Species *Xenotoca eiseni*	Size 6cm (2½in)

ORANGE-TAILED GOODEID

A bright orange to red patch appears on the caudal peduncle of this species, more intensely on the male. Coloration ahead of the dorsal fin is yellowish brown; rearwards the colour is metallic blue-green. A notch in the male anal fin is apparent, and his dorsal fin is often quite large and rounded. The lower jaw and throat regions may be pink.
• **HABITAT** Streams and rivers in the central highlands of Mexico.
• **REMARK** This species can be quarrelsome and it has a reputation for fin-nipping. Medium-hard water is preferred.
• **OTHER NAME** Red-tailed Goodeid.

dorsal fin set well back

CENTRAL AMERICA

♀

plumper female shape

orange-pink patch on caudal peduncle

notch in male anal fin

Diet Omnivorous	Tank levels All	Temperament

Family POECILIIDAE	Species *Xiphorus neuzalanahotl*	Size 6cm (2½in)

NORTHERN MOUNTAIN SWORDTAIL

The flanks of this creamy yellow fish are marked with erratic dark specklings, and some of the dark-edged scales join to form zigzag lines. The body shows some violet iridescences when viewed under sidelighting. Fins are clear with a hint of yellow and the dorsal fin has some speckling. The male carries a short "sword" which is edged in black, and the anal fin is rod-like. Females have fan-shaped anal fins.
• **HABITAT** Fast-flowing rivers in Mexico; adults stay in the middle of rivers, while juveniles and gravid females gather in the plants at the sides.
• **OTHER NAMES** Also known as Dwarf Livebearer, Dwarf Topminnow.

erratic speckling on creamy yellow flanks

CENTRAL AMERICA

slightly elongate body

"sword" on caudal fin of male

Diet Omnivorous	Tank levels All	Temperament

Family POECILIIDAE	Species *Poecilia reticulata*	Size 3cm (1¼in)

GUPPY

The wild Guppy is dark olive-green, shading to silver on the ventral surface. Aquarium-cultivated guppies conform to standards, but individual colours may differ greatly, as demonstrated by the selection shown here. Males are irregularly marked in red, orange, green, or black; no two males are exactly alike. Females are normally larger than males, and lack the coloration and extravagant finnage, although some females are now appearing with colours in the single fins. When gravid, the females take on extra body depth, and a dark area appears around the vent. The male anal fin, or gonopodium, is rod-shaped and used to fertilize the female internally.

• **HABITAT** Streams in Central America; also Trinidad and northern South America.

• **REMARK** To maintain colour strains, interbreeding should be avoided. Females store sperm internally.

• **OTHER NAMES** Millions Fish. Formerly classified as *Lebistes*.

CENTRAL AMERICA

GOLD COBRA GUPPY

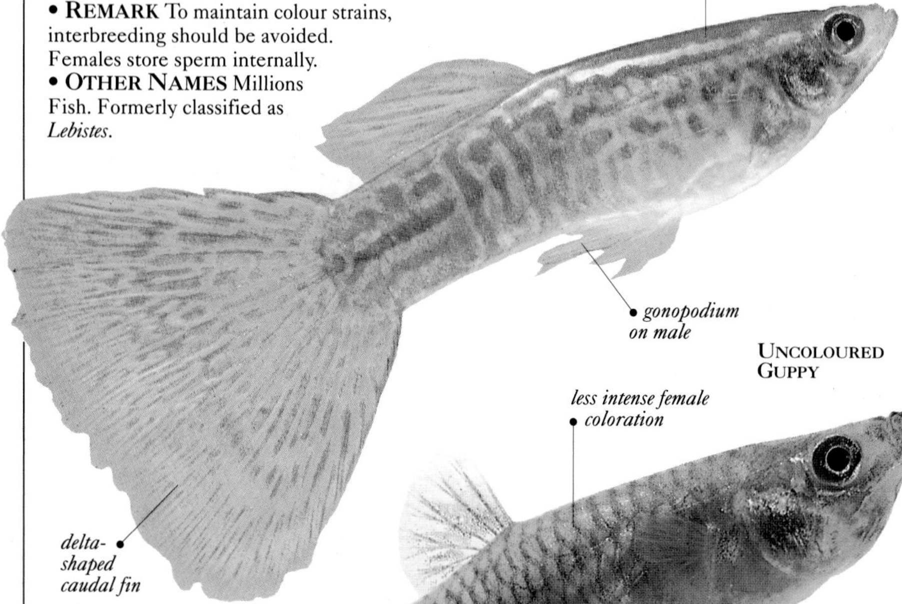

"snakeskin" markings

gonopodium on male

UNCOLOURED GUPPY

less intense female coloration

delta-shaped caudal fin

♀

dark spot when gravid

smaller female fins

Diet Omnivorous	Tank levels All	Temperament

long dorsal
• fin

**RED VARITAIL
GUPPY**

• varying
colour pattern

**RED-TAILED HALF-
BLACK GUPPY**

half-black
• body

flag-like
• dorsal fin

BLONDE GUPPY

• well-developed
caudal fin

• paler
ventral
surface

rounded
• caudal fin

Family POECILIIDAE	Species *Poecilia latipinna*	Size 10cm (4in)

SAILFIN MOLLY

All members of the family Poeciliidae, including the Sailfin Mollies, are stocky and fairly elongate. Many colour strains of this species have been developed by selective breeding, samples of which are shown below and opposite. Wild-caught mollies are coloured silvery green with some iridescences. The male dorsal fin is carried erect, like a sail, to impress females or challenge males. The male anal fin is adapted into a rod-like structure (the gonopodium) with which the female is internally fertilized; the female anal fin is fan-shaped.

• **HABITAT** Coastal brackish and marine waters of Mexico, including the Gulf of Mexico; also the United States south of Carolina.

• **REMARK** Clear water and regular supplies of vegetables are required for optimum development. A separate, well-planted tank is the best place for a female molly to give birth. Saline water can be tolerated.

CENTRAL AMERICA

GREEN MOLLY

• *rod-like anal fin*

PLATINUM SAILFIN

• *pointed snout*

plumper female body •

♀

erect "sail-like" • *dorsal fin*

• *clear fins*

GREEN SAILFIN MOLLY

Diet Omnivorous	Tank levels All	Temperament

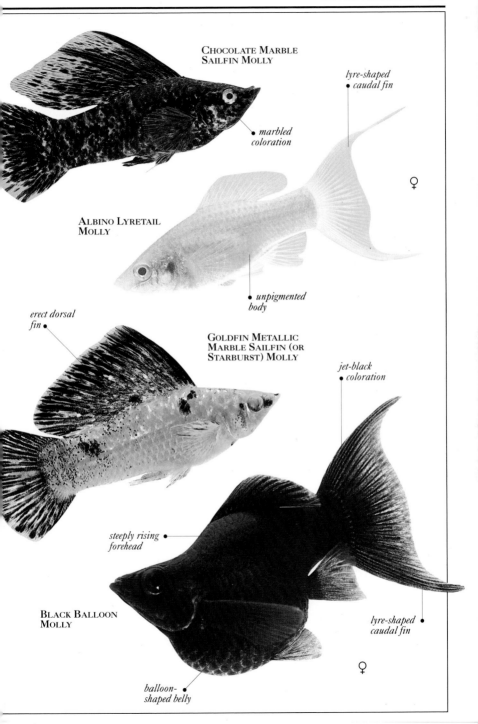

CHOCOLATE MARBLE
SAILFIN MOLLY

lyre-shaped
caudal fin

marbled
coloration

♀

ALBINO LYRETAIL
MOLLY

unpigmented
body

erect dorsal
fin

GOLDFIN METALLIC
MARBLE SAILFIN (OR
STARBURST) MOLLY

jet-black
coloration

steeply rising
forehead

BLACK BALLOON
MOLLY

lyre-shaped
caudal fin

♀

balloon-
shaped belly

Family POECILIIDAE	Species *Xiphophorus helleri*	Size 10cm (4in)

SWORDTAIL

The wild male Swordtail is green with a purple stripe along the side, and a yellow, sword-like caudal fin extension. The edges of the "sword" are black. Many different colour strains and finnage variants have been selectively bred, and examples are shown here. The female Green Swordtail, on this page, is closest to the original wild strain colour. The male anal fin forms a gonopodium, while the female is without a "sword", and her body is slightly larger.

• **HABITAT** Streams in Mexico, Honduras, and Guatemala.

• **REMARK** Males may quarrel among themselves. Occasionally females may switch sex in later life.

CENTRAL AMERICA

GREEN SWORDTAIL

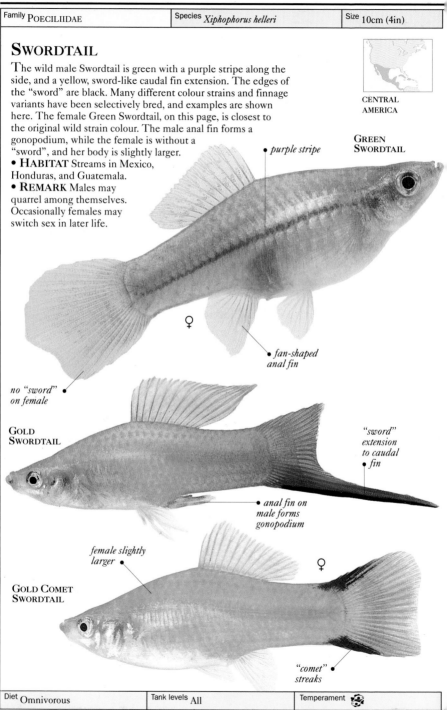

• *purple stripe*

♀

• *fan-shaped anal fin*

no "sword" on female •

GOLD SWORDTAIL

"sword" extension to caudal • *fin*

• *anal fin on male forms gonopodium*

female slightly larger •

♀

GOLD COMET SWORDTAIL

"comet" streaks •

Diet Omnivorous	Tank levels All	Temperament

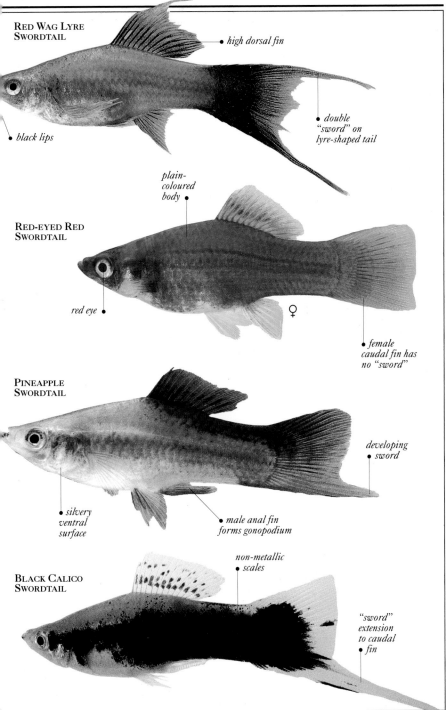

RED WAG LYRE SWORDTAIL

high dorsal fin

black lips

double "sword" on lyre-shaped tail

plain-coloured body

RED-EYED RED SWORDTAIL

red eye

♀

female caudal fin has no "sword"

PINEAPPLE SWORDTAIL

developing sword

silvery ventral surface

male anal fin forms gonopodium

non-metallic scales

BLACK CALICO SWORDTAIL

"sword" extension to caudal fin

| Family POECILIIDAE | Species *Xiphophorus maculatus* | Size 4cm (1½in) |

PLATY

The coloration of the wild Platy is grey with dark speckles and clear fins; there may be red in the dorsal fin. The Platy now appears in the aquarium in many cultivated variations, some of which are shown here. The "wagtail" is a very popular strain with a black mouth and black fins, and red or yellow body colours. The Red Wag Hi-fin Platy shown opposite is a fancy wagtail which has a tall dorsal fin. In all strains, the rod-like male anal fin is used to fertilize the female internally. She has a fan-shaped anal fin and becomes much larger when gravid.

• **HABITAT** Originally from Mexico, Guatemala, and Honduras, the Platy is now bred commercially in Florida and the Pacific Rim.

• **REMARK** The colours of this good community collection fish will degenerate unless breeding is strictly controlled.

CENTRAL AMERICA

GOLD COMET PLATY

♀

BLUE CORAL PLATY

• *"comet" streaks*

• *fan-shaped anal fin*

blue coral marking •

• *male anal fin forms gonopodium*

| Diet Omnivorous | Tank levels All | Temperament |

high dorsal fin

RED WAG HI-FIN PLATY

♀

black fins

plain-coloured body

RED HI-FIN PLATY

highly developed dorsal fin

male anal fin forms gonopodium

SUNSET MARIGOLD HI-FIN PLATY

darker rear of body

| Family POECILIIDAE | Species *Xiphophorus variatus* | Size 5cm (2in) |

VARIATUS PLATY

As with the related Swordtail and Platy (see pp.208–209 and pp.210–211), selective breeding has resulted in many colour strains of this fish, often with exaggerated finnage. Of the three female strains shown below, the top one is probably the closest in colour to the wild fish. The original wild form is greenish yellow with clearly defined, dark-edged scales, and possibly some dark flecks on the flanks. The body shape is more elongate than that of the Platy, but the male anal fins are similarly rod-like. Female fish are generally longer.
• **HABITAT** Originally found in streams in southern Mexico.

CENTRAL AMERICA

GREEN VARIATUS PLATY

greenish yellow body

clear edge of caudal fin •

CALICO PLATY

elongate caudal peduncle •

BLACK CALICO PLATY

pale ventral surface

colourless caudal fin

fan-shaped anal fin

| Diet Omnivorous | Tank levels All | Temperament |

COLDWATER FRESHWATER FISHES

SINGLE-TAILED GOLDFISHES

GOLDFISHES HAVE BEEN kept in captivity longer than any other fishes, and they remain popular due to the many varieties developed from the one original species, *Carassius auratus*.

This section is devoted to single-tailed varieties – hardy fishes that can over-winter outdoors. Their cultivation is generally limited to exaggerating fins or developing various colour strains.

Family CYPRINIDAE	Species *Carassius auratus*	Size Variable

COMMON GOLDFISH

Traditionally, the body colour of the Goldfish is metallic red-orange with matching fins. Young fish may be greenish bronze, changing to adult coloration after about one year. Dorsal and anal fins are relatively long-based and the caudal fin is forked and stiffly held. The lateral line is visible. Females usually appear plumper when they are viewed from above. At spawning time the male develops small white spots (tubercles) on the gill-covers and head.
• **REMARK** Goldfishes were first developed in 11th-century China from the occasional colourful or unusual specimen found among carp kept for food. Selective breeding established the distinguishing scale types: "metallic", "nacreous" (resembling mother-of-pearl), and "matt" (also known as calico).

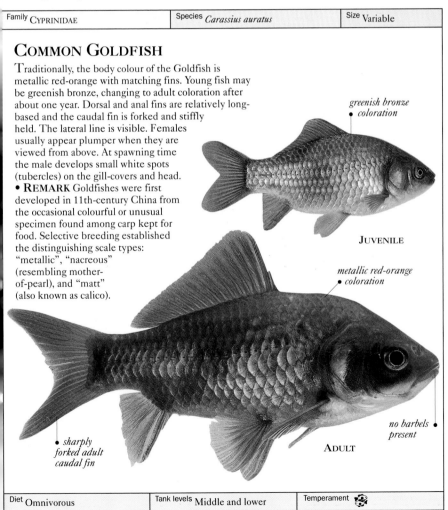

greenish bronze • coloration

JUVENILE

metallic red-orange • coloration

• no barbels present

• sharply forked adult caudal fin

ADULT

Diet Omnivorous	Tank levels Middle and lower	Temperament

Family CYPRINIDAE	Species *Carassius auratus*	Size Variable

COMET

The body shape of all Comets is elongate, with equally curved dorsal and ventral contours. It is not as deep as the Common Goldfish (see p.213). The colours of these fish depend on the strain, the most popular of which show red-orange and lemon-yellow colorations. The varieties shown here include an uncoloured juvenile Comet, a Gold (or Metallic) Comet, and an extremely popular strain, the Sarasa (or Red Cap) Comet, which has a white or silver base colour. A distinctive, cultivated feature of these varieties is the deeply forked caudal fin, which can be almost as long as the body.

• **REMARK** The Comet requires plenty of swimming room, and is capable of swimming very fast over short distances. It is a hardy fish and benefits from being kept outdoors in a pond all year round.

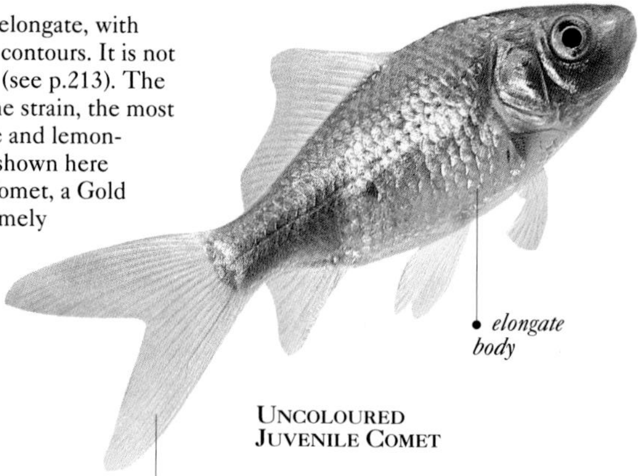

• *elongate body*

UNCOLOURED JUVENILE COMET

• *deeply forked caudal fin*

• *clear lobes of caudal fin*

GOLD COMET

• *darker front edges of fins*

• *terminal mouth*

• *red "cap"*

• *narrow caudal peduncle*

SARASA COMET

Diet Omnivorous	Tank levels All	Temperament

| Family CYPRINIDAE | Species *Carassius auratus* | Size Variable |

NYMPH

The shape of the Nymph is like that of the Fantail or the Veiltail (see pp.217 and 220), but this fish has single anal and caudal fins, unlike the double fins of the latter two strains. The variety shown here is a metallic red strain.
• **REMARK** The Nymph is usually found among the offspring of a Fantail or a Veiltail. In breeding terms, this fish is known as a "recessive".

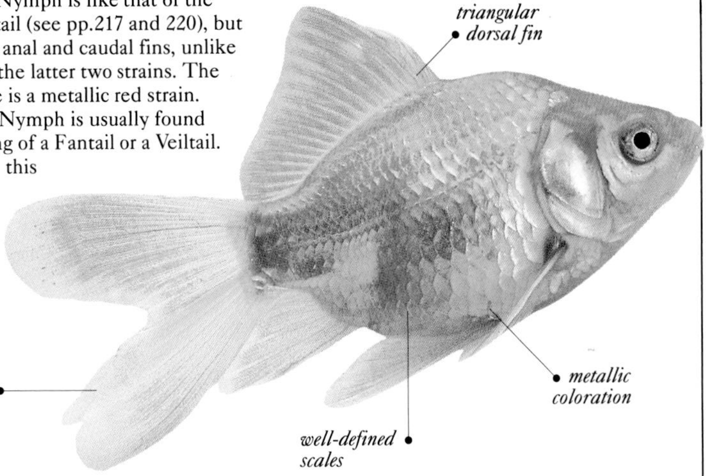

triangular dorsal fin

single clear caudal fin

well-defined scales

metallic coloration

| Diet Omnivorous | Tank levels All | Temperament |

| Family CYPRINIDAE | Species *Carassius auratus* | Size Variable |

SHUBUNKIN

The bodies of the Shubunkin varieties are slightly shorter than those of the Common Goldfish (see p.213), but they are similarly rounded. Shubunkin coloration depends very much on strain and on scale formation: the popular strains tend to show blacks, reds, purples, blues, and browns beneath nacreous or matt scales. The strain shown here is the Bristol Shubunkin, which features an extravagant caudal fin. Its pronounced, rounded lobes are carried without drooping on a good specimen.
• **REMARK** Another popular strain, the London Shubunkin, is the same shape as the Common Goldfish, but it is multi-coloured and lacks the metallic scales. Its fins have not been artificially developed.

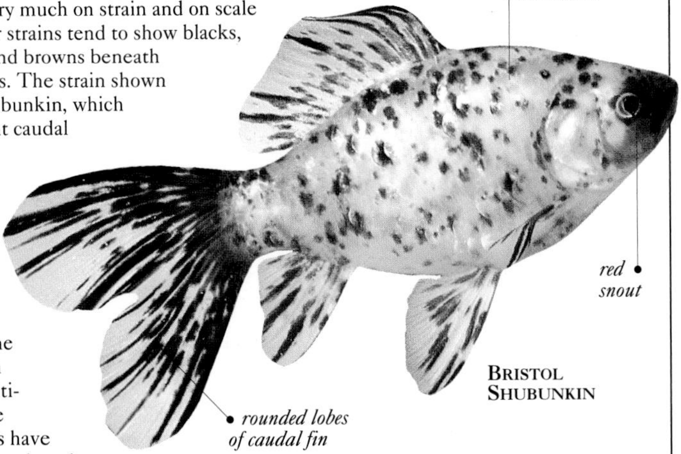

mottled coloration

red snout

BRISTOL SHUBUNKIN

rounded lobes of caudal fin

| Diet Omnivorous | Tank levels All | Temperament |

TWIN-TAILED GOLDFISHES

T HESE GOLDFISHES are termed "twintails" because their caudal and anal fins hang in double folds. Their aquarium-bred bodies become truncated and egg-shaped, and the ability to swim is gradually impaired as the form changes from the natural streamlined shape. These restrictions mean that twintails are not suited to outdoor ponds. They could not compete in the race for food, nor flee from predators. Their delicate fins may also become congested due to inferior water conditions. The maximum sizes twin-tailed goldfishes grow to depend on the size of the tank in which they are kept.

Family CYPRINIDAE	Species *Carassius auratus*	Size Variable

BUBBLE-EYE

The enlarged, fluid-filled sacs beneath the eyes of this variety of twintail are highly distinctive, and they sway as the fish swims. The rest of the body is roughly egg-shaped with a straight dorsal surface. The coloration varies but is usually metallic red-orange. The dorsal fin is absent and the anal and caudal fins are doubled, the extravagant caudal fin flowing from a down-turned caudal peduncle.

• **REMARK** The eye-sacs are prone to damage, so it is best to keep this strain in its own aquarium, without sharp-edged furnishings.

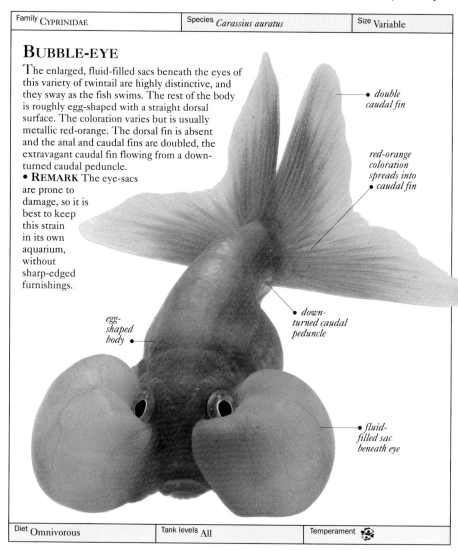

• *double caudal fin*

red-orange coloration spreads into • *caudal fin*

• *down-turned caudal peduncle*

egg-shaped body •

• *fluid-filled sac beneath eye*

Diet Omnivorous	Tank levels All	Temperament

Family CYPRINIDAE	Species *Carassius auratus*	Size Variable

CELESTIAL

The unusual eyes of this variety are directed permanently upwards due to fleshy growths beneath them. Coloration is usually metallic red-orange, although it can vary according to scale formation. The dorsal fin is absent, and the anal and caudal fins are doubled. A stiffly held caudal fin flows from a continuation of the dorsal surface.
• **REMARK** The eyes take several months from birth to assume their "celestial" glance. This fish is not hardy, and is therefore best kept in a separate indoor aquarium.

permanently upward vision •

• *fleshy growths support eyes*

*stiffly held •
caudal fin*

• *double anal fin*

Diet Omnivorous	Tank levels All	Temperament

Family CYPRINIDAE	Species *Carassius auratus*	Size Variable

FANTAIL

The coloration of the Fantail varies according to the scale formation and the relative differences in pigmentation. The dorsal fin is held high, and on good specimens it should measure half the body depth. Anal and caudal fins are doubled, and the caudal fin is carried above the horizontal line.
• **REMARK** This strain has no swimming difficulties and it can therefore be kept outside in ponds.

• *high dorsal fin*

• *variable, mottled colours*

*caudal fin •
held on
horizontal
line*

• *double anal fin*

Diet Omnivorous	Tank levels All	Temperament

Family CYPRINIDAE	Species *Carassius auratus*	Size Variable

LIONHEAD

The body of this fish is short and egg-shaped, and the dorsal surface lacks a dorsal fin. The raspberry-like growth on the head causes the Lionhead to resemble the Red-cap Oranda (opposite), but the double caudal fin is more stiffly held and is not as free flowing. The caudal peduncle is less down-turned on British specimens in comparison with Japanese strains.

stiffly held caudal fin

bare dorsal surface

• **REMARK** As with other highly developed Goldfish strains, the Lionhead is best kept indoors. Its ungainly method of swimming makes it unsuitable for outdoor ponds, and the conditions in the indoor aquarium can be kept at optimum levels more easily.

raspberry-like head growth

Diet Omnivorous	Tank levels All	Temperament

Family CYPRINIDAE	Species *Carassius auratus*	Size Variable

MOOR

The Moor is egg-shaped with a slightly down-turned caudal peduncle. The coloration is always black, hence the alternative name, Black Moor. The eyes may be normal or, in certain strains, "telescopic" (protruding on conical supports). The dorsal fin is set on the highest part of the back, and the anal fin is doubled. The extravagant double caudal fin hangs in folds and has a straight top edge.

high-set dorsal fin

• **REMARK** The best specimens are completely black; any sign of silver is penalized at fish shows and exhibitions. As a result of this, all competitive breeders cull fry that fail to meet the required colour standards.

extravagant caudal fin

eyes are "telescopic"

Diet Omnivorous	Tank levels All	Temperament

Family CYPRINIDAE	Species *Carassius auratus*	Size Variable

RED-CAP ORANDA

The Oranda is short compared with other cultivated Goldfish, and has a slightly down-turned caudal peduncle. The colour varies: this Oranda strain has a white body with a red cap on the head. The head growth is known as the "wen" and is peculiar to Orandas and to the Lionhead (opposite). The dorsal fin is high, and the anal and caudal fins are doubled and free flowing.

• **REMARK** Like other fancy strains, the Oranda needs a tank free of active or aggressive fishes, and it requires optimum water conditions to prevent fin damage and deterioration.

dorsal fin is held high

red cap, or "wen"

double anal fin

Diet Omnivorous	Tank levels All	Temperament

Family CYPRINIDAE	Species *Carassius auratus*	Size Variable

PEARLSCALE

This short, fancy Goldfish is very well-rounded with a short caudal peduncle. The colour varies depending on scale formation and corresponding pigmentation. It is similar in shape to the Fantail (see p.217) but this strain can be distinguished by the scale formation: each scale has a raised centre that is white or pearly coloured. The dorsal fin is held high, and the anal and caudal fins are doubled.

• **REMARK** This fish's natural plumpness and domed scales often resemble the symptoms of dropsy. Like all other highly developed strains, the Pearlscale is not an agile swimmer, and should be kept in a separate indoor aquarium.

distinctive domed scales

double caudal fin

short, well-rounded body

Diet Omnivorous	Tank levels All	Temperament

Family CYPRINIDAE	Species *Carassius auratus*	Size Variable

POM-PON

The scalation of this variety is usually metallic or nacreous, but it can vary. The Pom-pon is physically similar to the Lionhead (see p.218), but instead of a raspberry-like growth on the head, the nostril tissue has developed to form two distinct "pompons"; these hang down below the mouth on some varieties. On the original strain, the dorsal fin is absent. Recent strains retain it.

• **REMARK** Specialist care is needed if the delicate nasal growths are to be maintained in prime condition. It is best to keep these fish in a separate aquarium with good quality water.

• **OTHER NAME** Also spelt Pom-pom.

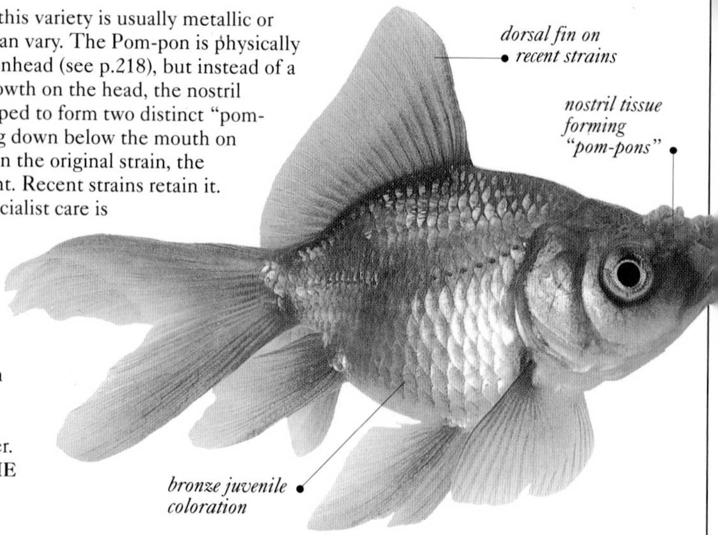

dorsal fin on recent strains

nostril tissue forming "pom-pons"

bronze juvenile coloration

Diet Omnivorous	Tank levels All	Temperament

Family CYPRINIDAE	Species *Carassius auratus*	Size Variable

VEILTAIL

The colour of the relatively deep-bodied Veiltail varies according to scale formation – a gold strain is shown here. Anal and caudal fins are doubled and hang in folds on good specimens. The dorsal fin is held high. Pectoral and pelvic fins are usually well produced and add to the gracefulness of the fish. The eyes can be normal or protuberant ("telescopic").

• **REMARK** The flowing fins require carefully monitored, good-quality water. The tank bottom should be kept free of detritus, and pond fish should be brought indoors during the winter months.

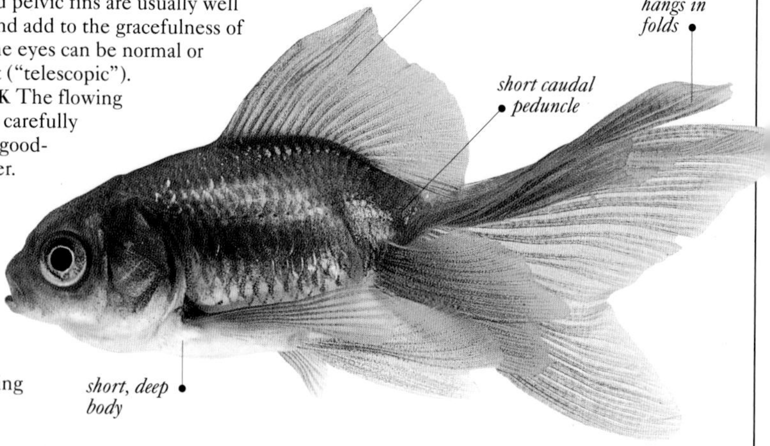

dorsal fin held high

caudal fin hangs in folds

short caudal peduncle

short, deep body

Diet Omnivorous	Tank levels All	Temperament

Family CYPRINIDAE	Species *Carassius auratus*	Size Variable

JAPANESE GOLDFISH STRAINS

A selection of twin-tailed strains cultivated in Japan are shown on the following two pages. Although there is no internationally accepted exhibiting standard for these twintails, they are becoming increasingly popular and readily available on the aquarium market.

• **REMARK** The names used to describe the shape of the "wen" – the fleshy head covering in the Lionhead (or Buffalo-head as it is called in Japan) – reflect the depth of Goldfish culture in Japan. "Tokin" is a Samurai helmet shape, "Bim-bari" denotes a side growth, and "Tatsugashira" means an overall head covering.

JAPANESE MOOR

double caudal fin

"telescopic" eyes

gold coloration

down-turned caudal peduncle

finless dorsal surface

RED AND WHITE LIONHEAD

rudimentary "wen" head covering

COMET SHUBUNKIN

large, forked caudal fin

multicoloured body

Diet Omnivorous	Tank levels All	Temperament

Family CYPRINIDAE	Species *Carassius auratus*	Size Variable

long-based dorsal fin •

egg-shaped • body

RED RYUKIN

RED AND WHITE RYUKIN

double caudal fin •

finless dorsal surface •

• two-tone coloration

• slightly protruding eyes

flattish • contour

RED RANCHU

colourless edge of caudal fin •

RED AND WHITE WAKIN

Diet Omnivorous	Tank levels All	Temperament

KOI

DESPITE THEIR long-term unsuitability for the indoor aquarium, there are many aquarium-bred strains of the ornamental Koi (*Cyprinus carpio*), and a selection is shown here. It is customary to view and judge these fish from above, and their colours and patterns have been developed accordingly. Koi originated in east Asia, but strains are now cultivated worldwide.

Family CYPRINIDAE	Species *Cyprinus carpio*	Size Variable

KOI

The shape of these classic, ornamental fish is elongate, with moderately arched dorsal profiles in juveniles. The adults are more torpedo-shaped, rounded, and powerfully built. A wide mouth carries two pairs of barbels on a large head. Colours are extremely variable as the Koi is a cultivated fish and not found in nature. The scalation of Koi also varies according to the strain. Strains with "doitsu" scalation, for example, carry only a few large scales, usually along the lateral line and on the dorsal surface. Strains with "matsuba" scalation have "pine-cone" effect scales; and those with "ginrin" covering feature shining metallic scales. The Asagi Koi shown here has a blue tone with matsuba scales; cheeks, fin bases, and chest areas are red. A selection of strains is shown overleaf.

• **REMARK** Koi quickly outgrow the indoor aquarium, developing optimum size and best colours outdoors. Their bright colours stand out well against the darkness of the pond bottom. Koi are hearty consumers (especially of plants) and their environment should have an efficient filter system to deal with the waste. Attention to water quality is important.

powerful caudal fin

ASAGI KOI

red fin bases

matsuba scales with bluish tone

EAST ASIA

red cheeks

Diet Omnivorous	Tank levels All	Temperament

Family CYPRINDAE	Species *Cyprinus carpio*	Size Variable

A colourful assortment of young Koi in an aquarium

powerful
caudal fin

single body
colour

ORENJI OGON

TAISHO SANKE

"pine-cone"
scales

dark edges on
caudal fin

KIN MATSUBA

metallic
sheen

stronger
yellow
on head

Diet Omnivorous	Tank levels All	Temperament

• *clear caudal fin*

red blotches on white body

red-orange tint in fins

KOHAKU

• *red and black on white body*

• *black speckling on white body*

• *metallic yellow sheen*

SHIRO-BEKKO

Koi patterns are judged from above

OTHER COLDWATER FRESHWATER FISHES

M ANY FISHKEEPERS' COLDWATER interests centre around Goldfish and Koi, but there are other attractions in this field of the hobby. In spite of their relative obscurity, it is easy to keep different North American fishes such as shiners and sunfish, along with bitterlings and some species from Asia Sunfish carry characteristic "ear flaps" which are extensions to the gill-cover.

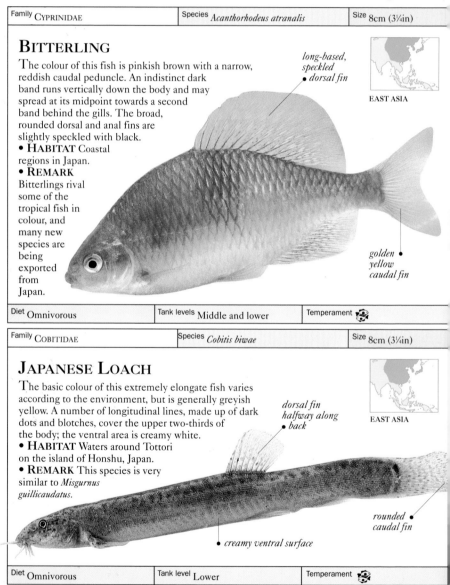

Family CYPRINIDAE	Species *Acanthorhodeus atranalis*	Size 8cm (3¼in)

BITTERLING

The colour of this fish is pinkish brown with a narrow, reddish caudal peduncle. An indistinct dark band runs vertically down the body and may spread at its midpoint towards a second band behind the gills. The broad, rounded dorsal and anal fins are slightly speckled with black.
• HABITAT Coastal regions in Japan.
• REMARK Bitterlings rival some of the tropical fish in colour, and many new species are being exported from Japan.

long-based, speckled
• *dorsal fin*

EAST ASIA

golden •
yellow
caudal fin

Diet Omnivorous	Tank levels Middle and lower	Temperament

Family COBITIDAE	Species *Cobitis biwae*	Size 8cm (3¼in)

JAPANESE LOACH

The basic colour of this extremely elongate fish varies according to the environment, but is generally greyish yellow. A number of longitudinal lines, made up of dark dots and blotches, cover the upper two-thirds of the body; the ventral area is creamy white.
• HABITAT Waters around Tottori on the island of Honshu, Japan.
• REMARK This species is very similar to *Misgurnus guillicaudatus*.

dorsal fin
halfway along
• *back*

EAST ASIA

rounded •
caudal fin

• *creamy ventral surface*

Diet Omnivorous	Tank level Lower	Temperament

Family GASTEROSTEIDAE	Species *Gasterosteus aculeatus*	Size 8cm (3¼in)

THREE-SPINE STICKLEBACK

Brown mottling covers the silvery body of this fish. There are three erectile spines in front of the dorsal fin, and bony plates along the flanks. The lower parts of the male's head, throat, and ventral region turn bright red during spawning.
• **HABITAT** Coastal waters of Europe; also of North America, northern Asia, and Algeria.
• **REMARK** The female deposits eggs in a tunnel nest, built by the male with plant matter. He fertilizes the eggs and guards them until they hatch. This fish requires live foods.

CENTRAL AND
W. EUROPE

*small, rounded
• caudal fin*

• bony plates

♀

*sharply •
pointed snout*

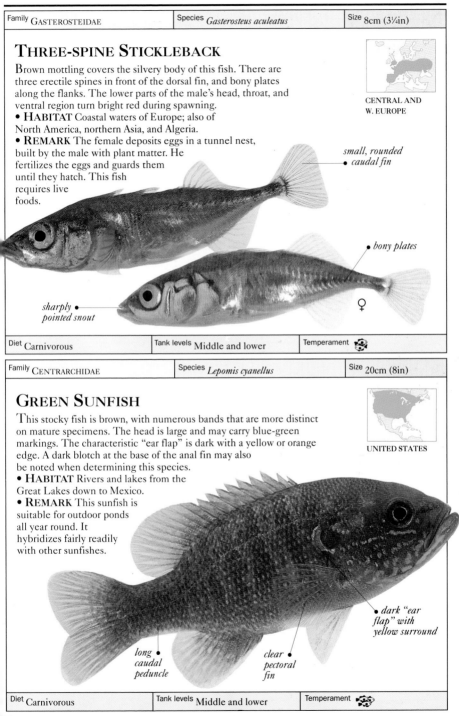

Diet Carnivorous	Tank levels Middle and lower	Temperament

Family CENTRARCHIDAE	Species *Lepomis cyanellus*	Size 20cm (8in)

GREEN SUNFISH

This stocky fish is brown, with numerous bands that are more distinct on mature specimens. The head is large and may carry blue-green markings. The characteristic "ear flap" is dark with a yellow or orange edge. A dark blotch at the base of the anal fin may also be noted when determining this species.
• **HABITAT** Rivers and lakes from the Great Lakes down to Mexico.
• **REMARK** This sunfish is suitable for outdoor ponds all year round. It hybridizes fairly readily with other sunfishes.

UNITED STATES

*dark "ear
flap" with
yellow surround*

*long •
caudal
peduncle*

*clear •
pectoral
fin*

Diet Carnivorous	Tank levels Middle and lower	Temperament

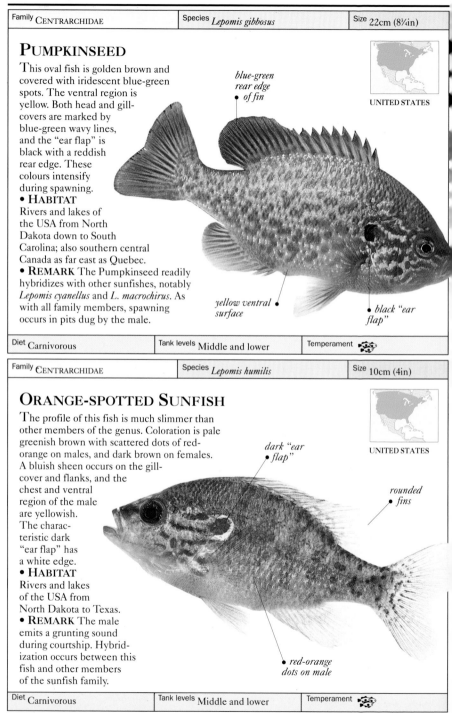

Family CENTRARCHIDAE	Species *Lepomis gibbosus*	Size 22cm (8¾in)

PUMPKINSEED

This oval fish is golden brown and covered with iridescent blue-green spots. The ventral region is yellow. Both head and gill-covers are marked by blue-green wavy lines, and the "ear flap" is black with a reddish rear edge. These colours intensify during spawning.
• **HABITAT**
Rivers and lakes of the USA from North Dakota down to South Carolina; also southern central Canada as far east as Quebec.
• **REMARK** The Pumpkinseed readily hybridizes with other sunfishes, notably *Lepomis cyanellus* and *L. macrochirus*. As with all family members, spawning occurs in pits dug by the male.

blue-green rear edge of fin

UNITED STATES

yellow ventral surface

black "ear flap"

Diet Carnivorous	Tank levels Middle and lower	Temperament

Family CENTRARCHIDAE	Species *Lepomis humilis*	Size 10cm (4in)

ORANGE-SPOTTED SUNFISH

The profile of this fish is much slimmer than other members of the genus. Coloration is pale greenish brown with scattered dots of red-orange on males, and dark brown on females. A bluish sheen occurs on the gill-cover and flanks, and the chest and ventral region of the male are yellowish. The charac-teristic dark "ear flap" has a white edge.
• **HABITAT**
Rivers and lakes of the USA from North Dakota to Texas.
• **REMARK** The male emits a grunting sound during courtship. Hybrid-ization occurs between this fish and other members of the sunfish family.

dark "ear flap"

UNITED STATES

rounded fins

red-orange dots on male

Diet Carnivorous	Tank levels Middle and lower	Temperament

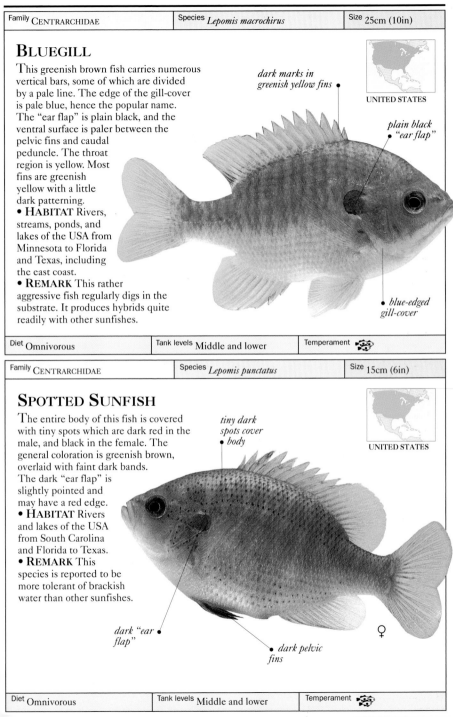

Family CENTRARCHIDAE	Species *Lepomis macrochirus*	Size 25cm (10in)

BLUEGILL

This greenish brown fish carries numerous vertical bars, some of which are divided by a pale line. The edge of the gill-cover is pale blue, hence the popular name. The "ear flap" is plain black, and the ventral surface is paler between the pelvic fins and caudal peduncle. The throat region is yellow. Most fins are greenish yellow with a little dark patterning.
• **HABITAT** Rivers, streams, ponds, and lakes of the USA from Minnesota to Florida and Texas, including the east coast.
• **REMARK** This rather aggressive fish regularly digs in the substrate. It produces hybrids quite readily with other sunfishes.

dark marks in greenish yellow fins •

UNITED STATES

plain black • "ear flap"

• blue-edged gill-cover

Diet Omnivorous	Tank levels Middle and lower	Temperament

Family CENTRARCHIDAE	Species *Lepomis punctatus*	Size 15cm (6in)

SPOTTED SUNFISH

The entire body of this fish is covered with tiny spots which are dark red in the male, and black in the female. The general coloration is greenish brown, overlaid with faint dark bands. The dark "ear flap" is slightly pointed and may have a red edge.
• **HABITAT** Rivers and lakes of the USA from South Carolina and Florida to Texas.
• **REMARK** This species is reported to be more tolerant of brackish water than other sunfishes.

tiny dark spots cover • body

UNITED STATES

dark "ear • flap"

• dark pelvic fins

♀

Diet Omnivorous	Tank levels Middle and lower	Temperament

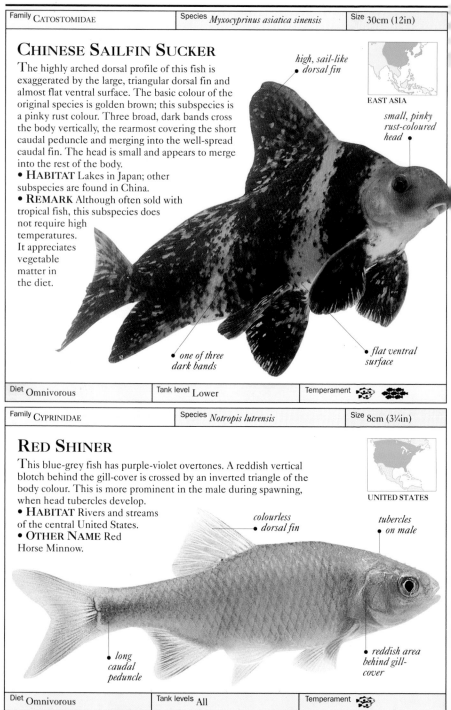

Family CATOSTOMIDAE	Species *Myxocyprinus asiatica sinensis*	Size 30cm (12in)

CHINESE SAILFIN SUCKER

The highly arched dorsal profile of this fish is
exaggerated by the large, triangular dorsal fin and
almost flat ventral surface. The basic colour of the
original species is golden brown; this subspecies is
a pinky rust colour. Three broad, dark bands cross
the body vertically, the rearmost covering the short
caudal peduncle and merging into the well-spread
caudal fin. The head is small and appears to merge
into the rest of the body.
• **HABITAT** Lakes in Japan; other
subspecies are found in China.
• **REMARK** Although often sold with
tropical fish, this subspecies does
not require high
temperatures.
It appreciates
vegetable
matter in
the diet.

*high, sail-like
dorsal fin*

EAST ASIA

*small, pinky
rust-coloured
head*

*one of three
dark bands*

*flat ventral
surface*

Diet Omnivorous	Tank level Lower	Temperament

Family CYPRINIDAE	Species *Notropis lutrensis*	Size 8cm (3¼in)

RED SHINER

This blue-grey fish has purple-violet overtones. A reddish vertical
blotch behind the gill-cover is crossed by an inverted triangle of the
body colour. This is more prominent in the male during spawning,
when head tubercles develop.
• **HABITAT** Rivers and streams
of the central United States.
• **OTHER NAME** Red
Horse Minnow.

UNITED STATES

*colourless
dorsal fin*

*tubercles
on male*

*long
caudal
peduncle*

*reddish area
behind gill-
cover*

Diet Omnivorous	Tank levels All	Temperament

| Family CYPRINIDAE | Species *Phoxinus phoxinus* | Size 14cm (5½in) |

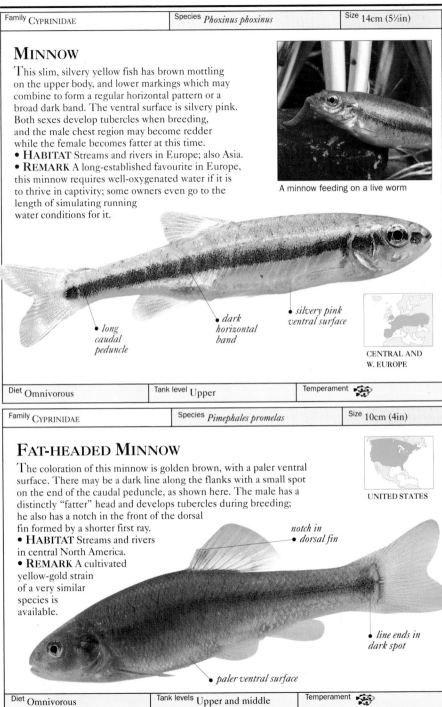

MINNOW

This slim, silvery yellow fish has brown mottling on the upper body, and lower markings which may combine to form a regular horizontal pattern or a broad dark band. The ventral surface is silvery pink. Both sexes develop tubercles when breeding, and the male chest region may become redder while the female becomes fatter at this time.
• **HABITAT** Streams and rivers in Europe; also Asia.
• **REMARK** A long-established favourite in Europe, this minnow requires well-oxygenated water if it is to thrive in captivity; some owners even go to the length of simulating running water conditions for it.

A minnow feeding on a live worm

• *long caudal peduncle*

• *dark horizontal band*

• *silvery pink ventral surface*

CENTRAL AND W. EUROPE

| Diet Omnivorous | Tank level Upper | Temperament |

| Family CYPRINIDAE | Species *Pimephales promelas* | Size 10cm (4in) |

FAT-HEADED MINNOW

The coloration of this minnow is golden brown, with a paler ventral surface. There may be a dark line along the flanks with a small spot on the end of the caudal peduncle, as shown here. The male has a distinctly "fatter" head and develops tubercles during breeding; he also has a notch in the front of the dorsal fin formed by a shorter first ray.
• **HABITAT** Streams and rivers in central North America.
• **REMARK** A cultivated yellow-gold strain of a very similar species is available.

UNITED STATES

notch in • *dorsal fin*

• *line ends in dark spot*

• *paler ventral surface*

| Diet Omnivorous | Tank levels Upper and middle | Temperament |

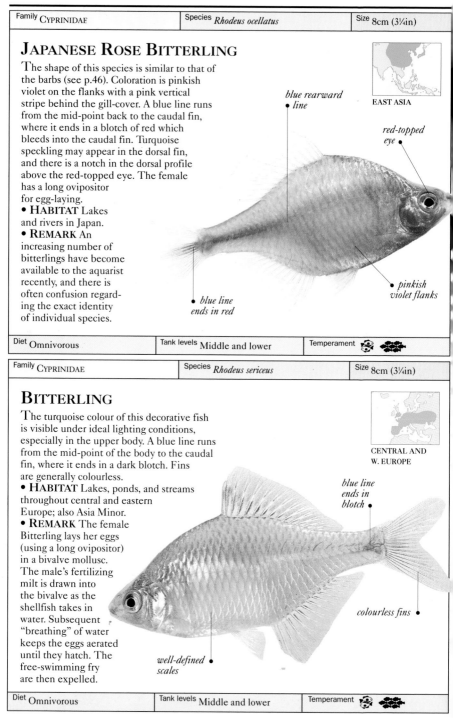

Family CYPRINIDAE	Species *Rhodeus ocellatus*	Size 8cm (3¼in)

JAPANESE ROSE BITTERLING

The shape of this species is similar to that of the barbs (see p.46). Coloration is pinkish violet on the flanks with a pink vertical stripe behind the gill-cover. A blue line runs from the mid-point back to the caudal fin, where it ends in a blotch of red which bleeds into the caudal fin. Turquoise speckling may appear in the dorsal fin, and there is a notch in the dorsal profile above the red-topped eye. The female has a long ovipositor for egg-laying.

• **HABITAT** Lakes and rivers in Japan.

• **REMARK** An increasing number of bitterlings have become available to the aquarist recently, and there is often confusion regarding the exact identity of individual species.

blue rearward • line

EAST ASIA

red-topped eye •

• pinkish violet flanks

• blue line ends in red

Diet Omnivorous	Tank levels Middle and lower	Temperament

Family CYPRINIDAE	Species *Rhodeus sericeus*	Size 8cm (3¼in)

BITTERLING

The turquoise colour of this decorative fish is visible under ideal lighting conditions, especially in the upper body. A blue line runs from the mid-point of the body to the caudal fin, where it ends in a dark blotch. Fins are generally colourless.

• **HABITAT** Lakes, ponds, and streams throughout central and eastern Europe; also Asia Minor.

• **REMARK** The female Bitterling lays her eggs (using a long ovipositor) in a bivalve mollusc. The male's fertilizing milt is drawn into the bivalve as the shellfish takes in water. Subsequent "breathing" of water keeps the eggs aerated until they hatch. The free-swimming fry are then expelled.

CENTRAL AND W. EUROPE

blue line ends in blotch •

colourless fins •

well-defined • scales

Diet Omnivorous	Tank levels Middle and lower	Temperament

| Family CYPRINIDAE | Species *Sarcocheilichthys sinensis* | Size 20cm (8in) |

OILY GUDGEON

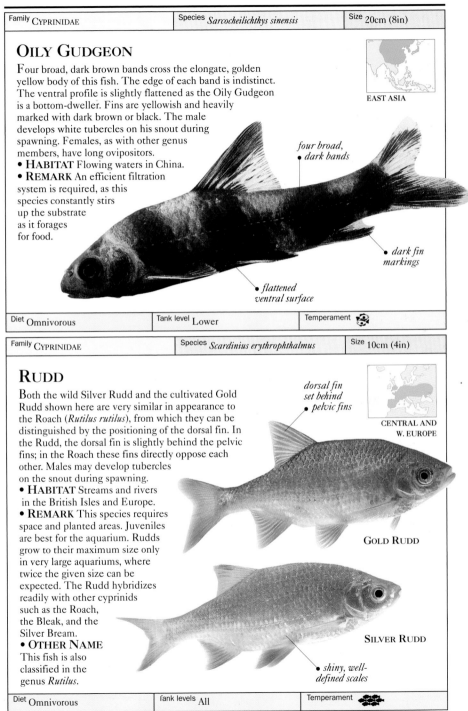

EAST ASIA

Four broad, dark brown bands cross the elongate, golden yellow body of this fish. The edge of each band is indistinct. The ventral profile is slightly flattened as the Oily Gudgeon is a bottom-dweller. Fins are yellowish and heavily marked with dark brown or black. The male develops white tubercles on his snout during spawning. Females, as with other genus members, have long ovipositors.
• **HABITAT** Flowing waters in China.
• **REMARK** An efficient filtration system is required, as this species constantly stirs up the substrate as it forages for food.

four broad, dark bands

dark fin markings

flattened ventral surface

| Diet Omnivorous | Tank level Lower | Temperament |

| Family CYPRINIDAE | Species *Scardinius erythrophthalmus* | Size 10cm (4in) |

RUDD

Both the wild Silver Rudd and the cultivated Gold Rudd shown here are very similar in appearance to the Roach (*Rutilus rutilus*), from which they can be distinguished by the positioning of the dorsal fin. In the Rudd, the dorsal fin is slightly behind the pelvic fins; in the Roach these fins directly oppose each other. Males may develop tubercles on the snout during spawning.
• **HABITAT** Streams and rivers in the British Isles and Europe.
• **REMARK** This species requires space and planted areas. Juveniles are best for the aquarium. Rudds grow to their maximum size only in very large aquariums, where twice the given size can be expected. The Rudd hybridizes readily with other cyprinids such as the Roach, the Bleak, and the Silver Bream.
• **OTHER NAME** This fish is also classified in the genus *Rutilus*.

dorsal fin set behind pelvic fins

CENTRAL AND W. EUROPE

GOLD RUDD

SILVER RUDD

shiny, well-defined scales

| Diet Omnivorous | Tank levels All | Temperament |

TROPICAL MARINE FISHES

ANEMONEFISHES

T HE FISHES in the family Poma-centridae that are referred to as "anemonefishes" derive the name from their relationship with sea anemones. The fish shelter within the tentacles of the anemones, protected from their poison by special skin mucus. Their ungainly swimming action has also earned them the name "clownfishes". These hardy fish are ideal starter fish.

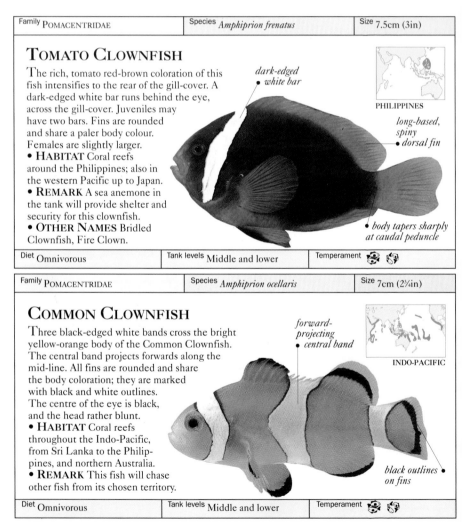

Family POMACENTRIDAE	Species *Amphiprion frenatus*	Size 7.5cm (3in)

TOMATO CLOWNFISH

The rich, tomato red-brown coloration of this fish intensifies to the rear of the gill-cover. A dark-edged white bar runs behind the eye, across the gill-cover. Juveniles may have two bars. Fins are rounded and share a paler body colour. Females are slightly larger.
• **HABITAT** Coral reefs around the Philippines; also in the western Pacific up to Japan.
• **REMARK** A sea anemone in the tank will provide shelter and security for this clownfish.
• **OTHER NAMES** Bridled Clownfish, Fire Clown.

dark-edged white bar

PHILIPPINES

long-based, spiny dorsal fin

body tapers sharply at caudal peduncle

Diet Omnivorous	Tank levels Middle and lower	Temperament

Family POMACENTRIDAE	Species *Amphiprion ocellaris*	Size 7cm (2¾in)

COMMON CLOWNFISH

Three black-edged white bands cross the bright yellow-orange body of the Common Clownfish. The central band projects forwards along the mid-line. All fins are rounded and share the body coloration; they are marked with black and white outlines. The centre of the eye is black, and the head rather blunt.
• **HABITAT** Coral reefs throughout the Indo-Pacific, from Sri Lanka to the Philip-pines, and northern Australia.
• **REMARK** This fish will chase other fish from its chosen territory.

forward-projecting central band

INDO-PACIFIC

black outlines on fins

Diet Omnivorous	Tank levels Middle and lower	Temperament

Family POMACENTRIDAE	Species *Amphiprion perideraion*	Size 7.5cm (3in)

PINK SKUNK CLOWNFISH

A narrow white stripe runs from the tip of this fish's snout, along the top of the delicate, golden pinkish body, to the end of the caudal peduncle. A narrower, dark-edged white band crosses the body vertically, covering the gill-cover. The dark eye has a gold rim around the pupil, and the rounded fins are a shade or two paler than the body. The dorsal and caudal fins of males have orange edges.
• **HABITAT** The Philippines; also coral reefs around Hong Kong, and from Thailand to northern Australia.
• **OTHER NAME** Salmon Clownfish.

Sea anemones provide valued shelter

white band along dorsal surface

rounded fins

PHILIPPINES

gold rim around eye

♀

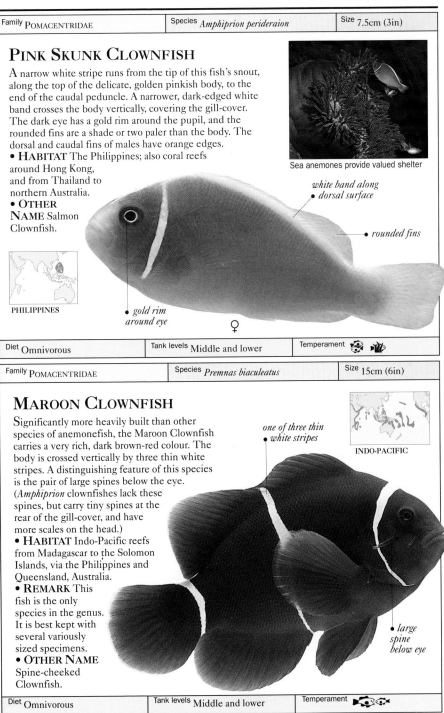

Diet Omnivorous	Tank levels Middle and lower	Temperament

Family POMACENTRIDAE	Species *Premnas biaculeatus*	Size 15cm (6in)

MAROON CLOWNFISH

Significantly more heavily built than other species of anemonefish, the Maroon Clownfish carries a very rich, dark brown-red colour. The body is crossed vertically by three thin white stripes. A distinguishing feature of this species is the pair of large spines below the eye. (*Amphiprion* clownfishes lack these spines, but carry tiny spines at the rear of the gill-cover, and have more scales on the head.)
• **HABITAT** Indo-Pacific reefs from Madagascar to the Solomon Islands, via the Philippines and Queensland, Australia.
• **REMARK** This fish is the only species in the genus. It is best kept with several variously sized specimens.
• **OTHER NAME** Spine-cheeked Clownfish.

one of three thin white stripes

INDO-PACIFIC

large spine below eye

Diet Omnivorous	Tank levels Middle and lower	Temperament

ANGELFISHES

T HE ANGELFISHES (family Poma-canthidae) can be distinguished from their relatives, the butterflyfishes, by the presence of a sharp spine on the rear of the gill-cover. There is also often a marked difference in coloration and patterning between juvenile and adult forms. Reproduction in angelfishes is by egg-scattering, although it is unlikely to occur in an average-sized aquarium, where fishes may be immature or where there is a lack of space. Members of the angelfish family are polyp feeders, consuming living corals and sponges, for example. These special dietary requirements are likely to exclude the more exotic species from most collections, but commercial foods that include required natural ingredients are increasingly available.

Family POMACANTHIDAE	Species *Centropyge argi*	Size 7.5cm (3in)

CHERUBFISH

The rich, dark blue body of this angelfish gives way to a yellow chest and head region. This region may vary from yellow to golden purple among subspecies from different locations. Long-based dorsal and anal fins share the body colour and have black streaks radiating out towards dark margins bordered by electric blue.
• **HABITAT** Coral reefs in the Caribbean; also the western Atlantic.
• **REMARK** This hardy fish does not require a large aquarium. Cherubfish tend to pair, so look for two fish that appear inseparable when purchasing.
• **OTHER NAMES** Purple Fireball, Pygmy Angelfish.

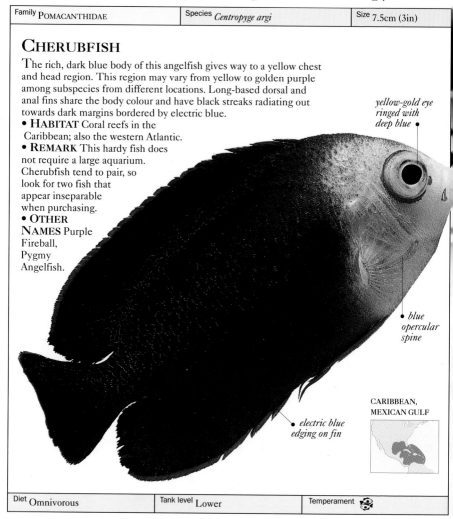

yellow-gold eye ringed with deep blue

• *blue opercular spine*

• *electric blue edging on fin*

CARIBBEAN, MEXICAN GULF

Diet Omnivorous	Tank level Lower	Temperament

| Family POMACANTHIDAE | Species *Centropyge bicolor* | Size 13cm (5in) |

BICOLOR CHERUB

The rear portion of this fish is deep blue and the front is bright yellow. The dark area is separated from the bright front portion and the caudal fin by narrow, vertical white bands. A small band of blue also crosses the forehead.

small blue band crosses forehead

INDO-PACIFIC

• **HABITAT** Coral reefs from the East Indies to Samoa; widespread in the western Pacific.
• **REMARK** The Bicolor Cherub is a harem spawner: a larger male breeds with several smaller females. Females will change sex to replace a single group male should he die or be withdrawn. This species is highly susceptible to copper poisoning.
• **OTHER NAMES** Blue and Gold Angelfish, Oriole Angelfish.

pale blue edge of anal fin

| Diet Omnivorous | Tank levels All | Temperament |

| Family POMACANTHIDAE | Species *Centropyge bispinosus* | Size 13cm (5in) |

CORAL BEAUTY

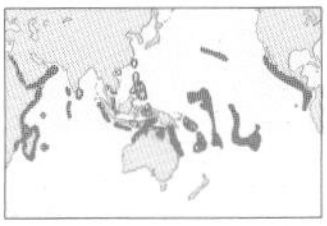

Generally, the colour of the Coral Beauty is a mix of red-gold and blue-purple, but coloration patterns can vary according to the environment. Vertical dark bars and speckles cover all tones. The dorsal, anal, and caudal fins carry dark patterns and pale blue edges. Pectoral fins are plain yellow, and pelvic fins are bright yellow-orange. Juveniles, as shown here, have more blue-purple colour than gold, but as the fish matures, the dark areas fade, leaving a brighter fish.

pale blue edges on dorsal fin

INDO-PACIFIC

• **HABITAT** Coral reefs of the East African coast, the East Indies, and Australasia to the mid-Pacific.
• **REMARK** This is a shy fish which needs plenty of retreats.
• **OTHER NAMES** Dusky Angelfish, Red and Blue Angelfish.

predominant blue-purple juvenile colour

| Diet Omnivorous | Tank levels All | Temperament |

| Family POMACANTHIDAE | Species *Centropyge eibli* | Size 15cm (6in) |

EIBL'S ANGELFISH

The majority of the body of this species is grey-gold, patterned by vertical, evenly spaced wavy lines. These lines are red-gold at the front of the body, but change to gold-black to the rear, where they eventually match the black portions of the dorsal fin, caudal peduncle, and caudal fin. Dorsal, anal, and caudal fins may have gold or pale blue edgings, depending on geographical location. Some gold flecks appear on both anal and dorsal fins. The eye is ringed with gold and blue, then gold again; the opercular spine is light blue.
• **HABITAT** Deep waters from the Maldive Islands to Australia, Indonesia, and the mid-Pacific.
• **REMARK** The juvenile Orange-gilled Surgeonfish (*Acanthurus pyroferus*) mimics the appearance and behaviour of this species.

wavy, • vertical lines

INDO-PACIFIC

• grey-gold body coloration

• yellow-edged anal fin

| Diet Omnivorous | Tank level Lower | Temperament |

| Family POMACANTHIDAE | Species *Centropyge loriculus* | Size 10cm (4in) |

FLAME ANGELFISH

The body of the Flame Angelfish, including most of the dorsal and anal fins, is an intense red-orange colour, while the area from behind the gills to the caudal peduncle, and the caudal fin itself, is golden yellow. There are four to five dark vertical bars partially crossing the golden area. The outer edges of the dorsal and anal fins are violet, and these broaden out and combine with black stripes on the rear areas of these two fins. Pectoral and pelvic fins and the opercular spine are red-orange.
• **HABITAT** Coral reefs of the western and central Pacific.
• **REMARK** This fish is hardy and easily managed, although it can be territorial. Keep it with larger fishes and provide plenty of retreats.

dark-coloured edges • of dorsal fin

PACIFIC OCEAN

• intense, flame-orange coloration

| Diet Omnivorous | Tank level Lower | Temperament |

Family POMACANTHIDAE	Species *Euxiphipops navarchus*	Size 25cm (10in)

BLUE-GIRDLED ANGELFISH

A broad saddle of yellow, dotted with blue, extends down over the middle third of the body. At either end of the saddle, separated by pale blue bands, there are two dark blue areas with lighter blue speckles. The rearmost area covers the caudal peduncle and anal fin, and a portion of the yellow dorsal fin; the forward portion makes an inverted triangle up to the head region. The lower part of the head and the opercular spine are a pale, creamy colour, and all the fins, excluding the pectoral fins, are edged with pale blue. Juveniles are dark blue with white vertical stripes.
• **HABITAT** Coral reefs of the Indo-Pacific, often solitary or in pairs.
• **REMARK** A popular if expensive species, the Blue-girdled Angelfish requires plenty of space and hiding places.

yellow saddle dotted with blue

INDO-PACIFIC

blue mouth

fins edged with pale blue

Diet Omnivorous	Tank levels Middle and lower	Temperament

Family POMACANTHIDAE	Species *Holacanthus ciliaris*	Size 45cm (17½in)

QUEEN ANGELFISH

The whole of this fish, be it juvenile or adult, is outlined in bright blue, with the exception of the plain yellow caudal fin. The overall ground colour can be changeable, depending on lighting conditions (and hybridization between similar species). This specimen is maturing. The adult fish has a golden brown to bright yellow-green body and well-defined scales. The rear edge of the gills and the base of the pectoral fins are bright blue. Small spines protect the gill-cover. The anal and dorsal fins are extremely well produced and sweep back towards the caudal fin.
• **HABITAT** Western Atlantic and the Caribbean, often in pairs over coral reefs.
• **REMARK** Native waters are of a higher specific gravity, so acclimatize this fish to a large aquarium carefully.

opercular spine

well-defined scales

WESTERN ATLANTIC

fins swept back

Diet Omnivorous	Tank levels Middle and lower	Temperament

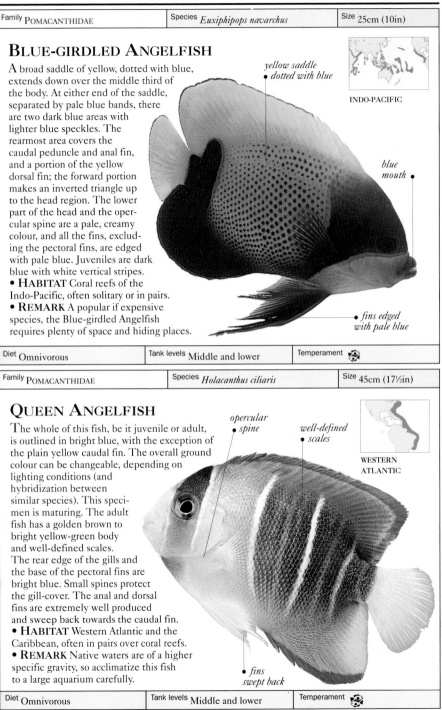

| Family POMACANTHIDAE | Species *Holacanthus tricolor* | Size 60cm (24in) |

ROCK BEAUTY

Juvenile Rock Beauties share the same coloration as the adult, but in different proportions: the juvenile is plain yellow, with a blue-edged, dark spot on the flanks below the rear of the dorsal fin. In the adult, this spot covers three-quarters of the body; only the head, chest, and nape areas remain yellow. The dark dorsal and anal fins are outlined in yellow-red, and the pectoral, pelvic, and caudal fins are yellow.
• **HABITAT** Coral reefs in the Caribbean and environs.
• **REMARK** This angelfish is aggressive towards its own kind in the aquarium, and should not be kept as a pair or in a group. Offer foods with a high natural sponge content when possible.

yellow-red fin outline

WESTERN ATLANTIC

dark spot covers most of adult body

blue shading around eye

| Diet Omnivorous | Tank level Lower | Temperament |

| Family POMACANTHIDAE | Species *Holacanthus trimaculatus* | Size 25cm (10in) |

THREE SPOT ANGELFISH

The major fins of this species are rounded, rather than pointed like those of other angelfish, accentuating the oval shape. The popular name refers to the three body spots: on the forehead and, less clearly, behind each gill-cover. Pectoral, pelvic, dorsal, and caudal fins share the body colour, but the outer arc of the anal fin is black; the portion nearest the body is a slightly paler yellow.
• **HABITAT** Widespread on coral reefs from East Africa to the Philippines.
• **REMARK** This fish requires high-quality water. A variety of foods is also needed, including greens.
• **OTHER NAME** Also classified as a member of the genus *Apolemichthys*.

spot on forehead

INDO-PACIFIC

blue mouth

black section of anal fin

| Diet Omnivorous | Tank level Lower | Temperament |

| Family POMACANTHIDAE | Species *Pomacanthus annularis* | Size 40cm (16in) |

BLUE RING ANGELFISH

Juveniles have a dark blue body with white, alternate, thick and thin vertical lines. The caudal fin is clear but may have pale spots. This colouring corresponds to that of the juvenile *Pomacanthus chrysurus*, except the latter has a yellow caudal fin. The adult is dark golden brown with royal blue lines; the common name describes the blue marking on the shoulder.
• **HABITAT** Sri Lanka to the Pacific Solomon Islands.
• **REMARK** Supply with algae.

blue ring on
• shoulder

INDO-PACIFIC

JUVENILE

• *lines curve into anal fin*

ADULT

yellow • edging on caudal fin

| Diet Mainly herbivorous | Tank level Lower | Temperament |

| Family POMACANTHIDAE | Species *Pomacanthus maculosus* | Size 40cm (16in) |

HALF MOON ANGELFISH

The juveniles of this species carry the typical blue and white angelfish markings. They take on the yellow "half moon" crescent shape of the adult as the white lines fade with maturity. The adult is purple-grey with dark speckling, especially to the rear of the head and above the gill-covers. The yellow crescent shape crosses the mid-point of the body. Dorsal and anal fins elongate with age, and often have extreme filaments.
• **HABITAT** Coral reefs of the Red Sea and through-out the western Indian Ocean.
• **OTHER NAMES** Purple Moon Angelfish, Red Sea Halfmoon Angelfish, Sea-bride, Yellowbar Angelfish.

yellow "half moon" • marking

INDIAN OCEAN

• *clear pectoral fin*

| Diet Mainly herbivorous | Tank level Lower | Temperament |

Family POMACANTHIDAE	Species *Pomacanthus imperator*	Size 30cm (12in)

EMPEROR ANGELFISH

The juvenile shown here is dark blue with concentric, slightly oval, white markings. In front of the gill-cover the lines are almost vertical with a slight backward sweep. Anal, dorsal, and caudal fins are marked with dark flecks. The adult Emperor Angel (below) has a plain yellow caudal fin and a yellow body crossed diagonally by pale blue-grey lines. These extend into the dorsal fin, which becomes pointed in mature fish. The anal fin, however, retains the dark blue of the juvenile. The mouth is pinky yellow, edged with pale blue (a colour repeated in the opercular spine). The pelvic fins carry some red colour among their basic blue.
• **HABITAT** Indo-Pacific from the East African coast (including the Red Sea) to Hawaii, and Australia.
• **REMARK** The relatively rare Emperor Angelfish can grow to an impressive size, and so requires a large aquarium. It prefers living with other large species.

young fish is dark blue with white markings

INDO-PACIFIC

JUVENILE

ADULT

eye masked by dark band

diagonal yellow lines on adult

plain yellow caudal fin

Diet Omnivorous	Tank levels Middle and lower	Temperament

Family POMACANTHIDAE	Species *Pomacanthus paru*	Size 30cm (12in)

FRENCH ANGELFISH

Juveniles are black with four or five striking yellow vertical stripes. As these fish approach adulthood, the yellow bands fade and the fish turns dark grey. At the same time, the major part of the body to the rear of the gill-covers becomes speckled. Limited speckling extends into the anal fin but more appears on the dorsal fin (which often has a pale-coloured tip).
• **HABITAT** Western Atlantic from Florida and the Caribbean to Brazil.
• **REMARK** Juveniles may quarrel among themselves in the aquarium. The adult is similar to the Grey Angelfish (*Pomacanthus arcuatus*), whose speckles are brighter and which has a yellow patch at the base of each pectoral fin.

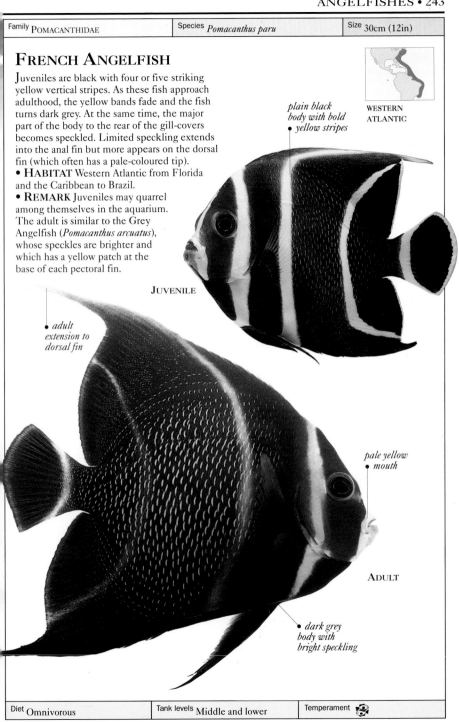

plain black body with bold • yellow stripes

WESTERN ATLANTIC

JUVENILE

• adult extension to dorsal fin

pale yellow • mouth

ADULT

• dark grey body with bright speckling

Diet Omnivorous	Tank levels Middle and lower	Temperament

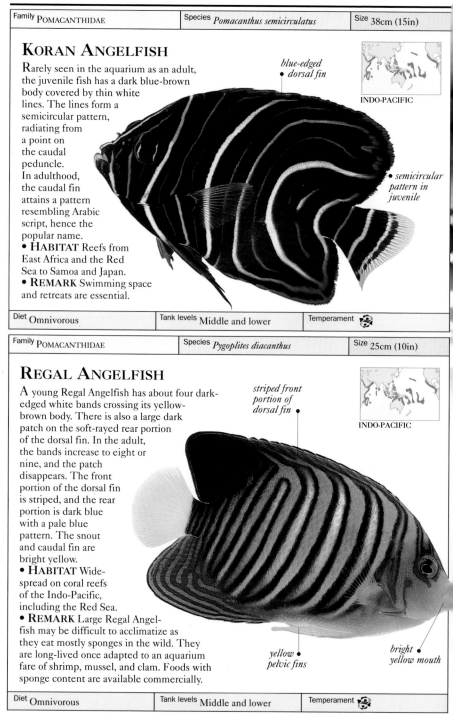

Family POMACANTHIDAE	Species *Pomacanthus semicirculatus*	Size 38cm (15in)

KORAN ANGELFISH

Rarely seen in the aquarium as an adult, the juvenile fish has a dark blue-brown body covered by thin white lines. The lines form a semicircular pattern, radiating from a point on the caudal peduncle. In adulthood, the caudal fin attains a pattern resembling Arabic script, hence the popular name.
• HABITAT Reefs from East Africa and the Red Sea to Samoa and Japan.
• REMARK Swimming space and retreats are essential.

blue-edged • dorsal fin

INDO-PACIFIC

• semicircular pattern in juvenile

Diet Omnivorous	Tank levels Middle and lower	Temperament

Family POMACANTHIDAE	Species *Pygoplites diacanthus*	Size 25cm (10in)

REGAL ANGELFISH

A young Regal Angelfish has about four dark-edged white bands crossing its yellow-brown body. There is also a large dark patch on the soft-rayed rear portion of the dorsal fin. In the adult, the bands increase to eight or nine, and the patch disappears. The front portion of the dorsal fin is striped, and the rear portion is dark blue with a pale blue pattern. The snout and caudal fin are bright yellow.
• HABITAT Widespread on coral reefs of the Indo-Pacific, including the Red Sea.
• REMARK Large Regal Angelfish may be difficult to acclimatize as they eat mostly sponges in the wild. They are long-lived once adapted to an aquarium fare of shrimp, mussel, and clam. Foods with sponge content are available commercially.

striped front portion of dorsal fin •

INDO-PACIFIC

yellow • pelvic fins

bright • yellow mouth

Diet Omnivorous	Tank levels Middle and lower	Temperament

BUTTERFLYFISHES

MEMBERS OF THE butterflyfish family (Chaetodontidae) share the dazzling colours and patterns of the angelfishes. Unless they are comfortable in the aquarium, however, they may hide from suspected dangers. Unfortunately, it is the more colourful varieties that often adjust poorly to captivity, although retreats and hideaways will aid acclimatization. Butterflyfishes prefer to retreat among coral at night, when they may change their patterns. These shy fishes may also lose out to other species at feeding time, so worms, dried foods, and algae should be carefully offered.

Family CHAETODONTIDAE	Species *Chaetodon auriga*	Size 20cm (8in)

THREADFIN BUTTERFLYFISH

Three-quarters of this fish is white, overlaid with two areas of opposing dark, diagonal lines. The rear, uppermost part of the body is darker where the diagonal bands seem to merge together. A dark vertical bar crosses the head, passing through the eye, and yellow lines cross the snout. The background colour of the spiky dorsal fin changes from white to yellow halfway back; the rear portion is plain yellow with an eye-spot in the upper rear corner. Juveniles have the eye-spot but paler colouring.

- **HABITAT** A very common species, widespread throughout reefs of the Indo-Pacific.
- **REMARK** This Butterflyfish is a popular choice and readily obtainable.

INDO-PACIFIC

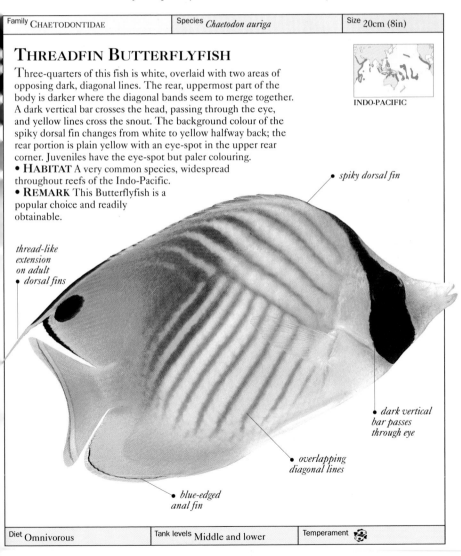

spiky dorsal fin

thread-like extension on adult dorsal fins

dark vertical bar passes through eye

overlapping diagonal lines

blue-edged anal fin

Diet Omnivorous	Tank levels Middle and lower	Temperament

Family CHAETODONTIDAE	Species *Chaetodon lunula*	Size 20cm (8in)

RACCOON BUTTERFLYFISH

The colour of this fish, including the fins, is yellow with dark diagonal lines crossing the body upwards from the pectoral fins. A dark saddle, bordered in front by a thin white line, and behind by a broad white band, crosses the forehead to mask each eye, giving the fish its raccoon-like appearance. There are distinct spines at the front of the dorsal and anal fins. Juveniles are paler ahead of the eye bar and have an eye-spot on the dorsal fin. These characteristics change with adulthood; the eye-spot fades while the pale area deepens to yellow.
• **HABITAT** Shallow waters from East Africa to Australia and Hawaii.
• **REMARK** *Chaetodon fasciatus,* a similar species, inhabits the Red Sea, but lacks the dark area on the caudal peduncle.

dark diagonal lines • cross the body

INDO-PACIFIC

• distinct spines in fin

"raccoon" mask crosses forehead

Diet Carnivorous	Tank levels Middle and lower	Temperament

Family CHAETODONTIDAE	Species *Chaetodon quadrimaculatus*	Size 20cm (8in)

HAWAIIAN TEARDROP BUTTERFLYFISH

The coloration is distinctly divided in two: the dark brown dorsal area shades to golden yellow midway down the body. Two white patches appear within the brown area below the dorsal fin, which has a brown base. Like the anal fin, it has a blue line along its mid-section. Fins are a golden reddish colour. The caudal peduncle is brown, with red at the base of the caudal fin. The eye is crossed by a dark-bordered, orange-red bar with a white-yellow bar behind it.
• **HABITAT** Coral reefs around Hawaii.
• **REMARK** This fish is very similar in appearance to the Teardrop Butterflyfish (*Chaetodon unimaculatus*), but it is not as common. A limited natural range, such as that of the Hawaiian Teardrop, often indicates a specialist feeder which, in turn, means problems in aquarium acclimatization. This may well be one of those species which is best left in its natural reef habitat until suitable foods can be commercially produced.

one of two dorsal white patches •

PACIFIC OCEAN

brown caudal • peduncle

Diet Carnivorous	Tank levels Middle and lower	Temperament

| Family CHAETODONTIDAE | Species *Chaetodon unimaculatus* | Size 20cm (8in) |

TEARDROP BUTTERFLYFISH

The body of this butterflyfish is yellow with a slightly paler area between the eye and the centre of the flanks. Yellow, obtuse-angled chevron patterning crosses the pale area. Midway along the body there is a large, dark "teardrop" marking. As the fish matures, the mark loses definition, and often becomes no more than a circular blob. A dark vertical bar passes through the eye; another crosses the caudal peduncle and the rear edges of the yellow anal and dorsal fins, bordered on each side by a narrow white margin. Juveniles are paler with a clearer teardrop.
• **HABITAT** Widespread from the Red Sea to Hawaii.
• **REMARK** This species adapts well to captivity. Offer plenty of live, worm-type foods or good quality frozen fish foods.

"teardrop"
• *marking*

INDO-PACIFIC

| Diet Carnivorous | Tank levels Middle and lower | Temperament |

| Family CHAETODONTIDAE | Species *Chaetodon decussatus* | Size 20cm (8in) |

BLACK-FINNED BUTTERFLYFISH

The pale cream body is overlaid in two areas with dark diagonal lines: one group rises from behind the head up to the dorsal region; the other runs from the first set of lines towards the rear of the anal fin. A dark vertical bar crosses the head and passes through the eye. The rear part of the body and the long-based anal and dorsal fins are mostly black. The yellow caudal fin has a black bar mid-way and a white edge. Pectoral fins are white.
• **HABITAT** A common species which is widespread in the Indo-Pacific.
• **REMARK** The Black-finned Butterflyfish is readily available, and is an ideal fish for the beginner.

two areas of dark
• *diagonal lines*

INDO-PACIFIC

dark bar through
• *eye*

• *yellow-edged anal fin*

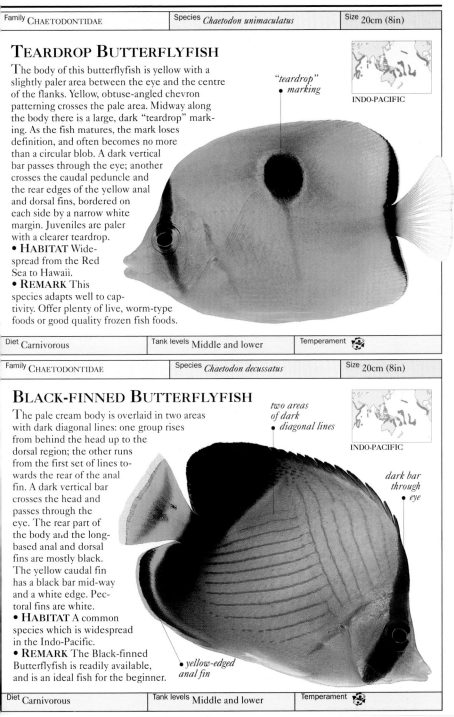

| Diet Carnivorous | Tank levels Middle and lower | Temperament |

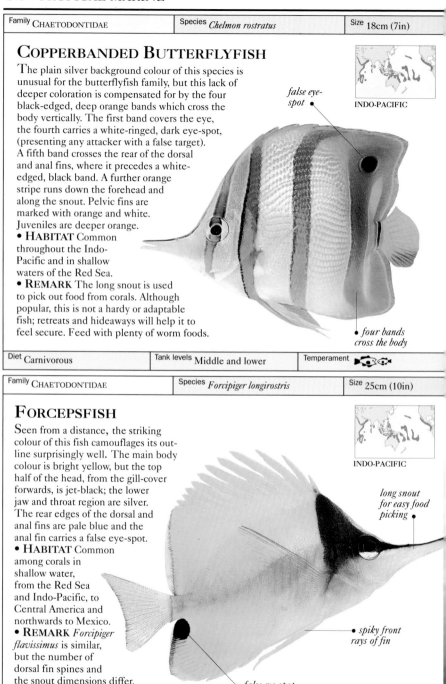

Family CHAETODONTIDAE	Species *Chelmon rostratus*	Size 18cm (7in)

COPPERBANDED BUTTERFLYFISH

The plain silver background colour of this species is unusual for the butterflyfish family, but this lack of deeper coloration is compensated for by the four black-edged, deep orange bands which cross the body vertically. The first band covers the eye, the fourth carries a white-ringed, dark eye-spot, (presenting any attacker with a false target). A fifth band crosses the rear of the dorsal and anal fins, where it precedes a white-edged, black band. A further orange stripe runs down the forehead and along the snout. Pelvic fins are marked with orange and white. Juveniles are deeper orange.
• **HABITAT** Common throughout the Indo-Pacific and in shallow waters of the Red Sea.
• **REMARK** The long snout is used to pick out food from corals. Although popular, this is not a hardy or adaptable fish; retreats and hideaways will help it to feel secure. Feed with plenty of worm foods.

false eye-spot

INDO-PACIFIC

four bands cross the body

Diet Carnivorous	Tank levels Middle and lower	Temperament

Family CHAETODONTIDAE	Species *Forcipiger longirostris*	Size 25cm (10in)

FORCEPSFISH

Seen from a distance, the striking colour of this fish camouflages its out-line surprisingly well. The main body colour is bright yellow, but the top half of the head, from the gill-cover forwards, is jet-black; the lower jaw and throat region are silver. The rear edges of the dorsal and anal fins are pale blue and the anal fin carries a false eye-spot.
• **HABITAT** Common among corals in shallow water, from the Red Sea and Indo-Pacific, to Central America and northwards to Mexico.
• **REMARK** *Forcipiger flavissimus* is similar, but the number of dorsal fin spines and the snout dimensions differ.

INDO-PACIFIC

long snout for easy food picking

spiky front rays of fin

false eye-spot

Diet Carnivorous	Tank levels Middle and lower	Temperament

Family CHAETODONTIDAE	Species *Heniochus acuminatus*	Size 18cm (7in)

WIMPLEFISH

The dorsal and anal fins make this a "high" rather than an elongate fish, in contrast with other members of this group. The body is white with two black bands sloping rearwards. The long, trailing top section of the dorsal fin, which resembles a medieval wimple, is white, as is the corresponding section of the anal fin. The soft-rayed rear part of the dorsal fin is bright yellow, a colour shared with the caudal fin. There may be small, horny protuberances above the eyes. Juveniles lack the long extension to the dorsal fin.

• **HABITAT** Red Sea and throughout the Indo-Pacific.

• **REMARK** A large aquarium is needed to keep several Wimplefish as one leader may bully the rest. Other species in the genus are seldom imported.

• **OTHER NAMES** Poor Man's Moorish Idol, Pennant Fish.

INDO-PACIFIC

long, trailing dorsal fin

black bands slope rearwards across the body

black "saddle" crosses eye

bright yellow caudal fin

Diet Omnivorous	Tank levels Middle and lower	Temperament

DAMSELFISHES

T HE MEMBERS of the family Pomacentridae in this section share the same reef habitat as anemonefishes, but, not having the same immunity to sea anemones, most do not venture into the venomous tentacles. Quarrels may occur between damselfishes unless space and aquarium retreats are provided. There is often confusion over the scientific names of these fish, particularly amongst the bright blue species.

Family POMACENTRIDAE	Species *Abudefduf oxyodon*	Size 8cm (3¼in)

BLACK NEON DAMSELFISH

The body of this damselfish is slightly more elongate than others in the family. Juvenile coloration is deep blue-black with a paler throat region. A single white and yellow bar crosses the body vertically just ahead of the dorsal fin. Electric blue lines also appear, particularly on the head, but these fade with age. The adult is a dark, dull grey.
• **HABITAT** Coral reefs of the western Pacific Ocean.
• **OTHER NAMES** This fish has recently been classified in the *Paraglyphidodon* genus. It is also known as the Blue-banded Sergeant Major.

electric blue lines fade with age

PACIFIC OCEAN

deep blue-black juvenile coloration

Diet Omnivorous	Tank levels Middle and lower	Temperament

Family POMACENTRIDAE	Species *Abudefduf saxatilis*	Size 18cm (7in)

SERGEANT MAJOR

This deep-bodied fish has a white or yellow background colour. Five or six blue bands cross the body vertically; the sixth band may be visible on the caudal peduncle. All fins are plain. Juveniles are brighter.
• **HABITAT** Coral reefs in the Indo-Pacific and Caribbean. Juveniles are also found in drifting seaweed in the Gulf Stream off the Atlantic coast.
• **REMARK** This shoaling species is territorial when spawning. No more than two or three Sergeant Majors should be kept together in a tank.

vertical dark bands

INDO-PACIFIC

well-defined scales

Diet Omnivorous	Tank levels Upper and middle	Temperament

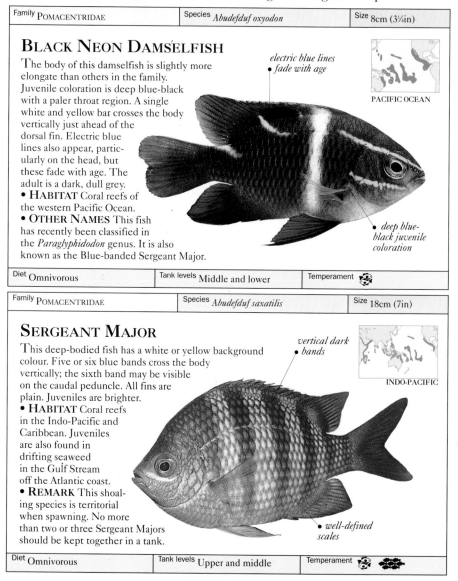

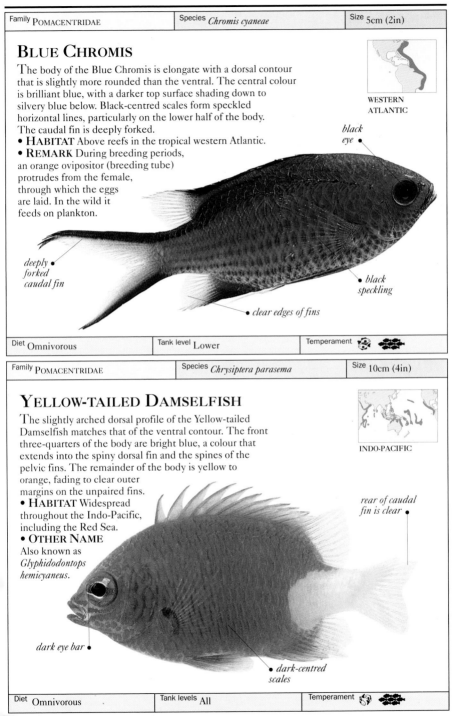

| Family POMACENTRIDAE | Species *Chromis cyaneae* | Size 5cm (2in) |

BLUE CHROMIS

The body of the Blue Chromis is elongate with a dorsal contour that is slightly more rounded than the ventral. The central colour is brilliant blue, with a darker top surface shading down to silvery blue below. Black-centred scales form speckled horizontal lines, particularly on the lower half of the body. The caudal fin is deeply forked.
• **HABITAT** Above reefs in the tropical western Atlantic.
• **REMARK** During breeding periods, an orange ovipositor (breeding tube) protrudes from the female, through which the eggs are laid. In the wild it feeds on plankton.

WESTERN
ATLANTIC

*black
eye*

*deeply
forked
caudal fin*

*black
speckling*

clear edges of fins

| Diet Omnivorous | Tank level Lower | Temperament |

| Family POMACENTRIDAE | Species *Chrysiptera parasema* | Size 10cm (4in) |

YELLOW-TAILED DAMSELFISH

The slightly arched dorsal profile of the Yellow-tailed Damselfish matches that of the ventral contour. The front three-quarters of the body are bright blue, a colour that extends into the spiny dorsal fin and the spines of the pelvic fins. The remainder of the body is yellow to orange, fading to clear outer margins on the unpaired fins.
• **HABITAT** Widespread throughout the Indo-Pacific, including the Red Sea.
• **OTHER NAME** Also known as *Glyphidodontops hemicyaneus*.

INDO-PACIFIC

*rear of caudal
fin is clear*

dark eye bar

*dark-centred
scales*

| Diet Omnivorous | Tank levels All | Temperament |

Family POMACENTRIDAE	Species *Dascyllus aruanus*	Size 8cm (3¼in)

HUMBUG DAMSELFISH

This damselfish is stocky with a steeply rising forehead. Three black stripes cross the white body. The first stripe runs from the mouth into the rays of the dorsal fin; the next includes the pelvic fins and crosses the body at a slight angle. The tail is clear, distinguishing this fish from the Black-tailed Humbug (opposite), which has a black caudal fin.
• **HABITAT** Among corals in the Indo-Pacific, including the Red Sea but not Hawaii.
• **REMARK** A commonly available, hardy species; ideal for the beginner.
• **OTHER NAMES** White-tailed Damselfish, Three-striped Damselfish.

one of three black stripes •

INDO-PACIFIC

• *white rear of caudal peduncle*

Diet Omnivorous	Tank levels All	Temperament

Family POMACENTRIDAE	Species *Dascyllus carneus*	Size 8cm (3¼in)

CLOUDY DAMSELFISH

The shape of the Cloudy Damselfish is typical of the family, but its colours are not as strong as those of many other damselfishes. An indistinct black stripe separates the darker, brown head area from the paler, creamy main body. Both head and body are spotted with blue. On some specimens a white blotch may appear on the dorsal surface. The caudal fin and rear edge of the otherwise dark dorsal fin are clear; all other fins are black.
• **HABITAT** Coral heads in the Indian Ocean and western Pacific Ocean.
• **REMARK** This fish is generally peaceful, but may quarrel with its own kind.

indistinct dark stripe •

INDO-PACIFIC

clear caudal fin •

• *blue spots over body*

Diet Carnivorous	Tank levels All	Temperament

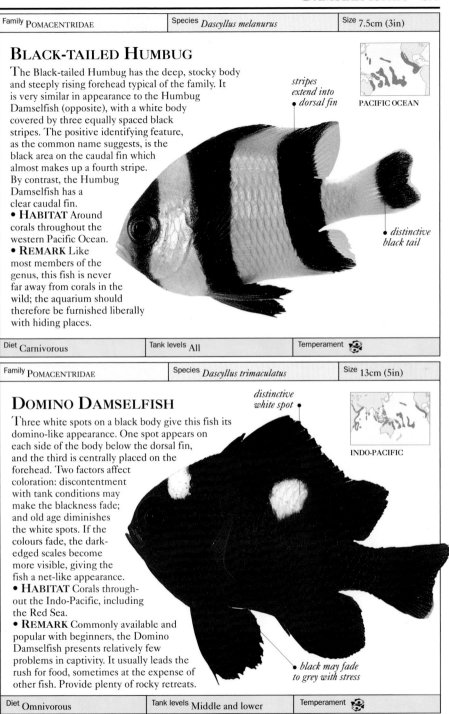

| Family POMACENTRIDAE | Species *Dascyllus melanurus* | Size 7.5cm (3in) |

BLACK-TAILED HUMBUG

The Black-tailed Humbug has the deep, stocky body
and steeply rising forehead typical of the family. It
is very similar in appearance to the Humbug
Damselfish (opposite), with a white body
covered by three equally spaced black
stripes. The positive identifying feature,
as the common name suggests, is the
black area on the caudal fin which
almost makes up a fourth stripe.
By contrast, the Humbug
Damselfish has a
clear caudal fin.
• **HABITAT** Around
corals throughout the
western Pacific Ocean.
• **REMARK** Like
most members of the
genus, this fish is never
far away from corals in the
wild; the aquarium should
therefore be furnished liberally
with hiding places.

*stripes
extend into
• dorsal fin*

PACIFIC OCEAN

*• distinctive
black tail*

| Diet Carnivorous | Tank levels All | Temperament |

| Family POMACENTRIDAE | Species *Dascyllus trimaculatus* | Size 13cm (5in) |

DOMINO DAMSELFISH

*distinctive
white spot •*

Three white spots on a black body give this fish its
domino-like appearance. One spot appears on
each side of the body below the dorsal fin,
and the third is centrally placed on the
forehead. Two factors affect
coloration: discontentment
with tank conditions may
make the blackness fade;
and old age diminishes
the white spots. If the
colours fade, the dark-
edged scales become
more visible, giving the
fish a net-like appearance.
• **HABITAT** Corals throughout the Indo-Pacific, including
the Red Sea.
• **REMARK** Commonly available and
popular with beginners, the Domino
Damselfish presents relatively few
problems in captivity. It usually leads the
rush for food, sometimes at the expense of
other fish. Provide plenty of rocky retreats.

INDO-PACIFIC

*• black may fade
to grey with stress*

| Diet Omnivorous | Tank levels Middle and lower | Temperament |

Family POMACENTRIDAE	Species *Microspathodon chrysurus*	Size 20cm (8in)

JEWEL FISH

The juvenile Jewel Fish is dark blue-black with bright blue spots. The dorsal, anal, and pelvic fins are dark with light blue edging, and the caudal fin is colourless. Adults lose the bright blue spots and develop a vivid yellow caudal fin.
• **HABITAT** Stands of fire coral in the Caribbean; also the tropical western Atlantic.
• **REMARK** Jewel Fish are unaffected by the stinging cells of fire coral, which they inhabit out of the reach of predators.

A Jewel Fish patrols a bed of fire coral

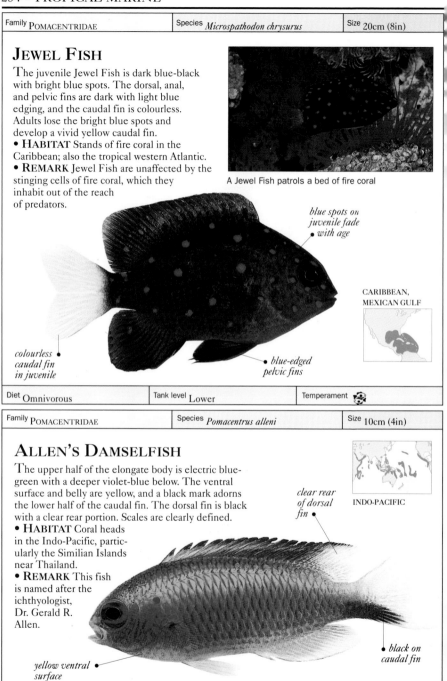

blue spots on
juvenile fade
• with age

CARIBBEAN,
MEXICAN GULF

colourless •
caudal fin
in juvenile

• blue-edged
pelvic fins

Diet Omnivorous	Tank level Lower	Temperament

Family POMACENTRIDAE	Species *Pomacentrus alleni*	Size 10cm (4in)

ALLEN'S DAMSELFISH

The upper half of the elongate body is electric blue-green with a deeper violet-blue below. The ventral surface and belly are yellow, and a black mark adorns the lower half of the caudal fin. The dorsal fin is black with a clear rear portion. Scales are clearly defined.
• **HABITAT** Coral heads in the Indo-Pacific, particularly the Similian Islands near Thailand.
• **REMARK** This fish is named after the ichthyologist, Dr. Gerald R. Allen.

clear rear
of dorsal
fin •

INDO-PACIFIC

• black on
caudal fin

yellow ventral •
surface

Diet Omnivorous	Tank levels All	Temperament

Family POMACENTRIDAE	Species *Pomacentrus caeruleus*	Size 10cm (4in)

BLUE DEVIL

The elongate body of this striking species is brilliant blue with a black mark at the rear of the long-based dorsal fin. A black line passes from the snout through the eye. Each scale has a central yellow-white mark.
• **HABITAT** Widespread throughout the Indo-Pacific.
• **REMARK** Positive identification is often confused as the dark markings may vary, and some specimens develop more yellow in later life.
• **OTHER NAMES** Also classified in the *Eupomacentrus* and *Glyphidodontops* genera.

INDO-PACIFIC

black line through eye •

clear caudal fin •

trailing pelvic fins •

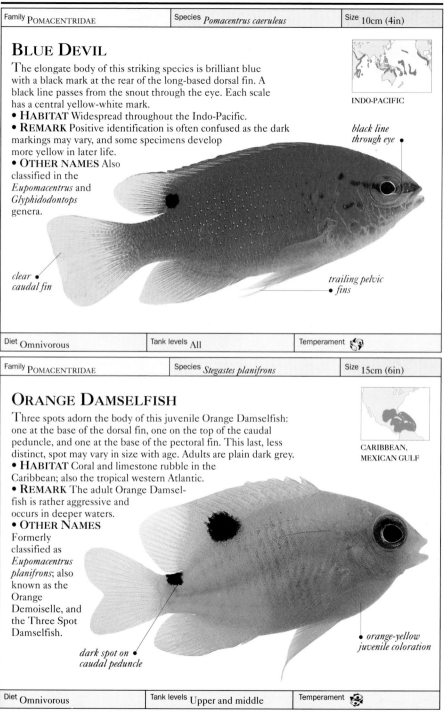

Diet Omnivorous	Tank levels All	Temperament

Family POMACENTRIDAE	Species *Stegastes planifrons*	Size 15cm (6in)

ORANGE DAMSELFISH

Three spots adorn the body of this juvenile Orange Damselfish: one at the base of the dorsal fin, one on the top of the caudal peduncle, and one at the base of the pectoral fin. This last, less distinct, spot may vary in size with age. Adults are plain dark grey.
• **HABITAT** Coral and limestone rubble in the Caribbean; also the tropical western Atlantic.
• **REMARK** The adult Orange Damselfish is rather aggressive and occurs in deeper waters.
• **OTHER NAMES** Formerly classified as *Eupomacentrus planifrons*; also known as the Orange Demoiselle, and the Three Spot Damselfish.

CARIBBEAN, MEXICAN GULF

dark spot on caudal peduncle •

orange-yellow juvenile coloration •

Diet Omnivorous	Tank levels Upper and middle	Temperament

SURGEONS AND TANGS

S EVERAL MEMBERS of the family Acanthuridae are quarrelsome, and some carry sharp spines near the tail, hence the names "surgeon" and "tang". Long-based dorsal and anal fins and a sloping forehead are other distinctive features. They need green foods, and spawn by egg-scattering.

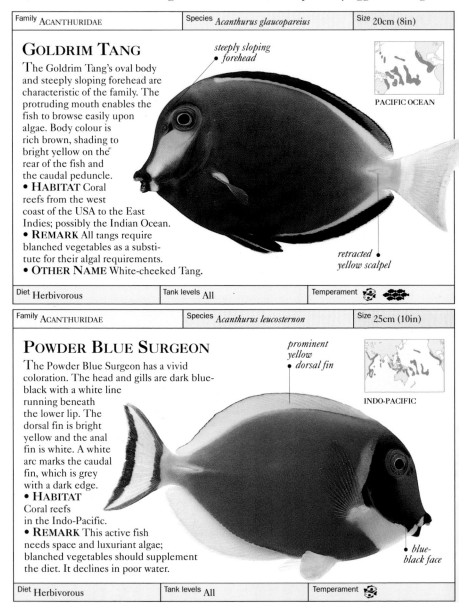

Family ACANTHURIDAE	Species *Acanthurus glaucopareius*	Size 20cm (8in)

GOLDRIM TANG

The Goldrim Tang's oval body and steeply sloping forehead are characteristic of the family. The protruding mouth enables the fish to browse easily upon algae. Body colour is rich brown, shading to bright yellow on the rear of the fish and the caudal peduncle.
• **HABITAT** Coral reefs from the west coast of the USA to the East Indies; possibly the Indian Ocean.
• **REMARK** All tangs require blanched vegetables as a substitute for their algal requirements.
• **OTHER NAME** White-cheeked Tang.

steeply sloping • forehead

PACIFIC OCEAN

retracted • yellow scalpel

Diet Herbivorous	Tank levels All	Temperament

Family ACANTHURIDAE	Species *Acanthurus leucosternon*	Size 25cm (10in)

POWDER BLUE SURGEON

The Powder Blue Surgeon has a vivid coloration. The head and gills are dark blue-black with a white line running beneath the lower lip. The dorsal fin is bright yellow and the anal fin is white. A white arc marks the caudal fin, which is grey with a dark edge.
• **HABITAT** Coral reefs in the Indo-Pacific.
• **REMARK** This active fish needs space and luxuriant algae; blanched vegetables should supplement the diet. It declines in poor water.

prominent yellow • dorsal fin

INDO-PACIFIC

• blue-black face

Diet Herbivorous	Tank levels All	Temperament

| Family ACANTHURIDAE | Species *Naso literatus* | Size 20cm (8in) |

JAPANESE TANG

The body of this pale brown-grey tang is sleekly streamlined. The mouth is accentuated by a combination of red and orange lips. Blue and brown lines on the gill-covers give a folded skin effect. This species carries two scalpels on each side. The caudal fin is crescent-shaped, and the rays on the top and bottom are extended into filaments.
• **HABITAT** Coral heads from the Red Sea and the Indian Ocean to Hawaii.
• **REMARK** The collective name for the *Naso* genus is Unicorn-fish, a reference to the protuberance that some species grow on the forehead. Plenty of green matter is needed.
• **OTHER NAMES** Smooth-head Unicorn, Lipstick Tang.

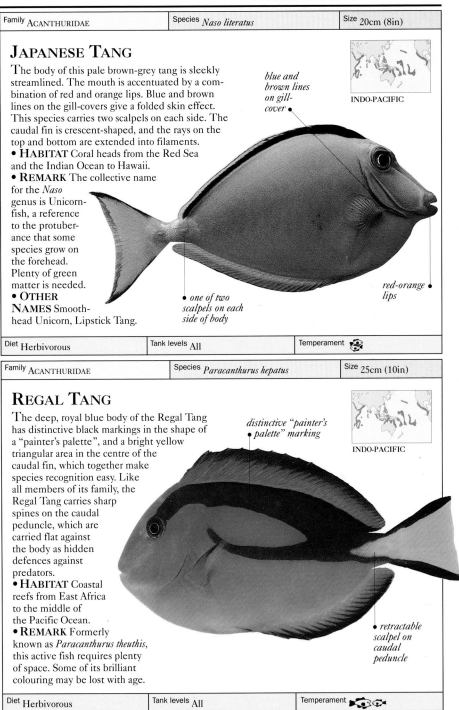

blue and brown lines on gill-cover

INDO-PACIFIC

red-orange lips

one of two scalpels on each side of body

| Diet Herbivorous | Tank levels All | Temperament |

| Family ACANTHURIDAE | Species *Paracanthurus hepatus* | Size 25cm (10in) |

REGAL TANG

The deep, royal blue body of the Regal Tang has distinctive black markings in the shape of a "painter's palette", and a bright yellow triangular area in the centre of the caudal fin, which together make species recognition easy. Like all members of its family, the Regal Tang carries sharp spines on the caudal peduncle, which are carried flat against the body as hidden defences against predators.
• **HABITAT** Coastal reefs from East Africa to the middle of the Pacific Ocean.
• **REMARK** Formerly known as *Paracanthurus theuthis*, this active fish requires plenty of space. Some of its brilliant colouring may be lost with age.

distinctive "painter's palette" marking

INDO-PACIFIC

retractable scalpel on caudal peduncle

| Diet Herbivorous | Tank levels All | Temperament |

| Family ACANTHURIDAE | Species *Zebrasoma flavescens* | Size 20cm (8in) |

YELLOW TANG

The oval body of this fish is exaggerated by the surrounding fins to give a disc-like appearance. The snout is relatively long, with a steeply sloping forehead and high-set eyes. The overall body colour is bright yellow, with paler coloration around the eyes, and white scalpels on the caudal peduncle. All fins are yellow, matching the body. Juveniles and adults share the same coloration, unlike some other members of the family. Small scales give the body a velvety appearance.
• **HABITAT** Shallow waters, particularly around Hawaii.
• **REMARK** The Yellow Tang is similar to the juvenile Blue Tang (*Acanthurus caeruleus*).
• **OTHER NAME** Lau'i-pala.

uniformly yellow fins

PACIFIC OCEAN

steeply sloping forehead and long snout

very small scales

| Diet Herbivorous | Tank levels All | Temperament 🐟 |

| Family ACANTHURIDAE | Species *Zebrasoma xanthurum* | Size 20cm (8in) |

PURPLE SAILFIN TANG

The body of the Purple Sailfin Tang is oval but looks disc-shaped because of the stiffly held fins. The snout is fairly well extended, the forehead is steep, and the eyes are high set. This tang is deep blue-purple with darker, purple-red dots and lines concentrated on the head and front of the body. These markings peter out gradually behind the dorsal fin. The dorsal and anal fins are blue-purple, like the body, and marked with little speckles and streaks. Retractable scalpels on the caudal peduncle are somewhat obscured, as they blend with the body colour. In contrast, the caudal fin is bright yellow.
• **HABITAT** Red Sea and Indian Ocean to the mid-Pacific.
• **REMARK** This fish is territorial and usually kept one to a tank, but some recommend keeping it in a shoal. It requires green foods, including blanched vegetables; algae-coated decorations provide an ideal grazing ground.

purple-red dots and lines

INDO-PACIFIC

bright yellow caudal fin

| Diet Herbivorous | Tank levels All | Temperament 🐟 |

TRIGGERFISHES

A PRINCIPAL FEATURE of the members of this family (Balistidae) is their ability to lock the first two dorsal fins in an upright position, providing a deterrent against being swallowed or dragged from crevices by predators. Swimming is achieved mainly by movements of the dorsal and anal fins. Triggerfishes spawn into pits dug in the sand. Some species guard their eggs.

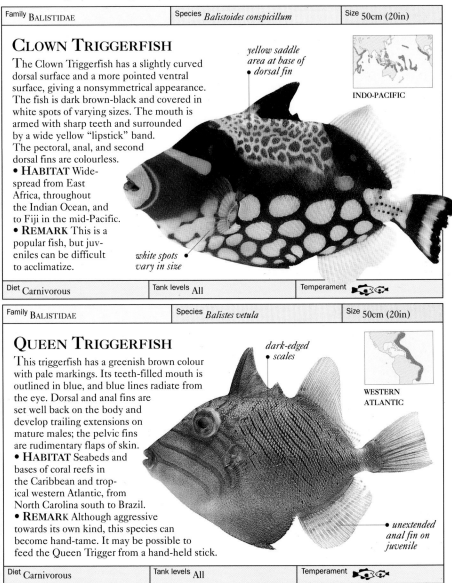

Family BALISTIDAE	Species *Balistoides conspicillum*	Size 50cm (20in)

CLOWN TRIGGERFISH

The Clown Triggerfish has a slightly curved dorsal surface and a more pointed ventral surface, giving a nonsymmetrical appearance. The fish is dark brown-black and covered in white spots of varying sizes. The mouth is armed with sharp teeth and surrounded by a wide yellow "lipstick" band. The pectoral, anal, and second dorsal fins are colourless.
• HABITAT Widespread from East Africa, throughout the Indian Ocean, and to Fiji in the mid-Pacific.
• REMARK This is a popular fish, but juveniles can be difficult to acclimatize.

yellow saddle area at base of dorsal fin

INDO-PACIFIC

white spots vary in size

Diet Carnivorous	Tank levels All	Temperament

Family BALISTIDAE	Species *Balistes vetula*	Size 50cm (20in)

QUEEN TRIGGERFISH

This triggerfish has a greenish brown colour with pale markings. Its teeth-filled mouth is outlined in blue, and blue lines radiate from the eye. Dorsal and anal fins are set well back on the body and develop trailing extensions on mature males; the pelvic fins are rudimentary flaps of skin.
• HABITAT Seabeds and bases of coral reefs in the Caribbean and tropical western Atlantic, from North Carolina south to Brazil.
• REMARK Although aggressive towards its own kind, this species can become hand-tame. It may be possible to feed the Queen Trigger from a hand-held stick.

dark-edged scales

WESTERN ATLANTIC

unextended anal fin on juvenile

Diet Carnivorous	Tank levels All	Temperament

| Family BALISTIDAE | Species *Odonus niger* | Size 50cm (20in) |

BLACK TRIGGERFISH

Despite its name, the body colour of this fish is not purely black; it may be a deep shade of brown, green, purple, or blue. The fish is not quite as angular in outline as other species in the family. Two dorsal fins are present, but the pelvic fins are reduced to stumps and perhaps a fold of skin. The large second dorsal fin and the anal fin provide the motive force for the fish, rather than the caudal fin, which is lyre-shaped and has elongated outer rays.
• **HABITAT** Red Sea, through the Indian Ocean, and east to the central Pacific.
• **REMARK** Specimens have spawned in captivity; eggs are laid, fertilized, and guarded in nests or burrows in the substrate.

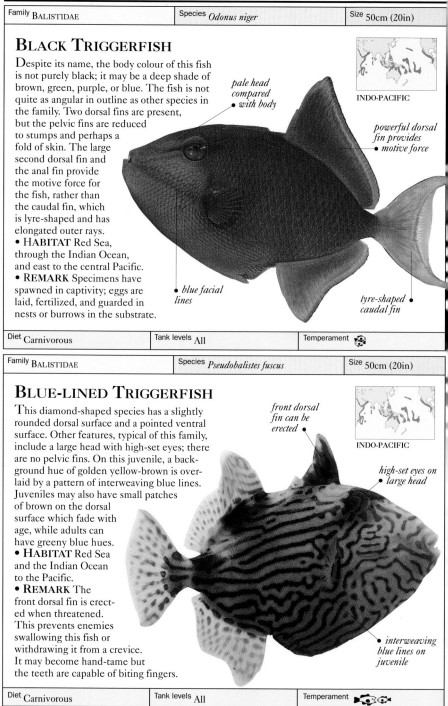

INDO-PACIFIC

pale head compared with body

powerful dorsal fin provides motive force

blue facial lines

lyre-shaped caudal fin

| Diet Carnivorous | Tank levels All | Temperament |

| Family BALISTIDAE | Species *Pseudobalistes fuscus* | Size 50cm (20in) |

BLUE-LINED TRIGGERFISH

This diamond-shaped species has a slightly rounded dorsal surface and a pointed ventral surface. Other features, typical of this family, include a large head with high-set eyes; there are no pelvic fins. On this juvenile, a background hue of golden yellow-brown is overlaid by a pattern of interweaving blue lines. Juveniles may also have small patches of brown on the dorsal surface which fade with age, while adults can have greeny blue hues.
• **HABITAT** Red Sea and the Indian Ocean to the Pacific.
• **REMARK** The front dorsal fin is erected when threatened. This prevents enemies swallowing this fish or withdrawing it from a crevice. It may become hand-tame but the teeth are capable of biting fingers.

INDO-PACIFIC

front dorsal fin can be erected

high-set eyes on large head

interweaving blue lines on juvenile

| Diet Carnivorous | Tank levels All | Temperament |

Family BALISTIDAE	Species *Rhinecanthus aculeatus*	Size 30cm (12in)

PICASSO TRIGGERFISH

The body of this fish is more elongate than other triggerfishes. Its popular name, Picasso, reflects its modernistic pattern. Yellow lines around the lips extend back past the gill-cover to join up with a dark blue-lined patch which runs across the eyes. This color-ation makes the mouth look deceptively larger, but it is no bigger than that of any other triggerfish.
• **HABITAT** Shallow waters in the Red Sea and the Indo-Pacific Oceans to Hawaii.
• **REMARK** Its drawn-out popular name in Hawaii, where it is the national fish, means "the fish which carries a needle, has a snout, and grunts like a pig".

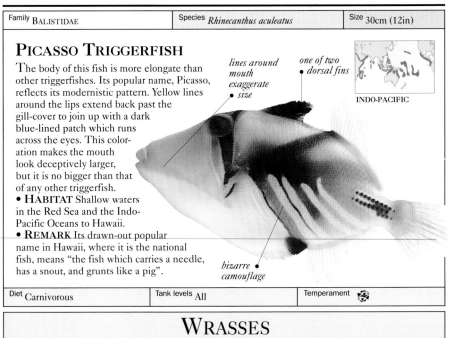

lines around mouth exaggerate • size

one of two • dorsal fins

INDO-PACIFIC

bizarre • camouflage

Diet Carnivorous	Tank levels All	Temperament

WRASSES

W RASSES, MEMBERS OF the Labridae family, have distinct behaviour patterns, including the removing of parasites or "cleaning" of other fishes, and the building of night-time, cocoon-like mucus structures. Sex reversal is common in single-sexed groups when required; spawning is by egg-scattering.

Family LABRIDAE	Species *Bodianus rufus*	Size 60cm (24in)

SPANISH HOGFISH

The upper body section of this juvenile Spanish Hogfish is purple-blue, from the eye almost to the rear of the dorsal fin. Adults are largely red with yellow on the lower flanks. Most aquarium specimens are juveniles, however, with either purple-blue or blue-brown on the dorsal surface, and yellow on the ventral surface and tail.
• **HABITAT** Rocky outcrops of the Caribbean and tropical western Atlantic.
• **REMARK** Juveniles may act as "cleaners".

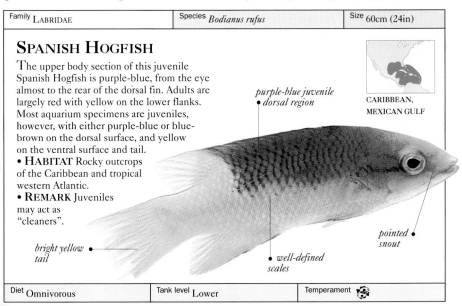

purple-blue juvenile • dorsal region

CARIBBEAN, MEXICAN GULF

bright yellow • tail

pointed • snout

• well-defined scales

Diet Omnivorous	Tank level Lower	Temperament

Family LABRIDAE	Species *Bodianus puchellus*	Size 25cm (10in)

CUBAN HOGFISH

Most of the body of the adult Cuban Hogfish is carmine-red, with some dark speckling. A tapering band of white runs from the bottom lip rearwards. The last few rays of the dorsal fin and the upper caudal fin are yellow. Juveniles are mostly yellow.
• **HABITAT** Rocky outcrops of the Caribbean; also the Western Atlantic.
• **REMARK** Juveniles may act as "cleaners" to other fishes.

CARIBBEAN, MEXICAN GULF

dark spot on tip of pectoral fin

tapering white band on adult

yellow rear portion

dark-edged scales

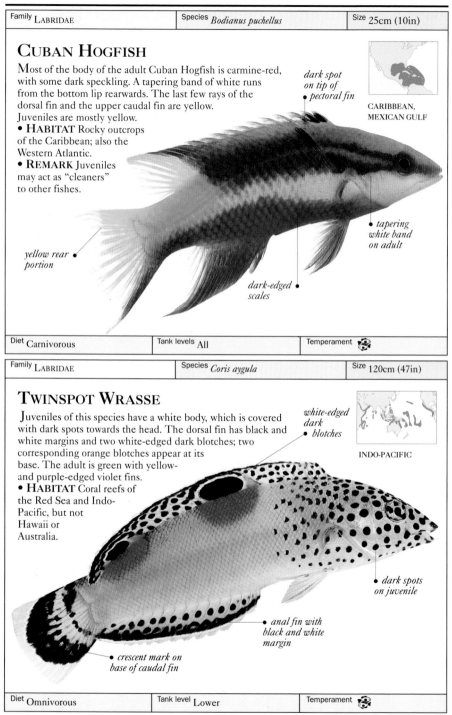

Diet Carnivorous	Tank levels All	Temperament

Family LABRIDAE	Species *Coris aygula*	Size 120cm (47in)

TWINSPOT WRASSE

Juveniles of this species have a white body, which is covered with dark spots towards the head. The dorsal fin has black and white margins and two white-edged dark blotches; two corresponding orange blotches appear at its base. The adult is green with yellow- and purple-edged violet fins.
• **HABITAT** Coral reefs of the Red Sea and Indo-Pacific, but not Hawaii or Australia.

INDO-PACIFIC

white-edged dark blotches

dark spots on juvenile

anal fin with black and white margin

crescent mark on base of caudal fin

Diet Omnivorous	Tank level Lower	Temperament

Family LABRIDAE	Species *Coris gaimardi*	Size 30cm (12in)

CLOWN WRASSE

The cylindrical body of this fish deepens with age; its colour also varies from juvenile to adult. Juveniles have bright red or orange bodies and fins with white markings. Adults have a dark brown-red body with blue speckles and blue-green facial markings; dorsal and anal fins are red, edged with blue, and the caudal section is yellow.
• **HABITAT** Coral reefs from the central Indian Ocean to Hawaii, but not Australia.
• **REMARK** *Coris gaimardi africana* is similarly coloured when adult, and inhabits coral reefs of the East African coast.

INDO-PACIFIC

white dorsal markings on juvenile •

first white • mark on juvenile

• dark-edged pale line crossing caudal fin

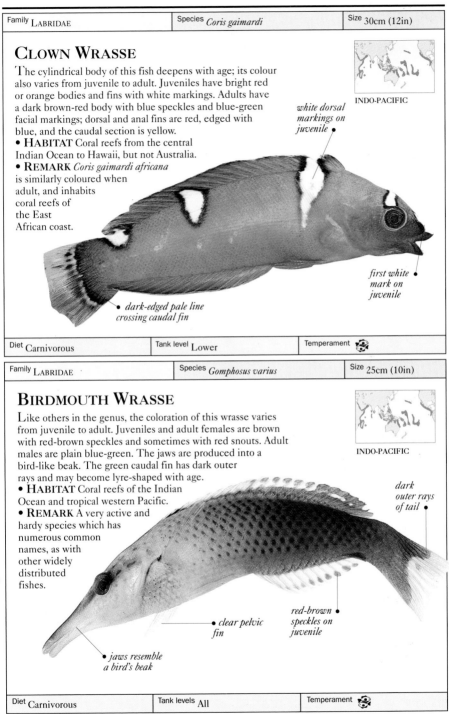

Diet Carnivorous	Tank level Lower	Temperament

Family LABRIDAE	Species *Gomphosus varius*	Size 25cm (10in)

BIRDMOUTH WRASSE

Like others in the genus, the coloration of this wrasse varies from juvenile to adult. Juveniles and adult females are brown with red-brown speckles and sometimes with red snouts. Adult males are plain blue-green. The jaws are produced into a bird-like beak. The green caudal fin has dark outer rays and may become lyre-shaped with age.
• **HABITAT** Coral reefs of the Indian Ocean and tropical western Pacific.
• **REMARK** A very active and hardy species which has numerous common names, as with other widely distributed fishes.

INDO-PACIFIC

dark outer rays of tail •

• clear pelvic fin

red-brown • speckles on juvenile

• jaws resemble a bird's beak

Diet Carnivorous	Tank levels All	Temperament

| Family LABRIDAE | Species *Labroides phthirophagus* | Size 10cm (4in) |

HAWAIIAN CLEANER WRASSE

This juvenile fish has a brightly coloured body, the front half of which is yellow. A dark central stripe runs back from the snout and broadens towards the rear to include the centre of the caudal fin. Dorsal and anal fins are blue, and the caudal fin has cerise top and bottom edges. Adults lose the brighter colours.
• **HABITAT** "Cleaning stations" are established on coral reefs around Hawaii and the western Pacific.
• **REMARK** Offer shellfish meat, or brine shrimp.

PACIFIC OCEAN

long-based • dorsal fin

• bright yellow front portion of juvenile

• squared-off caudal fin

| Diet Carnivorous | Tank levels All | Temperament |

| Family LABRIDAE | Species *Labroides dimidiatus* | Size 10cm (4in) |

CLEANER WRASSE

The dorsal surface of this fish is pale brown, shading to creamy white on the flanks and ventral surface. An increasingly wide black stripe runs from the tip of the snout to the rear of the caudal fin. Pale blue areas highlight the sides of the stripes towards the rear.
• **HABITAT** Widely distributed on coral reefs and in rock-pools of the Indo-Pacific, but not Hawaii.
• **REMARK** The main attraction of this species is its cleaning activity: it picks parasites from the skin, or even the inside of mouths and gills, of other fish. Be sure that the mouth is set at the tip of the snout, as the similar-looking blenny, *Aspidontus taeniatus*, rips the flesh of other fish with its underslung mouth.

Cleaner Wrasse cleans a butterflyfish

terminal • mouth on shallow head

• widening black stripe

• pale blue areas towards rear

INDO-PACIFIC

| Diet Carnivorous | Tank levels All | Temperament |

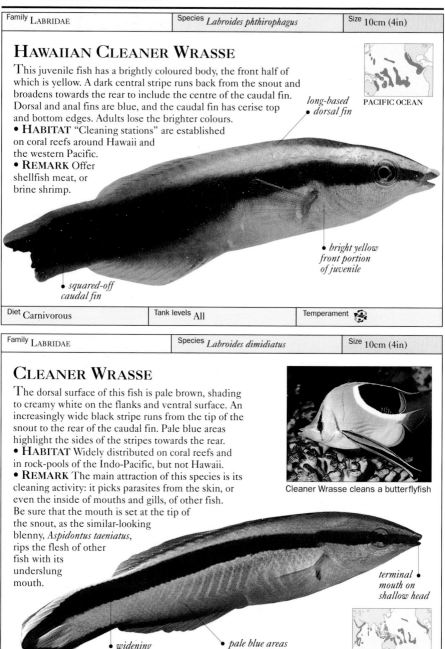

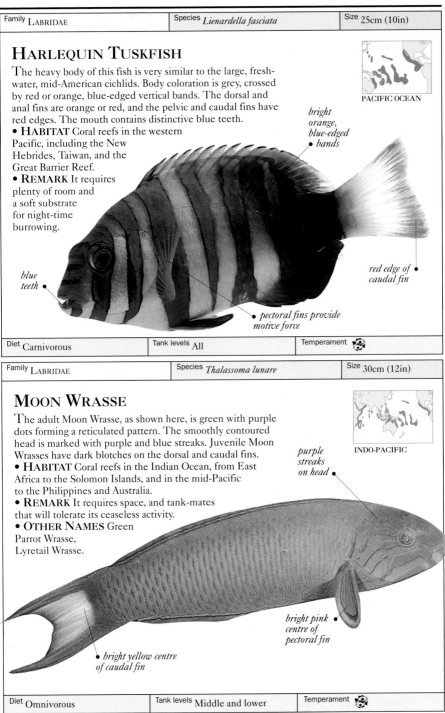

| Family LABRIDAE | Species *Lienardella fasciata* | Size 25cm (10in) |

HARLEQUIN TUSKFISH

The heavy body of this fish is very similar to the large, fresh-water, mid-American cichlids. Body coloration is grey, crossed by red or orange, blue-edged vertical bands. The dorsal and anal fins are orange or red, and the pelvic and caudal fins have red edges. The mouth contains distinctive blue teeth.
• **HABITAT** Coral reefs in the western Pacific, including the New Hebrides, Taiwan, and the Great Barrier Reef.
• **REMARK** It requires plenty of room and a soft substrate for night-time burrowing.

PACIFIC OCEAN

bright orange, blue-edged bands

red edge of caudal fin

blue teeth

pectoral fins provide motive force

| Diet Carnivorous | Tank levels All | Temperament |

| Family LABRIDAE | Species *Thalassoma lunare* | Size 30cm (12in) |

MOON WRASSE

The adult Moon Wrasse, as shown here, is green with purple dots forming a reticulated pattern. The smoothly contoured head is marked with purple and blue streaks. Juvenile Moon Wrasses have dark blotches on the dorsal and caudal fins.
• **HABITAT** Coral reefs in the Indian Ocean, from East Africa to the Solomon Islands, and in the mid-Pacific to the Philippines and Australia.
• **REMARK** It requires space, and tank-mates that will tolerate its ceaseless activity.
• **OTHER NAMES** Green Parrot Wrasse, Lyretail Wrasse.

INDO-PACIFIC

purple streaks on head

bright pink centre of pectoral fin

bright yellow centre of caudal fin

| Diet Omnivorous | Tank levels Middle and lower | Temperament |

BASSES AND GROUPERS

MANY MEMBERS OF THE family Serranidae (the sea basses and groupers) are extremely attractive, but only small specimens of these natural predators are suitable for the average-sized aquarium. Fortunately, some of the smallest family species, including the basslets, are the most brilliantly coloured. Sexing is difficult, as hermaphroditic changes occur during these fishes' lives: each fish has both male and female capabilities, but not simultaneously. Many species turn darker or paler, or take on a bicolour pattern, when breeding, and females become obviously distended with eggs.

Family SERRANIDAE	Species *Anthias squamipinnis*	Size 12cm (4¾in)

WRECKFISH

The golden pink body of this fish is covered with well-defined scales. The head is pink to violet and a thin, orange-gold band runs across the top of the mouth, through the bottom of the eye, and to the base of the pectoral fin. The dorsal fin is long-based and pink with gold speckles; that of the male has a long third ray. The caudal fin of both sexes is lyre-shaped and the female's may have a V-shaped pink blotch.
• **HABITAT** Very widespread, shoaling in great numbers around coral reefs from East Africa to the central Pacific.
• **REMARK** This fish may not accept dead food unless it can be fooled into thinking it is live (by introducing it in water currents or by jerking it on a thread). It does not thrive as a solitary specimen.
• **OTHER NAMES** Lyretail Coralfish, Pink Coralfish, Golden Jewelfish, Orange Sea Perch.

Wreckfish traverse the coral reef

extended third ray of male dorsal fin

lyre-shaped caudal fin

orange head band

reddish pectoral fins on male

INDO-PACIFIC

Diet Carnivorous	Tank levels All	Temperament

Family SERRANIDAE	Species *Chromileptis altivelis*	Size 60cm (24in)

POLKA-DOT GROUPER

Numerous black spots cover this grouper's creamy white body. These spots become more abundant with age. The pectoral fins are large as they are the primary means of propulsion. The long-based dorsal fin has a noticeable notch in front of the soft-rayed rear section.
• **HABITAT** Coral reefs of the Indian Ocean, coastal East Indies, Philippines, and Queensland, Australia.
• **REMARK** It swims head-down while prowling. Young fish acclimatize well if given space and retreats.
• **OTHER NAMES** Humped Rock Cod, Barramundi Cod, Pantherfish, Kerapu Sonoh.

notched section of dorsal fin

INDO-PACIFIC

eyes set high on small head

large, projecting mouth

dark dots in all fins

Diet Carnivorous	Tank levels Middle and lower	Temperament

Family SERRANIDAE	Species *Gramma loreto*	Size 13cm (5in)

ROYAL GRAMMA

The Royal Gramma's vivid body coloration is divided into a brilliant pink-violet front half and a bright yellow rear. The junction between the two colours is marked by yellow speckles. A dark blotch appears in the front rays of the dorsal fin.
• **HABITAT** Caves in coral reefs of the Caribbean and environs.
• **REMARK** The aquarium should be furnished with rocky retreats. Males protect a spawning cave and breed with various females almost daily. The adhesive eggs hatch after about two weeks, but the fry are difficult to raise.

spot in front rays of dorsal fin

CARIBBEAN, MEXICAN GULF

dark bar passes through eye

trailing pelvic fins

yellow speckles

Diet Plankton	Tank level Lower	Temperament

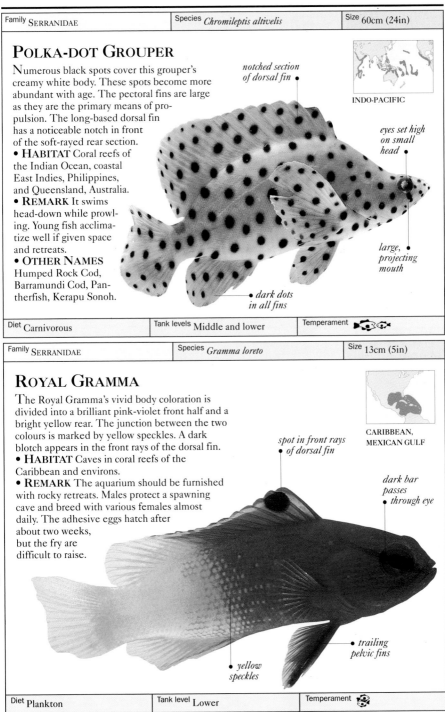

BATFISHES AND CARDINALFISHES

MEMBERS OF THE batfish family, (Platacidae) can be recognized by their wing-like fins, but species identification is difficult. Adult coloration is more drab, and speculation surrounds the classification of the colour forms. The cardinalfishes (Apogonidae) are mainly nocturnal. Mouth-brooding behaviour and the presence of two erect dorsal fins are their chief characteristics.

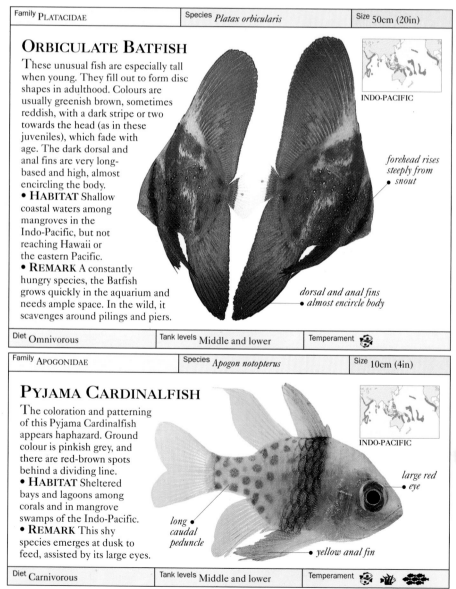

Family PLATACIDAE	Species *Platax orbicularis*	Size 50cm (20in)

ORBICULATE BATFISH

These unusual fish are especially tall when young. They fill out to form disc shapes in adulthood. Colours are usually greenish brown, sometimes reddish, with a dark stripe or two towards the head (as in these juveniles), which fade with age. The dark dorsal and anal fins are very long-based and high, almost encircling the body.
• **HABITAT** Shallow coastal waters among mangroves in the Indo-Pacific, but not reaching Hawaii or the eastern Pacific.
• **REMARK** A constantly hungry species, the Batfish grows quickly in the aquarium and needs ample space. In the wild, it scavenges around pilings and piers.

INDO-PACIFIC

forehead rises steeply from snout

dorsal and anal fins almost encircle body

Diet Omnivorous	Tank levels Middle and lower	Temperament

Family APOGONIDAE	Species *Apogon notopterus*	Size 10cm (4in)

PYJAMA CARDINALFISH

The coloration and patterning of this Pyjama Cardinalfish appears haphazard. Ground colour is pinkish grey, and there are red-brown spots behind a dividing line.
• **HABITAT** Sheltered bays and lagoons among corals and in mangrove swamps of the Indo-Pacific.
• **REMARK** This shy species emerges at dusk to feed, assisted by its large eyes.

INDO-PACIFIC

large red eye

long caudal peduncle

yellow anal fin

Diet Carnivorous	Tank levels Middle and lower	Temperament

BLENNIES

A COMMON FEATURE of the family Blenniidae is their slimy skin – blennies are sometimes called slimefishes. Many are bottom-dwellers, living on the seabed at the base of reefs, or around coral heads in the shallow waters just below the tide-line. The whisker-like growths, or cirri, above the eyes are sensory, and are not found in all blenny species.

Family BLENNIIDAE	Species *Ecsenius bicolor*	Size 10cm (4in)

BICOLOUR BLENNY

Only the front half of this fish is normally seen, as the golden rear is concealed when the fish hides among rocks or in the substrate. Its unusual dorsal fin runs the entire length of the body. When spawning, the male colouring changes to red with white bars, and after spawning he is often dark blue with pale blotches.
• **HABITAT** Coral reef bases and rocky shores throughout the Indo-Pacific.
• **REMARK** This fish browses on algae.

INDO-PACIFIC

dorsal fin runs entire • length of body

hair-like • cirri

golden • coloured rear section

Diet Omnivorous	Tank level Lower	Temperament

Family BLENNIIDAE	Species *Meiacanthus smithii*	Size 9cm (3½in)

SMITH'S SAWTAIL BLENNY

The dark rear rays on the caudal fin of this blenny provide the "sawtail" effect. The delicate grey colour shades to a paler pinkish hue on the ventral surface, and a black band runs the length of the dorsal fin.
• **HABITAT** Above coral reefs throughout the Indo-Pacific.
• **REMARK** *Meiacanthus plagiotremus* is similar, but lacks the diagonal eye stripe. Some authors place members of this genus in a separate family, the Meiacanthidae.

broad black stripe on dorsal fin •

INDO-PACIFIC

thread-like • pelvic fin

Diet Omnivorous	Tank level Lower	Temperament

BOXFISHES

THE BOX-SHAPED BODIES of members of the family Ostraciidae are covered by rigid plates. Pelvic fins are absent, and bony stumps may appear in their place on some species. All species are propelled slowly by movements of the dorsal, anal, and pectoral fins. When stressed, boxfishes excrete poison, and should, therefore, be settled into a new aquarium first.

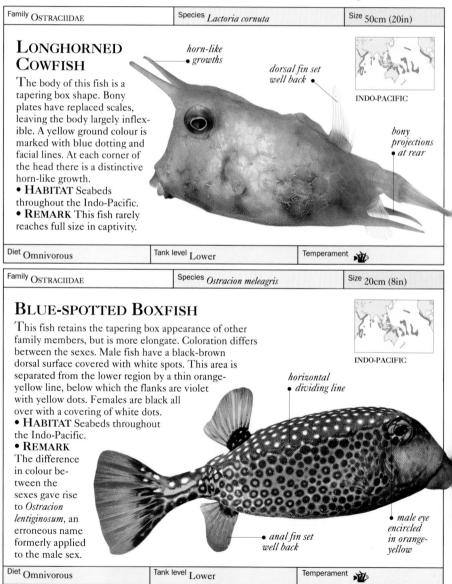

Family OSTRACIIDAE	Species *Lactoria cornuta*	Size 50cm (20in)

LONGHORNED COWFISH

The body of this fish is a tapering box shape. Bony plates have replaced scales, leaving the body largely inflexible. A yellow ground colour is marked with blue dotting and facial lines. At each corner of the head there is a distinctive horn-like growth.
• **HABITAT** Seabeds throughout the Indo-Pacific.
• **REMARK** This fish rarely reaches full size in captivity.

horn-like growths

dorsal fin set well back

INDO-PACIFIC

bony projections at rear

Diet Omnivorous	Tank level Lower	Temperament

Family OSTRACIIDAE	Species *Ostracion meleagris*	Size 20cm (8in)

BLUE-SPOTTED BOXFISH

This fish retains the tapering box appearance of other family members, but is more elongate. Coloration differs between the sexes. Male fish have a black-brown dorsal surface covered with white spots. This area is separated from the lower region by a thin orange-yellow line, below which the flanks are violet with yellow dots. Females are black all over with a covering of white dots.
• **HABITAT** Seabeds throughout the Indo-Pacific.
• **REMARK** The difference in colour between the sexes gave rise to *Ostracion lentiginosum*, an erroneous name formerly applied to the male sex.

INDO-PACIFIC

horizontal dividing line

anal fin set well back

male eye encircled in orange-yellow

Diet Omnivorous	Tank level Lower	Temperament

FILEFISHES

THE ROUGH SKIN of the mono-
canthids accounts for the
common name "filefishes", and for the
alternative popular name of "leather-
jackets". They are related to the triggerfishes, from which they differ by
being unable to lock the first dorsal
spine into an upright position.
Filefishes may swim head-down. In
the wild they feed on polyps and algae.

Family MONOCANTHIDAE	Species *Chaetoderma penicilligera*	Size 25cm (10in)

PRICKLY LEATHERJACKET

Grey-blue and yellow-gold tints
colour the rhomboid body of this
fish. A number of thin, dark, wavy
lines cross the entire body
horizontally. The main features
are the branched tentacles; they
grow along the ventral and dorsal
outlines and serve as camouflage.
• **HABITAT** Drifting seaweeds
in the western Pacific, from
the East Indies to Samoa.
• **REMARK** This fish is
particularly hardy and sociable.

PACIFIC OCEAN

dark, wavy lines

greyish fins carry dark spots

branched tentacle

Diet Carnivorous	Tank levels Upper and middle	Temperament

Family MONOCANTHIDAE	Species *Pervagor melanocephalus*	Size 13cm (5in)

LACE-FINNED LEATHERJACKET

The body colour of this filefish is divided
into two halves: the front half is purple,
shading through brown to a bright
yellow back at the caudal fin. Scales
are very small. The first of the two
dorsal fins comprises a single
spine. The second dorsal fin
is long-based and set above
the similarly constructed
anal fin. Pelvic fins are
merely single spines.
• **HABITAT** Drifting
seaweed throughout the
Indo-Pacific Ocean, including
the islands of Hawaii and Australia.
• **REMARK** Like other filefishes,
this species is generally smaller and less
active than the triggerfishes (see p.259).

single, upright spine

INDO-PACIFIC

streaked, fan-shaped caudal fin

pelvic spine

Diet Carnivorous	Tank levels Upper and middle	Temperament

GOBIES

MEMBERS OF THE FAMILY Gobiidae are very similar in body shape to those of the family Blennidae (see p.269). Gobies can be distinguished by their pelvic fins, which grow together to form a suction-disc, used to anchor the fish to a rock or other resting place. Some gobies are brilliantly coloured. They can be bred in the aquarium, but the tiny fry are difficult to raise.

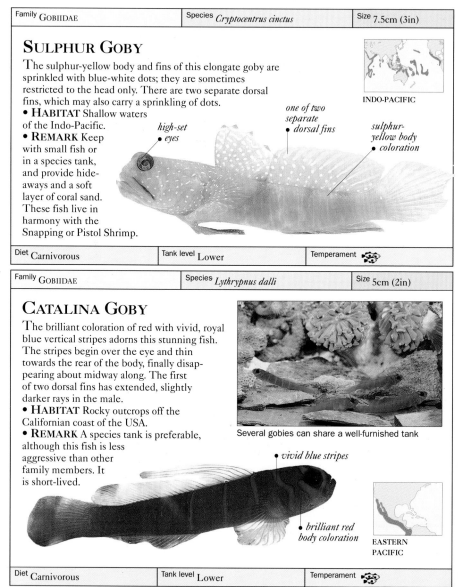

Family GOBIIDAE	Species *Cryptocentrus cinctus*	Size 7.5cm (3in)

SULPHUR GOBY

The sulphur-yellow body and fins of this elongate goby are sprinkled with blue-white dots; they are sometimes restricted to the head only. There are two separate dorsal fins, which may also carry a sprinkling of dots.
• **HABITAT** Shallow waters of the Indo-Pacific.
• **REMARK** Keep with small fish or in a species tank, and provide hide-aways and a soft layer of coral sand. These fish live in harmony with the Snapping or Pistol Shrimp.

INDO-PACIFIC

high-set eyes

one of two separate dorsal fins

sulphur-yellow body coloration

Diet Carnivorous	Tank level Lower	Temperament

Family GOBIIDAE	Species *Lythrypnus dalli*	Size 5cm (2in)

CATALINA GOBY

The brilliant coloration of red with vivid, royal blue vertical stripes adorns this stunning fish. The stripes begin over the eye and thin towards the rear of the body, finally disappearing about midway along. The first of two dorsal fins has extended, slightly darker rays in the male.
• **HABITAT** Rocky outcrops off the Californian coast of the USA.
• **REMARK** A species tank is preferable, although this fish is less aggressive than other family members. It is short-lived.

Several gobies can share a well-furnished tank

vivid blue stripes

brilliant red body coloration

EASTERN PACIFIC

Diet Carnivorous	Tank level Lower	Temperament

Family GOBIIDAE	Species *Nemateleotris decora*	Size 6cm (2½in)

PURPLE FIREFISH

The coloration of this fish is divided: the front half of the body is golden yellow, with violet on top of the head and along the dorsal surface, while the rear half of the body is brownish grey. The first few rays of the front dorsal fin are elongate and coloured black, violet, and red, as are the second dorsal fin, the anal fin, and the lyre-shaped caudal fin.
• **HABITAT** Caves in coral reefs from the central Indian Ocean to the central Pacific.
• **REMARK** As with related species, the pelvic fins are not fused but divided, as in the *Eleotris* genus. Retreats are essential.

INDO-PACIFIC

violet-coloured dorsal surface

striped colours on anal fin

long, violet-edged pelvic fin

Diet Carnivorous	Tank levels Middle and lower	Temperament

Family GOBIIDAE	Species *Nemateleotris magnifica*	Size 6cm (2½in)

FIREFISH

As with the Purple Firefish (above), the coloration of this species is divided into two areas: the front half of the body is pinky yellow, with a plain yellow area on the head, while the rear half is pinky orange, shading through red to a dark brown-red. The first few rays of the front dorsal fin are elongate and yellow, with a pink front edge. The second dorsal fin and the anal fin have a yellow base with a brown-red outer edge.
• **HABITAT** Coral reef caves from the central Indian Ocean to the central Pacific.
• **REMARK** The pelvic fins are split in two, not fused together.
• **OTHER NAME** Magnificent Hover Goby.

very long first ray of dorsal fin

INDO-PACIFIC

bold speckling around head

long pelvic fin

pinky yellow front section

Diet Carnivorous	Tank levels Middle and lower	Temperament

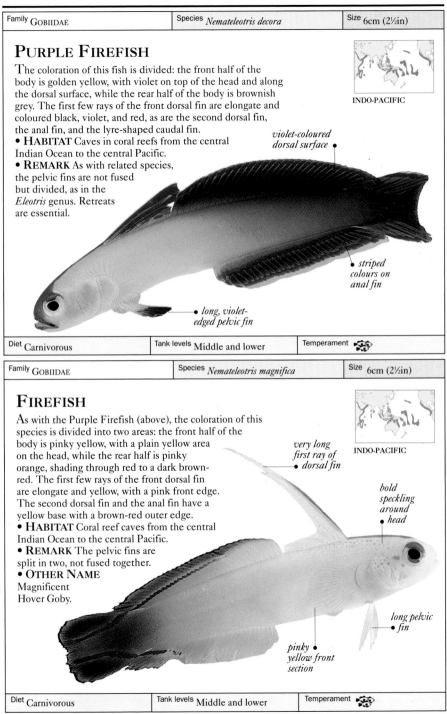

GRUNTS AND HAWKFISHES

L IKE THE BASSES and groupers, the grunts (family Pomadasyidae) usually grow too large for the average aquarium. Marked pattern changes occur between juvenile and adult stages. The hawkfishes (family Cirrhitidae), so named because they perch in wait for their prey like hawks, eat other fishes, but invertebrates are safe with them. They breed by egg-depositing.

Family POMADASYIDAE	Species *Anisotremus virginicus*	Size 30cm (12in)

PORKFISH

This juvenile Porkfish is bluish silver with dark horizontal stripes and a black blotch on the caudal peduncle. Adult coloration is bright blue and silver, with vivid yellow lines running back behind the second of two black bars that cross the head.
• **HABITAT** Around piers and rocks in the Caribbean.
• **REMARK** These fish make grunting sounds with their pharyngeal teeth when removed from water, hence the name of grunt. They are active at night.

dark horizontal stripes

WESTERN ATLANTIC

yellow head on juvenile

flattish ventral surface

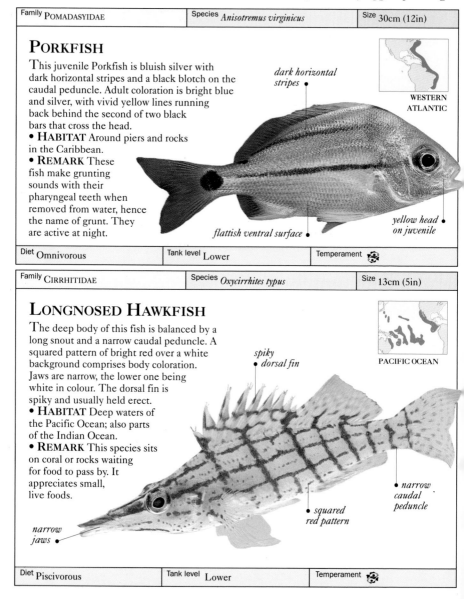

Diet Omnivorous	Tank level Lower	Temperament

Family CIRRHITIDAE	Species *Oxycirrhites typus*	Size 13cm (5in)

LONGNOSED HAWKFISH

The deep body of this fish is balanced by a long snout and a narrow caudal peduncle. A squared pattern of bright red over a white background comprises body coloration. Jaws are narrow, the lower one being white in colour. The dorsal fin is spiky and usually held erect.
• **HABITAT** Deep waters of the Pacific Ocean; also parts of the Indian Ocean.
• **REMARK** This species sits on coral or rocks waiting for food to pass by. It appreciates small, live foods.

spiky dorsal fin

PACIFIC OCEAN

narrow caudal peduncle

squared red pattern

narrow jaws

Diet Piscivorous	Tank level Lower	Temperament

JAWFISHES AND LIONFISHES

T HE MOST NOTABLE characteristic of jawfishes (family Opisthognathidae) is their habit of building burrows in the substrate, into which they retreat tail-first. The graceful swimming action of the lionfishes (family Scorpaenidae) conceals a stealthy, predatory instinct. Their fins contain a powerful venom and should be handled with extreme caution.

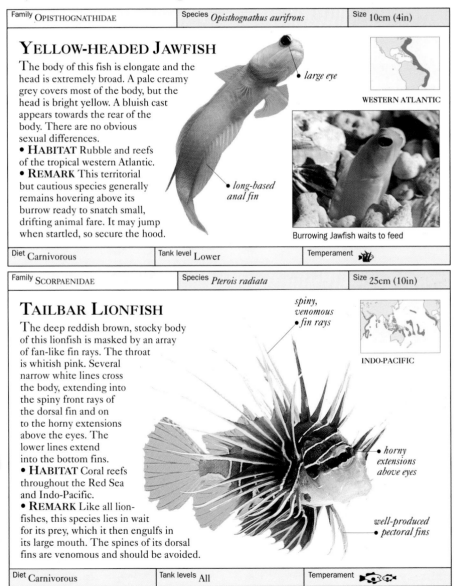

Family OPISTHOGNATHIDAE	Species *Opisthognathus aurifrons*	Size 10cm (4in)

YELLOW-HEADED JAWFISH

The body of this fish is elongate and the head is extremely broad. A pale creamy grey covers most of the body, but the head is bright yellow. A bluish cast appears towards the rear of the body. There are no obvious sexual differences.
• **HABITAT** Rubble and reefs of the tropical western Atlantic.
• **REMARK** This territorial but cautious species generally remains hovering above its burrow ready to snatch small, drifting animal fare. It may jump when startled, so secure the hood.

• *large eye*

WESTERN ATLANTIC

• *long-based anal fin*

Burrowing Jawfish waits to feed

Diet Carnivorous	Tank level Lower	Temperament

Family SCORPAENIDAE	Species *Pterois radiata*	Size 25cm (10in)

TAILBAR LIONFISH

The deep reddish brown, stocky body of this lionfish is masked by an array of fan-like fin rays. The throat is whitish pink. Several narrow white lines cross the body, extending into the spiny front rays of the dorsal fin and on to the horny extensions above the eyes. The lower lines extend into the bottom fins.
• **HABITAT** Coral reefs throughout the Red Sea and Indo-Pacific.
• **REMARK** Like all lionfishes, this species lies in wait for its prey, which it then engulfs in its large mouth. The spines of its dorsal fins are venomous and should be avoided.

spiny, venomous • *fin rays*

INDO-PACIFIC

• *horny extensions above eyes*

well-produced • *pectoral fins*

Diet Carnivorous	Tank levels All	Temperament

Family SCORPAENIDAE	Species *Pterois volitans*	Size 35cm (14in)

LIONFISH

The white body of this venom-ous fish is crossed vertically by light and dark brown-red bars. The eye is concealed by the pattern, beneath a pair of horn-like growths. The first spines of the dorsal fin are patterned with light and dark marks; they are spiny and very poisonous.
• **HABITAT** Red Sea and Indo-Pacific coral reefs.
• **REMARK** Handle with extreme caution and feed with living or dead, meaty foods but not red meat.

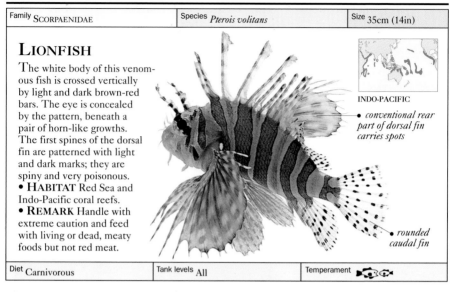

INDO-PACIFIC

• *conventional rear part of dorsal fin carries spots*

• *rounded caudal fin*

Diet Carnivorous	Tank levels All	Temperament

MANDARINFISHES

M ANDARINFISHES and the related dragonets belong to the family Callionymidae, comprising attractive, but shy, bottom-dwelling species. *Synchiropus splendidus* (below) is the most colourful example. Males are brighter and have extensions to the dorsal and anal fins. Fertilization is internal, before the eggs are scattered. They feed on small marine animals.

Family CALLIONYMIDAE	Species *Synchiropus splendidus*	Size 7.5cm (3in)

MANDARINFISH

The body of this species is bluish green-gold, with a random pattern of wide, dark-edged blue lines extending on to the fins. The eyes are gold and black, and the lower head is pale beneath a dark line which runs from the snout to the gold-spotted gill-cover.
• **HABITAT** Hideaways on reef bottoms in the Pacific, south to Australia.
• **REMARK** Keep the Mandarinfish in a quiet tank away from boisterous fishes.

elongate spine on • first dorsal fin

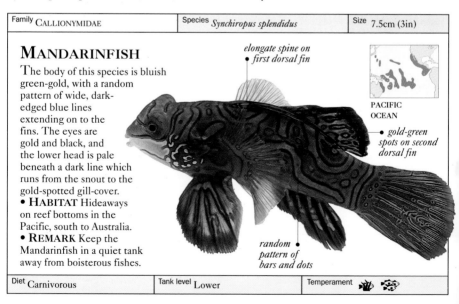

PACIFIC OCEAN

• *gold-green spots on second dorsal fin*

random • pattern of bars and dots

Diet Carnivorous	Tank level Lower	Temperament

MORAY EELS

MEMBERS OF THE family Muraen-idae, moray eels are only suitable for the largest aquariums, but make splendid attractions for those able to accommodate them. In the wild, they inhabit rocky caves and other retreats such as corals or shipwrecks. These fish must be handled with extreme care, as even the smallest bites can be painful. Only eels of large, unrestricted sizes are capable of breeding, and many morays eels need to migrate before spawning can occur. Never keep these predatory species with small fishes.

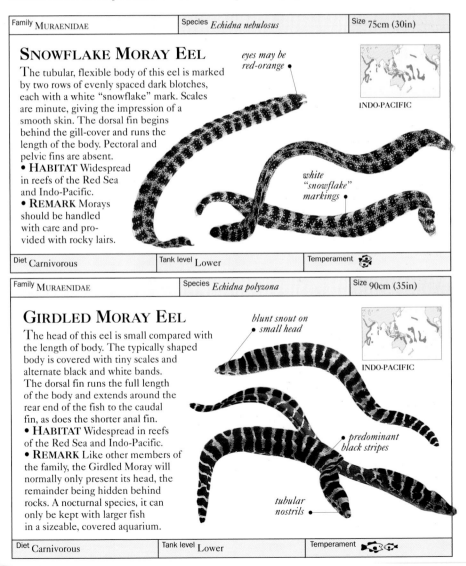

Family MURAENIDAE	Species *Echidna nebulosus*	Size 75cm (30in)

SNOWFLAKE MORAY EEL

The tubular, flexible body of this eel is marked by two rows of evenly spaced dark blotches, each with a white "snowflake" mark. Scales are minute, giving the impression of a smooth skin. The dorsal fin begins behind the gill-cover and runs the length of the body. Pectoral and pelvic fins are absent.
• **HABITAT** Widespread in reefs of the Red Sea and Indo-Pacific.
• **REMARK** Morays should be handled with care and provided with rocky lairs.

eyes may be red-orange

white "snowflake" markings

INDO-PACIFIC

Diet Carnivorous	Tank level Lower	Temperament

Family MURAENIDAE	Species *Echidna polyzona*	Size 90cm (35in)

GIRDLED MORAY EEL

The head of this eel is small compared with the length of body. The typically shaped body is covered with tiny scales and alternate black and white bands. The dorsal fin runs the full length of the body and extends around the rear end of the fish to the caudal fin, as does the shorter anal fin.
• **HABITAT** Widespread in reefs of the Red Sea and Indo-Pacific.
• **REMARK** Like other members of the family, the Girdled Moray will normally only present its head, the remainder being hidden behind rocks. A nocturnal species, it can only be kept with larger fish in a sizeable, covered aquarium.

blunt snout on small head

INDO-PACIFIC

predominant black stripes

tubular nostrils

Diet Carnivorous	Tank level Lower	Temperament

Family MURAENIDAE	Species *Muraena lentiginosa*	Size 60cm (24in)

JEWEL MORAY EEL

This brown eel is covered with dark-edged yellowish "stars"
which are arranged in rows and extend into the fins. The
dorsal, anal, and caudal fins are contiguous. There are no
scales, and the nostrils are characteristically tubular. The
powerful jaws are filled with sharp teeth.
• **HABITAT** Sea caves and crevices from the Gulf
of California down to Peru.
• **REMARK** A specimen
fish for the large
aquarium, the Jewel
Moray Eel should
be handled
with care.

*combined fins
begin ahead of
gill opening*

EASTERN
PACIFIC

*scale-less
body*

*powerful,
teeth-filled jaws*

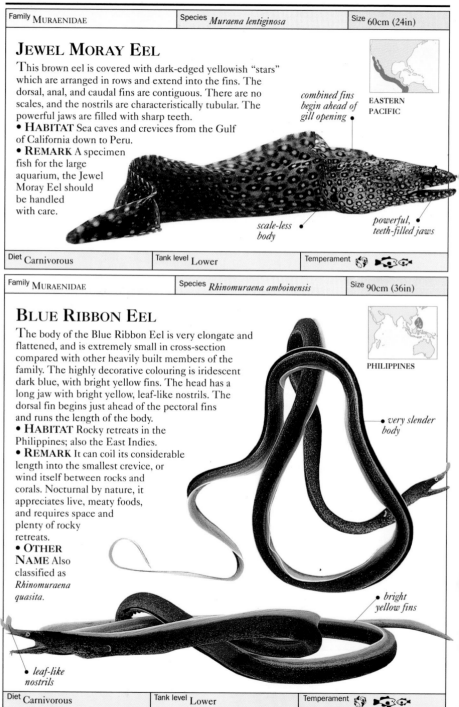

Diet Carnivorous	Tank level Lower	Temperament

Family MURAENIDAE	Species *Rhinomuraena amboinensis*	Size 90cm (36in)

BLUE RIBBON EEL

The body of the Blue Ribbon Eel is very elongate and
flattened, and is extremely small in cross-section
compared with other heavily built members of the
family. The highly decorative colouring is iridescent
dark blue, with bright yellow fins. The head has a
long jaw with bright yellow, leaf-like nostrils. The
dorsal fin begins just ahead of the pectoral fins
and runs the length of the body.
• **HABITAT** Rocky retreats in the
Philippines; also the East Indies.
• **REMARK** It can coil its considerable
length into the smallest crevice, or
wind itself between rocks and
corals. Nocturnal by nature, it
appreciates live, meaty foods,
and requires space and
plenty of rocky
retreats.
• **OTHER
NAME** Also
classified as
*Rhinomuraena
quasita.*

PHILIPPINES

*very slender
body*

*bright
yellow fins*

*leaf-like
nostrils*

Diet Carnivorous	Tank level Lower	Temperament

PIPEFISHES

T HE COLOURFUL MEMBERS of the pipefish and seahorse family (Syngnathidae) will live contentedly in reef-type aquariums in which invertebrates are present. Some pipefishes inhabit estuaries and are able to tolerate water of varying salt content. All these fishes have small mouths and require small types of live foods – brine shrimp and livebearer fry are ideal.

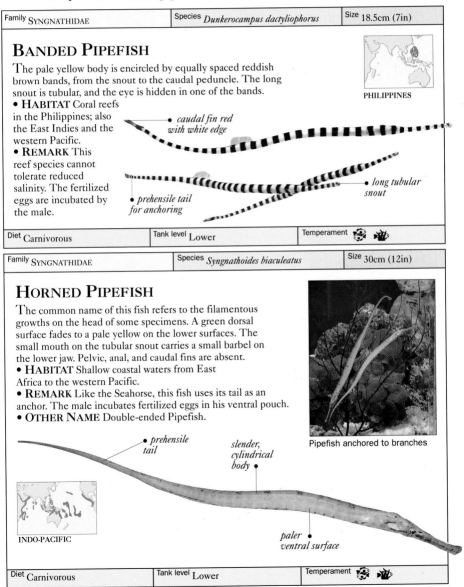

Family SYNGNATHIDAE	Species *Dunkerocampus dactyliophorus*	Size 18.5cm (7in)

BANDED PIPEFISH

The pale yellow body is encircled by equally spaced reddish brown bands, from the snout to the caudal peduncle. The long snout is tubular, and the eye is hidden in one of the bands.
• **HABITAT** Coral reefs in the Philippines; also the East Indies and the western Pacific.
• **REMARK** This reef species cannot tolerate reduced salinity. The fertilized eggs are incubated by the male.

PHILIPPINES

caudal fin red with white edge

long tubular snout

prehensile tail for anchoring

Diet Carnivorous	Tank level Lower	Temperament

Family SYNGNATHIDAE	Species *Syngnathoides biaculeatus*	Size 30cm (12in)

HORNED PIPEFISH

The common name of this fish refers to the filamentous growths on the head of some specimens. A green dorsal surface fades to a pale yellow on the lower surfaces. The small mouth on the tubular snout carries a small barbel on the lower jaw. Pelvic, anal, and caudal fins are absent.
• **HABITAT** Shallow coastal waters from East Africa to the western Pacific.
• **REMARK** Like the Seahorse, this fish uses its tail as an anchor. The male incubates fertilized eggs in his ventral pouch.
• **OTHER NAME** Double-ended Pipefish.

Pipefish anchored to branches

prehensile tail

slender, cylindrical body

INDO-PACIFIC

paler ventral surface

Diet Carnivorous	Tank level Lower	Temperament

Family SYNGNATHIDAE	Species *Hippocampus kuda*	Size 25cm (10in)

SEAHORSE

The Seahorse's swimming position is vertical, with only slight inclinations forwards or backwards depending on the direction of travel. The body is covered with armoured plates. An equine-like head set at right-angles to the body ends in a long tubular snout and expandable mouth. A bony "coronet" may develop on the head.
• **HABITAT** Shallow coastal waters throughout the Indo-Pacific.
• **REMARK** Live foods are required, preferably small fishes and crustaceans. Seahorses are best kept in species aquariums, with branches to cling to. Females deposit eggs in the male's abdominal pouch, from which the fry emerge weeks later.

INDO-PACIFIC

high-set eyes for good field of vision

bony "coronet"

equine-like head

long, tubular snout

ridges and rings of armoured plates

prehensile tail acts as anchor

Diet Small, live foods	Tank levels Middle and lower	Temperament

PORCUPINEFISHES AND PUFFERFISHES

T HE LATIN FAMILY name of the porcupinefishes, Diodontidae, means "two teeth", as the front teeth of these fishes are fused together, giving the impression of a single top and bottom tooth. The scales are covered with sharp spines which create a formidable deterrent against predators when the fish is inflated. Pufferfishes (family Tetradontidae) have four teeth – two on each jaw. Both families enjoy small, meaty foods.

Family DIODONTIDAE	Species *Diodon holocanthus*	Size 50cm (20in)

LONG-SPINED PORCUPINEFISH

T he golden brown body of the Long-spined Porcupinefish has a pale underside, and dark dots are widely spaced over the body. The pectoral fins are large but pelvic fins are absent. Dorsal and anal fins are set back on the body, and the caudal fin is rounded. This fish carries its spines folded against the body, but will inflate itself when frightened.
• **HABITAT** Seaweed and near-shore rocky beds in the Indo-Pacific; also the Atlantic Ocean.
• **REMARK** Crustaceans, shellfish, and other invertebrate life will be eaten, and should be excluded from the aquarium.

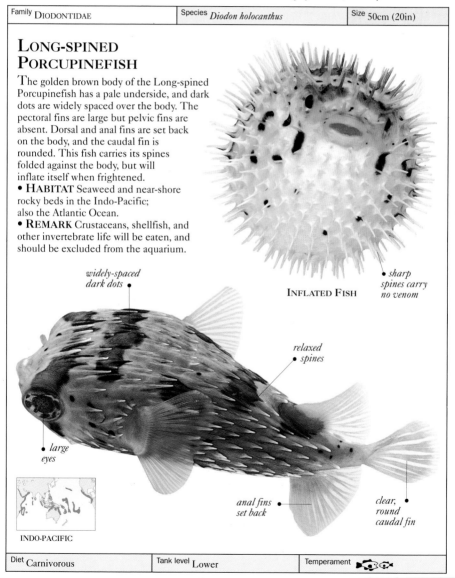

INFLATED FISH

sharp spines carry no venom

widely-spaced dark dots

relaxed spines

large eyes

anal fins set back

clear, round caudal fin

INDO-PACIFIC

Diet Carnivorous	Tank level Lower	Temperament

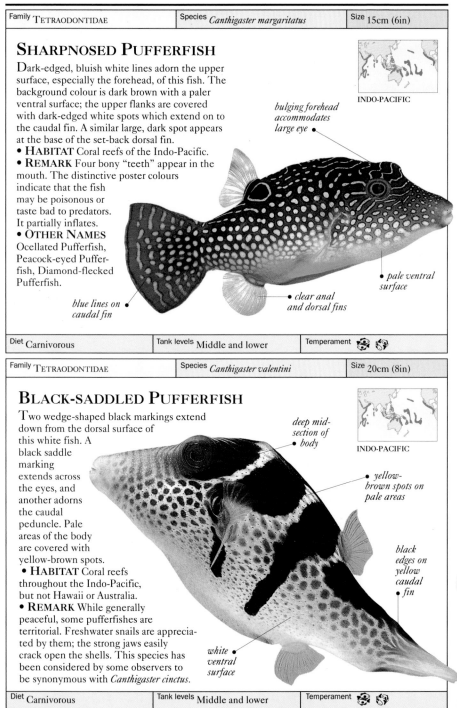

| Family TETRAODONTIDAE | Species *Canthigaster margaritatus* | Size 15cm (6in) |

SHARPNOSED PUFFERFISH

Dark-edged, bluish white lines adorn the upper surface, especially the forehead, of this fish. The background colour is dark brown with a paler ventral surface; the upper flanks are covered with dark-edged white spots which extend on to the caudal fin. A similar large, dark spot appears at the base of the set-back dorsal fin.
• **HABITAT** Coral reefs of the Indo-Pacific.
• **REMARK** Four bony "teeth" appear in the mouth. The distinctive poster colours indicate that the fish may be poisonous or taste bad to predators. It partially inflates.
• **OTHER NAMES** Ocellated Pufferfish, Peacock-eyed Pufferfish, Diamond-flecked Pufferfish.

INDO-PACIFIC

bulging forehead accommodates large eye

blue lines on caudal fin

clear anal and dorsal fins

pale ventral surface

| Diet Carnivorous | Tank levels Middle and lower | Temperament |

| Family TETRAODONTIDAE | Species *Canthigaster valentini* | Size 20cm (8in) |

BLACK-SADDLED PUFFERFISH

Two wedge-shaped black markings extend down from the dorsal surface of this white fish. A black saddle marking extends across the eyes, and another adorns the caudal peduncle. Pale areas of the body are covered with yellow-brown spots.
• **HABITAT** Coral reefs throughout the Indo-Pacific, but not Hawaii or Australia.
• **REMARK** While generally peaceful, some pufferfishes are territorial. Freshwater snails are appreciated by them; the strong jaws easily crack open the shells. This species has been considered by some observers to be synonymous with *Canthigaster cinctus*.

deep mid-section of body

INDO-PACIFIC

yellow-brown spots on pale areas

black edges on yellow caudal fin

white ventral surface

| Diet Carnivorous | Tank levels Middle and lower | Temperament |

RABBITFISHES AND RAZORFISHES

T HE RABBITFISHES (family Sigan-idae) carry poisonous spines on their dorsal and anal fins. Juveniles tend to be more colourful than adults, and all require space and vegetable foods. The razorfishes (family Centri-scidae) are adapted for concealment among sea urchin spines. Dorsal, cau-dal, and anal fins are hidden by a bony back covering, the tip of which is spiny.

Family SIGANIDAE	Species *Lo vulpinus*	Size 25cm (10in)

FOXFACE

The facial patterning of this fish is reminiscent of the badger's (hence the alternative name, Badgerfish). The small mouth is tubular and the eyes are set high on a black and white striped head. From the gill-covers backwards, the body and all fins are plain yellow.
• HABITAT Shallow waters among weeds from the East Indies to the Solomon Islands.

spiny dorsal fin

INDO-PACIFIC

badger-like facial marks

Diet Herbivorous	Tank levels Middle and lower	Temperament

Family CENTRISCIDAE	Species *Aeoliscus strigatus*	Size 15cm (6in)

RAZORFISH

The dorsal surface of the Razorfish is covered by protective bony plates. They extend past the end of the golden yellow body and over the tail fin, which terminates in a sharp spine. A dark band runs the length of the fish.
• HABITAT Coastal waters from the central Indian Ocean to Hawaii.
• REMARK This fish adopts a head-down position, as an adaptation for hiding among sea urchin spines. It should be kept in a species tank with invertebrates, and fed brine shrimp.

spiny back covering

colours match sea urchin spines

small eye on tubular snout

INDO-PACIFIC

Diet Omnivorous	Tank levels Middle and lower	Temperament

SQUIRRELFISHES

T HE FAMILY HOLOCENTRIDAE comprises large-eyed shoaling fishes. Its members are widely distributed in all warm seas. They patrol the aquarium in numbers at night, but generally hide away from view during the daytime. Squirrelfishes are usually red, although each species is distinguished by variations in a white patterning. Worm foods and small fish are enjoyed.

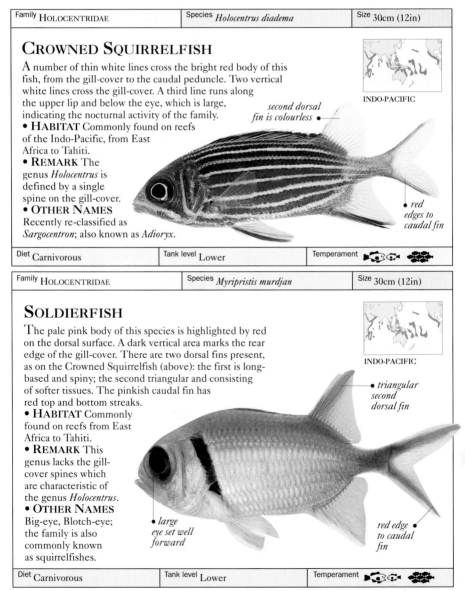

Family HOLOCENTRIDAE	Species *Holocentrus diadema*	Size 30cm (12in)

CROWNED SQUIRRELFISH

A number of thin white lines cross the bright red body of this fish, from the gill-cover to the caudal peduncle. Two vertical white lines cross the gill-cover. A third line runs along the upper lip and below the eye, which is large, indicating the nocturnal activity of the family.
• **HABITAT** Commonly found on reefs of the Indo-Pacific, from East Africa to Tahiti.
• **REMARK** The genus *Holocentrus* is defined by a single spine on the gill-cover.
• **OTHER NAMES** Recently re-classified as *Sargocentron*; also known as *Adioryx*.

INDO-PACIFIC

second dorsal fin is colourless

red edges to caudal fin

Diet Carnivorous	Tank level Lower	Temperament

Family HOLOCENTRIDAE	Species *Myripristis murdjan*	Size 30cm (12in)

SOLDIERFISH

The pale pink body of this species is highlighted by red on the dorsal surface. A dark vertical area marks the rear edge of the gill-cover. There are two dorsal fins present, as on the Crowned Squirrelfish (above): the first is long-based and spiny; the second triangular and consisting of softer tissues. The pinkish caudal fin has red top and bottom streaks.
• **HABITAT** Commonly found on reefs from East Africa to Tahiti.
• **REMARK** This genus lacks the gill-cover spines which are characteristic of the genus *Holocentrus*.
• **OTHER NAMES** Big-eye, Blotch-eye; the family is also commonly known as squirrelfishes.

INDO-PACIFIC

triangular second dorsal fin

large eye set well forward

red edge to caudal fin

Diet Carnivorous	Tank level Lower	Temperament

SWEETLIPS

J UVENILES OF THE family Hae-
mulidae, commonly known as
sweetlips, have an entirely different,
less vivid, coloration to that of adults.
Young sweetlips are excellent subjects
for a large aquarium. All species originate in the Indo-Pacific. They are shy,
slow eaters, requiring live foods.
Sweetlips are considered by some to be
a separate subfamily, Plectorhynchinae.

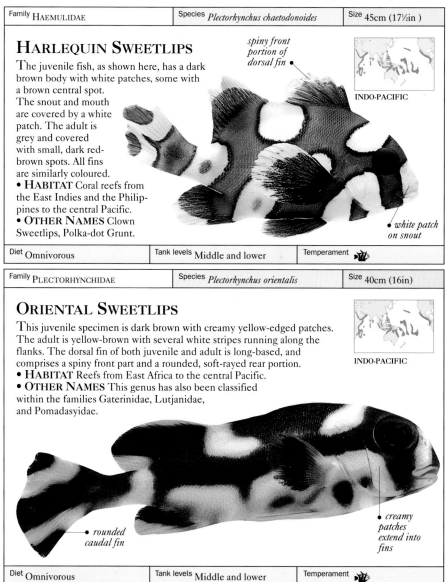

Family HAEMULIDAE	Species *Plectorhynchus chaetodonoides*	Size 45cm (17½in)

HARLEQUIN SWEETLIPS

The juvenile fish, as shown here, has a dark
brown body with white patches, some with
a brown central spot.
The snout and mouth
are covered by a white
patch. The adult is
grey and covered
with small, dark red-
brown spots. All fins
are similarly coloured.
• **HABITAT** Coral reefs from
the East Indies and the Philippines to the central Pacific.
• **OTHER NAMES** Clown
Sweetlips, Polka-dot Grunt.

*spiny front
portion of
dorsal fin*

INDO-PACIFIC

*white patch
on snout*

Diet Omnivorous	Tank levels Middle and lower	Temperament

Family PLECTORHYNCHIDAE	Species *Plectorhynchus orientalis*	Size 40cm (16in)

ORIENTAL SWEETLIPS

This juvenile specimen is dark brown with creamy yellow-edged patches.
The adult is yellow-brown with several white stripes running along the
flanks. The dorsal fin of both juvenile and adult is long-based, and
comprises a spiny front part and a rounded, soft-rayed rear portion.
• **HABITAT** Reefs from East Africa to the central Pacific.
• **OTHER NAMES** This genus has also been classified
within the families Gaterinidae, Lutjanidae,
and Pomadasyidae.

INDO-PACIFIC

*rounded
caudal fin*

*creamy
patches
extend into
fins*

Diet Omnivorous	Tank levels Middle and lower	Temperament

ZANCLIDAE

T HE MOORISH IDOL shown below is the only species in the family Zanclidae. Scientifically, it is related to the family Acanthuridae, comprising surgeons and tangs, as can be seen in the physical similarity of the young. Juvenile Moorish Idols, however, lack scalpels on the caudal peduncle. Moorish Idols are shoaling fishes, commonly found throughout the Indo-Pacific.

Family ZANCLIDAE	Species *Zanclus canescens*	Size 25cm (10in)

MOORISH IDOL

T his monotypic species is very tall and laterally compressed. The pale yellow and white body is crossed vertically by dark bands which extend into the dorsal and anal fins. A yellow mark adorns the top of the extended snout beneath the steeply rising forehead. The bottom jaw is black. The dorsal fin has very long, extended rays and is white, black, and yellow. Mature adults carry tiny, distinctive, horn-like growths above the eye.

• **HABITAT** Coral reefs throughout the Indo-Pacific.

• **REMARK** This popular species is often difficult to acclimatize. It will not feed in aquariums if damage is caused by transportation in polluted shipping bags, and may slowly decline from starvation.

• **OTHER NAME** Formerly classified as *Zanclus cornutus*.

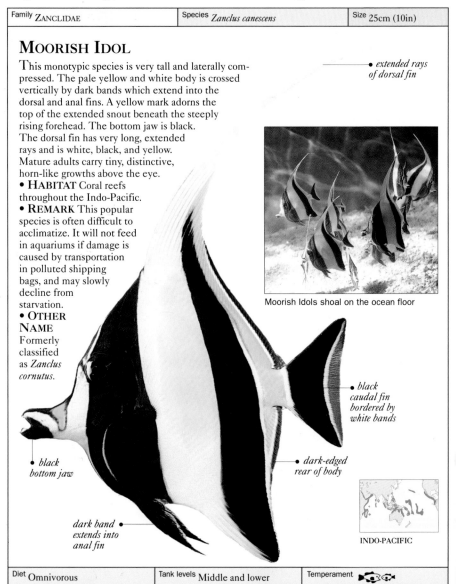

• *extended rays of dorsal fin*

Moorish Idols shoal on the ocean floor

• *black caudal fin bordered by white bands*

• *dark-edged rear of body*

• *black bottom jaw*

dark band • extends into anal fin

INDO-PACIFIC

Diet Omnivorous	Tank levels Middle and lower	Temperament

COLDWATER MARINE FISHES

BLENNIES

COLDWATER MEMBERS of the family Blenniidae are active little fishes, which scuttle around rocky crevices at the base of the aquarium. In nature, they are found in shallow coastal waters, often trapped in rockpools between tides. The characteristic growths (cirri) above the eye are one of the principal means of identification among these similarly coloured species.

Family BLENNIIDAE	Species *Blennius gattorugine*	Size 20cm (8in)

TOMPOT BLENNY

The head is the deepest part of this fish's stocky body, which is coloured with a combination of reddish brown and white cross-banding on the flanks. A steeply rising forehead leads away from a wide mouth. There are two branched, tentacle-like growths above the eyes known as cirri.
• **HABITAT** Shallow waters and rock-pools of the eastern Atlantic Ocean, including the Mediterranean to the north of Scotland, but not the North Sea.
• **REMARK** Although territorial and likely to worry smaller fishes, the Blenny may itself be intimidated by larger fishes. A species aquarium would suit it well. This fish requires plenty of rocky retreats, and feeds mainly on meaty foods. It often becomes hand-tame.

Blennies hide in rocky retreats

branched cirri above eyes •

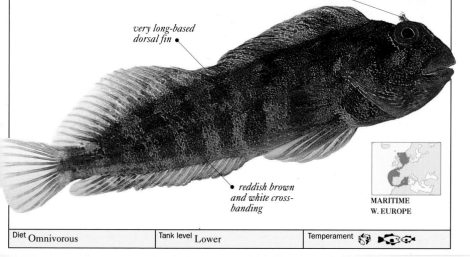

very long-based dorsal fin •

• *reddish brown and white cross-banding*

MARITIME W. EUROPE

Diet Omnivorous	Tank level Lower	Temperament

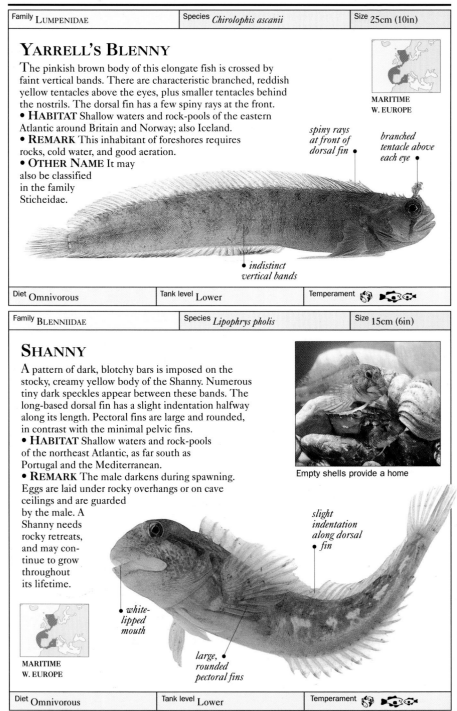

| Family LUMPENIDAE | Species *Chirolophis ascanii* | Size 25cm (10in) |

YARRELL'S BLENNY

The pinkish brown body of this elongate fish is crossed by faint vertical bands. There are characteristic branched, reddish yellow tentacles above the eyes, plus smaller tentacles behind the nostrils. The dorsal fin has a few spiny rays at the front.
• **HABITAT** Shallow waters and rock-pools of the eastern Atlantic around Britain and Norway; also Iceland.
• **REMARK** This inhabitant of foreshores requires rocks, cold water, and good aeration.
• **OTHER NAME** It may also be classified in the family Sticheidae.

MARITIME
W. EUROPE

spiny rays at front of dorsal fin •

branched tentacle above each eye •

• indistinct vertical bands

| Diet Omnivorous | Tank level Lower | Temperament |

| Family BLENNIIDAE | Species *Lipophrys pholis* | Size 15cm (6in) |

SHANNY

A pattern of dark, blotchy bars is imposed on the stocky, creamy yellow body of the Shanny. Numerous tiny dark speckles appear between these bands. The long-based dorsal fin has a slight indentation halfway along its length. Pectoral fins are large and rounded, in contrast with the minimal pelvic fins.
• **HABITAT** Shallow waters and rock-pools of the northeast Atlantic, as far south as Portugal and the Mediterranean.
• **REMARK** The male darkens during spawning. Eggs are laid under rocky overhangs or on cave ceilings and are guarded by the male. A Shanny needs rocky retreats, and may continue to grow throughout its lifetime.

Empty shells provide a home

slight indentation along dorsal • fin

MARITIME
W. EUROPE

• white-lipped mouth

large, • rounded pectoral fins

| Diet Omnivorous | Tank level Lower | Temperament |

GOBIES AND CLINGFISHES

T HE SCAVENGING MEMBERS of the goby family (Gobiidae) search constantly for food on rocky sea floors or in rock-pools. Although similar in appearance to blennies, clingfishes (family Gobiesocidae) and gobies are easily recognized by their brighter coloration, and by their pelvic fins, which combine to form suction discs. These discs prevent the fish from being dislodged by wave movements. Clingfishes spawn in the summer only.

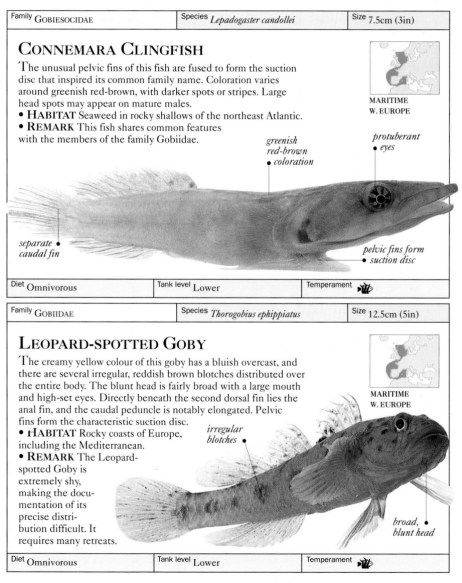

Family GOBIESOCIDAE	Species *Lepadogaster candollei*	Size 7.5cm (3in)

CONNEMARA CLINGFISH

The unusual pelvic fins of this fish are fused to form the suction disc that inspired its common family name. Coloration varies around greenish red-brown, with darker spots or stripes. Large head spots may appear on mature males.
• **HABITAT** Seaweed in rocky shallows of the northeast Atlantic.
• **REMARK** This fish shares common features with the members of the family Gobiidae.

MARITIME
W. EUROPE

greenish
red-brown
• coloration

protuberant
• eyes

separate •
caudal fin

pelvic fins form
• suction disc

Diet Omnivorous	Tank level Lower	Temperament

Family GOBIIDAE	Species *Thorogobius ephippiatus*	Size 12.5cm (5in)

LEOPARD-SPOTTED GOBY

The creamy yellow colour of this goby has a bluish overcast, and there are several irregular, reddish brown blotches distributed over the entire body. The blunt head is fairly broad with a large mouth and high-set eyes. Directly beneath the second dorsal fin lies the anal fin, and the caudal peduncle is notably elongated. Pelvic fins form the characteristic suction disc.
• **HABITAT** Rocky coasts of Europe, including the Mediterranean.
• **REMARK** The Leopard-spotted Goby is extremely shy, making the documentation of its precise distribution difficult. It requires many retreats.

MARITIME
W. EUROPE

irregular
blotches •

broad, •
blunt head

Diet Omnivorous	Tank level Lower	Temperament

WRASSES

T HE LARGE COLDWATER wrasse family (Labridae) offers a wide choice of species for aquarium culture, although in most cases only juveniles are suitable for captivity. A main attraction of the juveniles is the "cleaning" service they provide to other fish. Fortunately, the juvenile phase is often the most colourful period of the wrasses' lives. In adulthood, patterns and colours may change, and sometimes become much duller. Colours can vary between the sexes and sometimes alter with the fish's moods and the colour of the substrate. Males may alter colour at breeding times, and sex changes among these species are fairly common. Aquarium wrasses tend to be active during the day and bury themselves in the substrate at night.

Family LABRIDAE	Species *Centrolabrus exoletus*	Size 17.5cm (7in)

ROCK COCK

The coloration of this deep-bodied fish varies from brown on the dorsal surface to yellow on the flank, and silvery white on the belly. There may be some speckling. The flanks become iridescent blue on a spawning male. The terminally situated mouth is especially small, and violet lines adorn the throat. The anal fin has several spines at its front, and a dark bar crosses the base of the caudal peduncle.
• **HABITAT** Seaweed in shallows from Norway to the Bay of Biscay, excluding the southern North Sea.
• **REMARK** The Rock Cock is usually active during the day, but rests among rocks at night.
• **OTHER NAME** Small-mouthed Wrasse.

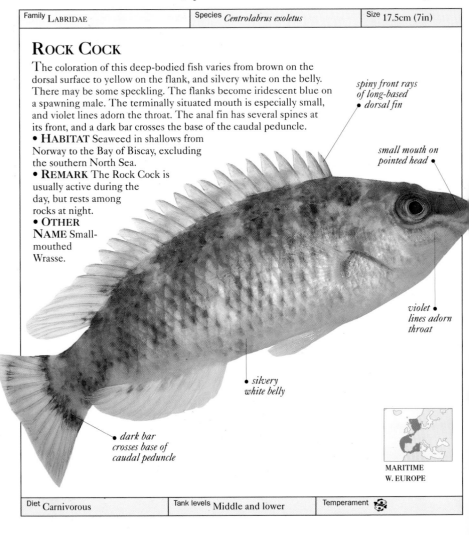

spiny front rays of long-based dorsal fin

small mouth on pointed head

violet lines adorn throat

silvery white belly

dark bar crosses base of caudal peduncle

MARITIME
W. EUROPE

Diet Carnivorous	Tank levels Middle and lower	Temperament

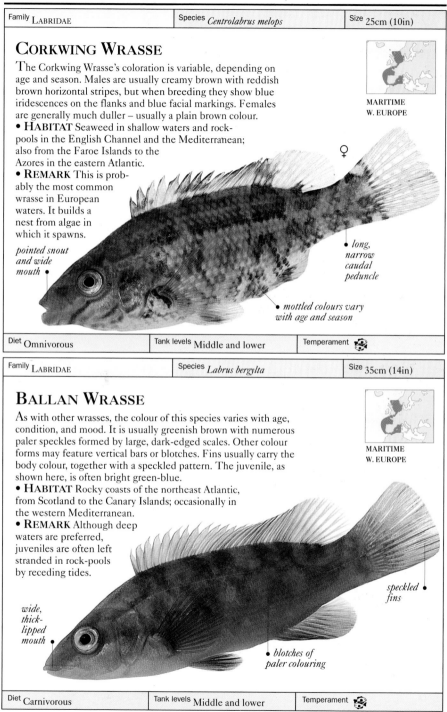

| Family LABRIDAE | Species *Centrolabrus melops* | Size 25cm (10in) |

CORKWING WRASSE

The Corkwing Wrasse's coloration is variable, depending on age and season. Males are usually creamy brown with reddish brown horizontal stripes, but when breeding they show blue iridescences on the flanks and blue facial markings. Females are generally much duller – usually a plain brown colour.

MARITIME
W. EUROPE

• **HABITAT** Seaweed in shallow waters and rock-pools in the English Channel and the Mediterranean; also from the Faroe Islands to the Azores in the eastern Atlantic.
• **REMARK** This is probably the most common wrasse in European waters. It builds a nest from algae in which it spawns.

♀

pointed snout and wide mouth •

• *long, narrow caudal peduncle*

• *mottled colours vary with age and season*

| Diet Omnivorous | Tank levels Middle and lower | Temperament |

| Family LABRIDAE | Species *Labrus bergylta* | Size 35cm (14in) |

BALLAN WRASSE

As with other wrasses, the colour of this species varies with age, condition, and mood. It is usually greenish brown with numerous paler speckles formed by large, dark-edged scales. Other colour forms may feature vertical bars or blotches. Fins usually carry the body colour, together with a speckled pattern. The juvenile, as shown here, is often bright green-blue.

MARITIME
W. EUROPE

• **HABITAT** Rocky coasts of the northeast Atlantic, from Scotland to the Canary Islands; occasionally in the western Mediterranean.
• **REMARK** Although deep waters are preferred, juveniles are often left stranded in rock-pools by receding tides.

speckled fins •

wide, thick-lipped mouth •

• *blotches of paler colouring*

| Diet Carnivorous | Tank levels Middle and lower | Temperament |

SCORPIONFISHES AND SEA SCORPIONS

T HE FAMILIES SCORPAENIDAE and Cottidae consist of sedentary fishes that lie on the substrate waiting for prey, in the form of other fishes, to pass by. They are effectively camouflaged with varying blotches and stripes. The decorative spines are highly venomous and should be handled with caution. It can be difficult to identify individual Scorpaenidae species.

Family SCORPAENIDAE	Species *Scorpaena species*	Size 25cm (10in)

SCORPIONFISH

This fish is generally reddish brown, with contrasting blotches and stripes that form camouflage, though colours do vary. A massive head carries a mouth of corresponding proportions. Above the oval eyes there are feathery growths, smaller versions of which appear on the nostrils. Venomous spines occur on and above the gill-covers.
• **HABITAT** Rocky shallows in the Mediterranean and the Bay of Biscay; also south to the Canary Islands.
• **REMARK** This highly predatory and venomous fish remains settled on the substrate.

long-based dorsal fin

MARITIME
W. EUROPE

camouflage markings

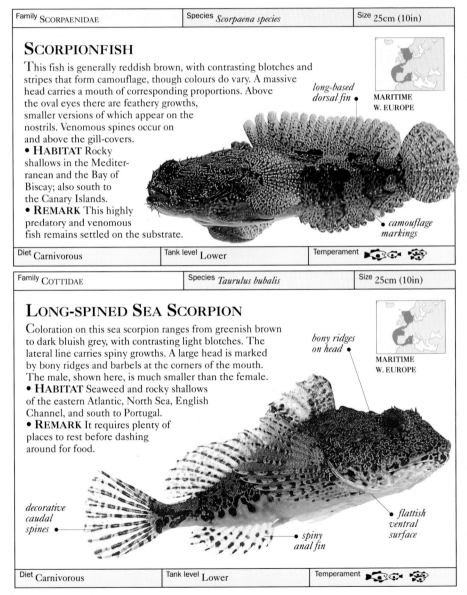

Diet Carnivorous	Tank level Lower	Temperament

Family COTTIDAE	Species *Taurulus bubalis*	Size 25cm (10in)

LONG-SPINED SEA SCORPION

Coloration on this sea scorpion ranges from greenish brown to dark bluish grey, with contrasting light blotches. The lateral line carries spiny growths. A large head is marked by bony ridges and barbels at the corners of the mouth. The male, shown here, is much smaller than the female.
• **HABITAT** Seaweed and rocky shallows of the eastern Atlantic, North Sea, English Channel, and south to Portugal.
• **REMARK** It requires plenty of places to rest before dashing around for food.

bony ridges on head

MARITIME
W. EUROPE

decorative caudal spines

spiny anal fin

flattish ventral surface

Diet Carnivorous	Tank level Lower	Temperament

OTHER COLDWATER MARINE FISHES

T HE FOLLOWING SELECTION comprises fishes that may be found in temperate rock-pools and coastal waters of Europe and its environs. It is presented as an inspirational token of the diverse and interesting species that can be sought from similar waters of other geographical locations. When collecting from the coast, however, it is always vital to leave the habitat undisturbed.

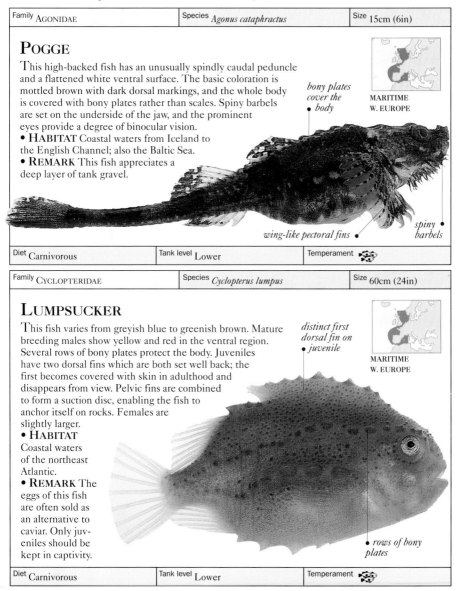

Family AGONIDAE	Species *Agonus cataphractus*	Size 15cm (6in)

POGGE

This high-backed fish has an unusually spindly caudal peduncle and a flattened white ventral surface. The basic coloration is mottled brown with dark dorsal markings, and the whole body is covered with bony plates rather than scales. Spiny barbels are set on the underside of the jaw, and the prominent eyes provide a degree of binocular vision.
• **HABITAT** Coastal waters from Iceland to the English Channel; also the Baltic Sea.
• **REMARK** This fish appreciates a deep layer of tank gravel.

bony plates cover the • body

MARITIME
W. EUROPE

wing-like pectoral fins •

spiny • barbels

Diet Carnivorous	Tank level Lower	Temperament

Family CYCLOPTERIDAE	Species *Cyclopterus lumpus*	Size 60cm (24in)

LUMPSUCKER

This fish varies from greyish blue to greenish brown. Mature breeding males show yellow and red in the ventral region. Several rows of bony plates protect the body. Juveniles have two dorsal fins which are both set well back; the first becomes covered with skin in adulthood and disappears from view. Pelvic fins are combined to form a suction disc, enabling the fish to anchor itself on rocks. Females are slightly larger.
• **HABITAT** Coastal waters of the northeast Atlantic.
• **REMARK** The eggs of this fish are often sold as an alternative to caviar. Only juveniles should be kept in captivity.

distinct first dorsal fin on • juvenile

MARITIME
W. EUROPE

• rows of bony plates

Diet Carnivorous	Tank level Lower	Temperament

Family GASTEROSTEIDAE	Species *Spinachia spinachia*	Size 20cm (8in)

FIFTEEN-SPINED STICKLEBACK

The fifteen spines that gave this fish its common name are the remnants of the spiny front of the dorsal fin. The body is spindly with a flattened head and long caudal peduncle. Coloration is dark greenish brown, but males show a bluish sheen when spawning. Small dorsal and anal fins are set opposite each other, well back on the body, and the rudimentary pelvic fin is composed of only a single spine and ray. The caudal fin is small and rounded.
• **HABITAT** Seaweed in shallows of the northeast Atlantic, from the Bay of Biscay to Norway, including the North and Baltic Seas.
• **REMARK** It can tolerate brackish water. All sticklebacks require small live foods.

MARITIME
W. EUROPE

spines along dorsal ridge

elongated jaws

colourless pectoral fin

small rounded caudal fin

long caudal peduncle

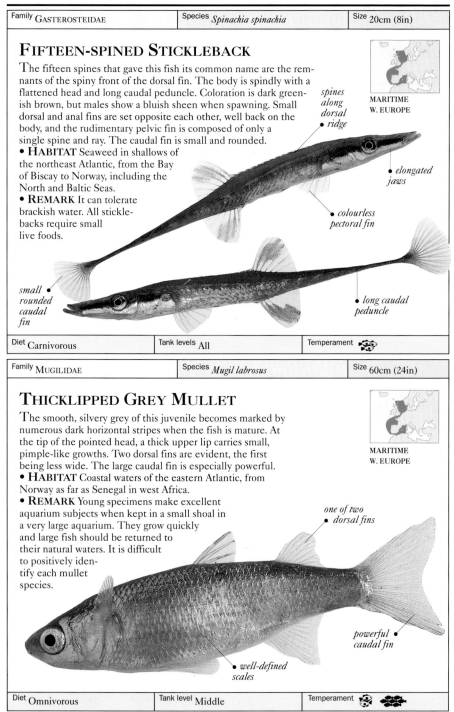

Diet Carnivorous	Tank levels All	Temperament

Family MUGILIDAE	Species *Mugil labrosus*	Size 60cm (24in)

THICKLIPPED GREY MULLET

The smooth, silvery grey of this juvenile becomes marked by numerous dark horizontal stripes when the fish is mature. At the tip of the pointed head, a thick upper lip carries small, pimple-like growths. Two dorsal fins are evident, the first being less wide. The large caudal fin is especially powerful.
• **HABITAT** Coastal waters of the eastern Atlantic, from Norway as far as Senegal in west Africa.
• **REMARK** Young specimens make excellent aquarium subjects when kept in a small shoal in a very large aquarium. They grow quickly and large fish should be returned to their natural waters. It is difficult to positively identify each mullet species.

MARITIME
W. EUROPE

one of two dorsal fins

powerful caudal fin

well-defined scales

Diet Omnivorous	Tank level Middle	Temperament

Family PHOLIDIDAE	Species *Pholis gunnellus*	Size 25cm (10in)

GUNNEL

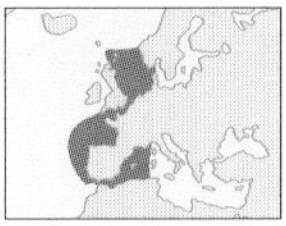

This heavily built, eel-like fish is gold and brown, with contrasting vertical bands that disappear as the fish matures. A number of pale-rimmed dark spots appear regularly along the long-based dorsal fin, and a dark bar runs through the eye. The dorsal, caudal, and anal fins are contiguous.

MARITIME
W. EUROPE

• **HABITAT** Sandy and muddy coastal waters, often under rocks, of the temperate eastern and western Atlantic.
• **REMARK** This extremely slim fish requires hiding places and meaty foods.
• **OTHER NAME** Butterfish.

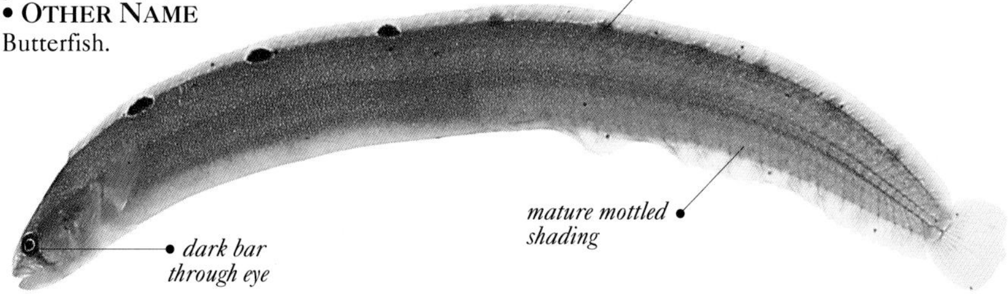

spots along dorsal fin

dark bar through eye

mature mottled shading

Diet Carnivorous	Tank level Lower	Temperament

Family POMACENTRIDAE	Species *Chromis chromis*	Size 15cm (6in)

MEDITERRANEAN DAMSELFISH

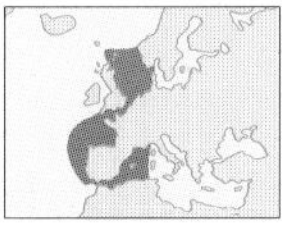

This fish is a rather deep, laterally compressed oval with a narrow caudal peduncle. Coloration is blue-green in juveniles, as shown here, and darker brown in adults. Adults have extended rays in their pelvic fins. All scales are large and dark-edged. The eye is set well forward on the head, close to the small, terminally situated mouth. The front section of the dorsal fin is spiny, whereas the rear section is soft-rayed.

spiny section of dorsal fin

MARITIME
W. EUROPE

• **HABITAT** Rocky outcrops in the Mediterranean and eastern Atlantic, from Portugal to west Africa.
• **REMARK** This shoaling fish spawns like a cichlid, laying eggs on selected and pre-cleaned sites. Eggs are guarded by the male.
• **OTHER NAME** Demoiselle.

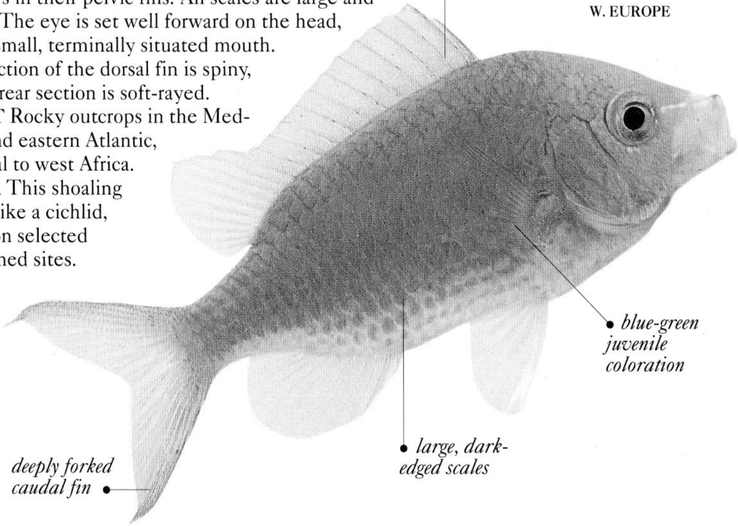

blue-green juvenile coloration

deeply forked caudal fin

large, dark-edged scales

Diet Omnivorous	Tank level Lower	Temperament

GLOSSARY

WORDS PRINTED in bold type have their own definition elsewhere in the glossary.

• **ACIDIC**
Condition of water often due to decomposing vegetation or filtration through peat; pH balance is below 7. *See also* **Soft water**.

• **ADIPOSE FIN**
Small extra fin in between **dorsal** and **caudal fins**.

• **ADSORB**
Collection of dissolved wastes by means of a suitable filter medium such as activated carbon.

• **ALKALINE**
Condition of water due to build up of dissolved salts, usually calcium and magnesium; pH balance is above 7. *See also* **Hard water**.

• **ANAL FIN**
Single, vertical fin beneath the rear of the body.

• **BARBEL**
Whisker-like growth around the mouth, used for locating food.

• **BRACKISH**
Mixture of fresh and salt water, found in estuaries.

• **BRINE SHRIMP**
Tiny saltwater crustaceans that make excellent first food for **fry**. Available live or frozen.

• **BUBBLE-NEST**
Raft of bubbles that some fish use to protect eggs and **fry**.

• **CAUDAL FIN**
Tail fin, often divided into lobes.

• **CAUDAL PEDUNCLE**
Slender, muscular rear part of body, adjoining the tail.

• **CIRRI**
Branched, tentacle-like growths above the eyes of some **coldwater** marine fishes.

• **COLDWATER FISH**
Generally refers to fish kept under ambient temperatures, without additional heating.

• **CULTIVATED**
Aquarium-developed **strains** or **varieties** of fish, not found in nature. *See also* **Fancy**.

• **DORSAL**
Pertaining to top surface of a fish.

• **DORSAL FIN**
Single fin on the **dorsal** surface.

• **EGG-LAYER**
Fish whose eggs are fertilized and hatch externally.

• **EGG-SPOTS**
Egg-shaped markings on the **anal fins** of male **mouth-brooders**.

• **FAMILY**
Group containing one or more **genera**. *See also* **Genus.**

• **FANCY**
Aquarium-developed **strains** or **varieties**. *See also* **Cultivated**.

• **FRY**
Newly hatched fish.

• **GENUS** (*pl.* **GENERA**)
Individual group within a **family**, containing one or more **species**.

• **GILL**
Respiratory organ used to extract dissolved oxygen from water.

• **GILL COVER**
See **Operculum**.

• **GONOPODIUM**
Modified **anal fin** of male **livebearing** fishes.

• **GRAVID**
Pregnant female **livebearer**, or female **egg-layer** full of ripe eggs.

• **GUANIN**
Crystals of urea deposited beneath the skin which bend and reflect light, causing iridescence.

• **HARD WATER**
Condition of water due to dissolved salts, usually of calcium and magnesium. *See also* **Alkaline**.

• **LABYRINTH ORGAN**
Auxiliary respiratory organ that allows some fish to "breathe" air.

• **LATERAL LINE**
Row of pores along the flanks, allowing the detection of vibrations, for navigation.

• **LENGTH**
Dimension of fish measured from snout to end of **caudal peduncle**; excludes **caudal fin.**

• **LIVEBEARER**
Fish that fertilizes and incubates eggs inside the female body.

• **MILT**
Fish sperm.

• **MORPH**
A natural colour variant.

• **MOUTH-BROODER**
Species that incubates externally fertilized eggs and protects fry within the female throat cavity.

• **NUCHAL HUMP**
Pronounced forehead on mature male cichlids.

• **OPERCULUM**
Shiny bone covering gill opening; also called **gill-cover**.

• **PECTORAL FINS**
Paired fins, one on each side of the head behind the **gill** opening.

• **PELVIC FINS**
Paired fins, ahead of the **anal fin**.

• **PHARYNGEAL TEETH**
Teeth in the throat of cyprinids.

• **RAY**
Tissue-supporting bone in fins.

• **SALT**
Usually refers to sodium chloride.

• **SALT-MIX**
Proprietary mixture of ingredients to make up artificial sea-water.

• **SCALE**
Small, protective platelet covering the fish's skin.

• **SCALPEL**
Sharp, retractable spine carried as a defence by surgeons and tangs.

• **SCUTE**
Overlapping bony plate (modified **scale**) covering the skin, found especially in catfishes.

• **SHOAL**
Collection of fish swimming together, usually of one **species**.

• **SOFT WATER**
Condition of water due to lack of dissolved salts. *See also* **Acidic**.

• **SPAWNING**
Breeding.

• **SPECIES**
Group within a **genus**, the members of which share similar characteristics and can breed successfully together.

• **SPECIFIC GRAVITY (SG)**
Density of a liquid containing dissolved minerals, compared with that of pure water.

• **STRAIN**
Aquarium-developed variant of a **species**. Same as **variety**.

• **SUBSPECIES**
Sub-group of a **species**, usually geographically separated.

• **SUBSTRATE**
Bottom material such as mud, gravel, rocks, or sand.

• **SWIM BLADDER**
Internal organ that automatically regulates neutral buoyancy.

• **TUBERCLE**
Small white pimple on the gill-covers of many cyprinids, usually **spawning** males.

• **VARIETY**
See **Strain**.

• **VENTRAL**
Pertaining to underside of a fish.

INDEX

ACKNOWLEDGMENTS

The author would like to thank the following, without whom this book could not have been produced: Jane Cooke, Louise Bruce, Lesley Malkin, Spencer Holbrook, Jonathan Metcalf, Mary-Clare Jerram, and Gill Della Casa at Dorling Kindersley, Richmond; Jerry Young, our intrepid photographer; and Dr. Chris Andrews and Dr. Robert J. Goldstein for authentication.

Thanks also go to the following for providing fish for photographing, and offering invaluable advice: Keith Lambert of Wildwoods; Barry Jackson of Jackamoors; Max Gibbs of The Goldfish Bowl; Terry Jones of Wholesale Tropicals; Jimmy Croft & Paul Thomas of Waterworld; Dave & Mark Watkinson of Reef World; Simon Langdale of Iver Fishworld; Derek Lambert of Viviparous; Len Eldridge of the West London section of the British Killifish Association; fellow hobbyists within the Federation of British Aquatic Societies; South Park Aquatic Study Society; Isle of Wight Aquarist Society; Mike Quarm of the Sea Life Centre, Weymouth; Vernon Hunt of Portsmouth Aquarist Society; Oliver Crimmens of the Natural History Museum, London; and Andy Houghton. Finally, I could not have produced such a book without the full support and understanding of my wife, Janet.

Dorling Kindersley would like to thank: Michael Allaby for compiling the index; Charles Astwood for page make-up assistance; Caroline Church for the endpapers; Neal Cobourne for the jacket design; Julia Pashley for picture research; Alastair Wardle for DTP management, maps, and fonts; Angeles Gavira, Lucinda Hawksley, Constance Novis, and Helen Townsend, for additional editorial assistance; Elaine Hewson, Chris Legee, Shaun Mc Nally, Sharon Moore, and Ann Thomson, for additional design assistance.

All specially commissioned photography by Jerry Young, except for the following (a=all, i=inset, m=main): Derek Lambert 100t, 193t, 198t, 199, 200b, 202b, 203b; The Goldfish Bowl 10tl, 20tl, 54b, 66b, 87b, 99t, 190t, 218t, 228b, 232t, 252b, 254, 255b; Jane Burton/Kim Taylor 15, 20bl, 22br, 23cr, 24, 25(all food pics), 28a, 29a, 31rb, 32a, 33a, 34, 262t, 263b, 276t, 295t; Colin Keates 34tr; Dave King 3, 8bl, 14br, 15tr, 15tl, 25br, 30l, 40tc, 44tc, 106b, 121b, 122, 178t, 186b, 196i, 242b, 243b, 248b, 259t, 271b, 281t, 283b, 292t, 297, 302.

The publishers would also like to thank the following for permission to reproduce the photographs and illustrations indicated below: Ardea 18br, 264i (P. Morris), 235i (Ron & Valerie Taylor); Camera Press Ltd 8br; Bruce Coleman 231t (John Anthony), 26tl, 62i, 80i, 85i, 194i, 214c, 288i (Jane Burton), 225i (Eric Crichton), 30b (C.B. & D.W. Frith), 27t (Jennifer Fry), 26bl (M.P. Price), 85b, 103t, 147i, 191i, 231 (Hans Reinhard), 30t (Carl Roessler), 287i (John Taylor), 16t (Kim Taylor), 265b (Bill Wood); Mary Evans Picture Library 7a; The Goldfish Bowl 9m, 11tr, 20r, 27b, 34cl, 54i, 66i, 67b, 88t, 90t, 110t, 113i, 128i, 141, 154i, 164i, 170i, 184i, 194, 224i, 234t, 240t, 258b, 260t, 262b, 263t, 266m, 270b, 272i, 274t, 276t, 279b, 279i, 282t, 286m; Michael Holford 6b; Derek Lambert 16b, 27c, 36b, 42b; Dick Mills 9i, 18bc, 18bl, 19t, 73b, 129t, 145t, 202t, 215b, 228t, 272b, 275i, 286i; Oxford Scientific Films 115i (Max Gibbs); Planet Earth Pictures 250b (Ken Lucas), 126i (Paulo Oliviera), 266i (Peter Scoones); William Tomey 90b, 91b, 104b, 151t; A. van den Nieuwenhuizen 16a, 57t, 94b, 103b, 104t, 185b, 254i.

Illustrations by: King & King Design Associates 11, 12t, 12bl, 13t; Linden Artists Ltd 21a (Stewart Lafford).